THE
RELATIVITY
OF
DEVIANCE

··········THIRD EDITION··········

THE
RELATIVITY
OF
DEVIANCE

············THIRD EDITION············

JOHN CURRA

Eastern Kentucky University

Los Angeles | London | New Delhi
Singapore | Washington DC

Los Angeles | London | New Delhi
Singapore | Washington DC

FOR INFORMATION:

SAGE Publications, Inc.
2455 Teller Road
Thousand Oaks, California 91320
E-mail: order@sagepub.com

SAGE Publications Ltd.
1 Oliver's Yard
55 City Road
London EC1Y 1SP
United Kingdom

SAGE Publications India Pvt. Ltd.
B 1/I 1 Mohan Cooperative Industrial Area
Mathura Road, New Delhi 110 044
India

SAGE Publications Asia-Pacific Pte. Ltd.
3 Church Street
#10-04 Samsung Hub
Singapore 048763

Copyright © 2014 by SAGE Publications, Inc.

Printed in the United States of America

Library of Congress Cataloging-in-Publication Data

Curra, John.

The relativity of deviance / John Curra, Eastern Kentucky University. — Third Edition.

pages cm
Includes bibliographical references and index.

ISBN 978-1-4522-0262-4 (alk. paper)

1. Deviant behavior. I. Title.

HM811.C87 2013
302.5'42—dc23   2013001178

This book is printed on acid-free paper.

Acquisitions Editor: Diane McDaniel
Editorial Assistant: Lauren Johnson
Production Editor: Jane Haenel
Copy Editor: Teresa Herlinger
Proofreader: Kristin Bergstad
Typesetter: C&M Digitals (P) Ltd.
Indexer: Terri Corry
Cover Designer: Gail Buschman
Permissions Editor: Karen Ehrmann
Marketing Manager: Jonathan Mason

SUSTAINABLE FORESTRY INITIATIVE

Certified Chain of Custody
Promoting Sustainable Forestry
www.sfiprogram.org
SFI-01268

SFI label applies to text stock

13 14 15 16 17 10 9 8 7 6 5 4 3 2 1

Brief Contents

Detailed Contents

Preface

Human attitudes, behaviors, and conditions—the ABCs of deviance—do not exist in a social vacuum; they are always of great interest and concern to others. Depending on time, place, situation, the particular temperament of the individuals involved, and a host of other factors, some attitudes, behaviors, and conditions are praised, some are condemned, and others are ignored, at least for a time. Readers of this book will see that what qualifies as deviance varies from place to place, time to time, and situation to situation. They will see that deviance cannot be understood apart from its social setting, and they will be introduced to many examples that show this to be true. What exists could almost always be otherwise, and a change in social settings and interpersonal relationships almost always produces a change in the nature of deviance. This book will be appealing to anyone who is fascinated by the great diversity in human experience and the even greater diversity in social representations or constructions of it. Readers will come to realize that no intrinsic or inherent qualities exist to separate deviance from nondeviance and that deviance is far from absolute and uniform. This book will encourage readers to evaluate critically their own understandings of deviance.

In this third edition, I have included new examples and concepts to demonstrate the relativity of deviance, while keeping what I hope is the best from previous editions. In the following pages, readers will meet the blue people of Kentucky, a woman who believes that she is a vampire, the thugs of India, tattooists, self-injurers, autoerotic asphyxiates, berdaches, terrorists, serial killers, and even a man who ate an entire airplane. Some of the examples are funny, some are sad, and some are shocking. These examples, however, are more than journalistic accounts of quirky events. They show that deviance is a social construction—an accomplishment—of individuals in particular situations at particular times. The only valuable way to understand deviance is to use variables such as power, conflict, norms, labeling, culture, vocabularies of motive, rationalizations, retrospective interpretation, stigma, accounts, ideologies, techniques of neutralization, and social reactions, so these concepts (and many more) are discussed in the following pages.

Chapter 1 explains how deviance can be understood as a socially constructed event by discussing egocentricity, ethnocentricity, culture, norms, sanctions, and ideologies. This chapter will show that we live in a world of multiple realities and that deviance must be understood as a situational, interactive, meaningful accomplishment of humans acting together. It explores the meaning of relativity and how relativity helps to illuminate the relationship between human diversity and social deviance. It also discusses theories of deviance that help in understanding its relative nature.

Each of the book's remaining chapters discusses a different facet of the relativity of deviance. Chapter 2 (dealing with identities, responsibility, and stigma) shows that people can be labeled deviant for things over which they have little control. It discusses physical appearance and its social construction, bodily adornment (e.g., tattooing), self-injurers, and eccentrics (and their eccentricities). Chapter 3 deals with the role played by both power and organizational networks in the social construction of deviance. It illustrates that individuals in organizations regularly use their social positions to hurt others, posing a threat to our collective and individual well-being. It also shows that some people's deviance is considered perfectly all right, whereas other people's deviance is criminalized and punished to the fullest extent of the law. Chapter 4 shows how human diversity, social conflicts, power, organizational interests and resources, social control, and naming and diagnosing all work together to construct that social deviance known as mental disorder. It demonstrates that deviance is a contested social terrain and that different groups will do all they can to define deviance in a way that best serves their own economic and political interests. This is particularly clear in the medicalization of deviance in which so much human diversity and pathos have been transformed into treatable disease. Chapter 5 examines predatory violence. It shows that even serious acts, which produce great harm, are not deviant at all times and in all places. Chapter 6 deals with sexual violence. It shows that serious violence erupting from sex and gender antagonisms and disagreements may still be widely viewed as both normal and normative. Chapter 7, on suicide, presents readers with information about the framing of social events. They will see that suicide is a socially constructed category with diverse meanings that are determined by time and place. Chapter 8 deals with sex, gender, and sexuality. It shows that sexual diversity—rooted in biology, psychology, culture, and society—is transformed into sexual deviance whenever humans and what they do, think, or feel in regard to things sexual are pigeonholed and then devalued. Few universals exist, and sexuality is a complex and ever-changing human experience. Chapter 9 discusses drugs and deviance. Readers will see that some groups initiate moral crusades to brand other people's drug use as sick and wholly unacceptable. The book contains what I hope are interesting and thought-provoking examples of social deviance, designed to show readers the great array in both human experience and social constructions of it.

I have added information about the worldwide economic crisis, deviance and social inequality, the killing of Osama bin Laden, and the Penn State sexual abuse scandal. I have also expanded the theoretical section. The discussions of terrorism, sexual deviance, and drugs and deviance have also been expanded, as well as the exploration of predatory violence. New information is included on sexual minorities (e.g., lesbians, gays, transgendered people, exotic dancers, prostitutes) as well as on far-side sexual deviances (e.g., paraphilias). New research from academic journals and books has also been added, which is why this third edition is longer than the previous two. I think all this strengthens the book, and I hope readers will agree.

The writing in this book is gender-neutral. When direct quotes of others are included, however, that was not always possible, especially when the authors lived and wrote at an earlier time in history. They were not always sensitive to the sexism in their language. These authors were inclined to use masculine pronouns to represent all humans, male and female. Although this is not acceptable now, in order to keep the meaning and flow of the original citation, when a direct quotation is included, the original language is unaltered.

1

The Dynamic
Nature of Deviance

Kids, Crocodiles, and Social Control

On January 2, 2004, Steve Irwin, crocodile hunter, snake wrangler, television personality, and naturalist, brought his 1-month-old son with him into a crocodile pen at Australia Zoo in Brisbane. He held his son in his left arm and a dead chicken in his right hand. While his wife, visitors to the zoo, and a camera crew looked on, Irwin extended the chicken to a 13-foot crocodile. The reptile lunged forward, snapped its massive jaws shut on the chicken, and ate the food. With his son held tightly in his arm, Irwin jumped safely away from the hungry animal. While the Irwins looked at the stunt as inconsequential, nothing more than a crocodile-feeding debut by the youngest member of a reptile-loving family, some other people were mightily upset by what happened. A film of the incident was shown several times on U.S. television, Steve Irwin was quizzed by various U.S. newscasters, and family services officials in Australia reprimanded the Irwins for what they had done. Legal charges could have been filed against them for child abuse.

Steve Irwin was astonished that anyone could think he would put his infant son in harm's way. The child was in no danger, Irwin insisted, and getting up close and personal with dangerous reptiles is what it means to be a member of the Irwin family. Steve Irwin's 30 years of experience, tracking and capturing highly dangerous creatures, gave him the confidence that his son would be perfectly safe. Irwin's surprise gave way to defiance and eventually to a modicum of public remorse, an apology, and a pledge that nothing like it would ever happen again. (Steve Irwin was killed in September 2006 during the making of a film on Australia's Great Barrier Reef. He startled a stingray and, in defense, the creature pierced Irwin's heart with the serrated, poisonous barb it carries in its tail. Irwin pulled the barb from his body just moments before he lost consciousness, eventually dying from the toxins and the physical damage to his heart.)

This incident involving kids, crocodiles, and social control illustrates central elements in the human social construction of deviance, especially showing that fundamental disagreements do exist over proper ways of acting, thinking, feeling, and being. Whose definition of the "crocodile stunt" is the "right" one? Were the Irwins bad parents, or were they carefully (and safely) exposing their child to a new and valuable experience? How different is this from what other parents do when they take their child for a ride in an airplane, for a trip by car, for a swim in an ocean, or for a horseback ride, any of which events could end disastrously? Some parents would be inclined to do with their child exactly what Irwin did with his, just as some parents would *not* do it with their child under any circumstances. Likewise, some individuals, while they would not actually *do* what Irwin did, would still think (and feel) that what he did was perfectly okay; other individuals would think (and feel) just as strongly that it most certainly was *not* okay. The elements we find in this social event—expectations, human interactions (and the associated thoughts and emotions), social evaluations and judgments—are the social "stuff" from which *any* social deviance originates. This incident involving kids and crocs has much to teach us about *all* social deviance and its relative and relational nature.

Relationships and Rule Breaking

The study of deviance involves *at its core* an understanding of how social meanings are constructed and attached to individuals (Schur, 1975). The study of social deviance must involve an understanding of the *origination* of human attitudes, behaviors, and conditions—the ABCs of deviance (Adler & Adler, 2009)—it is true, but it must also involve an understanding of socially constructed *perspectives* on human attitudes, behaviors, and conditions (Goffman, 1961).

> Deviance is not a self-evident category. It does not just float down from the skies applying itself to people who quite obviously are deviant. Deviance is a

historical term and its application and/or adoption can create a status which dwarfs all others in its consequences for the individual's existence. Even the most deviant of all deviants does not just "happen"; someone has to pass judgement, to portray, to stigmatize, to insult, to heap abuse, to exclude or to reject. (C. Sumner, 1994, p. 223)

Social reactions and cultural meanings strongly affect the type of deviance that exists in society, and patterns of deviance constantly evolve and change over time. What's more, the ABCs and characterizations of them don't always line up in uniform ways.

At one time or place, drinking alcohol is perfectly proper, while at another time or place, it is forbidden. At one time or place, smoking cigarettes is a sign of maturity and sophistication, while at some other time or place, it is a sign of immaturity and irresponsibility. The *deviancy* of some attitude, behavior, or condition cannot be determined simply by examining it closely and objectively. No one human attitude, behavior, or condition will be universally judged as proper or improper by people in all societies—large and small, industrial and nonindustrial—at all times. Very few, if any, human experiences exist in a social vacuum, and very few, if any, can be understood separately from social context.

Plainly, people throughout the ages have worried over—told tales about, made laws for, designed rituals around—situations that disturb the peace or threaten the communal fabric. Equally plainly, the coming to group attention of a specific threat has largely depended upon how that threat is publicly named, shaped, cast, categorized, and put in context. (Schwartz, 1997, p. 289)

Human beings are simply too inventive in assigning positive and negative labels to the many things that they do for us to ignore in our explanations of social deviance how groups judge and evaluate what other groups and the people in them are doing, thinking, feeling, and being (O'Brien, 2006, pp. 64–82; Spector & Kitsuse, 1977). Because we seek to understand deviance as a social relationship, we cannot stop with an *explanation* of human diversity. We must also examine the diversity of claims, labels, constructions, or characterizations of it.

Cultures and Subcultures

The word *culture* was first used in 1877 by the anthropologist Edward Tylor to describe the totality of humans' behavioral, material, intellectual, and spiritual products. It now refers to designs for living or shared understandings that members of a society use as they act together (Kluckhohn, 1949). Cultures are created by people at some place and time, and the designs or shared understandings are then transmitted from group to group (or generation to generation). People in a society (or a part of it) find that certain ways of acting, thinking, feeling, or being seem better than other ways, and these designs for living are then encouraged or even demanded. "Do unto others as you would have them do unto you" is part of U.S. culture, as is the injunction to "obey all traffic laws." If individuals internalize a culture, obey its rules, and honor its values, they are usually defined by other members of that society as civilized and responsible members of the group. Culture became one of the best ways to explain why people are the same in some ways but different in other ways.

Each society contains a multitude of groups, each having its own subculture (J. P. Williams, 2011). A *subculture* is a culture within a culture, identifiable by its distinctive constellation of information. Poker players are a subculture, as are attorneys, guitar players, and stamp collectors. Subcultures can be, and usually are in some respects, in conflict with one another. When you follow the rules and regulations of one subculture, it almost always means that you are violating the rules and regulations of a whole lot of other subcultures (Sellin, 1938). For example, youth culture contradicts other parts of U.S. culture in many ways, as it gives young people an outlet for some of the insecurities and anxieties that characterize adolescence (Danesi, 2010). When adolescents follow the rules of youth subculture—a reasonable thing for them to do—it can bring them into conflict with other subcultures (Haenfler, 2013).

Humans formulate cultural rules about "proper" and "improper" ways of thinking, acting, feeling, and being. These rules are called *norms*. The directive to "chew your food with the lips closed" is the statement of a norm, as is the sign found in many restaurants informing customers, "No shoes, no shirt, no service." Norms are usually coupled with *sanctions*. A *positive sanction* conveys approval and encourages norm-following activities; a *negative sanction* conveys disapproval and is designed to discourage norm-breaking activities. Norms are an important part of culture and subculture, helping us to understand regularities in human behavior better (Becker, 1982).

Rule enforcers are themselves governed by norms and shared understandings about how to sanction rule violators and to what degree (Horne, 2009). These *reactive norms* are shared understandings about what should happen, what will happen, and who should react to any given incident of rule breaking (Clark & Gibbs, 1965; Gibbs, 1966b). This is all different—or can be—from what actually *does* happen when rules are actually broken (Clark & Gibbs, 1965, p. 403). This is why occasions arise in everyday life when any objective observer must conclude that the reaction was disproportionate to whatever injury was caused by the trespass itself. Police were the ones to call, but they were too brutal in their treatment of the criminal. The reverse conclusion is also possible in which the reaction was appropriate but the reactor was not the one who should have done it. It is likely that groups (or individuals in them) will have competing views, for example, of police power or psychiatric intervention (or any other social reaction).

Being Centered

As newborns, we humans are *egocentric,* meaning we are wrapped in our own viewpoint (Piaget, 1948). We look out on the world and respond to the people in it, it is true, but early in life we have no external or outside position from which to view *ourselves* or to evaluate what we are and do. As we become more aware of others and participate in meaningful relationships with them, we start looking at our society and ourselves in new ways. We eventually come to think, feel, and act in *anticipation* of the impact we can have on others. It becomes less likely that we will intentionally hurt someone else, but it does not automatically guarantee that we won't. People—some more than others—will maintain some of their egocentricity throughout their lives (Kumbasar, Romney, & Batchelder, 1994, p. 499). They will continue to do what is good for them *as individuals,* even if it is contrary to the wishes and interests of others. In fact, humans have evolved in such a way that they are inclined toward individualism, being resistant to domination by others even while they may be emotionally tied to them (J. H. Turner & Maryanski, 2008).

Another kind of centeredness is *ethnocentrism,* which exists when members of some society or group come to believe that their culture or subculture—the system of values, norms, and customs—is better than everyone else's. If Americans were to decide that they were better than, say, Italians, because Americans play baseball better, this could easily be a reflection of ethnocentrism. A custom in one culture, baseball, is being used to evaluate and then belittle members of some other culture who have little or no knowledge of the sport. Using the values, norms, or customs of one culture to evaluate people of some other culture will usually produce a great deal of distortion and misunderstanding. Ethnocentrism makes it more likely that some people will define as inferior other people who are merely *different* from them or who do things differently from what they do. Difference is easily transformed into deviance, and deviance is easily transformed into abnormality or degeneracy.

Too much ethnocentrism or egocentrism makes it less likely that people will be able to—or willing to—look at the world through others' eyes.

Empathy (or *role taking*) is encouraged by the interactive process as we each mentally project ourselves into the positions of others and incorporate others' viewpoints into our selves (Mead, 1934). Some research exists—both suggestive and controversial—that indicates that humans have *mirror neurons* in their brains, which seem to play a role in the ability to empathize with others. Thus, the ability to do this skillfully may have some foundation in the brain (Iacoboni, 2009). We must be cautious in drawing too many conclusions from this research on mirror neurons, however. Empathy is not identical to sympathy, and just because we can identify with others, and maybe even understand their viewpoints, it does not mean we can feel their pain or that we care at all about what happens to them.

Some social scientists have been careful to avoid ethnocentrism. They have advanced an approach characterized by *relativity,* the insistence that human experiences and conditions must always be viewed within the social and cultural contexts within which they have originated and developed. These social scientists were careful to use the concept of culture *only* to describe and explain relationships and regularities in human experience. They refused to use culture to judge people or to compare people in different lands to one another. Franz Boas, for example, would not rank cultures from good to bad no matter how primitive some cultures might have appeared to outsiders (cited in Mintz, 1982, p. 501). He insisted that no universal standard or rule exists that can be used to decide exactly *which* attitudes, behaviors, or conditions are best. Boas's students, especially Ruth Benedict, Margaret Mead, and Melville Herskovits, carried on his legacy, believing that cultures had to be understood as being separate *and* equal to one another.

Although Boas and his students did reaffirm the importance and value of cultural relativity, their exaggerated devotion to it blinded them to its fundamental error: Just because all cultures are proclaimed to *be* equivalent doesn't mean that they actually *are.*

> Many would surely be troubled by the idea that the political systems of Iraq, Hitler's Germany, or the Khmer Rouge in Cambodia were, or are, as good as those in, say, Norway, Japan, or Switzerland. And they would probably react with disbelief to the assertion that there is no scientific basis for evaluating another society's practice of genocide, judicial torture or human sacrifice, for example, except as the people in that society themselves evaluate these practices. (Edgerton, 1992, p. 2)

As systems of power, knowledge, morality, and surveillance change, so do patterns of deviance (Ben-Yehuda, 2006; Foucault, 2003, pp. 55–75; Mills, 1943; Staples, 2000, pp. 15–39). This does not mean, however, that all human customs are equivalent to one another and identical in all ways (as Edgerton notes in the above quote). Norms forbidding slavery are different from norms that forbid nose picking or shoplifting. Some deviance is harmful and dangerous, or "hard," while other deviance is "soft," meaning it is unique and original, posing little threat to a society or the people in it (Raybeck, 1991, p. 54).

Sociological Relativity

Peter Berger, in his *Invitation to Sociology* (1963), showed the value of a *relativizing motif*. This demands that we keep foremost in our explanations of human experience the fact that identities, ideas, and customs are specific to a particular time and place.

> The sociological frame of reference, with its built-in procedure of looking for levels of reality other than those given in the official interpretations of society, carries with it a logical imperative to unmask the pretensions and the propaganda by which men cloak their actions with each other. (Berger, 1963, p. 38)

To fully explain—and therefore to fully understand—we must develop and then nourish whatever capacity we have to alternate from one perspective to another and to take account of meaning systems that stand in opposition to one another. This leads neither automatically nor inevitably to a greater tolerance of group or cultural differences. What it does lead to, however, is the willingness to scrutinize and then call into question what most other people take for granted (Portes, 2000).

A sociological relativist is unlikely to believe that anything goes (i.e., is acceptable) just because a majority of people says it does. However, he or she is likely to believe that a wide range of things *could* go. It is the belief in human *potentialities,* coupled with a determination to explain correctly, that characterizes sociological relativity.

Practically anything that can be done with the human body has been done with the human body, either as a source of individual pleasure or as a matter of group custom, by somebody (or somebodies), somewhere, sometime. This means an incredible diversity exists in human attitudes, behaviors, and conditions. An even greater diversity exists in the *judgments* and *evaluations* humans make of attitudes, behaviors, and conditions that they find (Cohen, 1974). Deviance is defined up and down all the time (Krauthammer, 1993; Moynihan, 1993). Definitions of deviance change over time, and as we move from one group to another at one point in time (Adler & Adler, 2006, p. 132). Things that were mightily upsetting to one generation are trivial to the next (i.e., defining deviancy down) and vice versa (i.e., defining deviancy up). Serious deviances in one group are routine and regular happenings in some other group. Goffman (1963) insisted that "normal" and "stigmatized" are not inherent qualities of individuals but *perspectives* on individuals (p. 138). If anything intrinsically real or objective may be found in the human condition, it is the intrinsically situational nature of both rules and reactions, producing a dynamic, negotiated social order (Becker, 1973, p. 196).

Deviance is not a quality of the act a person commits, Becker (1963, p. 9) instructs. It is a function of the application of rules and sanctions to a suspect individual. Those traits individuals possess that are objects of reverence to their friends are—or can be—objects of disgust to their enemies. The traits have not changed, but the meanings of them have. Such assessments depend as much or more on *who* is doing the evaluating than they do on what is being evaluated. "No trait is normal or pathological in itself but only acquires the quality of normality (or deviance) with regard to the environment in which it arises" (Horwitz, 2008, p. 366). How things look and get defined depends a lot on where you're standing. If any human universal has relevance for our understanding of social deviance, then it must surely be the human inclination to construct social differences and then to persecute anyone who seems to be out of step with everybody else (Moore, 1987).

Sociological relativity demands that social scientists who want to understand groups of people, even ones that are very different from their own, must suspend their moral judgments and look at the world through the eyes of the people whom they wish to understand (T. Turner, 1997, p. 275). This requires the "practice of putting yourself in your adversary's shoes, not in order to wear them as your own but in order to have some understanding (far short of approval) of why someone else might wear them" (Fish, 2001, p. A23). Relativists may be less likely to be ethnocentric or egocentric because looking through the eyes of people in a multitude of situations may increase a tolerance for practices different from their own. Goffman (1961) shows how this can work in the following:

> [T]he awesomeness, distastefulness, and barbarity of a foreign culture can decrease to the degree that the student becomes familiar with the point of view to life that is taken by his subjects. (p. 130)

Goffman's assertion is true, but it's not the whole truth. Although some things that initially seemed foreign or strange may become less so with greater familiarity, it is also possible for things that once seemed ordinary to look strange as an observer's familiarity with them increases.

A powerful tension exists between wanting to understand people and wanting to help them (Riesman, 1963, p. xviii), a tension that is at the core of a paradox that afflicts *any* relativistic approach. Sociologists (and anthropologists) must use tenets of relativism to understand and explain human experience correctly, but by using the tenets of relativism, they put themselves in a contradictory moral position. The *decrease* in ethnocentrism and the *increase* in tolerance that can come from a relativistic approach must be tempered by the knowledge that some of the things that an individual may find in the groups he or she is studying may be too maladaptive or damaging for them to be accepted or overlooked. Relativity is difficult to defend if it demands acceptance of things, such as murder, slavery, mutilation, or assassinations, all under the banner of a doctrinaire acceptance of cultural equivalency and celebration of diversity. If relativity becomes too relativistic, it invites criticism and rejection from nonrelativists for its moral indifference (Gibbs, 1966a, p. 11).

Contrary to the cultural relativity of Boas and his students, all customs are not equivalent. A well-played basketball game is different from a poorly played one; a well-run company is not identical to one that is inefficient; stealing other people's money is not the same as earning it; a badly written novel is not the same as a well-written one; getting a ship safely to port is not the same as smashing it into an iceberg; dishonesty is different from honesty; an interesting lecture is different from a dull one; and a silk purse is not the same as a sow's ear. Meanings are not always randomly or capriciously attached to human attitudes, behaviors, and conditions (Lemert, 1972). What if Steve Irwin had for some reason (e.g., confusion, insanity, or evilness) held the chicken in his left arm and actually fed his *son* to the crocodile? Can anyone seriously believe that relativists would view this as no different from what actually happened?

The Social Construction of Reality

Some human activities can exist independently from a socially constructed system of rules. Eating, breathing, drinking, sleeping, and waste elimination are regulated in all places and in all times by rules and understandings, but these activities would exist even without rules. Humans cough due to an involuntary muscular spasm in the throat that clears air passages. We get things stuck in our throats and cough. Coughing, however, involves more than an expulsion of air from the body. It involves rules that regulate it. Years ago (in the United States), the "correct" or "proper" way to cough was to expel air into an open hand that covered the mouth. The

H1N1 virus was an impetus to change how we cough (or, more correctly, how we *regulate* how we cough). Now it is the elbow that is the "correct" or "proper" target of the expelled air. Some kinds of human activity, however, are *constituted* by rules, not merely regulated by them. If the rules were nonexistent, the activity in question would be as well. For example, if you refuse to follow the rules of chess, then you are not playing the game (Searle, 1995, pp. 27–29).

Although all cultural rules—both regulative and constitutive—have a provisional quality (Troyer, 1992, p. 36), their conventional nature is sometimes easy to miss. The social world (or parts of it) can reach the point where it "thickens" and "hardens" (Berger & Luckmann, 1966; Kraaykamp & van Eijck, 2010, p. 225) so much that its members think and feel that it is natural and inevitable, no longer amenable to change. Particular people with particular interests may use their resources to portray certain social arrangements and cultural understandings as far better and more natural than all others (Bourdieu, 1991). It may be impossible to know if this is true or if these claims are merely the ideological rumblings of some particular group of people with self-interest on their minds (Boudon, 1994).

A major part of human development involves learning and internalizing *symbols,* physical gestures or sounds (i.e., words) that represent something else because of group agreement. Humans do not live only in a physical world of smells, sights, sounds, tastes, and touches. They live in a world of "hot and humid"; "felonies and misdemeanors"; "pepperoni pizzas"; "governments by the people and for the people"; and many other things, material and nonmaterial, that are identified and represented in a culture. Symbols make it possible for an individual to become an active and interactive member of a society. They also enable a language user to distinguish "real" from "not real" and "present" from "not present."

The separation between what is and what could be makes it possible for humans to separate "should do" from "does" and "should be" from "is." A parent may ask the youngest child, "Why can't you be more like your older brother?" The parent has an understanding made possible by his or her ability to organize experiences symbolically and to recognize that the younger child acts differently from the older child and from how the younger child *could* and *should* act. Humans are able to recognize the difference between what is, what was, and what should be. The human communication process is a powerful force, having the capacity to encourage both prosocial behaviors (e.g., healthy eating habits) and antisocial behaviors (e.g., crime or delinquency) (Gladwell, 2000; Rosenberg, 2011).

Deviants can be typified or conceptualized in such a way that their deviance offers no serious threat to the dominant construction of reality and the shared understandings on which it is based. If anything, the existence of deviance is used by supporters of the dominant culture to encourage an allegiance to conformity and conventionality (Reiman & Leighton, 2010). Deviance (and deviants) is branded as sick, evil, or abnormal, rather than as a cultural alternative or functional group difference. The definition of alternate realities as inauthentic, pathological, or just plain weird reinforces the dominant view of reality and makes it appear more immutable and concrete than it actually is. The construction of deviant labels and their assignment to particular individuals serve to mask social conflicts and make the labelers more confident that their way is the only *right* way (Parsons, 1951, p. 266).

During the New Orleans Mardi Gras, certain forms of *creative deviance* that might normally be forbidden become customary (Douglas, Rasmussen, & Flanagan, 1977, p. 238). One of these is "parade stripping," in which women expose their naked breasts to people on parade floats so that they will be thrown glass beads and trinkets. People who are not so accepting of the practice refer to these women as "beadwhores," and they tend to view parade stripping as unbridled exhibitionism. To those individuals who are caught up in the playful atmosphere of Mardi Gras, however, things are different (Forsyth, 1992, p. 395). Parade stripping represents a ritualized exchange of things of value. The float rider gets to see naked breasts, and the woman receives beads, trinkets, and confirmation that her breasts are grand enough to warrant a bestowing of gifts (Shrum & Kilburn, 1996, p. 444). In 1935, police officers in Atlantic City, New Jersey, arrested 42 *men* on the beach because they wore swimsuits without tops. Imagine what these officers would have done at Mardi Gras (or on a nude beach)!

Communities exist all across the world that provide alternate identities to their members that give them a sense of pride and significance even while they are deviant from the standpoint of other communities (Cross & Hernández, 2011). Cultural and subcultural rules exist that make it possible for people to do what is easy, smart, practical, simple, or fun, rather than what is proper (Freilich, 1991). Each relationship contains rules, understandings, and background assumptions that might very well seem odd to people from other relationships (Denzin, 1970, pp. 131–132).

A study of "catchout camp" by Wasserman and Clair (2010), a region in Birmingham, Alabama, populated by the homeless, shows how marginal people may display a creative resistance to what they see as a normative system that is really not for them. The residents of this camp found out that their way of life was going to be criticized or condemned by many different groups of people—police, social workers, religious zealots, shopkeepers, elites, ordinary citizens—under the cloak of care, concern, and compassion. They concluded, therefore, that they lived in a hostile social environment.

Residents did what they could to resist the imposition of labels attached to them and their lifestyle by others. Catchout camp inhabitants made their own world as best they could, one characterized by resilience, pride, independence, humor, and lively conversation (often about sports or sex).

Theoretical Views: The Old and the Not-So-Old

Bad Actors and Bad Acts

One of the earliest conceptions of deviance and the deviant was founded on a belief that deviants could be separated from nondeviants on the basis of inherent or intrinsic characteristics of the individual rule breaker (Devroye, 2010; Rafter, 1997). Usually, some biological or psychological factor, such as body chemistry, intelligence, or brain dysfunction, was identified and then blamed for the trespass (Bernard, Snipes, & Gerould, 2010; F. P. Williams & McShane, 2010). Because the deviance was almost always viewed as unacceptable and unnecessary, the temptation to see defect, abnormality, or degeneracy in the biology or psychology of deviants was too great to resist. Simply, deviants were viewed as both distinct (identifiable and all alike) and inferior, so deviance was anything that abnormal people did (or were).

The belief developed that with certain kinds of deviance (e.g., crime), the deviant had physical markers—an inherited taint—of his or her degeneracy that could be recognized by dispassionate observers (e.g., asymmetry of the face or brain, too-large jaws or cheekbones, too-large or too-small ears, abnormal teeth, too-long arms, extra fingers or toes). This kind of marginal thinking was not restricted only to marginal thinkers. A former U.S. Supreme Court Judge named Oliver Wendell Holmes, Jr., in a 1927 case (*Buck v. Bell*), upheld the forced sterilization of an adolescent female. She had been deemed by the state of Virginia to be both retarded and a deficient mother. Holmes reasoned that

> it is better for all the world if, instead of waiting to execute degenerate offspring for crime, or to let them starve for their imbecility, society can prevent those who are manifestly unfit from continuing their kind. . . . Three generations of imbeciles are enough. (Schnakenberg, 2009, pp. 46–47)

Some theorists focused on deviant acts instead of deviant individuals, classifying these acts as inherently or intrinsically deviant. For example, Parsons (1951) insisted that deviance produces a disturbance in the equilibrium of interactive systems, and Schwendinger and Schwendinger (1975) asserted that deviance is behavior that is harmful. As sociologists and anthropologists demonstrated the great array that exists in human customs and conditions, the meaning of deviance changed. Attention was less on deviants and what they did and more on the relativity of reactions and relationships (Best, 2004).

Relativity is found in the works of both Karl Marx and Émile Durkheim. Marx (1846/1978) was inclined to believe that the economic forms within which humans produce, consume, and exchange are transitory and historical. No final conclusion, theory, or premise exists that applies universally to all times, places, and circumstances. However, the first thorough-going application of relativity to an understanding of deviance is found in Durkheim's *The Rules of Sociological Method* (1895/1938) where he contrasts the "normal" with the "pathological." Durkheim asks us to imagine a society of saints where each individual is exemplary, so crimes such as murder, rape, or assault will not exist (pp. 68–69). This does not mean, however, that crime will be unknown. Offenses that might seem trivial and ordinary to us would appear quite scandalous in this saintly society. Durkheim was indicating that it is the *attitude* about, and *reaction* to, some social arrangement that is responsible for its categorization as criminal.

Relativity also appears in his *The Division of Labor in Society* (1893/ 1933), where Durkheim asserts that many acts are regarded as criminal even though they are not intrinsically harmful, such as touching a forbidden object, allowing a sacred fire to die out, or failing to make a required sacrifice (p. 72). Although we might now refuse to classify normative violations like these as crimes, Durkheim's point stands. Crime is whatever people say it is, and it is social reaction that establishes what is harmful, not the other way around. Deviance as an analytical and empirical category may be nearly universal, but the particular form that deviance takes is not (Ben-Yehuda, 1990, 2006).

The Chicago School

In the United States, a group of sociologists in the Department of Sociology at the University of Chicago were the first to use a relativistic approach to deviance (known as the Chicago School). They were to exert a tremendous amount of influence on practically all subsequent approaches to deviance and crime that had any sociological leanings (Lanier & Henry, 2010, pp. 232–233). Bernard et al. (2010, p. 147) declare that the Chicago School can be described as a gold mine that continues to enrich the study of crime even today. For representatives of the Chicago School, neither absolutes nor universal rules of human behavior existed (F. P. Williams & McShane, 2010).

The Chicago School emphasized the powerful role played by context and social setting in the creation of deviance and crime by showing that coexisting and yet incompatible subcultures could encourage different ways of acting, thinking, and feeling. The Chicago School also showed that different groups could evaluate the same conduct or social arrangement in different ways. As these Chicago sociologists moved from one locale or zone to another in the urban milieu, they found people acting, thinking, and feeling in different ways. What they found was that those urban regions, zones, or natural areas where deregulation and social disorganization were the highest were the places where all kinds of deviance were too.

The Chicago School, embodied particularly in the works of Edwin Hardin Sutherland (1947), clarified how differential association makes it possible for some individuals to learn things that other individuals do not. By focusing on symbolic interaction and learned behavior, Sutherland gave a social and interactive understanding of the development of crime, while he offered a contextual understanding of shared rules and subcultural variation. This transformed the meaning of social disorganization into something closer to what actually exists in the real world: differential social organization. This helped to erode even further the idea that deviants were degenerate and that deviance was inherently abnormal. Rapid social and political change, as well as changes in the distribution of scarce resources, can produce confusion and deregulation, which can lead to deviance and crime (Zhao & Cao, 2010, pp. 1223–1224).

The principal factor in understanding why some people break the law, Sutherland (1947) insisted, is to be found in the meanings or definitions they give to events in the social world. Most juvenile delinquency, for example, is learned from others with whom the juvenile has meaningful and rewarding contacts. It is rarely an outcome of fractured interpersonal relationships or a response to isolation and despair (Smångs, 2010, pp. 620–625). Having delinquent companions is one of the best and most consistent predictors of teenagers' delinquent activity (Warr, 1993, 2002). Deviant acts may be the expression of *subterranean values,* such as autonomy, daring, street smartness, avenging masculinity, and conspicuous consumption (Matza & Sykes, 1961, p. 716).

Sutherland believed that face-to-face interaction was the only way that definitions favorable to violating the law could be learned. However, in this day and age, where the information superhighway is so wide and long, television (and movies, to a lesser extent) and cell phones play a prominent role in our lives. Restricting interaction exclusively to face-to-face relationships is unwarranted. Many of us are now part of *portable communities* (Chayko, 2008, p. 8), networks of interactants who are connected through online and mobile technologies, regardless of whether we meet face-to-face frequently, infrequently, or never.

With the passage of time, Sutherland's view of learning was fleshed out by adding newly developed (and still developing) ideas from psychology and social psychology about how humans learn (Tibbetts & Hemmens, 2010, pp. 443–448). One of the more important reformulations of Sutherland's differential association theory has been done by Burgess and Akers (1966), which itself was expanded by Akers (1985). These theorists contributed additional (and valuable) information about how humans acquired deviant behaviors through imitation and vicarious learning.

Norms and Naughtiness

In the middle of the twentieth century, more sociologists reached the conclusion that deviance was never going to be suitably understood by looking at intrinsic or essential qualities of deviants that distinguished them from nondeviants. Attitudes, behaviors, and conditions are simply too relative and dynamic to be pigeonholed into two mutually exclusive categories of abnormality and normality. The concept of norm was adopted as a better way—or so it seemed—to explain and understand the nature of social deviance than any account based on the notion of degeneracy or abnormality.

William Graham Sumner's (1906) discussion of folkways, a type of norm, had indicated that they are inherited from the past and that they direct human behavior almost automatically. When rules are followed, they facilitate the adjustment of individuals to life conditions and to the particular demands of time and place. It was an easy leap to the view that deviance is a normative departure and that norms could make anything right or wrong, depending on the case (Gibbs, 1966a, p. 14; W. G. Sumner, 1906, pp. 521–522). Becker (1963) retained the idea of norm but changed the thinking about responsibility. It was no longer the rule breaker who was at fault. Becker reasoned that it is the group *itself* that creates deviance by making rules whose violation qualifies as deviance, identifying rule breakers, and treating them as outsiders (p. 163).

One valuable conclusion from these is that we must see deviance as an outcome of a process of interaction between people, some of whom in their own interests make and enforce rules that catch others who are doing (or being) something that gets them labeled as deviants and treated accordingly.

A successful, and enforceable, social construction of a particular label of deviance depends on the ability of one, or more, groups to use (or generate) enough power so as to enforce *their* definition and version of morality on others. . . . Deviance . . . always results from negotiations about morality *and* the configuration of power relationships. (Ben-Yehuda, 1990, pp. 6–7)

Some of these moral crusades are very successful, having enduring effects, while others are short-lived, dying quickly and with little fanfare.

No longer were norms necessarily viewed as reflective of a society-wide consensus or a universal morality. C. Wright Mills (1943), one of the most influential sociologists in the history of the discipline (Oakes, 2011), showed that the prevailing norms *always* reflect some *specific* group's biased view of what is proper or improper; norms reflect the power, interests, and outlooks of the groups that create them. Under Mills's gaze, not only did norms produce efficiency and predictability in human behavior, but they also served as smokescreens to hide the wellspring of power and class interests. Norms are "propaganda for conformity," embodying and demanding adherence to standards that are biased, reflecting a confluence of class, status, and power (1943, p. 179).

The Labeling or Social Reactions Perspective

Once theoretical explanations of deviance were sensitive to the role played by the "other" in the construction of deviance, a whole new world of possibilities was opened. It could be maintained with credibility and confidence that social control *itself* has the ironic effect of actually creating deviance and channeling the direction that it takes (Lemert, 1972, p. 49). Tannenbaum (1938) insisted that social labels (and other social reactions) actually create deviance: "The process of making the criminal, therefore, is a process of tagging, defining, identifying, segregating, describing, emphasizing, making conscious and self-conscious; it becomes a way of stimulating, suggesting, emphasizing, and evoking the very traits that are complained of" (pp. 19–20). A new wrinkle had been added: The understanding of social deviance required an analysis of the processes by which persons come to be defined and treated *as deviant* by others. The definition of deviance changed to reflect this new understanding: "Deviance is not a property *inherent in* certain forms of behavior; it is a property *conferred upon* these forms by the audiences which directly or indirectly witness them" (Erikson, 1962, p. 308).

How can social control create deviance? One way is by naming, labeling, or categorizing some attitudes, behaviors, or conditions as types of deviance, separating them from other attitudes, behaviors, or conditions that are considered to be proper or even desirable.

> Deviance may be conceived as a process by which the members of a group, community, or society (1) interpret behavior as deviant, (2) define persons who so behave as a certain kind of deviant, and (3) accord them the treatment considered appropriate to such deviants. (Kitsuse, 1962, p. 248)

A second possibility is that the *reactions* of other people to an individual's initial or primary deviance—what these others say, do, or believe—can powerfully impact the nature and form of all subsequent deviant behavior.

> [W]e start with the idea that persons and groups are differentiated in various ways, some of which result in social penalties, rejection and segregation. These penalties and segregative reactions of society or the community are dynamic factors which increase, decrease, and condition the form which the initial differentiation or deviation takes. (Lemert, 1951, p. 22)

According to Lemert's (1951, 1972) *secondary deviance proposition*, an individual's deviant behavior evolves to the point where it is constructed *principally* as a means of defense, attack, or adaptation to the problems created by the real or anticipated disapproving, degradational, or isolating reactions of others.

About the same time that Lemert was exploring the role of secondary processes in human deviance, Merton was exploring how collective events (i.e., human actions, decisions, or beliefs) can have unanticipated consequences. One possibility, which Merton (1948, p. 195) called the "self-fulfilling prophecy," is that a *false* or *incorrect* definition of a situation changes subsequent events sufficiently that the originally false definition of a situation actually becomes true. Students, for example, convinced that they are destined to fail an exam, become so nervous and anxious that they worry more than they study, and they do fail. Merton (1968) also acknowledged, though he spent no time developing the idea, that beliefs (and reactions based on them) can be self-destroying, an idea he credited to John Venn, a nineteenth-century logician (p. 182). Merton (1948) called this a "suicidal prophecy" (p. 196). The suicidal prophecy *prevents* or "kills off" the fulfillment of an outcome that would otherwise have developed. The hare in the famous fable about its race against the tortoise demonstrates a suicidal prophecy. The rabbit was so certain that it would beat the slow-moving reptile that it behaved imprudently, and it did not win the race. Another example is found in the situation where a teacher tells a student that he or she will never amount to anything, which results in the pupil working hard to prove the teacher wrong.

These two prophecies have not been treated equally in subsequent analyses of deviance. Becker (1963), for example, only felt obliged to use a self-fulfilling prophecy in his analysis of deviant careers (failing to credit Merton when he did). This gave the false or at least distorted impression that the only situations of importance to an analysis of deviance are when social mechanisms work together to shape individuals into the images that people have of them. Although it is true that sometimes an individual's deviance is amplified by the reactions of others, this is not the only possibility.

The Normality of Deviance

Deviance came to be viewed as an inevitable and rather ordinary feature of life in a pluralistic society, and deviants came to be viewed as more sinned against than sinning. In fact, siding with deviants became as defensible as siding with representatives of conventional society, such as police, judges, or psychiatrists. The deviant's right to be different and to be free from stigma and harassment was actively defended. Deviance was defined increasingly in political terms. Power—the power to label and the power to legitimate one's own view of proper and improper—emerged as a central explanatory variable in understanding deviance (Young, 2011). Deviance was conceptualized more than ever as a name, label, category, definition, vocabulary, discourse, or narrative that was applied to individuals and what they think, do, and are (Dellwing, 2011).

The emergence of a radical view of deviance meant that some theorists took the side of deviants with a vengeance. Not only did these theorists defend the right of deviants to be different, but they also condemned representatives of conventional society and branded them as the dangerous, odd, or misguided ones. Life in an unequal, competitive, insecure, acquisitive society, they believed, was brutalizing for some people, and brutal conditions generate brutal behaviors. Radicals viewed deviance as one of the choices that people consciously make in order to manage some of the difficulties posed for them by life in a contradictory society (Taylor, Walton, & Young, 1973, p. 271).

Radicals insist that the control of deviants and the suppression of deviance are both principal ways that threats to the economic and political systems are counteracted so that the status quo is preserved for the benefit of powerful groups (Quinney, 1970, 1974; Reiman & Leighton, 2010). Quinney (1973, p. 60) went so far as to claim that the really bad people in a society are those who make laws to protect their own interests and to legitimate their suppression of threatening groups. Radical deviance theorists, as well as others who consider power and social conflict to be at the heart of both social deviance and any understanding of it, now are inclined to use the term "postmodern" to identify their work (Cote, 2002, p. 228; F. P. Williams & McShane, 2010, p. 142). (Arrigo and Bernard [1997], however, concluded that postmodern criminology is an independent orientation and method of analysis despite having some areas of agreement with conflict criminology and radical criminology.)

Postmodernists (Arrigo & Bernard, 1997; Ferrell, 1999; Henry & Milovanovic, 1991, 1996; Katz, 1988; Milovanovic, 1997) conceptualize deviance as a joint construction of social actors, and a core theme is postmodernists' refusal to reduce social deviance down to the concrete and discrete action of one individual (i.e., a deviant) that is then followed by the concrete and discrete reaction of another individual (i.e., a control agent) (Henry & Milovanovic, 1991). Postmodernists assert that the meanings, definitions, discourses, and narratives used to describe and understand both deviance and control of it are always problematic and contentious, just like the social world itself (Henry & Milovanovic, 1996; Lyman & Scott, 1989, p. 7). They adopt a viewpoint of appreciative relativism, which is inclined to see all points of view as equally valid and reliable (Bernard et al., 2010, p. 280).

Postmodernists focus on how humans jointly produce social deviance (crime in particular) through modes of discourse that they conveniently forget they have jointly produced. Structures of control, as well as that which is being controlled (i.e., deviance), are shaped by human collective actions, interactions, and the discourses that are all such an essential part of the reproduction of what is being described. Postmodernists give great importance to the means of linguistic production because of their view that all knowledge—human thoughts and emotions particularly—is inseparable from language and shared systems of discourse. We must always have a clear understanding of exactly who the individuals are that are deciding that something is deviant, why they are making their claims about it, and their level of success in convincing others that they are authorities on the issue in question (Best, 1990, pp. 11–13; Spector & Kitsuse, 1977). We must also have a clear understanding of how these discourses or narratives change those individuals who make them in the first place in terms of their evolving understandings, actions, and reactions.

Language itself is far from neutral, privileging some points of view while invalidating others (Bernard et al., 2010, p. 275; Foucault, 2003). Agents of social control try to make what they do to control others appear to be the only reasonable way to proceed, as a way to help the people being controlled to lead better, more productive lives. This is a fiction, according to postmodernists. The principal objective of control agents is to control any troublesome population wherever and whenever it is found, an enterprise in which a constellation of interlocking agencies from different institutions work together to maintain the status quo and to keep it from being changed or altered (Foucault, 1977; Henry & Milovanovic, 1991).

It may be the *functionality* of both deviance and deviant—serving as an object of persecution—for those groups that benefit from the status quo that is a principal reason for both the existence and persistence of deviance. Conventional groups do things to ensure that deviance exists— some intentionally and some unintentionally—because, despite surface appearances or public proclamations, deviance actually contributes in many ways to preservation of the status quo. The war on crime, for example, justifies the existence of police, courts, and prisons (Reiman & Leighton, 2010). It is the same for other kinds of deviance. Groups and organizations that have the mandate to eliminate deviance benefit too much from its existence to do the job well enough to make much of a difference. Deviants can be used as scapegoats to explain away continuing or worsening social problems (Gamson, 1995, p. 17). Both under-conformity (being too "bad") to norms and over-conformity (being too "good") can evoke negative reactions from powerful individuals when these reactors conclude that their interests are being threatened (Heckert & Heckert, 2002, p. 468). (Though being too bad is more likely to be defined as a problem than is being too good.)

Relativity and Social Deviance

Pathology, Harm, and Basic Human Rights

To describe some culture, society, social arrangement, group, or individual as degenerate, pathological, or abnormal may be convenient, but none of these terms adds very much to our understanding of social deviance (Matza, 1969, pp. 41–42).

> If persons are miserable, they may be so designated, and the quality of that misery described. Nothing but confusion is added by rendering that misery a pathology. But at the same time much that is essential to the phenomenon may be lost by neglecting to mention the misery. (p. 43)

We do not need to categorize something as degenerate, pathological, or abnormal in order to recognize that it is something that humans would be better off without.

The principal defect of either pathologizing diversity or romanticizing it is that either position fails to explain correctly the phenomena under consideration (Matza, 1969, p. 44). When social arrangements are pathologized, it makes it far more difficult to entertain the possibility that they are, despite surface appearances, functional or even valuable accomplishments. When they are romanticized, it misrepresents or misses the genuine tragedy, pathos, and harm that certain social arrangements actually produce.

Preservation of basic human rights emerged as a global concern, principally in response to the Holocaust and World War II. These rights were formalized in the Universal Declaration of Human Rights (UDHR) of the United Nations (1948). This document is premised on the idea that all human beings should have the same fundamental rights no matter where they live (T. Turner, 1997, p. 276; Zechenter, 1997, p. 320). The UDHR was ratified by each member country of the United Nations in 1948, and it continues to be an important standard against which human decency is measured (Nagengast & Turner, 1997, p. 269).

Before the Second World War, most people thought human rights protection would occur at the level of the nation-state and that it was a domestic, not international, issue. The atrocities of the war changed that. They showed that individuals were at a distinct disadvantage when confronted with malevolent governmental power, and they needed more protections against governmental abuse than the legal system of any one nation could provide.

Provisions of the UDHR prohibit murder, torture, and slavery, while they guarantee freedom of conscience, speech, and dissent. Specific sections provide guarantees to employment and fair working conditions; to health, food, and social security; to education; and to participation in the cultural life of the community (United Nations, 1948). The history of a global concern with human rights has been uneven, precarious, difficult, and protracted. A "Responsibility to Protect" doctrine has been evolving in spurts and fits (Moyn, 2010). This doctrine is founded on the idea that human rights are universal, so every state or government should do what it can to protect them. If a political entity drags its feet or fails to protect its citizens altogether, other political entities (e.g., the United Nations) should step in to do the job.

Indigenous populations have been thrown off of their lands, legally and illegally; women have been denied equal access to food, health care, and other medical necessities; individuals (especially women and children) have been forced to perform slave labor; people across the planet have been deprived of both property and liberty without due process; and people have been tortured and killed merely because they were defined as political threats by powerful elites (Hagan & Rymond-Richmond, 2009; Levy & Sznaider, 2010). Some nations further their economic, political, and cultural interests in ways that are destructive to the sanctity and well-being of people worldwide (Ritzer, 2008, pp. 164–168; T. Turner, 1997, p. 283). The actions of some groups within a given society do threaten fundamental human rights of other groups in that society (Gross, 2010).

We must be able to identify how and when human rights are being violated, by whom, for what reasons, and with what consequences. Attention to the existence of harm is a valuable contribution to our understanding of deviance (Costello, 2006, 2009). It would be a mistake, however, to conclude that a harm-based conception of deviance invalidates sociological relativity. A government, because of its monopolization of power, can blame individuals for harms that are really no different from the harms imposed by the government itself (Kennedy, 1976, p. 62). It can also blame individuals for harms that are really not their fault. Decisions about harm—what qualifies and who is at fault—are subject to a great deal of relativity (Ghatak, 2011).

Human rights seem to be less a problem of the legal formulations of rights and duties than they are a problem of human classification, of who is counted as a complete human being, deserving of the full range of human rights (Agier, 2011). The global push for human rights must start with an understanding of how individuals in different societies construct their own social realities, cultural meanings, and personal identities (Findlay & Henham, 2010). Human rights are a function of inclusion and exclusion, a matter of truly belonging to a nation, society, or group. This cannot happen unless members of a nation recognize and accept one another as full citizens (Glenn, 2011, pp. 3–9). Between the extremes of essentialism on the one hand and relativity on the other, a middle ground must be found to mediate between narrow, universalist claims and broad, cultural relativist counter-claims (Messer, 1997, pp. 310–311). It is no easy task to develop a concept of universal human rights in the face of such profound and enduring cultural and social conflicts and disagreements in regard to moral and ethical norms (Zechenter, 1997, p. 320).

Being a relativist does not inevitably dull one's moral sensibilities, and relativists can be as passionately committed as anyone else to ending human suffering. As Berger (1963) notes, a use of relativity to better understand human experience frees no one from finding his or her own way morally (pp. 158–159). Even though we might be able to understand that one nation's terrorist is another nation's freedom fighter, it certainly does not mean that we must cast an approving eye toward the attacks on the U.S. World Trade Center on September 11, 2001. Likewise, even though we can understand that laws against theft are culturally specific and historically based, reflecting some groups' interest and power more than others', it does not mean that we have to grin and bear it when our homes are burglarized and our possessions taken. We can still commit to the intellectual position of sociological relativity and yet be passionately committed to one course of action instead of another. It is "possible to be fully aware of the relativity and the precariousness of the way by which men organize their sexuality, and yet commit oneself absolutely to one's own marriage" (p. 159). We do the "right" thing because we can, justifying it on the basis of neither nature nor necessity.

Relativity does not require moral indifference, and it does not mean that we can never be upset or horrified by what we see or experience in another group or society (Goode & Ben-Yehuda, 1994, p. 73). Relativity just reminds us that our personal beliefs or our cultural understandings are not necessarily found everywhere. If we condemn some practice, we must be certain that we are doing it for reasons other than our own particular ethnocentric or egocentric biases. Our biases cannot be avoided completely, it is true, but relativity allows us the best chance to recognize them for the partialities that they are.

The Serious Implications of Taking Relativity Seriously

Relativity in the sociology of deviance led to a rejection of correctionalism, which is founded on strong and abiding faith in the goodness and necessity of prevailing standards and an even stronger faith in the abnormality and pathology of individual rule breakers. Correctionalism was replaced by naturalism, which is founded on a view of the human being as a self-conscious, reflexive being who engages in meaningful activity. Naturalism combines the scientific method of observation with empathy, intuition, and experience. According to Matza (1969), the sociology of deviance encourages an appreciation of human diversity and a rejection of the simplistic notion that deviants are inherently pathological (pp. 8–10).

> The growth of a sociological view of deviant phenomena involved, as major phases, the replacement of a correctional stance by an *appreciation* of the deviant subject, the tacit purging of a conception of pathology by new stress on human *diversity,* and the erosion of a simple distinction between deviant and conventional phenomena, resulting from more intimate familiarity with the world as it is, which yielded a more sophisticated view stressing *complexity.* (p. 10)

Social scientists, just like the humans they study, must be able to deal with—and construct theories that make sense of—the ambiguity and uncertainty of social life. Sociology itself, Goode (2003) asserts, is "wedded" to the concept of deviance (pp. 519–520). If the marriage works, it is due in no small part to the relativity that is at the core of both.

Humans have a remarkable capacity to make practically anything proper or improper, as the case may be. The world is constantly in flux, and people have done, are doing, and will continue to do a multitude of things that will lead to the delight, indifference, or dismay of others (Gibbs, 1994). A colleague of mine once observed that the ties that bind—traditions and customs, ways of doing things, standard notions of proper and improper—also qualify as the ties that *blind*. Human beings assign meaning to practically everything that can be seen, felt, smelled, tasted, or heard. Once this is done, it tends to blind them to other possibilities and to alternate ways of thinking, feeling, acting, or being. One individual's object of outrage or disgust might be, and probably is, another individual's object of reverence, worship, or desire; one individual's revulsion might be another individual's attraction; and the object or objects of hatred for members of one human society just might be, and probably are, the objects of adoration for members of another society (Winther, personal communication, 1994).

Culture shock is the feeling of disorientation or uneasiness that one might experience when traveling to a different place and being forced to accommodate to new ways of thinking, feeling, or acting. Sometimes the culture shock is mild. If you went from a hot climate, such as one finds in Southern California or Florida, to a much colder climate, such as one finds in Illinois or New York, you might experience things in the winter to which you were unaccustomed. People would seem to be dressing in unusual ways and doing unusual things, such as buying snow blowers and snow shovels, but it would be easy to adjust to these changes. They would be only temporarily disorienting. What if you were told, however, that the stew you had just eaten was made with dog meat, horse meat, sheep eyes, or the flesh of recently killed rattlesnakes? How would you feel if you were told that the crunchy snack you had just eaten was not a party mix but baked locusts and termites? In these cases, culture shock may be acute and quite unsettling. Sometimes it is an experience an individual will never forget.

Berger (1963) observed that sociological discovery is culture shock without geographical displacement (p. 23). Just as travelers to another land may experience a sense of uneasiness, disorientation, or surprise when faced with people whose customs are different from their own, so can we be shocked by seeing familiar happenings in a new way. This culture shock may propel us in the direction of greater ethnocentrism. No way, we tell ourselves, would we ever do *that*; we would have to be sick, crazy, or out of our heads. Yet we must fight this centeredness and make every effort to understand the context of action. We must understand that if we had been raised in a culture where people eat dogs, horses, sheep eyes, rattlesnakes, locusts, or termites, we would, in all likelihood, be eating and enjoying them, too.

Viewing deviance as something that can produce culture shock but that is not intrinsically bad or inherently sick is valuable. Just as we might study any form of behavior in a foreign land, we can study deviance "at home"—even in our own homes—as part of changing social relationships and alternating cultural meanings. Because our goal is to understand the context of behavior and how and why it is defined and evaluated the way it is, we will not spend much time trying to decide if deviance is abnormal or sick, in need of cure or correction. Just as it would be too ethnocentric to conclude that eating dog meat instead of cow meat is abnormal or sick, it is too ethnocentric to conclude that people who inhale certain kinds of substances (e.g., marijuana) are more abnormal or sicker than people who inhale other kinds of substances (e.g., tobacco). Deviance in practically all its forms is a normal feature of human societies, and we must fight the temptation to equate deviance with disease or abnormality. Some deviance is unsettling or shocking to people who are unfamiliar with it, but this does not mean that deviance is essentially or necessarily abnormal or sick everywhere and at all times.

Whose Side Are We On?

The concept of sentimentality (Becker, 1963, 1964, 1967) offers a powerful reminder that sides exist in deciding who or what is deviant, and it matters greatly whose side is taken. Becker (1964) defined *sentimentality* as a disposition on the part of a researcher to leave certain variables in a research problem unexamined or to refuse to consider alternate views of some social happening or distasteful possibilities (pp. 4–5). Becker borrowed the term from Freidson's (1961) study of physicians and their patients. Freidson was willing to give credibility and authority to patients' views of their physicians even when these views were at odds with what physicians thought of themselves. Sides exist even in the seemingly straightforward relationship between physician and patient, and it is possible that a patient's view is more credible than is the physician's.

Sometimes, a researcher's bias is to side with representatives of the official world (e.g., police, judges, or psychiatrists), in which case he or she is adopting *conventional sentimentality*; at other times, a researcher's bias is to side with representatives of deviant worlds (e.g., criminals or the mentally ill), in which case he or she is adopting *unconventional sentimentality* (Becker, 1964, p. 5). Researchers are sentimental when they overidentify with either conventional or unconventional human beings only because they do not want to face the possibility that some cherished sympathy of theirs could be shown to be untrue (Becker, 1967, p. 246). Alternation between these two different sides will increase the chances of developing an actor-relevant, naturalistic understanding of both rule breakers *and* rule makers.

Social scientists are required by the demands of their disciplines to understand as fully as possible the social systems they are studying. This means that they will almost always have to uncover and critically evaluate the myths, ideologies, and verbal smoke screens that humans use to hide, distort, or legitimate whatever they are doing (Berger, 1963, p. 41–42). Carried to extremes, romanticizing or glorifying diversity will have the unfortunate outcome of making it more difficult to see and deal with the extreme suffering that deviance can cause in the lives of people who are adversely affected by it (Matza, 1969, p. 44). We must not be relativistic in the extreme, because it would hamper our ability to understand social deviance (Rafter, 1992, p. 38).

The social construction of values and norms is often accidental and arbitrary, but it is also (or can be) rational and reasonable (Bloom, 1987). By restricting ourselves to one particular group and time, the acts, attributes, ideas, and identities can be ranked in some rough fashion from good to bad, appropriate to inappropriate, or injurious to benign. To act as if it is unimportant exactly *what* attitudes, behaviors, and conditions individuals profess, display, or have would be a mistake. Feeding a dead chicken to a crocodile is identifiably different from, and morally superior to, feeding your infant son to the reptile. The issue gets murky, however, when you try to compare customs from different cultures or time periods along some universal dimension of goodness and badness. What one group calls a "freedom fighter" or "martyr," another group calls a "terrorist," and it does little good to try to figure out who is right independent from a consideration of who exactly is making the determination and why.

Elites in sovereign nations justify and excuse everything they do by insisting that they should be allowed to do anything they want because they are sovereign nations. This represents not so much the tenets of relativism as their misuse. A conflict can exist between the rights (or lack thereof) of citizens of any particular society or nation-state and their rights in the global community (Moyn, 2010). Countries that violate the human rights of their population most often are the ones that justify their actions in the international arena by appealing to sovereignty and cultural relativity (Nagengast & Turner, 1997, p. 270). They defend practices such as corporal or capital punishment, the abuse of women (including genital mutilation), sexism and racism, and violence by claiming that their critics are ethnocentric or indifferent to the integrity of local customs.

The concept of relativity in sociology (and anthropology), which was developed partly to encourage an awareness of and respect for human variability and diversity, has returned to haunt us. Relativity has been used to justify the differential treatment of indigenous groups, women, and minorities, as well as to excuse human rights abuses (Nagengast, 1997, p. 352). Self-interest can be masked as the common good, and socially constructed roles can serve as alibis for acts of personal cruelty or cowardice (Berger, 1963, p. 160). It is quite proper—and not at all inconsistent with sociological relativity—to be critical of sovereign nations whenever they have institutionalized practices that interfere with human rights for reasons unrelated to community survival or the safety and security of their citizens. Customs that are a product of ideological thinking (e.g., male dominance) or stark economic inequalities are the ones that are most in need of a relativist analysis.

Conclusions

The egocentricity of childhood, in which we are concerned principally with ourselves, is eventually replaced with the ethnocentricity of adulthood, in which we come to evaluate the customs and standards of other people against those of our own groups. Cultural understandings are acquired in the context of socialization, in which each individual learns the social heritage of his or her society. An important part of this process is the acquisition of symbols and the language of which they are a part. The great diversity in human behavior is produced by the interplay of biological, psychological, and sociocultural factors.

Theories of deviance have evolved over time. Early views were based on a belief that intrinsic characteristics separated both deviants and deviance from their opposites. They assumed that deviance is what abnormal people do. Attention ultimately shifted to norms and then to labels and social reactions. Social deviance came to be viewed as a regular feature of life in a pluralistic society that could be caused by social control itself. Deviance emerges from social differentiation, social conflict, and social disagreement, and the meanings of deviance are always problematic.

A great deal of diversity can be found as we move from society to society or group to group. Relativity is a way of examining standards and customs by understanding their context. Deviance, like beauty, is in the eye of the beholder. It exists because some groups decide that other groups ought not to be doing and being what they are, in fact, doing and being. Deviance results from dynamic relationships among many people; it is not an unchanging or immutable condition with intrinsic or inherent qualities. We must remember that all things are transitory and impermanent, including human understandings about proper and improper ways of acting, thinking, feeling, and being.

Victor Hugo claimed that nothing is as powerful as an idea whose time has come. This is certainly true for sociological relativity. Sometimes, examples of deviance will be found—glaring examples of inhumanity and incivility—that will shock our sensibilities so much that we will be inclined toward intolerance and a quest for harsher and swifter penalties for deviants. Some individuals or groups will do things that are so harmful or outlandish that they push practically everyone else into a strong defense of the status quo and conventional morality. However, it is relativity that offers social scientists—especially sociologists—the best hope for understanding the social construction of both reality and social deviance.

Because relativity is so central to sociological consciousness, it must be a central part of practically all of our understandings of human experience. Sociological relativity's vision of society (socially constructed), vision of human nature (broad and flexible), scientific methodology (actor-relevant and empathic), and moral stance (unsentimental) all offer great power and potential to anyone who wants to understand and explain social deviance. Sociological relativity is just too powerful an idea and too much a part of what makes the sociological imagination important and valuable for it to be dumped in the intellectual waste bin.

References

Adler, P., & Adler, P. (2006). The deviance society. *Deviant Behavior, 27,* 129–148.

Adler, P., & Adler, P. (2009). Defining deviance. In P. Adler & P. Adler (Eds.), *Constructions of deviance: Social power, context, and interaction* (6th ed., pp. 11–15). Belmont, CA: Thomson/Wadsworth.

Agier, M. (2011). *Managing the undesirables: Refugee camps and humanitarian government.* Cambridge, UK: Polity Press.

Akers, R. L. (1985). *Deviant behavior: A social learning approach* (3rd ed.). Belmont, CA: Wadsworth.

Arrigo, B. A., & Bernard, T. J. (1997). Postmodern criminology in relation to radical and conflict criminology. *Critical Criminology, 8,* 39–60.

Becker, H. (1963). *Outsiders: Studies in the sociology of deviance.* New York, NY: Free Press.

Becker, H. (1964). Introduction. In H. Becker (Ed.), *The other side: Perspectives on deviance* (pp. 1–6). New York, NY: Free Press.

Becker, H. (1967). Whose side are we on? *Social Problems, 14,* 239–247.

Becker, H. (1973). Labeling theory reconsidered. In H. Becker (Ed.), *Outsiders: Studies in the sociology of deviance* (pp. 177–212). New York, NY: Free Press.

Becker, H. (1982). Culture: A sociological view. *Yale Review, 71,* 513–527.

Ben-Yehuda, N. (1990). *The politics and morality of deviance: Moral panics, drug abuse, deviant science, and reversed stigmatization.* Albany: State University of New York Press.

Ben-Yehuda, N. (2006). Contextualizing deviance within social change and stability, morality, and power. *Sociological Spectrum, 26,* 559–580.

Berger, P. (1963). *Invitation to sociology: A humanistic perspective.* Garden City, NY: Anchor.

Berger, P., & Luckmann, T. (1966). *The social construction of reality.* Garden City, NY: Anchor.

Bernard, T. J., Snipes, J. B., & Gerould, A. L. (2010). *Vold's theoretical criminology* (6th ed.). New York, NY: Oxford University Press.

Best, J. (1990). *Threatened children: Rhetoric and concern about child victims.* Chicago, IL: University of Chicago Press.

Best, J. (2004). *Deviance: Career of a concept.* Belmont, CA: Thomson/Wadsworth.

Bloom, A. (1987). *The closing of the American mind.* New York, NY: Simon & Schuster.

Boudon, R. (1994). *The art of self-expression: The social explanation of false beliefs* (M. Slater, Trans.). Cambridge, UK: Polity.

Bourdieu, P. (1991). *Language and symbolic power* (G. Raymond & M. Adamson, Trans.). Cambridge, MA: Harvard University Press.

Burgess, R. L., & Akers, R. L. (1966). A differential association-reinforcement theory of criminal behavior. *Social Problems, 14,* 128–147.

Chayko, M. (2008). *Portable communities: The social dynamics of online and mobile connectedness.* New York: State University of New York Press.

Clark, A. L., & Gibbs, J. P. (1965). Social control: A reformulation. *Social Problems, 12,* 398–415.

Cohen, A. (1974). *The elasticity of evil: Changes in the social definition of deviance.* Oxford, UK: Basil Blackwell.

Costello, B. (2006). Cultural relativism and the study of deviance. *Sociological Spectrum, 26,* 581–594.

Costello, B. (2009). Against relativism: A harm-based conception of deviance. In P. Adler & P. Adler (Eds.), *Constructions of deviance: Social power, context, and interaction* (6th ed., pp. 46–52). Belmont, CA: Thomson/Wadsworth.

Cote, S. (Ed.). (2002). *Criminological theories: Bridging the past to the future.* Thousand Oaks, CA: Sage.

Cross, J. C., & Hernández, A. H. (2011). Place, identity, and deviance: A community-based approach to understanding the relationship between deviance and place. *Deviant Behavior, 32,* 503–537.

Danesi, M. (2010). *Geeks, goths, and gangstas: Youth culture and the evolution of modern society.* Toronto, Ontario, Canada: Canadian Scholars' Press.

Dellwing, M. (2011). Truth in labeling: Are descriptions all we have? *Deviant Behavior, 32,* 653–675.

Denzin, N. (1970). Rules of conduct and the study of deviant behavior: Some notes on the social relationship. In J. Douglas (Ed.), *Deviance and respectability: The social construction of moral meanings* (pp. 120–159). New York, NY: Basic Books.

Devroye, J. (2010). The rise and fall of the American Institute of Criminal Law and Criminology. *The Journal of Criminal Law & Criminology, 100,* 7–32.

Douglas, J., Rasmussen, P., & Flanagan, C. (1977). *The nude beach.* Beverly Hills, CA: Sage.

Durkheim, E. (1933). *The division of labor in society* (G. Simpson, Trans.). New York, NY: Free Press. (Original work published 1893)

Durkheim, E. (1938). *The rules of sociological method* (8th ed.; George Catlin, Ed.; S. Solovay & John Mueller, Trans.). New York, NY: Free Press. (Original work published 1895)

Edgerton, R. (1992). *Sick societies: Challenging the myth of primitive harmony.* New York, NY: Free Press.

Erikson, K. (1962). Notes on the sociology of deviance. *Social Problems, 9,* 307–314.

Ferrell, J. (1999). Cultural criminology. *Annual Review of Sociology, 25,* 395–418.

Findlay, M., & Henham, R. (2010). *Beyond punishment: Achieving international criminal justice.* Basingstoke, UK: Palgrave Macmillan.

Fish, S. (2001, October 15). Condemnation without absolutes. *New York Times,* p. A23.

Forsyth, C. (1992). Parade strippers: A note on being naked in public. *Deviant Behavior, 13,* 391–403.

Foucault, M. (1977). *Discipline and punish: The birth of the prison* (A. Sheridan, Trans.). New York, NY: Pantheon.

Foucault, M. (2003). *Abnormal: Lectures at the Collège de France* (V. Marchetti & A. Salomoni, Eds.; G. Burchell, Trans.). New York, NY: Picador.

Freidson, E. (1961). *Patients' view of medical practice.* New York, NY: Russell Sage Foundation.

Freilich, M. (1991). Smart rules and proper rules: A journey through deviance. In M. Freilich, D. Raybeck, & J. Savishinsky (Eds.), *Deviance: Anthropological perspectives* (pp. 27–50). New York, NY: Bergin & Garvey.

Gamson, W. (1995). Hiroshima, the Holocaust, and the politics of exclusion (1994 presidential address). *American Sociological Review, 60,* 1–20.

Ghatak, S. (2011). *Threat perceptions: The policing of dangers from eugenics to the war on terrorism.* Lanham, MD: Lexington Books.

Gibbs, J. (1966a). Conceptions of deviant behavior: The old and the new. *Pacific Sociological Review, 9,* 9–14.

Gibbs, J. (1966b). Sanctions. *Social Problems, 14,* 147–159.

Gibbs, J. (1994). *A theory about control.* Boulder, CO: Westview Press.

Gladwell, M. (2000). *The tipping point: How little things can make a big difference.* Boston, MA: Little, Brown.

Glenn, E. N. (2011). Constructing citizenship: Exclusion, subordination, and resistance (2010 presidential address). *American Sociological Review, 76,* 1–24.

Goffman, E. (1961). *Asylums.* Garden City, NY: Doubleday.

Goffman, E. (1963). *Stigma: Notes on the management of spoiled identity.* Englewood Cliffs, NJ: Prentice Hall.

Goode, E. (2003). The MacGuffin that refuses to die: An investigation into the condition of the sociology of deviance. *Deviant Behavior, 24,* 507–533.

Goode, E., & Ben-Yehuda, N. (1994). *Moral panics: The social construction of deviance.* Oxford, UK: Basil Blackwell.

Gross, J. A. (2010). *A shameful business: The case for human rights in the American workplace.* Ithaca, NY: Cornell University Press.

Haenfler, R. (2013). *Goths, gamers, grrrls: Deviance and youth subcultures* (2nd ed.). New York, NY: Oxford University Press.

Hagan, J., & Rymond-Richmond, W. (2009). *Dafur and the crime of genocide*. New York, NY: Cambridge University Press.

Heckert, A., & Heckert, D. M. (2002). A new typology of deviance: Integrating normative and reactivist definitions of deviance. *Deviant Behavior, 23,* 449–479.

Henry, S., & Milovanovic, D. (1991). Constitutive criminology: The maturation of critical theory. *Criminology, 29,* 293–315.

Henry, S., & Milovanovic, D. (1996). *Constitutive criminology: Beyond postmodernism*. London, UK: Sage.

Horne, C. (2009). *The rewards of punishment: A relational theory of norm enforcement*. Palo Alto, CA: Stanford University Press.

Horwitz, A. (2008). Keyword: Normality. In J. Goodwin & J. Jasper (Eds.), *The contexts reader* (pp. 363–367). New York, NY: Norton.

Iacoboni, M. (2009). *Mirroring people: The science of empathy and how we connect with others*. New York, NY: Picador/Farrar, Straus & Giroux.

Katz, J. (1988). *Seductions of crime: Moral and sensual attractions in doing evil*. New York, NY: Basic Books.

Kennedy, M. (1976). Beyond incrimination: Some neglected facets of the theory of punishment. In W. Chambliss & M. Mankoff (Eds.), *Whose law? What order?* (pp. 34–65). New York, NY: Wiley.

Kitsuse, J. (1962). Societal reaction to deviant behavior: Problems of theory and method. *Social Problems, 9,* 247–257.

Kluckhohn, C. (1949). *Mirror for man: The relation of anthropology to modern life*. New York, NY: McGraw-Hill.

Kraaykamp, G., & van Eijck, K. (2010). The intergenerational reproduction of cultural capital: A threefold perspective. *Social Forces, 89,* 209–232.

Krauthammer, C. (1993, November 22). Defining deviancy up. *New Republic,* 20–25.

Kumbasar, E., Romney, A. K., & Batchelder, W. H. (1994). Systematic biases in social perception. *American Journal of Sociology, 100,* 477–505.

Lanier, M. M., & Henry, S. (2010). *Essential criminology* (3rd ed.). Boulder, CO: Westview Press.

Lemert, E. (1951). *Social pathology*. New York, NY: McGraw-Hill.

Lemert, E. (1972). *Human deviance, social problems, and social control* (2nd ed.). Englewood Cliffs, NJ: Prentice Hall.

Levy, D., & Sznaider, N. (2010). *Human rights and memory: Essays on human rights*. University Park: Pennsylvania State University Press.

Lyman, S., & Scott, M. (1989). *A sociology of the absurd* (2nd ed.). Dix Hills, NY: General Hall.

Marx, K. (1978). Society and economy in history. In R. Tucker (Ed.), *The Marx–Engels reader* (2nd ed., pp. 136–142). New York, NY: Norton. (Original work published 1846)

Matza, D. (1969). *Becoming deviant*. Englewood Cliffs, NJ: Prentice Hall.

Matza, D., & Sykes, G. M. (1961). Juvenile delinquency and subterranean values. *American Sociological Review, 26,* 712–719.

Mead, G. H. (1934). *Mind, self, and society: From the standpoint of a social behaviorist.* Chicago, IL: University of Chicago Press.

Merton, R. K. (1948). The self-fulfilling prophecy. *Antioch Review, 8,* 193–210.

Merton, R. K. (1968). Introduction. In R. K. Merton, *Social theory and social structure* (enlarged ed., pp. 175–184). New York, NY: Free Press.

Messer, E. (1997). Pluralist approaches to human rights. *Journal of Anthropological Research, 53,* 293–317.

Mills, C. W. (1943). The professional ideology of social pathologists. *American Journal of Sociology, 49,* 165–180.

Milovanovic, D. (1997). *Postmodern criminology.* New York, NY: Garland.

Mintz, S. (1982). Culture: An anthropological view. *Yale Review, 71,* 499–512.

Moore, R. I. (1987). *The formation of a persecuting society: Power and deviance in Western Europe, 950–1250.* New York, NY: Basil Blackwell.

Moyn, S. (2010). *The last utopia: Human rights in history.* Cambridge, MA: Belknap Press of Harvard University Press.

Moynihan, D. P. (1993). Defining deviancy down. *American Scholar, 64,* 25–33.

Nagengast, C. (1997). Women, minorities, and indigenous peoples: Universalism and cultural relativity. *Journal of Anthropological Research, 53,* 349–369.

Nagengast, C., & Turner, T. (1997). Introduction: Universal human rights versus cultural relativity. *Journal of Anthropological Research, 53,* 269–272.

Oakes, G. (2011). Mr. Big. *Contemporary Sociology, 40,* 549–552.

O'Brien, J. (2006). Shared meaning as the basis of humanness. In J. O'Brien (Ed.), *The production of reality* (4th ed., pp. 64–82). Thousand Oaks, CA: Pine Forge/Sage.

Parsons, T. (1951). *The social system.* New York, NY: Free Press.

Piaget, J. (1948). *The moral judgment of the child.* New York, NY: Free Press.

Portes, A. (2000). The hidden abode: Sociology as an analysis of the unexpected (1999 presidential address). *American Sociological Review, 65,* 1–18.

Quinney, R. (1970). *The social reality of crime.* Boston, MA: Little, Brown.

Quinney, R. (1973). There are a lot of folks grateful to the Lone Ranger: With some notes on the rise and fall of American criminology. *Insurgent Sociologist, 4,* 56–64.

Quinney, R. (1974). *Critique of the legal order: Crime control in capitalist society.* Boston, MA: Little, Brown.

Rafter, N. (1992). Some consequences of strict constructionism. *Social Problems, 39,* 38–39.

Rafter, N. (1997). *Creating born criminals.* Chicago: University of Illinois Press.

Raybeck, D. (1991). Hard versus soft deviance: Anthropology and labeling theory. In M. Freilich, D. Raybeck, & J. Savishinsky (Eds.), *Deviance: Anthropological perspectives* (pp. 51–73). New York, NY: Bergin & Garvey.

Reiman, J., & Leighton, P. (2010). *The rich get richer and the poor get prison: Ideology, class, and criminal justice* (9th ed.). Boston, MA: Pearson/Allyn & Bacon.

Riesman, D. (1963). Foreword. In E. S. Bowen, *Return to laughter* (pp. ix–xviii). Garden City, NY: Anchor/Doubleday.

Ritzer, G. (2008). *The McDonaldization of society* (5th ed.). Thousand Oaks, CA: Pine Forge/Sage.

Rosenberg, T. (2011). *Join the club: How peer pressure can transform the world.* New York, NY: Norton.

Schnakenberg, R. (2009). *Secret lives of the Supreme Court: What your teachers never told you about America's legendary justices.* Philadelphia, PA: Quirk Books.

Schur, E. (1975). Comments. In W. Gove (Ed.), *The labelling of deviance: Evaluating a perspective* (pp. 285–294). Beverly Hills, CA: Sage.

Schwartz, H. (1997). On the origin of the phrase "social problems." *Social Problems, 44,* 276–296.

Schwendinger, H., & Schwendinger, J. (1975). Defenders of order or guardians of human rights? In I. Taylor, P. Walton, & J. Young (Eds.), *Critical criminology* (pp. 113–146). London, UK: Routledge/Kegan Paul.

Searle, J. (1995). *The construction of social reality.* New York, NY: Free Press.

Sellin, T. (1938). *Culture conflict and crime* (Bulletin 41). New York, NY: Social Science Research Council.

Shrum, W., & Kilburn, J. (1996). Ritual disrobement at Mardi Gras: Ceremonial exchange and moral order. *Social Forces, 72,* 423–458.

Smångs, M. (2010). Delinquency, social skills and the structure of peer relations: Assessing criminological theories by social network theory. *Social Forces, 89,* 609–632.

Spector, M., & Kitsuse, J. (1977). *Constructing social problems.* Menlo Park, CA: Cummings.

Staples, W. (2000). *Everyday surveillance: Vigilance and visibility in postmodern life.* Lanham, MD: Rowman & Littlefield.

Sumner, C. (1994). *The sociology of deviance: An obituary.* New York, NY: Continuum.

Sumner, W. G. (1906). *Folkways: A study of the sociological importance of usages, manners, customs, mores, and morals.* Boston, MA: Ginn.

Sutherland, E. H. (1947). *Principles of criminology* (4th ed.). Philadelphia, PA: J. B. Lippincott.

Tannenbaum, F. (1938). *Crime and the community.* Boston, MA: Ginn.

Taylor, I., Walton, P., & Young, J. (1973). *The new criminology: For a social theory of deviance.* New York, NY: Harper & Row.

Tibbetts, S. G., & Hemmens, C. (2010). *Criminological theory: A text/reader.* Thousand Oaks, CA: Sage.

Troyer, R. (1992). Some consequences of contextual constructionism. *Social Problems, 39,* 35–37.

Turner, J. H., & Maryanski, A. (2008). *On the origin of societies by natural selection.* Boulder, CO: Paradigm.

Turner, T. (1997). Human rights, human difference: Anthropology's contribution to an emancipatory cultural politics. *Journal of Anthropological Research, 53,* 273–291.

United Nations. (1948). *The universal declaration of human rights.* Adopted and proclaimed by General Assembly Resolution 217 A (III) of 10 December 1948. [Online]. Retrieved January 18, 2013, from http://www.un.org/en/documents/udhr/index.shtml

Warr, M. (1993). Age, peers, and delinquency. *Criminology, 31,* 17–40.

Warr, M. (2002). *Companions in crime: The social aspects of criminal conduct.* New York, NY: Cambridge University Press.

Wasserman, J. A., & Clair, J. M. (2010). *At home on the street: People, poverty & a hidden culture of homelessness.* Boulder, CO: Lynne Rienner.

Williams, F. P., III, & McShane, M. (2009). *Criminological theory* (5th ed.). Upper Saddle River, NJ: Prentice Hall.

Williams, J. P. (2011). *Subcultural theory: Traditions and concepts.* Malden, MA: Polity Press.

Young, J. (2011). Moral panics and the transgressive other. *Crime, Media, Culture, 7,* 245–258.

Zechenter, E. (1997). In the name of culture: Cultural relativism and the abuse of the individual. *Journal of Anthropological Research, 53,* 319–347.

Zhao, R., & Cao, L. (2010). Social change and anomie: A cross-national study. *Social Forces, 88,* 1209–1230.

2

Being Deviant

The Original Blue Man (and Woman) Group

Over six generations ago, Martin Fugate and his bride settled on the banks of eastern Kentucky's Troublesome Creek. They had children, who had children, who had children. Most of them were healthy and lived well into old age. Not terribly long ago, Martin Fugate's great-great-great-great grandson was born. The boy was as healthy as a newborn could be, but he did have one curious trait: dark blue skin, the color of a plum or denim blue jeans. The attending physicians were very concerned. Did the child have a blood disorder? The child's grandmother told them not to worry. Many of the Fugates had blue skin (Trost, 1982).

A young hematologist from the University of Kentucky was curious about the reason for the unusual skin color. With the help of a nurse (who shared his interest) and a blue couple, the physician eventually uncovered the reason for the blue tint. It was caused by a hereditary condition that allowed too much methemoglobin (which is blue) to accumulate in the blood. The blue people, it seemed, lacked an enzyme that is necessary for the regulation of methemoglobin. It was either a quirk of fate or an affair of the heart that accounted for the original spark that generated the blueness of the Fugates. Martin Fugate married a woman who carried the same recessive gene for blueness that he did. Because members of the Fugate line were content to remain where they were born, people with the recessive gene that caused the blueness often married and had children with others who had the same hereditary trait. As a result, the number of blue people in this region of Kentucky increased.

The physician and the nurse had more than an academic interest in the blue skin color. As befitted their medical training, they were really hoping to find a "cure" for it. Once they knew the reason for the skin color, it was easy enough for them to find an "antidote." Methylene blue is a chemical that changes the color of methemoglobin. When it was injected into the blue people, it had the desired effect: Their skin turned pink. However, for the transformation to last, the *former* blue people of Kentucky would have to take a pill every day because the effects of methylene blue are short-lived (Trost, 1982). What could show the relative nature of deviance better than the fact that people can be stigmatized for characteristics over which they have little or no control? If being blue among a bunch of other blue people can be labeled as deviant and in need of change, then anything can be.

Being and Doing

An individual's identity contains two separable parts (Goffman, 1971, p. 189). One part is *social identity,* which consists of general social statuses, such as gender, race, class, and nativity. The other part is *personal identity,* which is more idiosyncratic and requires familiarity with an individual for it to be known. It includes an individual's name and appearance, as well as distinctive attributes, traits, or marks. These two identities, of course, complement one another, and social identity is always "fleshed out" by personal identity. Although being a "mother" is part of social identity, each mother has unique characteristics that make up her personal identity (e.g., *this* mom likes to mow the lawn and jog 5 miles a day). Some relationships are *pegged* or *anchored,* and interactants know one another personally and know that they are known in both their social and personal identities. Other relationships, however, are *anonymous,* and interactants know one another only in terms of social identity (p. 189).

Social and personal identities do not always complement one another. It is very possible, especially with a deeply discrediting act or attribute, for an individual to do all he or she can to keep it hidden entirely or restricted to personal identity alone so that only a relative few will be aware of it. It may be a central part of one's life to keep discrediting parts of personal identity from contaminating social identity (and vice versa). Some of what we are we embrace willingly and fully, while other parts we take on reluctantly, as something imposed upon us against our wills. The human body is both a possession and a prison (Kosut & Moore, 2010, p. 2).

A deviant's social identity (e.g., ethnicity, race, sex) can coalesce with cultural stereotypes in ways that influence how the individual is treated. For example, Harris, Evans, and Beckett (2011, pp. 248–252) found that Latino defendants in a court of law receive the harshest penalties when they are found guilty of having committed *stereotype-congruent offenses* (i.e., those that are "expected" or deemed to be the most likely for a given racial or ethnic population to commit). In this study, stereotype-congruent offenses meant drug offenses. Deviants can be the target of both formal and informal negative sanctions that cause varying levels of stress and interpersonal difficulties for them (Mustaine & Tewksbury, 2011).

Humans create new features of their identities and reaffirm old ones as they express themselves at home, in the community, or at work (Burke & Stets, 2009; MacKinnon & Heise, 2010). Deviants from all walks of life must manage impressions and manipulate what cues they can in order to construct identities that appear to be unexceptional, normal, and ordinary (Force, 2010). Most deviants, most of the time, do things that are far more normal than they are abnormal. Social and personal identities are in many ways a negotiated reality, being flexible, contingent, and relative to time and place (Richardson, 2010).

Garot (2010) studied gang memberships of students in an alternative school (named Choices Alternative Academy) in an area characterized by some of the highest levels of crime and poverty in the western United States. These students had histories of violence, drug use, truancy, dropping out of school, and teen pregnancy. Garot's subjects, who were mostly African Americans or Latinos, were rough and tough, the baddest of the bad. They knew how to take care of themselves, regularly using violence to do so (p. 15). Garot found, however, that gangs were not filled with ruthless killers, bent on carrying out whatever missions their leaders demanded of them. Gang members were individuals—more normal than not—who were trying to construct identities in social environments that they found irrelevant and alienating. Gang membership was a dynamic, interactive, situational feature of their identities that interpenetrated other parts of their lives (and vice versa). Whatever gang members are, they are more than just members of gangs.

People can be labeled and then negatively sanctioned for what they are (or for what they believe), not simply for what they do. The experiences of people who are treated as deviant for what they *are*—their shame, guilt, rejection by others—may not be appreciably different from the experiences of people who are treated as deviant for what they *do*. Both human behaviors *and* human beings must be part of our understanding of deviance, because deviance is sometimes a matter of being rather than of doing (Sagarin, 1975, p. 9).

> The belief that one is a certain thing, particularly when the concept of isness carries with it a sense of destiny, a part of oneself or one's very identity, creates a feeling of immutability in that role. The language reinforces both the identity and the immutability, and the role occupant at that point finds it impossible to believe that he can be or is other than what he has defined himself as being. (p. 152)

The experience of being labeled and rejected for something that one is can be particularly difficult for an individual so labeled, especially when it seems impossible to deny. *Role engulfment* can occur in which an individual feels trapped in some particular role and powerless to leave it (Schur, 1971, pp. 69–81). At this point, the labeled individual, as well as those with whom he or she interacts, may conclude that he or she is only what the person is said to be (Hills, 1980, p. 50). We sometimes do feel imprisoned by our bodies rather than liberated by them, and human bodies are imbued with all kinds of meanings and understandings, coming from both the self and others (Moore & Kosut, 2010). It is also true, however, that some groups have more power to construct cultural understandings about body images than other groups (Etorre, 2010, p. 155).

The surveillance and regulation of children and adolescents by adults is a central part of the process of social differentiation, which is associated with historical changes in conceptions of childhood and youth (Colls & Hörschelman, 2009, pp. 11–12). This process, however, is not restricted to the young. Richeson and Trawalter (2005) concluded that after O. J. Simpson's arrest in 1994 for the brutal killings of Ron Goldman and Nicole Brown-Simpson, Simpson's picture on the cover of *Time* magazine was darkened to make him appear more African American than white. Simpson's appearance may have "blackened" in the minds of the public, too (p. 517). Saperstein and Penner (2010), using data from the 1979 National Youth Survey, showed that a criminal record can be a lens through which perceptions of race are filtered. A record of arrest and imprisonment changes how a person is viewed by others, as well as how the individual views him- or herself.

Deviance and Responsibility

Attaching Blame

The *fundamental attribution error* (FAE) is the mistake of attaching responsibility for some happening to an individual (or individuals) rather than to the social situation within which the happening occurs; it is the error of giving too much responsibility to individual disposition and not enough to environmental factors (Nisbett & Ross, 1991; O'Brien, 2006, p. 68). In one experiment, observers were asked to view two teams of equally talented basketball players. One team was playing in a gymnasium that had plenty of light, and the second team was playing in a poorly lit gym (and doing far worse at making shots). The observers were asked to rate the players, and they decided that the players in the brighter gym were the best (Gladwell, 2000, p. 160). They confused context with character, deciding that it was players' *character traits* that explained what happened rather than obvious and important differences in environmental factors.

Although we should never miss the role played by individual factors in what humans are, we must also be fully aware of the power of context. We will find, more often than not, that what we do and are, as well as how what we do and are is evaluated, reflects context more than anything else. We may be more fun at parties—and viewed that way by others—precisely because *parties* are fun. If we found ourselves in a bar fight, however, all this would change. We wouldn't be fun people at all (nor would we be viewed that way by others).

The attribution of responsibility is strongly influenced by whether deviance is considered to be ascribed or achieved. *Ascribed deviance* exists if a rule breaker is defined or labeled as having a physical or visible impairment, and the individual can acquire that status regardless of his or her behavior or wishes. By contrast, *achieved deviance* involves some intentional or deliberate activity on the part of a rule breaker. Ascribed deviance would cover the situation of individuals who are rejected for physical disabilities, and achieved deviance would cover embezzlers or marijuana users. Unlike the ascribed, the achieved have had to achieve rule-breaking status, at least to some extent, on the strength of what they do (Mankoff, 1976, pp. 241–242).

If deviance is ascribed, it is more likely to be viewed as a misfortune—devalued perhaps, but not in the same category as achieved deviance. With achieved deviance, because something has indeed been done, negative reactions are more likely to be warranted and are easier to justify. It practically goes without saying that *behavior* that breaks rules or violates expectations will regularly be viewed as achieved, and *conditions* or *attributes* that break rules or violate expectations are more likely to be viewed as ascribed. It is possible for individuals to fall somewhere in between, displaying something that is defined as *voluntary,* but still what one *is* rather than what one *does* (Sagarin, 1975, p. 269). An individual who is hard of hearing but who refuses to get a hearing aid falls in this category. Because the individual could hear better by purchasing a hearing aid but chooses not to get one, he or she is perceived to be "deaf by choice." The deviance, however, exists, not because the individual is hard of hearing, but because he or she is defined by others as being able to do something to hear better but choosing not to. It is generally true, however, that "isness" is less blameworthy than "didness."

Some individuals get labeled as deviant and negatively sanctioned because they are viewed by others as a bothersome annoyance. In Irwin's (1985) words, they are *rabble*. Rabble are viewed by others as both detached and disreputable. *Detached* means they are isolated from conventional or mainstream communities, being separate and apart from those institutions, organizations, or social networks that define the social life of the mainstream. *Disreputable* means they display unacceptable behaviors or unusual ideas. If rabble keep to themselves and cause nobody any trouble, they are given little attention. However, if they end their detachment and take their disreputable behavior to places where they do not belong according to the majority, police will usually be called to return them to places where rabble are more likely to be tolerated or to cart them off to jail (Fitzpatrick & Myrstol, 2011). It is not their danger but their offensiveness to conventional moral standards and propriety that mobilizes the forces of social control against them.

When it comes to issues of deviance and responsibility, cause and blame are sometimes confused, but they are not the same thing (Felson, 1991). Cause is objective and verifiable, referring to observed patterns of association and ordering. If drinking ethyl alcohol causes poor driving ability, it is because the drinking precedes erratic driving and is responsible for it. Blame (or the assessment of responsibility) is a value-laden term, more moralistic and judgmental than a scientific determination based on logic and observation. If an individual had been in the World Trade Center on September 11, 2001, and was killed in the terrorist attack on that day, one *cause* of his or her death would have been that the individual decided to enter the building. However, the individual should not be *blamed* for what happened. Goode (2011) clarifies matters when he notes that, "[i]f I take a plane to Los Angeles and the plane crashes and I die, my taking the plane is one *cause* of my death—but I should not be *blamed* for my death" (p. 130).

No perfect correlation exists between cause and blame, and blaming someone for some trespass is different from identifying its cause. Though we may agree, from our observation of changes in variables, about what causes what, attaching blame is a more contentious issue. Different groups can have very different understandings about who is at fault for some untoward event (even while group members might agree on its cause). Not every moral trespass or impropriety, even if it is done in public and by celebrated individuals, qualifies as a scandal. In order for an event to be seen as a scandal, witnesses must be willing to overlook that they have probably seen things like this before (e.g., sexual improprieties by governmental officials). They must also be willing to overlook just how routine scandalous behaviors by prominent people are in the life of a society long enough for them to be scandalized once again (Kipnis, 2010, p. 13). In this process, celebrities can become villains (Penfold-Mounce, 2009).

Discreditable and Discredited Deviants

Deviance is a *personally discreditable* departure from a group's or society's expectations (Schur, 1971, p. 24). *Discreditable* attitudes, behaviors, or conditions could lead to social censure and stigma if they ever reach the light of day, so they must be expressed or performed in private and in secretive ways (Goffman, 1963). An example of discreditable behavior is ritualized self-injury. In the sample of 25 self-injurers studied by Adler and Adler (2009), the majority (80 percent) engaged in their acts of self-mutilation while they were alone, and they most frequently cut themselves, although they also burned, branded, and shocked themselves. By physically hurting themselves in private, it actually made it easier for them to deal with the pain, loneliness, boredom, and depression that they carried with them because of their strained relationships with others. Because the injurers could control where, when, and how the pain occurred, it replaced—at least temporarily—all the other pain in their lives, actually giving them a measure of comfort and relief.

Pain in the right circumstances and done ritually proved to self-injurers that they were strong enough to be able to tolerate the kind of discomfort that others could not even contemplate tolerating (Atkinson & Young, 2008). The ability to endure pain was, to the injurers, an indicator of strong character, bravery, and personal integrity. It was a "warrior mark," less an unfortunate consequence of the experience than one of its central objectives. The discreditable nature of self-injury creates a self-perpetuating cycle. The absorption of self-injurers in their own private world of injury and secrecy leads to greater and greater isolation from others and, if discovered, strong pressures for them to stop the injury, which leads ultimately to greater loneliness, which is the principal reason that they began to injure themselves in the first place.

Passing as something other than a deviant requires impression management and strategic interaction (Goffman, 1959, 1969). One strategy of passing is to construct a public self that is neither stigmatized nor condemned. Social identity is kept free from the taint of personal identity. A second strategy is to avoid interaction (behavioral or verbal) with others so that they will remain ignorant about who or what the individual trying to pass is (in terms of character) or has done. Passing involves information control and the manipulation of others in the interest of presenting a fabricated self (Shippee, 2011).

A qualitative study of 73 participants in the bondage/discipline/sadism/masochism subculture (BDSM), by Stiles and Clark (2011), reports that these sexual deviants were inclined to conceal their deviance from others whenever they could. They hid information about their sexual interests and practices, as well as about their deviant identity, when interacting with people whom they deemed likely to be both offended and judgmental. The largest portion of the sample (38 percent) told nobody outside of the subculture, following a strict need-to-know decision rule ("absolute concealment"). The rest told only close friends or family members. Only a small percentage (1 percent) was completely open about their sexual activities. Some of the sample (8 percent) had been forced out of the closet ("outed") against their wishes. The principal reasons members of this sample opted for concealment were self-protection and to protect others from information that these sexual deviants thought might be upsetting or unpleasant for them.

Individuals who have been caught and labeled for trespasses find themselves in a different situation from the discreditable. They are now *discredited deviants,* and their main problem is managing tension during social contacts with individuals who do not share their condition (Goffman, 1963, p. 42). Goffman relates the case of a 16-year-old female who wrote to "Miss Lonelyhearts," asking for advice about a "problem." The teenager told the columnist that she would like to go out on dates like everyone else, but males won't take her out even though she is a good dancer, wears nice clothes, and has a nice figure. The reason males avoid her as a dating partner is because she was born without a nose, having a "big hole" in the middle of her face. Her main question for the columnist is whether she should take her own life. In situations as extreme as this one, the discrediting trait is very difficult, if not impossible, to manage successfully, no matter how much an individual tries. Some people are quick to judge and quick to reject anyone who is perceived to be different from them, while others are much more accepting and inclusive (Edgell & Tranby, 2010).

A study by Rassin (2011) of individuals with HIV in the largest AIDS clinic in Israel shows that the division between the discredited and the discreditable falls apart in the real world. Because the demands of passing are so intense for individuals who must do it on a continual basis, *both* tension control and information control are required for anyone trying to conceal part of his or her identity from others. Part of the reason that these HIV sufferers decided to keep their condition a secret is that the initial reaction of family members who had been told of the diagnosis was prejudicial, discriminatory, and hurtful. Even those HIV sufferers who had received a favorable response had reasons to hide their disease from most others. They feared that their families might become the target of hostility or persecution. Life was difficult for these patients and not just because they had a life-threatening disease. Most of them reported that hiding the disease was necessary because it made it possible for them to continue to lead a normal life for as long as they could.

Responsibility and Moral Careers

McHugh (1970) identified two decision rules that observers use to attach moral responsibility or blame to individuals for their untoward attitudes, behaviors, or conditions. The first decision rule, called *conventionality* (pp. 66–73), refers to whether observers believe that the attitude, behavior, or condition "could have been otherwise." If, in their opinion, it could have been, then it is conventional and a good candidate for consideration as something deviant instead of something accidental, coerced, or miraculous. It is the perceived inevitability of nonconventional events that makes the difference. Slipping on ice and falling, getting hurt in the process, is a different event from the standpoint of conventionality than is using your body in a game of football to block an opponent. The extent of the injuries may be identical, but slipping is an accident—nonconventional—while body blocking in an athletic contest is something that did not have to happen. McHugh's second decision rule is *theoreticity* (pp. 73–78). It concerns whether the untoward attitude, behavior, or condition is viewed as having been intentional, unfolding according to some plan or purpose (making it "theoretic" instead of "practical" action). Individuals who deviate in a conventional and theoretic way are held responsible (i.e., blamed) for disrupting the social order. They are expected to show that they do understand the wrongfulness of their trespass. They are also expected to repair the damage they've done to the social order and the moral understandings on which it is based.

These two rules are neat and tidy—sort of—but the real world is far more complicated. The boys still won't ask the teenager with no nose out on dates, and she anguishes over her physical condition so much that she contemplates suicide. She can take some small comfort in knowing that had she intentionally removed her own nose (when she did not have to), her lot would have been even worse. She herself would have been held entirely responsible for her plight (or it would have been claimed she was not in her right mind). We see that even in the absence of the assessment that an individual is responsible for his or her deviance or disability, it is still possible for a great deal of embarrassment, stigma, and misery to result from being different from everyone else.

We must include in our understanding of deviance a category called *involuntary deviants*. These are individuals who are not held responsible for either their devalued traits or the social reactions based upon them (Montanino & Sagarin, 1977, p. 3). They are still devalued and stigmatized, however, for conditions that they are viewed as having had no responsibility in creating (Butera & Levine, 2009). In fact, people with disabilities are the target of both hate and violence because of their disabilities, and *disablism*—prejudice against people with disabilities—is a far-too-frequent fact of life for these involuntary deviants (Sherry, 2010). They may be viewed as disabled people instead of people with disabilities (Cahill & Eggleston, 2005; Campbell, 2009).

Disagreements exist over whether something is conventional or theoretic, and who or what is to blame is a contentious issue (as noted previously). A child is asked by a father to carry a plate of cookies, but the child then drops it. The mother may think that her husband is at fault for expecting capabilities beyond most children; the father, however, may think the child is to blame for not paying sufficient attention to the task at hand to do it correctly. An important factor in how a deviant is judged and reacted to is whether he or she is trying to evade the norms secretly, making him or her a *cynical deviant,* or openly defying them, making him or her an *enemy deviant* (Gusfield, 1967). Other things being equal, cynical deviants, because they are not openly challenging the status quo, are generally easier to deal with and easier to accept than are enemy deviants. Both the cynical and enemy deviants are different from a deviant like the cookie-dropper, who is neither intentionally resistant to, nor stubbornly defiant of, the normative system.

Individuals who view obesity as deviant are the ones who are most likely to define it as a result of individual laziness and weak will, a failure by overweight people to exercise often enough or to exert sufficient personal control over their eating habits (Sobal, 1995). These negative evaluators view obesity as a blemish of character, as well as of body, instead of the operation of forces over which an individual has little or no control (e.g., glandular malfunction) (Goode, 2002, 2011). They view it as both voluntary and undesirable, something that could and should be changed. The obese body is more than a lump of flesh and bone; it is a moral area and a contested terrain that is viewed in different ways by different audiences or groups, some accepting of it and some not (Badger, 2010, p. 152; English, 1993; Kwan, 2009).

The U.S. media usually offer a biased view of eating problems. Obesity is portrayed as nothing other than an individual problem with roots in fundamentally bad choices. Social factors (e.g., class, race, gender, ethnicity, opportunity, accessibility, affordability), despite their clear role in how, what, and how much we eat, are given little attention (Roberts & Edwards, 2010). Blame and responsibility are attached differently to the too-thin and the too-fat. Overeaters or binge eaters are looked at as morally defective, while anorexics and bulimics are looked at as victims of social or biological forces beyond their control. Thin bodies, though extreme, are still viewed as associated with responsibility and self-denial, albeit it of a perverse form, while fat bodies are viewed as the epitome of gluttony and irresponsibility (Saguy & Gruys, 2010, pp. 239–247). In the public realm, fat bodies are viewed as something that must be changed in order to make other bodily functions and individual accomplishments possible (Saguy, Gruys, & Gong, 2010). The fat body is the contaminated body, crying out in a multitude of ways to be saved from itself (Kent, 2010, p. 371).

The Social Construction of Spoiled Identities

Appearance and the Sociocultural Matrix

Physical appearance is one of the more obvious and immediate cues that people bring to their encounters with others, a fundamental element in personal identity. It is used as a signifier of other, more difficult-to-measure personal factors, and it plays an important role in patterns of social interaction and in the differential treatment that people receive. Physical attractiveness is both valued and valuable for an individual who is defined as having it (Vecitis, 2011, p. 451). The determination that someone is beautiful or ugly (or any gradation in between) involves selective viewing, definition, classification, and evaluation. Beauty, just like deviance, is in the eye of the beholder, and *attentional adhesion*—the difficulty of pulling one's attention or gaze away from a particular individual—is a documented fact (Maner, Gailliot, Rouby, & Miller, 2007). Appearance norms exist in all cultures, and violations of these norms can lead to the assessment that something deviant—or at least devalued—has occurred (Schur, 1983).

Studies have been done in which images of composite faces were constructed on a computer from individual pictures of faces. The greater the number of pictures of faces that went into the construction of the composite photo, the more average or symmetrical the composite became. So, if eight separate photos were used to make the composite, the composite was more symmetrical, typical, or average than if four separate photos had been used to make it. The central finding was that the composite image constructed from 32 separate pictures of faces was ranked as more attractive than a composite made from 16, 8, or 4 separate pictures of faces (Buss, 1994, p. 54).

The equating of facial symmetry with beauty and asymmetry with ugliness is interesting but flawed. People use things other than the face to determine attractiveness (figure, health cues, character, personality, age), and we can certainly think of times when a symmetrical face would *not* be judged particularly attractive.

Most of us suspect that the world's "most beautiful people" have gotten that way by being more than just average. Using *symmetrical* to mean "average" is not the same as using it to mean "ideal" or "flawless," and perhaps these words are closer to what is meant by *beautiful*. When American men and women are given the task of constructing an ideal or perfect human face, they seem to agree. The ideal or perfect female face is a very youthful one with full lips and a narrow mouth. The perfect male face (based on the responses of American female undergraduates) has large eyes, a large chin, a small nose, and prominent cheekbones. It is an open, pleasant face with rugged features (Small, 1995, p. 143).

None of these traits seems extraordinary, but maybe it is unusual to find so many diverse indicators of female attractiveness on the same female or of male attractiveness on the same male. What is true about sexual selection—a fact of which Darwin was fully aware—is that if females show a specific preference in selecting mates, then males with the desirable trait will be at a reproductive advantage. They will leave a greater number of offspring, and the frequency of that trait will increase in a population (Jones & Ratterman, 2009, p. 10002).

Are uniform and universal cues for beauty and ugliness to be found? Some traits—festering sores, hacking coughs, incessant sneezes, unpleasant body odors—are probably widely defined as unattractive or ugly, and they could easily repel potential mates in practically any situation. Other traits—youthfulness, vitality, sincerity, integrity, kindness, poise, intelligence, joviality—are likely to be viewed as attractive, and they may be used to classify people as beautiful. However, that is a far cry from the claim that objective and universal beauty cues exist that have been programmed into our biology and psychology to ensure reproductive success (Buss, 1994, pp. 53–54; Ridley, 1993, p. 280). Just because people say that they find some particular qualities attractive in a mate does not necessarily mean that their fantasies are echoes of some genetic predisposition established long ago (Small, 1995, p. 148).

How beautiful or ugly a partner looks to us depends on our needs, our interests, the nature of our relationship to him or her, and—importantly—our relationship to other "hims" or "hers." We may have an ideal image of beauty in our minds, but it is usually broad and alterable. Though a partner's age and health are supposed to be important indicators of beauty or handsomeness in long-term relationships oriented toward reproduction, it may be just those relationships in which they are the least important. People do not usually divorce or separate on the grounds that their partner is too old or too sick. In fact, growing old together may enhance the quality of the relationship for both partners. It is almost certain that if we looked, we could find *both* beautiful and ugly things in every person on earth, and a trait that looks ugly at one time may look beautiful at another.

Learning must certainly play a big role in what and whom people find attractive, and culture must have an impact on what a group defines as beautiful or ugly that parallels or surpasses any influence of biology. Women and men want mates who are enjoyable to be around, who will make them feel special and needed, and who are accommodating enough and sensitive enough to be responsive to their wants and needs. In the absence of these, a partner's youth, health, fecundity, or high social status will matter very little. However, what draws us to a relationship (attentional adhesion) may be very different from what keeps it going for any length of time. The evaluation of potential mates and actual partners is a flexible, ongoing enterprise.

All the different body forms, skin colors, nose shapes, ear designs, and facial configurations, along with all the deliberate modifications of the human form, make it hard to believe that any universal and uniform standard of beauty and ugliness could ever be found.

> A cross-cultural survey of notions of beauty is sure to include such "oddities" as a preference for cross-eyes (Mayans), flattened heads (Kwakiutl), black gums and tongue (Maasai), black teeth (Yapese), joined eyebrows (Syrians), absence of eyebrows and eyelashes (Mongo), enormously protruding navels (Ila), pendulous breasts (Ganda), gigantic buttocks (Hottentot), fat calves (Tiv), crippled feet (Chinese), and so on. (Gregersen, 1983, p. 81)

Certainly, it is not hard to find examples that challenge the claim that standards for beauty are universal and programmed into us at birth.

The erotic potential of female genitalia is found throughout the world, but the Tswana-Kgatla (Africa) put their own spin on the whole affair:

> With the onset of puberty Kgatla girls start pulling their labia and sometimes will ask a girlfriend to help. If the labia do not get longer as quickly as desired, the girls resort to magic. They kill a bat and cut off its wings, which they then burn. The ashes are ground up and mixed with fat. Each girl makes little cuts around her labia and smears the bat-ash ointment into the cuts. (Gregersen, 1983, p. 92)

This little bit of magic is designed to get the labia to grow quickly to the size of bat wings.

Teeth are an important part of one's appearance, and having a "nice" smile is usually considered an asset. The existence of "best smile" contests suggests that judges know a great smile when they see one (or believe that they do). Yet, what qualifies as a "great smile" varies across the globe. Teeth have been permanently colored, knocked out, dug out, filed down, decorated, drilled, and chipped in order to heighten their attractiveness (Gregersen, 1983, p. 97). U.S. models and actresses (and others, thanks to the influence of television advertising) spend time and money on the whitening of their teeth. The Nilotes of East Africa would find these efforts at whitening incomprehensible. Beauty for them involves knocking out the lower front teeth (up to six), usually at the start of adolescence (p. 97).

Standards for the "proper" girth and weight for individuals to meet are variable things, too. In places where food and a full stomach are both luxuries, corpulence is coveted, and thinness is taken as a sign of poverty or sickness, not self-control and good form (Brownmiller, 1984, p. 49).

> In Mexico, for example, people are significantly less concerned than U.S. citizens about their own weight and are more accepting of overweight people. In Niger, being overweight—ideally with rolls of fat, stretch marks, and a large behind—is considered an essential part of female beauty. Women who aren't sufficiently round are considered unfit for marriage. In Mauritania, girls as young as 5 and as old as 19 are sometimes forced by their parents to drink five gallons of fat-rich camel's milk each day so they become fat. Among the Calabari people of southeastern Nigeria, soon-to-be brides are sent to farms where caretakers feed them huge amounts of food to fatten them up for the wedding day. (Newman, 2008, p. 161)

The existence of cross-cultural differences in appearance norms for body size ratifies the truth of novelist Erica Jong's (1990, p. 296) Proverb Number One for Free Women: "You're not too fat; you're just in the wrong country" (p. 296). If she's right, it means that finding that one's body proportions are not only accepted, but even admired, has more to do with *where* an individual is than with the size of an individual's stomach.

A study of 57 college women in a large, public university in the western United States shows that some of them are so dedicated to staying thin that they are willing to resort to heavy and potentially dangerous drug use to help maintain it (Vecitis, 2011). They overidentify with a specific and highly inflexible set of cultural understandings about physical attractiveness, and they do all they can to control information to hide from practically everyone just how desperately they try to stay thin. The possibility of disclosure of their obsession with thinness produced fear and anxiety among these women that they would be publicly caught and stigmatized for what they were doing.

Even males—some, at any rate—can be so committed to thinness that they starve themselves to a point where their health is put in jeopardy. Atkinson's (2011) study of male athletes who were participants in a range of sports (e.g., marathon running, wrestling, swimming, tennis) reported that dangerous eating practices were justified by these men as both normal and desirable. They viewed their emaciation as a sign of self-reliance and emotional maturity, which meant that they had low levels of stigma and guilt over their risky behaviors. For them, "risky" did not mean the same thing as "deviant."

Most adult women in the Western world have at some time in their lives been displeased to a greater or lesser extent with the shape and weight of their bodies, and they have tried to alter them in one way or another by reducing their food intake (Grogan, 2009, p. 42). Studies in the United States, Australia, and Great Britain, using Figural Rating Scales (various silhouettes of a body, going from very thin to very fat), indicate that respondents were inclined to find as most attractive a body shape that was thinner than their own (pp. 42–43). Slenderness and confidence are positively linked for most women, and most can more easily identify something wrong with their bodies than find something right with them (p. 43). Glass, Hass, and Reither (2010) report from their research done in Wisconsin that heavy females in their sample were less inclined than lighter females to pursue post-secondary schooling, even though they were just as academically capable. An important part of the reason that heavy women avoided advanced education was low self-esteem, depression, and a fear of failing.

Physical appearance cues do influence how individuals are treated. For males, being tall helps increase their earnings throughout their careers, and tall men are viewed as better dating partners than are short men. For females, physical attractiveness doesn't directly affect their earnings, but it does eventually serve to facilitate entrance into occupations with greater prestige. For both sexes, facial attractiveness has a positive influence on marriageability but no influence on the social standing of one's spouse. Although both males and females may dislike getting old, more females than males report that they do not want to *look* old. A double standard exists that works to the advantage of older men, who can still be viewed as "distinguished," even well into old age, in a way that few women can achieve (Jaeger, 2011, pp. 993–998). Most women surveyed—heterosexual ones, at any rate—profess that an important factor that makes them think they look old is that they no longer receive approving attention from men (Slevin, 2010, p. 1015).

It is a long way from laboratory studies of symmetry and attentional adhesion to the real world of finding and uniting with a desired partner. A few things—a very few things—*might* be universally viewed as beautiful/ attractive or as ugly. However, what appears to be most important is the total package a person brings to a relationship—or the other's perception of that package. Having a beautiful face—or any other specific trait—is not that important, at least not for long, or at least not in long-term relationships. Many things—opportunity, accessibility, availability, personal objectives, individual motives, physical qualities, psychological and emotional factors, personality characteristics, social attributes (e.g., status)—are assessed by people as they form relationships. Humans find a wide range of things attractive and beautiful, some of which reflect cultural meanings and some of which reflect more idiosyncratic preferences. No matter whom we are with or what we find attractive, most of us realize that if we'd come to a different fork in the road and taken a different path, our partners would have been different from who they now are.

Status and Stigma

Each individual is a cluster of different attributes and appearance cues (in both social and personal identities), and each person displays a large number of different behaviors during the course of his or her life. We must wonder, therefore, why certain designations or characterizations are used more often than others to describe us, and why some of them stick to us more readily in describing what we are and what we do. E. C. Hughes (1945) coined the term *master status* to describe a status that evolves into the dominant way an individual is interpreted and categorized by others. A person's sex is usually a master status, as are skin color and occupation. These are major identity pegs, and they play a role in most human relationships. The status of deviant, Becker (1963, pp. 33–34) informs us, is also a master status. If an individual is defined as a deviant, this status can predominate over many others that the individual occupies and can become a controlling one in his or her relationships to others (Pager, 2007). A strong possibility exists that as a deviant identity evolves into a master status, the level of social censure will increase and the individual will experience stigma (Goffman, 1963, pp. 43–44).

At one time, the word *stigma* was used to mean a distinguishing mark or brand cut into an individual's flesh for the purpose of identifying him or her as a tainted or despised individual. Now, stigma means *any* attribute—a physical sign or character cue—that is accompanied by shame or disgrace. Too-tall Jones is identified by body, and Otis the town drunk is identified by character. Stigma can also have little directly to do with body or character: It can exist because a person is a member of a persecuted or despised group, what Goffman (1963) called *tribal stigma*. He reminds us that when speaking of stigma, what is really needed is a language of relationships rather than of attributes, because no attribute is automatically crediting or discrediting. Stigma always involves a relationship between an attribute and its perception and symbolization by others. "Normal" and "stigmatized" are not persons but *perspectives* on persons (p. 138).

A tattoo, for example, may be either a *stigma symbol* (i.e., discrediting) or a *prestige symbol* (i.e., status-enhancing), depending on who the tattooee is, what the tattoo represents, where the tattoo is placed, and the nature of the relationship between the tattooee and his or her evaluating others. Tattoos have been used to identify social outcasts and to make it more difficult for them to blend in with others. In Japan in the sixth century, criminals were tattooed on the arms and face, and in the 1800s, convicts in correctional facilities in Massachusetts had "Mass S.P." and the date of their release tattooed on their left arms (Sanders, 1996, p. 376). Even in these cases, however, the tattoos were not automatically discrediting. It depended strongly on the beliefs of the audience that witnessed them.

Some individuals today collect tattoos on their bodies, viewing these markings as a fundamental and attractive part of their personal and social identities. They use a tattoo to increase their feelings of self-worth and to transform their identities in the eyes of others (Goode & Vail, 2008, pp. 2–32; Sanders, 1996, p. 375). In fact, for some individuals, tattoos are said to be like potato chips in that one is not nearly enough (Vail, 2008, pp. 5–14).

Tattoos are defined by some individuals as tarnished cultural products, an indication that the tattooed individual lacks self-restraint and enough maturity to be able to consider the consequences of his or her actions (J. Adams, 2012, p. 150). Tattoos on teenagers are still stigmatizing, indicating to the general public that the bearer is unconventional in outlooks and interests. Adolescents with tattoos are reported to be more inclined toward deviance, less academically oriented than adolescents without tattoos, and less interested in attending college (Silver, Silver, Siennick, & Farkas, 2011, p. 552).

How tattoos are viewed by others, especially by those inclined to view them as disreputable, cannot be separated from the tattoo industry itself. Tattoo artists have not had the same level of success as practitioners in related industries (e.g., cosmetic surgeons, cosmetologists, barbers, beauticians, manicurists) in changing the public image that they are engaged in what E. C. Hughes (1951) called *dirty work*. This is work that is defined as unpleasant, with clients or customers who are defined as unsavory or immoral (J. Adams, 2012). In November 2012, a tattoo artist (the way Walter Smith describes himself) was disallowed from sharing information about tattooing with students during "Career Day" at Clearwater Fundamental Middle School (Clearwater, Florida). His daughter was a student at the school, and Smith had participated in years past. The reason cited by the school principal (David Rosenberger) for the ban was parental complaints that Smith would be promoting an alternative lifestyle.

Stigma may be an outcome of having "bad" companions or associates (or those defined as bad), a stigma by association called *courtesy stigma* (Goffman, 1963). (A daughter who is embarrassed because her father is viewed as the town drunk is suffering from this kind of stigma.) A study of stigma by association, experienced by Hollywood artists and performers during the "Red Scare" of the 1950s, illustrates how this can work. After the Second World War (circa 1945–1960), some powerful and influential people in Hollywood became convinced—or acted is if they were—that the film industry had been infiltrated by communists and communist sympathizers. Of the approximately 30,000 artists (31,781, to be exact) who worked in Hollywood during those years, 300 were officially blacklisted and kept from performing. Some of them were defined as a national security threat. The damning of actors during the Red Scare had a ripple effect. Practically anyone who had any connections with them, no matter how slight, also became the target of persecution, discovering that they, too, had trouble finding work. One contact with a tainted individual was usually enough to have adverse consequences for a performer's career. Even contact with a blacklisted writer proved to be a liability (Pontikes, Negro, & Rao, 2010).

The social construction of a spoiled identity usually includes a process called *retrospective interpretation*. This exists when an accused deviant's past behavior and experiences are redefined in light of the emergent information about his or her current deviance (Kitsuse, 1962, p. 253). In retrospective interpretation, an accused deviant's biography is scrutinized, and what is learned is used to reinterpret his or her current identity. Prior relationships with the accused are played over in memory, searching for anything that might help to account for the individual's current display of deviance. The rule breaker is recast in the eyes of others, and he or she is viewed in a new way (Schur, 1971, p. 52). What was once viewed as normal in the identity of the individual comes to be viewed as a façade that was actually hiding a deeper, more sinister, more authentic constellation of traits and attributes (Garfinkel, 1956).

Retrospective interpretation leads almost directly to the conclusion that the character traits that are being held responsible for the current trespass actually had been present all along. The human capacity for narration and memory means that we take bits and pieces of an individual's biographical information and fit them together into something that approximates a consistent view or biographical structuration of an individual (Schafer, Ferraro, & Mustillo, 2011, pp. 1081–1084). Retrospective interpretation works to create order out of what seems to be disorder. It allows observers to understand better how a seemingly ordinary person could do or be something unusual. This individual is found to be not as ordinary as was originally thought; despite surface appearances, he or she actually had been a deviant all along.

One aspect of the retrospective interpretation process is that of discovery. If something is found in the accused deviant's personal history that can explain the deviance, even remotely, it becomes part of the reconstructed biographical record. We may discover, for example, that a mass murderer had an abusive childhood and liked guns very much, information that would never have come to light—or been given much significance—if the individual had not committed random acts of violence. The process of retrospective interpretation is selective, and factors that might refute, challenge, or complicate the biographical sketch may be ignored, dismissed, or downgraded. It is also possible for the biographical reconstruction to involve fabrication or even outright lying. For example, a deviant's parents might be defined as having been abusive when they really were not. All deviants may undergo processes of retrospective interpretation when the need is great to explain or understand what seems to be inexplicable.

Deviants *themselves* may engage in an autobiographical retrospective interpretation as they search through their own life experiences to come to some understanding of why they can't be like everybody else or even why others are so annoyed by them. A study of 10 street prostitutes, who were in rehabilitation for their heavy drug use while trying to disengage from sex work, shows how this works. They used their former drug addictions as a way to explain and therefore handle some of the stigma associated with prostitution. They retrospectively made sense of their own involvement in prostitution by tying their sex work and their drug abuse together, and presenting it as a remnant of a former life with its corresponding former self (McCray, Wesely, & Rasche, 2011). This retrospective interpretation allowed them to move from a deviant to a nondeviant identity more easily. They were, in the words of Gusfield (1967), "repentant deviants."

Managing Stigma

Deviance Avowal

Individuals are objects of their own experience, holding opinions and making evaluations of their personal attributes and social identities. Just because other people may condemn an individual for some behavior or attribute does not mean that he or she must share their opinions (LeBel, 2012). Individuals may take pleasure and pride in what they are precisely because some other people do condemn it, or they may simply be indifferent to the reactions of others, marching to the beat of a different drummer. Stigma is based on negotiated understandings and situational factors, not universal and absolute decision rules (Haenfler, 2013, p. 94).

People with devalued attributes can still maintain a positive self-image, not only by hiding or covering the troubling condition, but also by believing that their personal condition is actually a good and valued trait, regardless of what others may think. They may view their condition as righteous, requiring neither apology nor regret (Rogers & Buffalo, 1974). Usually, individuals find that maintaining an identity that is discrediting—actually or potentially—requires a great deal of skillful interpersonal work if they are to maintain any kind of self-respect in the face of scornful reactions from others (G. Hughes & Degher, 1993, pp. 300–312; Kipnis, 2010). In some cases, stigmatized individuals find ways to exploit their condition for positive gains (Herman & Miall, 2005).

People will sometimes accept (or actively pursue) a deviant label because they see some advantage in it. They will transform negative labels into positive ones through a process of reinterpretation so that a once-stigmatizing label no longer is ("I'm bald *and* beautiful"). It is also possible for a once-stigmatizing trait to be redefined by others as something positive (or vice versa). Women with naturally curly hair are mightily pleased with what sits atop their heads until standards change and straight hair is all the rage. Little evidence exists that people who are defined as deviant by others *inevitably* hold poor opinions of themselves.

Whether negative reactions from others lead to reduced feelings of self-worth depends a lot on the type of deviance it is, how committed the individual is to the deviance, how involved the individual is with conventional society, the nature of the relationship between the accusers and the accused, and whether the condition is shared with others. Certain kinds of deviance are actually status enhancing, and deviants readily avow their deviance (Turner, 1972). *Deviance avowal* exists when people actually desire to occupy a deviant status and actively pursue it if they can. This reminds us that deviance can be functional, even righteous, for individuals. In fact, nondeviants may fake or exaggerate unrespectability (Ball, 1970, pp. 334–335).

Kitsuse (1980) proposed the term *tertiary deviation* to cover all those situations in which deviants embrace a deviant status but reject the negative identity and stigma implied by disapproving labels. This transforms a deviant identity into something that is both positive and desirable. He refers to individuals who do this successfully as the "new deviants":

> Fat people, little people, ugly people, old people, and a growing number of others—who have called into question the very concept of "deviant," not by denying what they are, but by affirming and claiming it as a valued identity deserving of the rights accorded any member of society. (p. 8)

One thing that tertiary deviants may do is to join with other devalued or deviant people to collectively fight against or resist the societal exclusion, segregation, prejudice, and discrimination to which they are subject.

At one time, people with certain types of spoiled identity—they used to be called "freaks"—could find a place in the world of popular entertainment and amusement. Siamese twins, bearded ladies, tattooed men, giants, dwarfs, armless men, the obese, the extremely thin—you name them, they were there. Though some were exploited, most of them were performers and entertainers who were applauded for having turned a potential liability into a profitable and valuable identity peg. According to Bogdan (1988), these human exhibits had no objection to being put on display; in fact, most of them enjoyed the attention. They were comfortable with what they were, and though they were called freaks, they did not believe they were freakish. Their view of themselves was different from that of Joseph Carey Merrick, nicknamed "the Elephant Man." He believed he needed to hide his physical deformities under a mask whenever he could. (He is thought to have suffered from von Recklinghausen disease.)

By the beginning of the twentieth century, the display of human oddities for amusement had fallen into disrepute in the United States. Part of the reason was the growing fear that these individuals might reproduce and transmit their physical traits to future generations. The other major factor was that after physicians organized into the American Medical Association (in 1847), they worked to establish their claim that they had special expertise in regard to understanding and treating *all* human deviation. Human oddities, like those displayed in the freak shows, came to be medicalized as sick and in need of cure rather than as exotic exhibits for the amusement of paying customers (Bogdan, 1988, p. 66).

Some attributes of individuals, though potentially discrediting, are tolerated or even accepted because they are assessed in light of other attributes of these individuals. A different cluster of attributes would have produced different reactions from others. Consider the following letter to "Dear Abby" from a "Happy Wife" (Van Buren, 1981, p. 175).

Dear Abby:

When our daughter was a baby, I found her pacifier in our bed. I thought it had dropped out of her mouth while she was in our bed, but later I found the pacifier in the drawer of our nightstand table, and I couldn't for the life of me figure out how it got there.

Then one morning I woke up early and saw my husband sound asleep with the pacifier in his mouth! We had a good laugh over it, and that evening when I fixed the baby's bottle I jokingly asked him if he wanted a bottle too. He said yes, so I fixed him one.

He loved it, so I kept fixing him a bottle right along with the baby's. I took the baby off the bottle when she was fourteen months old, but my husband still has one every night, and he is thirty-seven. Please don't use our names as my husband is well known here. He works on the space program. Thank you.

How can the husband *not* be a deviant? The wife is embarrassed to have their name printed, and both she and her husband seem to realize that most other fathers are not nursing on their baby's pacifier or drinking from baby bottles. Yet how can he *be* deviant? Both the wife and husband laugh over the husband's acts, and the wife really seems to experience very little consternation over her spouse's fondness for infant paraphernalia. Other characteristics in his cluster of traits (employee on the space program, good provider, good sense of humor) seem to be sufficient for his wife to be tolerant of his less commendable traits.

Deviance and Respectability

Audiences differ on what they accept or reject in others and on what they consider respectable. The larger the number of competing views about what qualifies as respectability, the harder it will be to appear respectable to all of the people all of the time. In November 1996, a 13-year-old female student named Karla Chapman did what she had done many times before. She went to class at the Runyon Elementary School in Pike County, Kentucky. This day, however, she was declared to be a distraction by Rosa Wolfe, the principal. Three times the principal had warned her, and three times Karla Chapman had defied the principal's authority. The problem? Karla Chapman wore *black* lipstick. At another time or place, with different people, this probably would have been no big deal. However, at this time and place, with these people, it developed into a very big deal indeed.

Karla found that her choice of lipstick color (which she insisted was her business, not the school's), coupled with her refusal to wipe the stuff off as ordered, got her suspended for 3 days. On the day that her suspension ended, Karla got ready for school, donned a different-colored lipstick, and arrived at the elementary school ready for classes to start. However, she was once again reprimanded and prohibited from entering the school, because her new choice of lipstick color—dark purple—was still unacceptable to school personnel. Because the principal would brook no opposition, Karla was put in a difficult situation. If she did not return to school, she would be considered a truant—which at Karla's age qualified her as a delinquent—but she could not return to school if she continued to wear lipstick that was considered distracting by the principal (Mueller, 1996).

It is difficult for an outsider to this incident to understand what it is about black lipstick that makes it so distracting and what exactly made Karla Chapman such a problem to the principal. Certainly, nothing unique to black lipstick makes it more upsetting than any other color of lipstick. Even red lipstick could be distracting on a 13-year-old (depending, of course, on how it was applied). Yet a principal does have an obligation to keep the school setting calm and orderly. One wonders if the problem was not so much the black lips as the fact that a teenager would refuse to comply with orders to wipe the stuff off (and thereby challenge the authority of those who have the power to decide what qualifies as a respectable appearance).

If Karla Chapman had been *born* with black lips, it is the principal who would have found herself in a difficult situation in trying to expel her. Though Karla still would have been sporting a "distracting" color, the attribute would be viewed as something over which Chapman had little or no control. The power and authority of school administrators would not have been challenged directly by a young person's *deliberate* act of insubordination, and they could have afforded to be more gracious and understanding than they were in this particular instance. Clearly, stigma (and other unpleasant consequences) is one possible outcome of the negotiations between people about the propriety of conditions that some of them find upsetting and unnecessary.

Deviants can encounter two different types of potentially supporting or confirming others. Goffman (1963) refers to one group as *the own*—individuals who also have the deviant's devalued trait. Although these individuals are more likely than others to be accepting of people like themselves, this is not guaranteed. Bullies don't like other bullies very much, and hyperactive people are not automatically more accepting of people like themselves. The stigmatized may, in fact, stigmatize others. The other group is *the wise*. These are individuals who do not themselves possess the devalued trait but who are familiar enough with the plight of deviants to be both understanding and accepting of them (pp. 20–28).

Bogdan and Taylor (1989) studied individuals who were in a caring and accepting relationship with persons who had severe and debilitating mental retardations and physical disabilities. These individuals with disabilities sometimes drooled, soiled themselves, and could not talk or walk well. How was it possible for caretakers to be accepting and loving toward individuals who were so visibly impaired? First, the individual with a disability was granted the capacity for thinking and feeling, as being more aware and responsive than he or she might appear. Second, the individual with a disability was viewed as someone who had a unique personality, specific likes and dislikes, and a personal history—all of which underscored the person's specialness or exceptionality. Third, the individual with a disability was defined as an active participant in social life. He or she was seen as fun, important, and someone with whom people without disabilities enjoyed interacting. Finally, a social place was reserved for the individual with a disability. He or she was defined as an important member of the family (or group), and he or she was included in its routines and rituals. The wise are able to avoid stigmatizing, stereotyping, and rejecting others, even those who have obvious and debilitating conditions, by seeing them as equals and as enjoyable instead of inferior and annoying.

The wise are not always as wise as they could be (or as wise as someone trying to assimilate would like them to be). A study of Greek organizations at three different East Coast universities over a 3-year period (2003 to 2006) focused on nonwhite students ($n = 31$) who were members of white fraternities or sororities (and had been for at least one full semester). Though the experiences in regard to race and ethnicity are not identical to the experiences of social deviants, the study is still instructive. The interview data showed example after example of the "paradox of participation" of these nonwhites. Their chance to be viewed as full-fledged members of the organization—as genuinely equal members of the brother- or sisterhood—was cobbled directly on their racial/ethnic identities as essentially different from, and generally inferior to, whites in the organization (Hughey, 2010, p. 674). When nonwhites attempted to assimilate or fit in, they faced the charge that they were acting in ways that were "uppity" or "phony." Nonwhites who wanted to be members of white Greek organizations had to deal on a continual basis with racial and ethnic stereotypes held by individuals who believed they held no stereotypes at all.

Neutralization and Stigma Management

An individual may find it necessary to manage or lessen whatever stigma he or she is experiencing through the use of *techniques of neutralization* (Sykes & Matza, 1957). These techniques, regardless of their specific form, are verbalizations that make it possible for individuals to temporarily suspend forces of social control, making them inoperative or insignificant (though neutralization could persist indefinitely). This makes it possible for an individual to engage in deviance without experiencing serious damage to his or her self-concept and without feeling constrained by feelings of stigma or embarrassment. Sykes and Matza identified five techniques of neutralization:

1. *Denial of responsibility:* The deviant insists that whatever happens is not his or her fault.

2. *Denial of injury:* The deviant insists that what happened hurt nobody.

3. *Denial of victim:* The deviant insists the victim was actually the one responsible for the deviance that occurred.

4. *Condemnation of the condemners:* The deviant insists that those who are criticizing him or her have no legitimacy, and it is they who are the real deviants.

5. *Appeal to higher loyalties:* The deviant insists that what he or she did was actually for the good of the whole—the nation, the society, the community, the gang—to achieve some higher purpose.

Some deviants will deny responsibility, thereby neutralizing whatever tension they might otherwise experience; others will insist that nobody was hurt or that the victim deserved what he or she got; still others will condemn those who condemn them and portray these others as stupid, spiteful, or mean; and still others will manage tension by claiming that they march to the beat of a different drummer (i.e., appeal to higher loyalties).

Neutralization techniques can also serve as *rationalizations*. These come *after* some untoward act occurs, and they help a deviant handle whatever tension or stigma might come from the trespass ("They had it coming, so what's the harm?"). The use of what Hitlin (2008) calls *lawyer logic* ("I did it, but they can't prove it") fulfills a rationalizing function. What kind of deviance occurs has a lot to do with the kind of neutralization techniques and rationalizations an individual is able to muster.

When it comes to stigma, it may not be so much that the deviant *did* (or *was*) the wrong thing as that the deviant failed to *present* what he or she did in the most appropriate, socially acceptable way. Some people can get away with things that other people cannot, because they are skilled at managing impressions for the benefit of others. One thing that a deviant can do is to perform *atonement*. This means doing the "right" thing immediately after it was done "wrongly." I once saw a tape of a weather report in which the reporter incorrectly informed her viewing audience that "from the north came cold mares' asses," while pointing to a map of the United States. She paused momentarily and then said it again, the right way: "From the north came cold air masses." Her atonement helped lessen some of the discomfort that her initial misstatement could have caused, both for the audience and for her. Another thing that deviants can do is to use an *apology* (Goffman, 1971, pp. 113–114). An apology is functional, both for the group and the individual who offers it. It shows that the individual realizes the wrongfulness of the trespass, tacitly supporting the normative order and the values on which it is based, while indicating that the rule breaking will never happen again. When successful, an apology promises a new self in an old body, one that will be more diligent in honoring the social contract.

Accused deviants can account for their trespass (Scott & Lyman, 1968). An *account* is a verbal statement that functions to relieve individuals of responsibility for what they have done. Two types of accounts exist, *excuses* and *justifications:*

> An excuse is an admission that the act in question was bad, wrong, or inept, coupled with a denial of full responsibility. A justification is an admission of full responsibility for the act in question, coupled with a denial that it was wrongful. (Lyman & Scott, 1989, p. 136)

If a defendant in a court of law were to claim that he or she was insane at the time of the crime, this would be an excuse. The defendant is claiming that he or she did not know the difference between right and wrong and so should not be held responsible for what happened. If, however, a defendant were to claim that he or she broke into a stranger's cabin to avoid an impending blizzard, this is a justification (called *necessity* in a U.S. court of law). The accused is not claiming that something external (or internal) negated personal *responsibility* for the breaking and entering; the intruder knew fully and exactly what he or she was doing. However, in this situation, the possibility of greater harm (death by freezing) is being used to justify the illegal entry (i.e., breaking and entering) of someone else's cabin. Humans, even when they are *outside* a courtroom, will use similar strategies to convince others (or try to) that they were not responsible for whatever happened or even that the deviance was actually necessary (i.e., justified) under the circumstances.

An exception to following rules that are viewed as important and necessary is a regular part of human encounters. When excuses "work" (i.e., are accepted as reasonable claims), the individual who might have been held responsible for the deviance is let off the hook, because it is concluded that the reason for the trespass was some factor (external or internal) over which the rule breaker had no control. When justifications "work" (i.e., are accepted as reasonable claims), a rule breaker is forgiven for the trespass, because it is concluded that it was actually demanded by the situation, being therefore unavoidable and thus blameless. We are prepared to exonerate some individuals for some rule breaking *if* they are able to account for these trespasses in acceptable ways. Individuals who refuse to offer accounts to others for their trespasses—or fail to apologize for them—face the prospect of not being reintegrated back into the group (Young & Thompson, 2011).

One of the best things for a rule breaker—better than apologizing, atoning, or accounting—is to be in a situation where nobody even knows that something untoward has happened, even those who have suffered some loss because of it. This is the case with *hidden* or *secret deviants.* They need not worry about dealing with injured parties who may demand restitution or even want the rule breaker punished for what was done to them. It is possible, however, for rule breakers to take advantage of others in one way or another, causing losses for them, but still keep them from realizing that they have been intentionally victimized. Turk (1969, pp. 58–61) used the word *sophistication* to refer to a knowledge of patterns of behavior of others that can be used to control or manipulate them. This may involve what Goffman (1952) called "cooling the mark out."

The various methods of *cooling the mark out* all boil down to a nudging of a victim, injured party, or offended individual in the direction of believing that what happened to him or her was nobody's fault. It was simply bad luck or coincidence. Though Goffman's (1952) principal objective was to show how victims are encouraged by coolers to adapt to failure and live with their losses (i.e., loss of status or security) in cases of criminal fraud (i.e., confidence games), his analysis has wider applications. "Persons who participate in what is recognized as a confidence game are found in only a few social settings, but persons who have to be cooled out are found in many" (pp. 452–453). Whenever a rule breaker is sophisticated enough to be able to cool the mark out successfully, no other strategies are necessary (such as apologizing, atoning, or accounting).

The sense of being conned or duped—often resulting in a loss of status—is a regular feature of social life. Anytime a person's expectations have been built up and then abruptly altered, he or she must find ways to adapt to the failure and mortification of self that are likely to follow. "The mark must therefore be supplied with a new set of apologies for himself, a new framework in which to see himself and judge himself" (Goffman, 1952, p. 456). This redefinition is what the cooler can help the mark develop while helping himself or herself, too. The victim is nudged by the cooler in the direction of defining himself or herself as having been an unfortunate victim of impersonal and inevitable forces and so not a mark at all. One example is when an individual who has been cheated during a game of cards, losing both money and self-respect, comes to believe that the outcome was simply a matter of bad luck and thus was nobody's fault.

Square Pegs and Round Holes: Eccentrics and Eccentricities

Danielle Willis is a vampire, or so she claims. She sleeps by day; works by night (she's a fiction writer); and drinks human blood, partly for nourishment and partly because it excites her. She paid her dentist to install a permanent set of porcelain fangs over her incisors. She does not change into a bat and then bite hapless victims on the neck, however. What she does is use a syringe to extract blood from a willing partner (whom she is confident has no blood-borne diseases) and then drink it, either right on the spot or at some later time. For Willis, the consumption of the bodily fluids of another is an expression of intimacy and trust. Hundreds of vampires like Willis live throughout the United States, and some of them believe (or at least hope) that drinking blood ensures their immortality ("Interview With a Vampirette," 1997). Are these people real bats, just batty, or something else?

Eccentrics are quirky or even odd people who have thrown off the bonds of conformity and who pursue whatever wild hair intrigues them. Some eccentrics are successful people, and their eccentricities are just part of what they are. Other eccentrics have gained fame and fortune because of their eccentricities, which shape their lives and their identities (Nash, 1982, p. xix). Still other eccentrics are abysmal failures at practically everything they do, partly because they are obsessed with their eccentricities. If an individual has the forbearance, ability, or good luck to triumph in some field, his or her eccentricity is likely to be overlooked or even admired. However, if an eccentric fails to gain prominence in some valued field of human endeavor, then his or her oddness is more likely to be disturbing to others, and he or she is more likely to be condemned or ridiculed (Wallace, 1957, pp. 11–12).

The label of eccentric—like all labels—is relative, and the ground rules for what makes one eccentric change all the time. Alexander Wortley had a deep suspicion of zippers in men's trousers, so he removed them from any pair he purchased. The reason? He did not want a lightning conductor so close to such a sensitive body part (S. Adams & Riley, 1988, p. 217). Wortley's anxiety over genital shocks is not at all unreasonable; it is how he went about protecting himself from electrocution that seems strange. The Reverend George H. Munday was a renowned Quaker preacher in nineteenth-century Philadelphia. Parishioners gathered by the hundreds to hear his sermons but mostly to observe his odd trait: He refused to wear a hat at a time when all male Quakers did (Sifakis, 1984, pp. xvi–xvii). Joseph Palmer moved to the city of Fitchburg, Massachusetts, in 1830. Some of his new neighbors shunned him, and others threw rocks at him (and at his house). Businesspeople refused to cater to him, and religious people prayed for his redemption. Women avoided and feared him, often crossing to the other side of the road when they saw him coming. What was Palmer's problem? He was one of the first individuals in the United States to grow a long beard. This was so upsetting to others that one day four men armed with scissors and a razor attacked him, threw him to the ground, and tried to shave him forcibly. Through all his trials and tribulations, he steadfastly kept his beard. His gravestone in Evergreen Cemetery in Leominster, Massachusetts, tells the story. It reads, "Persecuted for wearing the beard" (Sifakis, 1984, pp. 69–70).

Some eccentrics are what they are because accidents of birth made their pursuit of novelty more likely. Michel Lotito (1950–2007), also known as Monsieur Mangetout ("Mister Eat Everything"), a Frenchman from Grenoble, had an amazing ability: He could eat practically anything. When he was 16, he was drinking mint tea with friends at a French cafe, and the rim of the glass accidentally broke off in his mouth. Instead of spitting the piece out and complaining about the defective glass, he chewed the piece up and swallowed it. Because he experienced no adverse effects, he soon realized that he had a special talent (Flaherty, 1992, pp. 129–130). He went on to become a professional entertainer whose performance consisted of eating his way through things, such as television sets, aluminum skis, supermarket carts, bicycles (he liked the chain the best), razor blades, coins, glasses, bottles, bullets, and phonograph records. He even ate an entire airplane—a Cessna two-seater—piece by piece. Lotito would cut objects into bite-size pieces, lubricate his digestive tract liberally with mineral oil, and drink lots of water as he ate the debris. Surprisingly enough, though he could eat stuff that would kill an ordinary person, he had difficulty digesting bananas and eggs (S. Adams & Riley, 1988, p. 231). Lotito was awarded a brass plaque by the *Guinness Book of World Records* to commemorate his eating eccentricities. He was so honored that he ate it (Flaherty, 1992, p. 130). (*Gourmandizing*, which is excessive eating, was popular in the United States in the early 1900s as a form of freak entertainment. Now it is a competitive sport, and contests are regularly held, with winners receiving prizes worth thousands of dollars. An International Federation of Competitive Eating even exists to promote the sport.)

Other eccentrics methodically plan ways to be different and systematically carry them out. One such person is Ashrita Furman (born Keith Furman), who as of this writing has the most records in the Guinness Book of World Records held by a single individual. He has traveled to about 30 different countries to try to break records. One of the ways he gets in the book is by inventing new things to do that will establish a record, such as the fastest mile by someone balancing a baseball bat or underwater pogo stick jumping. Sometimes, Furman does ordinary things in extraordinary ways or in unusual places. For example, in 1979, he set his first record by doing 27,000 jumping jacks, and in 1986, he did somersaults along the same twelve-and-one-quarter miles that was traveled by Paul Revere on his famous ride in Massachusetts in 1775.

One of the most irrepressible traits of eccentrics is that they pay little attention to the derision and ridicule that they often receive from others. In some cases, they are unaware of what others think of them, but most times they are just unconcerned with the views of others. Weeks and James (1995) found some common traits in the eccentrics they studied. In general, they were (1) nonconforming; (2) creative; (3) curious; (4) idealistic; and (5) happily involved with one or more quirky hobbies or obsessions, usually five or six. In addition, they (6) felt different from others (and had since childhood), and they were (7) intelligent; (8) dogmatic; (9) independent; (10) unusual in living and eating practices; and (11) isolated from contacts with others and indifferent to their opinions. They also (12) had a mischievous sense of humor and were typically (13) single, (14) either the oldest child in a family or an only child, and (15) had poor spelling ability. The first five were found in *every* eccentric in the study, and the list of 15 goes from the most frequently found to the least. Some of these character traits are little more than synonyms for *eccentric* (nonconforming, creative, obsessive, opinionated, with peculiar living arrangements or eating habits), and others (isolated, unmarried, independent) are probably a response to how others have reacted to them.

Eccentrics occupy an indeterminate status. They are fascinating to others (and may even be a source of envy), while they are also upsetting to them. Eccentrics believe that they are right in what they do, and they are not usually unhappy with their unconventionality. They tend to do exactly as they please, and they are usually unconcerned with what is proper or what others want them to do.

Eccentrics are people who take boundless joy in life, immoderate men and women who refuse to violate their ideals. Their minds are always buzzing furiously with ideas. . . . At the root of eccentricity is a healthy and determined irreverence. (Weeks & James, 1995, p. 254)

The eccentric's unbridled freedom and independence of thought and action (or is it irresponsibility or some slavish obedience to the goal of being weird?) may rub others the wrong way. What gives eccentrics the right to do what they want when the rest of us cannot?

Eccentrics may actually be more alarming than other kinds of deviants. To be sure, their eccentricities rarely break the law, but this does not mean that eccentrics are simply amusing oafs, providing the spice of life. Whereas most deviants know the difference between right and wrong and do not flaunt or challenge the rules openly (Sykes & Matza, 1957), the eccentric seems to be out of touch with the ordinary concerns of the ordinary folk. Not only is the eccentric odd in the eyes of the beholders, but he or she also goes to great lengths to be different and separate from others, defends his or her oddness as perfectly proper, is indifferent to the expectations and wishes of others, and appears unable or unwilling to understand why others would be upset by him or her. Whatever tensions might exist between individual desires and the forces of social control have been resolved successfully by the eccentric in favor of his or her own interests (Suran, 1978). Eccentrics' trespasses may be minor and relatively benign, but they do them with such gusto, irreverence, self-centeredness, assurance, and guiltlessness that their trespasses can take on an ominous and foreboding quality.

Conclusions

This chapter has shown that attributes (the principal element in "conditions" in the ABCs of deviance) are themselves a source of categorization and judgment. People are stigmatized for things over which they have little or no control. "Normal" and "stigmatized" are *perspectives* on persons, so we always will need a language of relationships to be able to discuss and understand any discrediting or discreditable attributes. An error occurs when observers attribute the cause for some happening to individual character instead of to the context in which it occurs. Cause and blame are not identical, but *decisions* about blame and responsibility always have direct implications for who and what is deviant.

When the label of deviance is attached to some attitude, behavior, or condition, it usually involves some fundamental decisions about conventionality (Could it have been otherwise?) and theoreticity (Does or did the individual know what he or she is doing?). These decision rules help assess responsibility for some event, which leads quite easily into decisions about who or what is deviant. Such interpersonal processes are responsible for the social construction of spoiled identities and the stigma that ensues from it. Deviance can easily evolve into a master status and be accompanied by a great deal of shame and embarrassment. Reputations can be tarnished or even irreparably damaged. Retrospective interpretation is a dynamic process in which a person's social identity is reconstituted in the eyes of others. It is possible for accused deviants to impact what happens to them by using neutralizations, rationalizations, atonements, apologies, accounts, or cooling out strategies. When any of these is successful, it is possible to have a great deal of deliberate rule breaking without anyone being held responsible for it.

References

Adams, J. (2012). Cleaning up the dirty work: Professionalization and the management of stigma in the cosmetic surgery and tattoo industries. *Deviant Behavior, 33*, 149–167.

Adams, S., & Riley, L. (1988). *Facts and fallacies.* New York, NY: Reader's Digest Association.

Adler, P., & Adler, P. (2009). Self-injurers. In P. Adler & P. Adler (Eds.), *Constructions of deviance: Social power, context, and interaction* (6th ed., pp. 379–386). Belmont, CA: Thomson/Wadsworth.

Atkinson, M. (2011). Male athletes and the cult(ure) of thinness in sport. *Deviant Behavior, 32*, 224–256.

Atkinson, M., & Young, K. (2008). Flesh journeys: The radical body modification of neoprimitives. In E. Goode & D. A. Vail (Eds.), *Extreme deviance* (pp. 15–26). Thousand Oaks, CA: Pine Forge/Sage.

Badger, S. (2010). "Where the excess grows": Demarcating "normal" and "pathologically" obese bodies. In E. Etorre (Ed.), *Culture, bodies and the sociology of health* (pp. 137–154). Burlington, VT: Ashgate.

Ball, D. (1970). The problematics of respectability. In J. Douglas (Ed.), *Deviance and respectability: The social construction of moral meanings* (pp. 326–371). New York, NY: Basic Books.

Becker, H. (1963). *Outsiders: Studies in the sociology of deviance.* New York, NY: Free Press.

Bogdan, R. (1988). *Freak show: Presenting human oddities for amusement and profit.* Chicago, IL: University of Chicago Press.

Bogdan, R., & Taylor, S. (1989). Relationships with severely disabled people: The social construction of humanness. *Social Problems, 36*, 135–148.

Brownmiller, S. (1984). *Femininity.* New York, NY: Linden.

Burke, P. J., & Stets, J. E. (2009). *Identity theory.* New York, NY: Oxford University Press.

Buss, D. (1994). *The evolution of desire: Strategies of human mating.* New York, NY: Basic Books.

Butera, F., & Levine, J. M. (Eds.). (2009). *Coping with minority status: Responses to exclusion and inclusion.* New York, NY: Cambridge University Press.

Cahill, S., & Eggleston, R. (2005). Wheelchair users. In E. Rubington & M. Weinberg (Eds.), *Deviance: The interactionist perspective* (9th ed., pp. 26–41). Boston, MA: Pearson/Allyn & Bacon.

Campbell, F. K. (2009). *Contours of ableism: The production of disability and ableness.* New York, NY: Palgrave Macmillan.

Colls, R., & Hörschelman, K. (2009). Introduction: Contested bodies of childhood and youth. In R. Colls & K. Hörschelmann (Eds.), *Contested bodies of childhood and youth* (pp. 1–21). New York, NY: Palgrave Macmillan.

Edgell, P., & Tranby, E. (2010). Shared visions? Diversity and cultural membership in American life. *Social Problems, 57,* 175–204.

English, C. (1993). Gaining and losing weight: Identity transformations. *Deviant Behavior, 14,* 227–241.

Etorre, E. (2010). Bodies, drugs and reproductive regimes. In E. Etorre (Ed.), *Culture, bodies and the sociology of health* (pp. 155–172). Burlington, VT: Ashgate.

Felson, R. (1991). Blame analysis: Accounting for the behavior of protected groups. *American Sociologist, 22,* 5–23.

Fitzpatrick, K. M., & Myrstol, B. (2011). The jailing of America's homeless: Evaluating the rabble management thesis. *Crime & Delinquency, 57,* 271–297. (Originally published online August 25, 2008)

Flaherty, T. (1992). *Odd and eccentric people.* Alexandria, VA: Time-Life Books.

Force, W. R. (2010). The code of Harry: Performing normativity in *Dexter. Crime, Media, Culture, 6,* 329–345.

Garfinkel, H. (1956). Conditions of successful degradation ceremonies. *American Journal of Sociology, 61,* 420–424.

Garot, R. (2010). *Who you claim: Performing gang identity in school and on the streets.* New York: New York University Press.

Gladwell, M. (2000). *The tipping point: How little things can make a big difference.* Boston, MA: Little, Brown.

Glass, C., Haas, S., & Reither, E. N. (2010). The skinny on success: Body mass, gender and occupational standing across the life course. *Social Forces, 88,* 1777–1806.

Goffman, E. (1952). On cooling the mark out. *Psychiatry, 15,* 451–463.

Goffman, E. (1959). *The presentation of self in everyday life.* Garden City, NY: Doubleday Anchor.

Goffman, E. (1963). *Stigma: Notes on the management of spoiled identity.* Englewood Cliffs, NJ: Prentice Hall.

Goffman, E. (1969). *Strategic interaction.* New York, NY: Ballantine.

Goffman, E. (1971). *Relations in public: Microstudies of the public order.* New York, NY: Harper & Row.

Goode, E. (2002). Sexual involvement and social research in a fat civil rights organization. *Qualitative Sociology, 25,* 501–534.

Goode, E. (2011). *Deviant behavior* (9th ed.). Upper Saddle River, NJ: Pearson/ Prentice Hall.

Goode, E., & Vail, D. A. (Eds.). (2008). *Extreme deviance*. Thousand Oaks, CA: Pine Forge/Sage.

Gregersen, E. (1983). *Sexual practices: The story of human sexuality*. New York, NY: Franklin Watts.

Grogan, S. (2009). Femininity and body image: Promoting positive body image in the "culture of slenderness." In R. Colls & K. Hörschelmann (Eds.), *Contested bodies of childhood and youth* (pp. 41–52). New York, NY: Palgrave Macmillan.

Gusfield, J. (1967). Moral passage: The symbolic process in public designations of deviance. *Social Problems, 15,* 175–188.

Haenfler, R. (2013). *Goths, gamers, grrrls: Deviance and youth subcultures* (2nd ed.). New York, NY: Oxford University Press.

Harris, A., Evans, H., & Beckett, K. (2011). Courtesy stigma and monetary sanctions: Toward a socio-cultural theory of punishment. *American Sociological Review, 76,* 234–264.

Herman, N., & Miall, C. (2005). The positive consequences of stigma. In E. Rubington & M. Weinberg (Eds.), *Deviance: The interactionist perspective* (9th ed., pp. 237–249). Boston, MA: Pearson/Allyn & Bacon.

Hills, S. L. (1980). *Demystifying social deviance*. New York, NY: McGraw-Hill.

Hitlin, S. (2008). *Moral selves, evil selves: The social psychology of conscience*. New York, NY: Palgrave Macmillan.

Hughes, E. C. (1945). Dilemmas and contradictions of status. *American Journal of Sociology, 50,* 353–359.

Hughes, E. C. (1951). Work and the self. In J. Roher & M. Sherif (Eds.), *Social psychology at the crossroads* (pp. 313–323). New York, NY: Harper & Brothers.

Hughes, G., & Degher, D. (1993). Coping with a deviant identity. *Deviant Behavior, 14,* 297–315.

Hughey, M. W. (2010). A paradox of participation: Nonwhites in white sororities and fraternities. *Social Problems, 57,* 653–679.

Interview with a vampirette. (1997, February 9). *New York Times Magazine,* p. 17.

Irwin, J. (1985). *Managing the underclass in American society*. Berkeley: University of California Press.

Jaeger, M. M. (2011). "A thing of beauty is a joy forever"? Returns to physical attractiveness over the life course. *Social Forces, 89,* 983–1004.

Jones, A., & Ratterman, N. (2009). Mate choice and sexual selection: What have we learned since Darwin? *Proceedings of the National Academy of Sciences of the United States of America, 106*(Supp. 1), 10001–10008.

Jong, E. (1990). *Any woman's blues*. New York, NY: Harper & Row.

Kent, L. (2010). Fighting abjection: Representing fat women. In L. J. Moore & M. Kosut (Eds.), *The body reader: Essential social and cultural readings* (pp. 367–383). New York: New York University Press.

Kipnis, L. (2010). *How to become a scandal: Adventures in bad behavior*. New York, NY: Metropolitan Books.

Kitsuse, J. (1962). Societal reactions to deviant behavior: Problems of theory and method. *Social Problems, 9,* 247–257.

Kitsuse, J. (1980). Coming out all over: Deviants and the politics of social problems. *Social Problems, 28,* 1–13.

Kosut, M., & Moore, L. J. (2010). Introduction: Not just the reflexive reflex. Flesh and bone in the social sciences. In L. J. Moore & M. Kosut (Eds.), *The body reader: Essential social and cultural readings* (pp. 1–26). New York: New York University Press.

Kwan, S. (2009). Framing the fat body: Contested meanings between government, activists, and industry. *Sociological Inquiry, 79,* 25–50.

LeBel, T. P. (2012). Invisible stripes? Formerly incarcerated persons' perceptions of stigma. *Deviant Behavior, 33,* 89–107.

Lyman, S., & Scott, M. (1989). *Sociology of the absurd* (2nd ed.). New York, NY: General Hall.

MacKinnon, N. J., & Heise, D. R. (2010). *Self, identity, and social institutions.* New York, NY: Palgrave Macmillan.

Maner, J., Gailliot, M., Rouby, D., & Miller, S. (2007). Can't take my eyes off you: Attentional adhesion to mates and rivals. *Journal of Personality and Social Psychology, 93,* 389–401.

Mankoff, M. (1976). Societal reaction and career deviance: A critical analysis. In W. Chambliss & M. Mankoff (Eds.), *Whose law? What order?* (pp. 240–256). New York, NY: Wiley.

McCray, K., Wesely, J. K., & Rasche, C. E. (2011). Rehab retrospect: Former prostitutes and the (re)construction of deviance. *Deviant Behavior, 32,* 743–768.

McHugh, P. (1970). A common-sense conception of deviance. In J. Douglas (Ed.), *Deviance and respectability: The social construction of moral meanings* (pp. 61–88). New York, NY: Basic Books.

Montanino, F., & Sagarin, E. (1977). Deviants: Voluntarism and responsibility. In E. Sagarin & F. Montanino (Eds.), *Deviants: Voluntary actors in a hostile world* (pp. 1–15). Morristown, NJ: General Learning Press/Scott, Foresman.

Moore, L. J., & Kosut, M. (Eds.). (2010). *The body reader: Essential social and cultural readings.* New York: New York University Press.

Mueller, L. (1996, November 19). Father of black-lipsticked girl arrested. *Lexington Herald-Leader,* pp. A1, A8.

Mustaine, E., & Tewksbury, R. (2011). Assessing informal control against the highly stigmatized. *Deviant Behavior, 32,* 944–960.

Nash, J. R. (1982). *Zanies: The world's greatest eccentrics.* Piscataway, NJ: New Century.

Newman, D. (2008). *Sociology: Exploring the architecture of everyday life* (7th ed.). Thousand Oaks, CA: Pine Forge/Sage.

Nisbett, R. E., & Ross, L. (1991). *The person and the situation.* Philadelphia, PA: Temple University Press.

O'Brien, J. (2006). Shared meaning as the basis of humanness. In J. O'Brien (Ed.), *The production of reality* (4th ed., pp. 64–82). Thousand Oaks, CA: Pine Forge/Sage.

Pager, D. (2007). *Marked: Race, crime, and finding work in an era of mass incarceration.* Chicago, IL: University of Chicago Press.

Penfold-Mounce, R. (2009). *Celebrity culture and crime: The joy of transgression.* New York, NY: Palgrave Macmillan.

Pontikes, E., Negro, G., & Rao, H. (2010). Stained red. A study of stigma by association to blacklisted artists during the "Red Scare" in Hollywood, 1945 to 1960. *American Sociological Review, 75,* 456–478.

Rassin, M. (2011). Tactics of concealment among people living with HIV. *Deviant Behavior, 32,* 101–114.

Richardson, N. (2010). *Transgressive bodies: Representations in film and popular culture.* Burlington, VT: Ashgate.

Richeson, J. A., & Trawalter, S. (2005). On the categorization of admired and disliked exemplars of admired and disliked racial groups. *Journal of Personality and Social Psychology, 89,* 517–530.

Ridley, M. (1993). *The Red Queen: Sex and the evolution of human nature.* New York, NY: Penguin.

Roberts, I., & Edwards, P. (2010). *The energy glut: Climate change and the politics of fatness.* New York, NY: Zed Books.

Rogers, J., & Buffalo, M. D. (1974). Fighting back: Nine modes of adaptation to a deviant label. *Social Problems, 22,* 101–118.

Sagarin, E. (1975). *Deviants and deviance: An introduction to the study of disvalued people and behavior.* New York, NY: Praeger.

Saguy, A. C., & Gruys, K. (2010). Morality and health: News media constructions of overweight and eating disorders. *Social Problems, 57,* 231–250.

Saguy, A. C., Gruys, K., & Gong, S. (2010). Social problem construction and national context: News reporting on "overweight" and "obesity" in the United States and France. *Social Problems, 57,* 586–610.

Sanders, C. (1996). Getting a tattoo. In E. Rubington & M. Weinberg (Eds.), *Deviance: The interactionist perspective* (6th ed., pp. 364–377). Boston, MA: Allyn & Bacon.

Saperstein, A., & Penner, A. M. (2010). The race of a criminal record: How incarceration colors racial perceptions. *Social Problems, 57,* 92–113.

Schafer, M. H., Ferraro, K. F., & Mustillo, S. (2011). Children of misfortune: Early adversity and cumulative inequality in perceived life trajectories. *American Journal of Sociology, 116,* 1053–1091.

Schur, E. (1971). *Labeling deviant behavior: Its sociological implications.* New York, NY: Harper & Row.

Schur, E. (1983). *Labeling women deviant.* Philadelphia, PA: Temple University Press.

Scott, M., & Lyman, S. (1968). Accounts. *American Sociological Review, 33,* 46–62.

Sherry, M. (2010). *Disability hate crimes: Does anyone really hate disabled people?* Burlington, VT: Ashgate.

Shippee, N. D. (2011). Gay, straight, and who I am: Passing within the frames for everyday life. *Deviant Behavior, 32,* 115–157.

Sifakis, C. (1984). *American eccentrics.* New York, NY: Facts on File.

Silver, E., Silver, S. R., Siennick, S., & Farkas, G. (2011). Bodily signs of academic success: An empirical examination of tattoos and grooming. *Social Problems, 58,* 538–564.

Slevin, K. F. (2010). "If I had lots of money . . . I'd have a body makeover": Managing the aging body. *Social Forces, 88,* 1003–1020.

Small, M. (1995). *What's love got to do with it? The evolution of human mating.* New York, NY: Anchor.

Sobal, J. (1995). The medicalization and demedicalization of obesity. In D. Maurer & J. Sobal (Eds.), *Eating agendas: Food and nutrition as social problems* (pp. 67–90). New York, NY: Aldine de Gruyter.

Stiles, B. L., & Clark, R. E. (2011). BDSM: A subcultural analysis of sacrifices and delights. *Deviant Behavior, 32,* 158–189.

Suran, B. (1978). *Oddballs: The social maverick and the dynamics of individuality.* Chicago, IL: Nelson Hall.

Sykes, G., & Matza, D. (1957). Techniques of neutralization: A theory of delinquency. *American Sociological Review, 22,* 664–670.

Trost, C. (1982). The blue people of Troublesome Creek. *Science, 82,* 34–39.

Turk, A. (1969). *Criminality and legal order.* Chicago, IL: Rand McNally.

Turner, R. (1972). Deviance avowal as neutralization of commitment. *Social Problems, 19,* 308–321.

Vail, D. A. (2008). Tattoos are like potato chips . . . you can't have just one: The process of becoming and being a collector. In E. Goode & D. A. Vail (Eds.), *Extreme deviance* (pp. 5–14). Thousand Oaks, CA: Pine Forge/Sage.

Van Buren, A. (1981). *The best of Dear Abby.* Kansas City, MO: Andrews & McMeel.

Vecitis, K. S. (2011). Young women's accounts of instrumental drug use for weight control. *Deviant Behavior, 32,* 451–474.

Wallace, I. (1957). *The square pegs: Some Americans who dared to be different.* New York, NY: Knopf.

Weeks, D., & James, J. (1995). *Eccentrics: A study of sanity and strangeness.* New York, NY: Villard.

Young, R. L., & Thompson, C. Y. (2011). Gender, attributions of responsibility, and negotiation of deviant labels in small groups. *Deviant Behavior, 32,* 626–652.

3

Power, Social Networks, and Organizational Deviance

The Plunder of Poletown

Community Integration and Corporate Growth

A community in Detroit, Michigan—once known as Poletown—could trace its roots back to the 1880s. It started as a low-income, working-class, well-integrated, close-knit community whose residents had migrated from areas in Poland under Russian, Austrian, or German control. It developed into an area with strong community spirit, occupied by people who had a faith in the future. However, it all came to an end because Poletown, its residents, and much of what they owned—homes, businesses, hospitals, schools, churches, restaurants, laundromats—stood in the way of the interests of the privileged and the powerful.

In June of 1980, just before Ronald Reagan began his first term as president, Coleman Young, the mayor of Detroit, and Thomas Murphy, the chair of General Motors (GM), announced that a new Cadillac plant (the Hamtramck plant) would soon be built in Detroit on a site that would include a large portion of Poletown. The plant was packaged as a renovation project for Detroit that would create jobs (GM claimed that 6,000 workers would eventually be employed at the plant) and bring new prosperity to a city hit hard by economic recession and corporate flight. All seemed right with the world, and GM representatives and political officials apparently expected that everyone would be as pleased as they were with the prospects of a partnership between General Motors and the Detroit City Council.

The city council believed that it could iron out any wrinkles in the plan, pacify disgruntled Poletowners, and smoothly and quickly take care of business for General Motors. However, the best-laid plans often go awry. Almost as soon as the plan was unveiled, it was criticized by those people who defined it as nothing more than a land grab to make one of the richest companies on earth even richer. Members of Detroit's city council seemed befuddled to the point of amazement by the censure that they, General Motors, and the plan received. Some of them expressed both surprise and shock over the Poletowners' reaction to what they believed was one of the best things ever to happen to the city of Detroit. Others on the city council expressed anger over the attacks they received. The mayor of Detroit even went so far as to characterize attacking General Motors as equivalent to shooting Santa Claus (Wylie, 1989, p. 201).

It is hard for an outside observer to understand how anyone on the city council could reasonably believe that they would *not* be savagely attacked for what they proposed to do to the Poletowners. The building of the plant was to require the taking (stealing?) of 465 acres from residents of Poletown, where their homes, businesses, churches, and schools—their memories and traditions—were located. Even if residents could convince themselves that the coming of new jobs to the area somehow justified the taking of most of what they held dear, a problem still existed: The proposed plant would not employ anywhere near what was projected because it was designed to be highly automated. Machines, rather than men and women, would do much of the work, and what new employees would be required would come from two older Cadillac plants that were scheduled to be closed by General Motors. This would mean job retention more than job creation, and it undercut the only legitimate reason—more jobs in Detroit—for the close alliance between the city council and General Motors.

Because corporate boosters successfully steered much of the attention to the jobs that would (supposedly) come to Detroit and away from the destruction and damage that would be done to community integrity (and the profits that GM would make from the deal), GM's demands fell on receptive ears. In fact, General Motors held most of the cards and called most of the shots. GM wanted $350 million, which was to come from local, state, and federal taxpayers. It also wanted the city to give it tax abatements; necessary permits (air, water, and waste); land rezoning; and city-funded roads, rail lines, highways, sewage-removal facilities, and street lights (Wylie, 1989, p. 52).

Detroit officials had to obtain the title to Poletown's 1,400 homes, 144 businesses, 2 schools, 1 hospital, and 16 churches, and destroy them within 10 months—by May 1, 1981—or GM would probably cancel the deal and go elsewhere. The city of Detroit would have to pay for the seized property; it would have to pay the relocation costs for more than 4,200 residents who had been evicted; and it would have to level all the buildings, clean the entire area of debris, and prepare the grounds for the new plant construction. All this meant that it was unlikely that the city would *ever* recoup its investment in the GM deal. It had no guarantee that it would ever receive any revenues from GM to invest in schools, garbage collection, police, or other important municipal services (Wylie, 1989, p. 109). However, city officials were between a rock and a hard place. Either they give in to GM's demands, or they could be branded as antibusiness and lose the GM deal.

General Motors, Detroit officials, and other power brokers lined up against Poletown, using every device at their disposal to get exactly what they all wanted. The community was characterized by GM executives as a depressed area, filled with dilapidated homes and deteriorating businesses. Executives at GM publicly claimed that it was city officials who were responsible for the seizure and destruction of the community that would serve as the future site of their Cadillac plant, while they disparaged the community and its residents. Any resistance by Poletowners was branded as unreasonable and unfair; anything that GM and Detroit city officials did was portrayed as necessary and in the public interest.

A strong ally of the powerful interests that had gathered against Poletown—as is often the case—was the legal institution. A new law had been created in Detroit that made it perfectly legal to take private property for public use *if* it could be shown that some public purpose would be achieved. The new law was used for the first time in the Poletown relocation. The law was broad enough that the GM Cadillac plant could be portrayed as something that would serve a public purpose, so Poletowners could be legally evicted. The law also included a "quick-take" clause that made it possible for city officials to seize private property rapidly, relocate the residents, and make the area fit for new construction. Even if former residents had protested and won in court, all they would have received would have been extra monies for their property. They would never get their property returned to them. On March 31, 1981, the Michigan Supreme Court ruled in a 5-to-2 decision that the city acted legally in taking Poletowners' property.

Resistance and Retaliation

The saga of the residents' struggle against such an awesome set of opponents is a complex one. Despite the size and power of the opponent, Poletown residents did have some things working for them: grit, determination, and a belief in the righteousness of their cause. Much like protesters and insurgents at other times and places (della Porta & Piazza, 2008; Traugott, 2010), Poletowners' struggle created a sense of duty and purpose among them, leading to feelings of solidarity and identity. They believed that America was a place where people who fought against powerful interests had to win to prove that people still had a voice in public affairs. It is through community that humans deal with difficulties and contradictions that changing power relationships can cause for them (Collins, 2010, p. 24).

Poletowners did practically everything they could to save their community. They wrote letters, held meetings, contacted people they thought might serve as allies, gave interviews, and publicly protested. Ralph Nader sent five of his staff to Poletown, and some of them became passionately involved in the residents' struggles. Maggie Kuhn, organizer of the Gray Panthers, offered the symbolic support of her organization to the Poletown struggle. Max Gail, one of the stars of the once-popular *Barney Miller* television show, spent many days in Poletown, discussing the proposed plant with media representatives and Poletown residents. If any protesters should have been successful, it was these, because they used many of the strategies that have worked in similar protests (King, 2011). However, the Poletowners received no major institutional support, so their struggles may have been doomed from the start:

> Residents attempted to contact the chief executives at General Motors, the mayor and his staff . . . the cardinal and his adjuncts at the archdiocese, the local and high court judges, news editors and station managers, officials at the United Auto Workers, Detroit area clergy, community groups, and members of the Left. None took the time to respond in a genuine manner. None even advocated a meeting of all parties to discuss possible compromises. For a variety of reasons, all of which could be reduced to a collusion of class, the power brokers in Detroit embraced GM's Cadillac project. (Wylie, 1989, p. 84)

The Catholic archdiocese even sold two of the community churches, an act that Poletowners defined as betrayal and that disheartened them greatly.

Short-term residents were the ones most likely to accept the city's offer of 80 percent of the assessed value of their property, and they left early. Others, however, refused to move. Vandalism and arson increased in Poletown, and it seemed that some organized effort was under way to destroy the community so that it could be condemned. The smoke, the fire, and the fear of victimization did eventually drive out practically all of the residents. However, those that remained were a tenacious and determined bunch. They decided to try to save the Immaculate Conception Church from the wrecking ball. Some of them moved into the church illegally and barricaded themselves. The city responded by slowing down and eventually stopping utility services in the church. Phones were cut off, along with water and electricity. The protesters used flashlights and candles and slept on mattresses in the basement.

On July 14, 1981, city officials were fed up, and they moved on the church. The Special Weapons Attack Team (SWAT) was summoned, and police dogs were used to patrol the area. The police attached a chain to the sanctuary side door and used a tow truck to rip it off its hinges. The protesters fled to the basement and locked the door. The basement door was eventually ripped off, and 20 police officers swarmed into the room, prepared to deal with the protesters. During the eviction, the women—some of whom were in their seventies—were told to leave, and some of the men were verbally harassed and then arrested (a few of the arrestees even had their clothing ripped in the process). When the women refused to leave the basement, they too were arrested. The police transported 12 people to the Seventh Precinct, locked in the back of a paddy wagon. The men were fingerprinted, booked, and eventually moved to a jail downtown, but the women refused to leave the station house. After about 6 hours, both the women and men were released, and all charges were dropped—a small victory, but a victory nonetheless.

With the protesters removed, the demolition of the church could proceed with a vengeance. An 8-foot fence was erected around the church to keep out protesters, and police were dispatched around the perimeter; police helicopters scouted for troublemakers. A crowd of 200 people eventually gathered outside the fence. As the razing of the church proceeded, they prayed, cried, verbally protested, and commiserated with one another. Skirmishes erupted. One man jumped on top of a bulldozer, and he was taken to jail. Some people climbed onto a truck that was trying to remove the church bells, and they were threatened with arrest. Flowers were woven through the fence as a symbolic protest. People pulled on the fence, and police pulled them off and threw some to the ground. A man managed to break into the church, and demolition stopped until he could be found, arrested, and taken to jail. An East Indian family—husband, wife, and two young children—snuck under the fence in the predawn hours, but as they tried to reach the church, they were intercepted by police and arrested. The wife's sari was torn and her glasses were trampled. She was cursed by police; handcuffed; put in a squad car; and told that because of what she had done, her children would be taken permanently away from her. Her husband was handcuffed, placed in another police vehicle, and taken to jail. These acts of resistance, however, were little more than dust in the wind. The church was eventually leveled, and, in time, so was the rest of Poletown.

The ultimate irony, and thus the ultimate tragedy, is that none of this needed to have happened. The plant could have been built without tearing down the community. In fact, some of the Poletown residents who came to be the strongest resisters were not initially against the plant. Why would they be? If the plant brought jobs and led to a revitalization of their community, it would be a blessing to them. Richard Ridley, a Washington architect, devised several plans that would have allowed the plant to exist with the community left intact. Because Poletown was to be destroyed to create either greenspace around the plant or parking areas, several options presented themselves. What could have been done without too much trouble was to move the proposed site a bit to the north, rotate it so that it faced in a different direction than the one initially proposed, or build a multilevel parking structure and reduce or eliminate entirely the amount of greenspace (Wylie, 1989, p. 141). But neither General Motors nor the Detroit City Council was in an accommodating mood. The protesters called into question the freedom of General Motors to go where it wanted and do what it wanted, unfettered by any outside restrictions. This "good corporate citizen" had no intention of changing its game plan when it had the resources, interest, and enough influential allies on the team to play real hardball. As the economic and political powers of corporations increase and the power and influence of voters and workers decrease, it seems likely that confrontations like the ones in Poletown will become more common (Soule, 2009).

Power Corrupts, and Absolute Power Corrupts Absolutely

Social Structure and Self-Interest

Deviance that occurs principally because of organizational resources or the institutional structure of a society—as did the plunder of Poletown—has a prominent place in the sociology of deviance and for any relativistic approach. *Opportunity structure* is an important variable in understanding what kind of deviance occurs and why (J. W. Coleman, 1987, 2006; Merton, 1938). Only police can engage in police brutality, only politicians can engage in political corruption, and only members of corporations can commit corporate crime. Organizational and institutional dynamics powerfully affect the attitudes and behaviors of individuals who work in these organizations and institutions (Fullerton & Villemez, 2011). Representatives of organizations may protect one another, concealing and covering up any organizational deviance or crime that occurs.

Individuals regularly act to feather their own nests instead of doing what is politically correct or morally just. Some individuals may head to shopping malls to steal things from department stores; others may embezzle funds from their employers, take automobiles that do not belong to them, or break into people's homes or businesses; and still others may rob hapless strangers at gun- or knifepoint. The principal reason is the lure of getting other people's money and valuables in a quick and easy way. Other reasons are a sense of accomplishment, fun and excitement, and opportunities for control over other people and the increased sense of power that this can generate (Tunnell, 1992, pp. 39–50). Sometimes taking other people's valuables is an act of resistance to mainstream culture and the values it contains, especially those values that revere hard work, delayed gratification, job stability, and responsibility (Tunnell, 2006, p. 64). However, if people have power because of their social or organizational positions or interpersonal networks, it is easier for them to get what they want regardless of whom it hurts, and then to portray their actions as reasonable and necessary (Prechel & Morris, 2010). These efforts at legitimation, when successful, help to free these powerful individuals from the kind of blame and derision that would befall thieves of lesser means. Organizational men and women are more likely to commit acts of deviance and crime when they believe that these kinds of trespasses are widespread among their business associates (Tavits, 2010).

The worldwide financial crisis that started in 2007 and as of this writing continues to generate worldwide problems, is well known but still poorly understood despite a large number of books and other publications that are available to describe and explain it. One thing is beyond dispute: A significant variable was the too-cozy relationship between policy makers and regulators on the one hand and the financial community on the other (Smith, 2010). The Financial Crisis Inquiry Commission concluded in its final report, issued in January 2011, that the principal cause of the financial meltdown of 2008 and 2009 was the failure of federal regulators to exercise sufficient oversight and control of Wall Street's reckless profiteering (Rooney, 2011). Problems with corporate governance and risk management were also cited. The report did strongly contradict the claim (coming from Wall Street and parts of Washington) that the financial crisis could not have been predicted.

The institutional drive in banking to make money—lots of it and as quickly as possible—created incredible financial growth, but it was almost entirely based on U.S. home mortgages. Home mortgages were increasingly based on a predatory lending strategy that encouraged a Hobbesian war of all against all and a Darwinian social world in which it was not the fittest but the greediest, most ruthless, and least restrained that survived. The financial products took advantage of information asymmetries and lacked any reasonable notion of transparency.

> But while everything seemed to be falling apart at the same time, there was a common source: the reckless lending of the financial sector, which had led the housing bubble, which eventually burst. What was unfolding was the predictable and predicted consequences of the bursting of the bubble. Such bubbles and their aftermath are as old as capitalism and banking itself. It was just that the United States had been spared such bubbles for decades after the Great Depression because of the regulations the government had put in place after that trauma. Once deregulation had taken hold, it was only a matter of time before these horrors of the past would return. (Stiglitz, 2010, p. 27)

While private profits of some individuals and the wealth of banks increased, most everyone else was injured by the increase in collective risk (Smith, 2010). The declaration that the market is always rational was shown to be a mythical construction (Fox, 2009).

Bankers acted recklessly and greedily because they had both opportunities and incentives to do so. Repeal of the Glass-Steagall Act (in 1999), a 1933 creation of the New Deal reform movement that had prohibited commercial banks, investment firms, and insurance companies from merging into one company, is one of the things that led to the economic meltdown. Its repeal made it possible for large banks to get even larger, reaching a point where they were in every sense of the term just too large to fail. This is a condition that Stiglitz (2010, p. 135) labels *ersatz capitalism,* an economic system that generates private gains and collective losses. Executives could take whatever risks they wanted with other people's money, knowing that whatever happened, it would not affect their own personal fortunes. This provided the incentive for excessive and unbridled risk taking (Posner, 2010). If this was the motivator, the opportunity was provided by an economic climate of deregulation and lax governmental oversight. Additional factors were a housing epidemic in which too many houses were built, risky lending practices in which too much money was given out too easily, and racial and ethnic segregation in the housing market (Harvey, 2010; Rugh & Massey, 2010).

Money handed out under TARP (Troubled Assets Recovery Program), which was supposed to be used to recapitalize and provide credit to those who needed it, was used instead to pay out huge bonuses. It was as if the record losses were not losses at all and that taxpayers' generosity meant that it was business as usual. Much of what was not squandered in bonuses was used to pay shareholders in the form of dividends, a monetary way to share profits. In this case, however, no profits existed, only taxpayers' handouts. In fact, nine lenders that had combined losses of almost $100 billion were given $175 billion in bailout money from the government. Of this, they paid almost $33 billion in bonuses (which included giving $1 million to *each* of almost 5,000 employees, a total of nearly 5,000 *million* dollars); much of the rest went to pay dividends to stockholders (Stiglitz, 2010, p. 80).

Interest rates were deregulated, too, which allowed banks to offer higher-than-average interest rates to depositors in order to attract both business and capital. This put banks under greater and greater pressure to generate sufficient funds to pay higher dividends. The search for more and more capital led directly (and predictably) to pursuit of high-risk ventures, high costs for borrowers, risky loans, subprime mortgages, influx of capital from countries outside the United States, and the purchase of U.S. debt by foreign investors. This infusion of capital helped to manage the U.S. national debt that had increased so much during periods when tax cuts were increasing and so was military spending (Krippner, 2011).

The paradox of thrift (Keynes, 1930) shows us that what helps us as individuals may not help us as members of societies. An individual can improve his or her financial situation by saving as much of his or her paycheck as possible. The more an individual can save, the better off he or she will be when money is needed. However, what works for an individual does not work for societies as a whole, especially during economic downturns (i.e., recessions or depressions). If everyone saves and nobody spends, then unemployment eventually rises and productivity falls. (One remedy for economic problems, according to Keynesian economics, is for governments to step in during difficult economic times and spend money to compensate for reduced consumer spending, even if they have to borrow to do so.) If the value of the money being saved exceeds the value of what is being spent and invested, then productivity, employment, and incomes drop.

Power and Inequality

We cannot separate our understanding of the relativity of deviance from our understanding of *power*—who has it, how much they have, and how it affects the ebb and flow of social life (Davis, 1980; Kendall, 2008; Sherwood, 2010). Power over others is based partly on an individual's knowledge and skills—and in the case of a deviant, on his or her willingness to con or defraud others (Robbins, 2008). For example, in a game of three-card monte, a bettor must find the queen when it and two kings are thrown face down on a table and all three cards are mixed. Sometimes, it is not a game of chance at all because the card tosser uses sleight of hand to manipulate the cards so it is practically impossible for a bettor to win (Scarne, 1974). It would improve a bettor's chances if he or she did not even watch the cards being thrown and just randomly picked one. The card tosser, then, has power over bettors because the thief knows how to use sleight of hand to manipulate the cards. Some scams require greater skill and knowledge than others. It is more difficult, for example, to maintain one's composure during a high-stakes poker game while cheating others— bottom-dealing, holding out cards, stacking a deck, undoing the cut—than it is to master the throw used in the game of three-card monte (Prus & Sharper, 1977).

A more enduring and important source of power comes from an individual's social networks and opportunity structures that enable him or her to do things that affect the lives of others. Conan the Barbarian has a certain amount of power because he is big and strong; the chief executive officer (CEO) of General Motors (even in troubled economic times), however, has infinitely more power, even though the CEO may have small stature and be unable to lift a feather. When powerful people with interests in common unite to accomplish their objectives and establish ties to other powerful groups, they can move mountains. They can also use their power and resources in harmful or malicious ways.

A fish rots from the head first, claims an ancient proverb (which originated in either China or Italy), reminding us to consider that it is those who have the *most* resources who are responsible for a substantial amount of deviance (Samuel, 2010). We live in an *asymmetric society* in which the power of large organizations (e.g., corporations) far outweighs the power of the ordinary person (J. S. Coleman, 1982). Power, an important variable in an understanding of any kind of deviance, is particularly valuable in analyzing the organizational deviance that is regularly perpetrated by more privileged members of a society.

A transnational class now exists, characterized by global interconnections. Just as corporate influence and mass communications are no longer confined to just one country, so too, this transnational class scours the globe in search of the most hospitable climate for its economic interests to flourish. The power of this class comes from the spread of consumerism, new information technology, and the international electronic economy. This class is dominated by Europeans and North Americans, leading to global hegemony (Carroll, 2010). Globalization has made it more difficult for national governments to deal with problems within their borders, and governmental power has eroded (Rothkopf, 2012, p. 16). Big Business manipulates what it can to work one country against another (and one region against other regions in the *same* country) to obtain lower taxes, looser regulations, and an abundance of low-cost, uncomplaining laborers. Part of the reason that social inequality persists is that people have concluded that accumulation is more valuable than restraint and that individual suffering is an inevitable feature of the human condition (Dorling, 2010).

Some of the individuals in large organizations use their organizational positions to commit deviance, having both the opportunity to do so and the resources and interests to hide their deviance from others. They may experience a more intense sense of *subjective* or *relative deprivation,* increasing substantially their motivations to take what doesn't belong to them. Differential opportunity and relative deprivation can coalesce to make it more likely that the powerful will engage in harmful acts of deviance more frequently than will the powerless (Thio, 2009, p. 46). The powerful may deny that anyone was harmed by what they did, blame their deviance on some external factor over which they have no control, or convince themselves that they deserve the rewards that their deviance brought them (J. W. Coleman, 1987). They may use their resources to mask their untoward behaviors and to direct attention to the deviance of others.

The powerful benefit from a *shield of elitist invisibility* (Simon, 2008, p. 38) or *cloak of immunity* (Box, 1983, p. 99), such that their rule breaking either is not uncovered or, if it is uncovered, it is accorded a milder penalty than it deserves. According to Box, "The process of law enforcement, in its broadest possible interpretation, operates in such a way as to *conceal* crimes of the powerful against the powerless, but to *reveal* and *exaggerate* crimes of the powerless against 'everyone'" (p. 5). The ruin caused by powerful individuals in powerful organizations has a good chance of being peddled as an accident, as an isolated event (and therefore less harmful), or as the result of the antisocial behaviors of just a few "bad apples" (Poveda, 1994). The bad apple narrative, by blaming individuals instead of organizations, protects the economy and the state apparatus from a more sweeping condemnation (Cavender, Gray, & Miller, 2010). The blowout of the Deep Horizon oil well in the Gulf of Mexico (April 22, 2010) took place in a forbidding terrain, the site of dangerous hurricanes and precarious drilling conditions. The terrain didn't help, but to call this environmental catastrophe an accident misses much of what allowed it to happen. The opportunity of a private corporation to amass great profits (due in part to generous tax breaks) by supplying a commodity that the world either will not or cannot give up, made it possible for BP to cut corners and ignore safety regulations (Freudenberg & Gramling, 2011).

The Deviant Elite

Organizational deviants are able to capitalize on their organizational positions and resources to operate in secrecy and to develop vocabularies of motive and rationalizations to make deviance seem more reasonable and necessary. Lesser crooks, operating in isolation from one another, may find it more difficult to formulate the motives, intents, rationalizations, and neutralizations that allow them to use their resources and opportunities to do whatever benefits them the most. In fact, Hightower (2003) declares the United States of the twenty-first century to be a *kleptocrat nation,* a nation ruled by thieves where money and power are consistently taken from the many to enrich the few. In this process, liberty, justice, political integrity, equality, and opportunity are continually threatened. Little doubt exists that some economic elites are so prominent and powerful in the global economy that they are able to influence money flow, debt, and credit sufficiently that these core resources are manipulated to create private benefits and social costs (Lendman, 2011).

Klein (2007) sees the United States shifting more and more in the direction of what she calls *disaster capitalism.* This is a society in which groups and organizations orchestrate raids on the public sector in the wake of catastrophic events, treating both human-made catastrophes (e.g., the terrorist attacks of September 11, 2001) and natural disasters (e.g., Hurricane Katrina) as little more than an opportunity to amass greater and greater wealth (Freudenberg, Gramling, Laska, & Erikson, 2009). What better time to move swiftly to implement strategies to accrue great profit than during episodes of confusion and social chaos? What in calmer times would be soberly analyzed and rejected is accepted in a doctrinaire fashion during periods of social stress and collapse. In some cases, not only are the changes made swiftly—perhaps too swiftly—but they are also practically impossible to reverse or alter once they are implemented. The changes ushered in by disaster capitalism are founded on the core elements of increasing private profits at public expense and making it more difficult for government to do its work to increase the public good.

Democracy and free markets are not inevitable traveling companions. While they do at times play complementary roles, at other times they do not. Leaving something like health care or environmental integrity to market forces can do more harm than good. Markets have no morality, and they do not guarantee either opportunity or equality for all people. Markets encourage whatever produces profitability, which rewards size, which generates a concentration of economic and political power in the hands of the relative few. Ultimately, this leads to an undermining of both democracy and free enterprise. The obsessive pursuit of self-interest is justified as serving the common good even when it does not. Reining in the power of government is not always a victory for democracy and individual freedoms. What it does is to allow power to erupt elsewhere, usually in the private sector. This sector usually finds that its freedoms have indeed increased if what is meant by freedom is the right to go practically anywhere and to do practically anything that makes money for its owners.

In the last quarter of the twentieth century, the U.S. federal government did try to become more market-like in that it sought to downsize, outsource, deregulate, and dismantle (Blau, 1999). Working Americans, with no other option available, embraced the market with the hopes that it would benefit them and their families. However, this is not what happened (Martin, 2008). Large businesses and some of the wealthiest individuals in U.S. society continued to prosper, but practically everyone else did not (Brady, 2009). Workers' share of national incomes in capitalist democracies has decreased during the last 40 years or so, due principally to the deterioration in their bargaining power vis-á-vis their bosses in the economic arena (Kristal, 2010; Mouw & Kalleberg, 2010). The growing national debt and demands of consumerism have also led to an ever-widening gap between the wealthy and everyone else (Reich, 2010).

Collectivizing Risk

Risk has been shifted to the backs and shoulders of members of the working class, and laborers have found to their dismay that even a good education, hard work, and strong family ties no longer provide the protection from economic ruination that they once did (Gosselin, 2009). U.S. workers are being expected to do more and more with and for less and less, leading to both worker alienation and their exploitation (Juravich, 2009). The increase in income inequality in the United States has led to increased income segregation by making it possible for those with high incomes to flee areas populated by lower-income individuals (Reardon & Bischoff, 2011).

The turn to the market has not only been generally unrewarding for most of the people who hoped to benefit from it, but it has had other unfortunate consequences as well:

> Markets are well-known for deftness and agility in getting prices right, but they are less commendable for their tendency to put a price on everything. Civic disengagement, health care and prisons for profit, the malling of suburban America, the epidemic of corporate advertising in public space, and the torrent of private money in public life all testify to a coarsening of American

politics and culture. Competition to get the price right may be the hallmark of our economic system, but competition to put a price on everything produces a war of all against all. In this wartime condition, race and class tightly circumscribe communities, and the capacity to empathize with other people is fragile or nonexistent. (Blau, 1999, p. 4)

When what matters most is how much money some policy or practice produces for its corporate owners, many unsavory things can occur. Our collective and individual fears are manipulated by some individuals to get them what they want and to create the kind of society that they see as better for them and their interests. In a profit-oriented society, private corporations engage in price gouging, taking advantage of unusual events to peddle their products and services at the highest possible price to the most vulnerable and desperate (Simon, 2008, pp. 98–103). Employees are "liquidated"—fired or let go—to increase the value of corporate stocks and market control (Ho, 2009).

The flight of industry to countries outside of the United States has made it harder and harder for U.S. workers to find jobs. This means that more and more Americans are either unemployed or underemployed, being either without jobs completely or without jobs that pay a living wage. Added to this are the high prices of practically everything (e.g., gas, food, health care, energy, education, entertainment). Some of an individual's problems are, of course, related in part to character and personality in that some individuals do have poor work ethics or possess skills in low demand. However, many of the problems we now face can be traced in one way or another to the effects of globalization, free trade agreements, tax incentives for companies to move production out of the United States, deregulation, and privatization of more and more services that governments once provided for citizens (Goldsmith & Blakely, 2010).

What we are seeing in the United States is the emergence of a corporatist society in which the principal feature is a huge transfer of public wealth to private hands and a widening gap between the superrich and everyone else (Carroll, 2010). The inherent contradictions, however, of such a fundamentally destructive way of organizing human behavior and human experience make it unstable, requiring increases in the culture of surveillance, increases in social control (e.g., imprisonment and incarceration), and decreases of civil liberties (Staples, 2000). Social insecurity itself is created and sustained through strategies in which the poor and powerless are handled and controlled through both prisons and the transformation of welfare into workfare (Wacquant, 2009). Greater social and economic equality makes for stronger, more robust societies (Stiglitz, 2012; Wilkenson & Pickett, 2010).

U.S. history during the last 50 years or so is not simply a reflection of failed policies due to political incompetence or self-serving behaviors of elected officials. It is also a result of policies that were designed and implemented to produce total corporate liberation from public accountability, along with the violence and totalitarianism that result from this. The wars being waged by the United States are described by the "talking heads" on the evening news as righteous struggles to bring freedom and democracy to nations that lack them. This plays better with the public than describing them as what they also are: wars for the advancement of pure capitalism, unfettered by public interference or political oversight (Klein, 2007, p. 26).

Though great fortunes should not be condemned on principle alone (Kahan, 2010), we should not allow ourselves to be taken in by public relations campaigns that portray the superrich as those among us who deserve the very best due to their strong characters, principled behaviors, hard work, and boundless energy. A few businesspeople do embody these principles, but most do not. Great success in business is based principally on making great deals in which much comes from little in a short period of time and with little or no risk. To accomplish this, it almost always requires being at the right place at the right time and a willingness to exploit others without reservation. Using other people's ideas and talents to enrich oneself is at the heart of most personal fortunes, coupled with the interpersonal skills to keep these dishonorable activities as invisible as possible (Villette & Vuillermot, 2009). Advantage, deserved or not, once attained can lead to further advantage (called the *Matthew effect*; see Rigney, 2010).

The "rugged individualism" and "frontier spirit" that are such a central part of U.S. culture are more an idealization of our history than an accurate reflection of it (Vela-McConnell, 1999, p. 226). The West was tamed by people working together, not some lone gunslinger or high-kicking Texas Ranger (Charbeneau, 1992, p. 132). Almost always, great success of the few only comes from group efforts and contributions of the many.

> In most job settings . . . any individual's performance—indeed, any individual's apparent skill—depends subtly on communication and collaboration with co-workers, including supervisors. Great dancers need supportive partners; great journalists lean on skilled editors. (Tilly, 1998, p. 101)

Even great athletes or successful performers would not have gone very far without a supportive team or adoring public. Groysberg (2010) showed that successful financial analysts in any given Wall Street firm usually do not experience the same level of success when they move to a rival firm *unless* they are able to take their crew or team with them. Apparently, talent and success are not entirely portable, and the claim that individual merit and individual success are closely and inevitably aligned is less fact than fancy (O'Flynn, 2009). It practically goes without saying that what is valuable at one place and time may be valueless at some other place and time.

The Carrier's Case: Other People's Belongings and the Crime of Theft

Though it may seem natural to want to own things and to protect them from others, laws protecting property as we know them now were nonexistent before the fifteenth century. Their creation had practically nothing to do with a belief in the divine right of all persons to be safe and secure in their possessions. The laws regarding theft—which transformed taking other people's belongings into a crime—were established by powerful individuals for the purpose of furthering their own interests. Any benefit that these laws may have had for others was purely coincidental. This reminds us once again of the relativity of deviance in that certain kinds of taking are considered appropriate and in the public interest (e.g., the plunder of Poletown), while other kinds are labeled as criminal and steps are taken to punish the perpetrators. Whenever "deviance" is reconfigured as "crime," an important social event has occurred. The perpetrator of the untoward act now has a different status—criminal—and what a criminal does can be formally and forcefully sanctioned with the full weight of government (Chambliss & Seidman, 1982).

The case that is responsible for the creation of the crime of theft occurred in England in 1473 and is known as the *carrier's case*. A man was hired to carry bales of cloth to Southampton. Instead of completing the job, he broke the bales open and took off with their contents, intending them for his own use. He was eventually caught and taken into a court of law for magistrate review. The judges were in total agreement about what the carrier had done in terms of the details of his act, and they were also in total agreement that what the carrier had done was entirely legal. Because the carrier had been given the bales lawfully by his employer, nothing that he did after he took possession violated any existing law. Theft at the time was defined in terms of illegal trespass, and nobody who had been given property by its owner could trespass against it. Legally, it was the owner who was at fault for not employing a more trustworthy carrier (Hall, 1952, p. 5).

The judges were under great pressure, however, to craft the necessary legislation to transform what the carrier did into something more sinister and harmful. They decided that a crime *had* occurred after all. When the carrier broke open the bales, the judges figured, the property instantly reverted back to its owner. By absconding with the contents, the carrier was guilty of a form of trespass, and he could be treated as a criminal (Hall, 1952, p. 10). Curiously enough, if the carrier had somehow known what the judges were going to do, he could simply have taken *all* of the bales without breaking them open (but then the law would probably have been crafted differently). The judges portrayed the new law and the new understandings of "crime" and "criminal" that it established as just one more example of the strict application of legal precedent.

Why would the judges in the carrier's case invent a new law? It was not because they felt sorry for this particular owner or even because they wanted to encourage this particular carrier to walk the straight and narrow. Feudalism and its system of relationships based on sentiments of fidelity and obligation between serf and master were evaporating, being replaced by mercantilism and a middle class that owed its livelihood to commerce and trade. Any threat to the transportation of goods was a blow to this burgeoning economic system. King Edward IV, the ruling monarch at the time of the carrier's case, was highly supportive of trade, and he assiduously courted business interests. The owner of the property that the carrier stole was an Italian merchant who had been assured of safe passage for his cargo by King Edward himself. The bales contained wool (or some other cloth), merchandise of great importance to England's budding economy. The fact that the material was stolen while in transport to Southampton was even worse because it undermined business confidence in the security of a major English trading center and shipping port. As if that weren't enough, the goods were stolen by a professional carrier. Merchants were finding it increasingly difficult to use their own servants to transport goods and were being forced to rely more often on carriers. If carriers could not be trusted to deliver safely the cargo they were given, trade would be adversely affected.

When the carrier stole the contents of the bales, he was doing much more than depriving a solitary foreign merchant of his goods. He was threatening the economic interests of the textile industry, one of the most powerful and important businesses in all of England. He was also challenging the interests of the Crown, both personally and as a warrantor of the safety of economic transactions in the British state. King Edward IV exerted a great deal of influence over public officials, so the courts were likely to adopt any legislation that he wanted. What the new law of theft did, enforced by the courts, was to make taking property without consent of the owner a felony so that guilty parties were subject to severe penalties. During the centuries following the carrier's case, laws of theft were expanded to the point that the taking of money or property by cashiers and clerks eventually became illegal (called embezzlement), as did the receiving of stolen property.

The law is a tool that powerful groups can use to give themselves superior moral as well as coercive power in their conflicts with others (Chambliss & Seidman, 1982). Law is symbolic: It sets the broad parameters of correct and incorrect ways of acting in a society. Whether the law is actually followed is less important than the fact that practically everybody knows it is *supposed* to be followed. Law is also instrumental: It encourages people to follow the rules under the threat of unpleasant penalties. The law of theft that was created in 1473 in Britain was a concession to powerful interests. It gave influential individuals who felt victimized a way to protect themselves from the trespasses of others. It also provided a new understanding about proper and improper ways of doing business. Merchants' interests were protected and reinforced, while the interests and self-serving behaviors of the carriers were singled out for control and correction.

The carrier's case suggests that anything could be made illegal—and the new rules and sanctions could be justified as customary and reasonable—if the groups that create and enforce laws want this to happen. A corollary is that nothing will be illegal unless groups of people with sufficient resources are willing to take the time and trouble to criminalize those things that they do not like. (At times, the poor or powerless can work together to advance their interests and influence what kind of laws and judicial routines are implemented [Routledge & Cumbers, 2009].)

White-Collar Rule Breaking: Corporate Skullduggery and Political Racketeering

The American Sociological Society (ASS) held its thirty-fourth annual meeting jointly with the American Economic Society's (AES) fifty-second meeting in December 1939 in Philadelphia. The president of the AES, Jacob Viner (1940), addressed the audience first, talking about the relationship between public policy and economic doctrine. After he finished, Edwin Hardin Sutherland (1883–1950), the president-elect of the ASS, advanced to the podium and spoke about white-collar crime. (In 1959, the organization changed its name to the American Sociological *Association,* because it had become fashionable to use acronyms for professional organizations, and "ASA" made a much better acronym.) Sutherland (1940) defined *white-collar crime* as any crime committed by a person or persons of respectability and high social status in the context of professional activities, occupations, or jobs. This included crooked practices in occupations, professions, businesses, corporations, and even politics.

Sutherland (1940) traced the causes of white-collar crime to the structure of a society. Differential social organization and differential association create a situation in which some people encounter group supports and the values, motives, rationalizations, techniques, and definitions that make crime more likely. Sutherland believed that the demands of a business organization can create strong in-group loyalties that can lead to an indifference to the demands of legal or moral norms. This, in turn, can lead to an insensitivity to the interests or needs of outside groups, such as the public, customers, or other business organizations.

The message of Sutherland's (1940) address was clear to his audience: White-collar crime is real crime, it causes tremendous destruction, the perpetrators have a wanton disregard for the consequences of their actions, and the victims of it are both unsuspecting and severely damaged. White-collar crime rips the fabric of society, Sutherland believed, and its perpetrators deserve the ultimate in scorn, derision, and punishment. More than scientific interest prompted his concern with white-collar crime. He was outraged by the egregious acts of corporate representatives, and his sense of social decency was offended (Green, 1997, p. 6). Crimes of this variety are often made possible by the trust, actual or implied, that the eventual victim puts in the victimizer. Offenders do all they can to keep secret the existence of their offenses while still working to continue to occupy positions of trust (Menard, Morris, Gerber, & Covey, 2011).

Sutherland's own experiences in getting his ideas published support much of what he believed about the benefits of privilege and power (Geis & Goff, 1983). He had amassed a great deal of incriminating information about the collective and individual harms caused by some of the largest and most powerful companies on earth. His writings about the predations of these organizations were filled with the names and histories of the offending companies. However, his editors at Dryden Press balked at Sutherland's intention to describe the companies as criminal even though neither they nor any of their representatives had ever been actually convicted of any crimes. The administrators at Indiana University in Bloomington, where Sutherland taught, were also made skittish by Sutherland's plan to reveal in writing the names of offending corporations. They apparently feared that donations from these companies might stop. Sutherland (1949) eventually succumbed to the pressure and allowed his work to be published without the names of the offending companies. It was not until 1983 that a different publisher came out with an uncut version of Sutherland's book in which the names were finally revealed.

Many years after Sutherland's address to the ASS on white-collar crime, Clinard and Quinney (1973, p. 188) discerned two distinct types of crime covered by Sutherland's omnibus term: corporate and occupational. The crux of the distinction is who benefits from the antisocial activity. *Corporate criminal behavior* directly benefits an organization itself, even though agents of the corporation carry out the acts. *Occupational criminal behavior* is done by a person of respectability and high social status who is himself or herself the primary beneficiary. Even if the rule breaking takes place in a group setting, the deviant is acting primarily on his or her own to further his or her selfish interests. The organization is not responsible; in fact, the organization itself can be a victim (Belbot, 1995).

Because white-collar crime is not the prerogative of the corporate sector—it can be found in politics, the military, labor unions, medicine, law, churches, universities, and so on—it may be wise to replace the words *corporate crime* with *organizational crime* (J. W. Coleman, 2006, p. 12). We must also remember that organizations themselves do not operate in a social vacuum, and many instances of white-collar crime or elite deviance are made possible by supportive linkages between representatives of the corporate world and state functionaries (Kramer, Michalowski, & Kauzlarich, 2002). Without the linkages between the Detroit City Council, General Motors, the Roman Catholic Church, and the United Auto Workers, the plunder of Poletown would not have been possible. It was principally because the residents of the community received no major institutional support that it was possible for their community to be taken from them.

In most of the white-collar crimes that have plagued us through the ages, the distinction between occupational and organizational crime has been irrelevant because *both* the organization and its representatives have benefited from the ongoing deviances (Roy, 1997). These violations of norms help the organization and its members compete in a system where survival is never guaranteed and where objective indicators of personal and professional success are few and far between. Nolan Bushnell, founder of Atari, embodied this sentiment when he noted that business is a good game—lots of competition and a minimum of rules, a game in which score is kept with money. Large corporations have become both the sites of acts of major rule breaking and the instruments used to carry them out (Tillman & Pontell, 1995).

The text of Sutherland's (1940) address to the ASS shows that he believed that politicians presented a lesser threat than representatives of the business world (p. 4). Would he still think that way if he were alive today? It is hard to be at all familiar with political rackets and not have a suspicion that far too many politicians view the government as their own private cash cow that can be milked whenever the need arises. If there is a difference between political rackets and other kinds of trespass, it is to be found in opportunity structures, levels of accountability, and organizational supports, not in the greater morality or integrity of politicians as compared to other kinds of white-collar crooks.

American political life is replete with corruption, duplicity, and excessive self-interest. An arrogance of power and a shield of elitist invisibility can work together to allow destructive acts to flourish, undefined and unchecked, because of the privilege and power of those who commit them (Gross, 1996; Rosoff, Pontell, & Tillman, 2004). The great irony in the study of deviance— which, however, is of no surprise to relativists—is that certain people can cause great harm without being generally viewed as dangerous individuals or having their actions defined as harmful. The structure of relations in political organizations blurs responsibility, and it is difficult to know who did what. Top officials deny responsibility by claiming that they had no knowledge of how things were being implemented, and low-level employees deny responsibility by claiming that they were following orders. If blame is assessed, it is usually placed on this individual or that, not on organizational structure (Cavender, Jurik, & Cohen, 1993, pp. 157–159).

According to Franken (2003), politicians are guilty of campaign corruption and the illegal raising of funds to run them, lying, indifference to the needs of voters, conceit, cronyism, ignorance, and mismanagement of the governmental apparatus. Their greatest sins may be their waste of valuable resources and their taking and squandering (with the full protection of the law) of other people's belongings (Gross, 1996, pp. 7–8). Almost every politician tries to reward certain constituents by throwing special projects their way (called "pork"). This practice is rampant and almost wholly unaccountable, an example of stealing without stigma. Politicians take our money from us, money we may very well not wish to give up, and they then use it in ways over which we have little to no control. How is this any different from the depredations of a garden-variety thief? If a difference can be found between pork and theft, it is primarily in who has the power to say what is legal and what is not.

Sutherland (1940) claimed in his presidential address that the "inventive geniuses" for many kinds of white-collar crime are attorneys (p. 11). If only he could see us now, he would realize how prophetic his words have turned out to be. Without the assistance of lawyers who know how to use legal procedures to benefit their clients, it is unlikely that the wealthy would have fared as well as they have (Lauderdale & Cruit, 1993).

> The crimes of the upper class either result in no official action at all, or result in suits for damages in civil courts, or are handled by inspectors, and by

administrative boards or commissions, with penal sanctions in the form of warnings, orders to cease and desist, occasionally the loss of a license, and only in extreme cases by fines or prison sentences. (Sutherland, 1940, pp. 7–8)

Attorneys make it possible for some people to take other people's belongings with little or no accountability (Nader & Smith, 1996).

As a result of this special treatment, Sutherland (1945) declared, white-collar crooks are not viewed as real criminals by the general public or even by themselves. They may have done something technically illegal, but they do not believe that they are real criminals (Conklin, 1977). Even if they are charged with a crime, their resources make it easier for them to rebuke the charges against them. A study of defendants charged with bribery in Swedish courts showed that these individuals attempted to make themselves look less blameworthy by constructing a folk logic in which they were not culpable because everyone in their same situation was doing the same thing. They insisted that they were highly moral people despite the trespasses (Jacobsson, 2012).

Unsurprisingly, corporate representatives who break the law do all they can to keep themselves free from accountability and punishment for their wrongdoings. This is true despite the fact that their profiteering has done grave damage to those among us who have been injured by environmental pollution, defective automobiles, unsafe appliances, carcinogens in tobacco, and other dangerous products (Sutherland, 1945). Money, hype, and monotonous repetition are used to perpetuate a false image that corporations face a barrage of frivolous lawsuits and pay huge and undeserved fines. The truth is that corporations are *not* the target of a flood of lawsuits from consumers. If an increase in lawsuits against businesses does exist, it is due to businesses suing other businesses, a form of litigation that will undoubtedly continue. Juries are far from antibusiness, and they award punitive damages to an injured citizen only if it is clear that a corporation acted with glaring disregard for the consequences of its actions (Nader & Smith, 1996, pp. 278–279).

In February of 1992, Stella Liebeck, age 79, was a front-seat passenger in her grandson's car when they pulled into a McDonald's restaurant in Albuquerque, New Mexico, so that Ms. Liebeck could order coffee. Once it was served, she tried to remove the lid from the cup to add cream and sugar—the vehicle was motionless—and the entire contents spilled on her lap. She experienced third-degree burns on her thighs, groin, and buttocks, and she was permanently scarred on 16 percent of her body. These injuries were clearly serious, and it took more than 2 years for her to recover fully. Ms. Liebeck wanted some compensation for her emotional ordeal, some help with her medical bills, and some recognition by McDonald's of the dangers lurking in those cups of coffee for other unsuspecting customers. However, when she appealed to restaurant executives for help, they were unmoved by her pain and suffering. They refused to pay anything close to what her operations had cost (about $20,000). All they did was offer Ms. Liebeck $800. In desperation, she hired a lawyer, and a lawsuit was filed.

At the trial, at least initially, Ms. Liebeck faced a skeptical jury. Members of the jury believed that a lawsuit over a cup of coffee was a waste of their time, being both frivolous and malicious. They certainly had no discernible animosity toward McDonald's. However, as the details of the case unfolded in the week-long trial, McDonald's reputation was tarnished. Testimony was introduced that corporate headquarters required that the temperature of the coffee be maintained at between 180 and 190 degrees Fahrenheit to make it taste better for longer periods. (Many other restaurants keep the temperature of their coffee at 160 degrees.) At this high temperature, severe burning and tissue destruction occur within seconds in the case of a spill. Making matters worse was the quality of the McDonald's cup. It has exceptional insulating properties, so coffee drinkers are unable to appreciate just how hot their coffee really is until they start drinking it. The jury concluded that McDonald's did keep the temperature of the coffee much too high for human consumption and that customers were given insufficient warnings about the potential dangers. The jury settled on compensatory damages of $200,000, which it then reduced to $160,000 because it believed Ms. Liebeck had to bear some of the responsibility for spilling the coffee on herself.

The jury awarded an additional $2.7 million in punitive damages to Ms. Liebeck. Why? The answer is simple: McDonald's had shown a wanton disregard for the well-being of its customers. It came to light that 700 other people had experienced a fate similar to Ms. Liebeck's between 1982 and 1992; this included some children who had been severely burned in accidents involving the too-hot coffee when adults accidentally knocked cups over or dropped them, and the contents spilled on the youngsters. Executives of the restaurant chain believed that no compelling reason existed to turn down the heat because, considering all the coffee that their restaurant chain served, 700 burns were insignificant to them. The jury concluded that anyone who ordered a cup of McDonald's too-hot coffee was a potential burn victim. The jury's principal objective was to get McDonald's attention and force its executives to reduce the temperature of the coffee. The jury came up with the $2.7 million figure because that is about how much McDonald's made from 2 days of selling coffee worldwide. The judge decided that the punitive damages were too high, so he reduced them to $480,000, three times greater than the compensatory damages. McDonald's had intended to appeal the $640,000 award, but it finally agreed to settle for an undisclosed amount if the details of the arrangement were kept silent forever by Ms. Liebeck and her attorney. (Ms. Liebeck died in 2004, but she and her story live on in the 2011 movie titled *Hot Coffee*.)

The Relativity of Terrorism

One Nation's Terrorist . . .

Terrorism is widely viewed as loathsome behavior—practically by definition, to call something terrorism is to condemn it as the ultimate evil—but disagreement still exists over the exact meaning of the term and to which specific acts or individuals the label is most appropriately applied (Feniger & Yuchtman-Yaar, 2010). The consensus view is that if the targets of violence are selected randomly and are nonmilitary, civilian targets, to generate fear in an entire population, it qualifies as "terrorism" (Jenkins, 2003, p. 27). Though this definition is valuable, allowing some precision in regard to classifying acts of terrorism, the terms *terrorist* and *terrorism* do have a measure of relativity. What looks like terrorism to one nation may look like freedom fighting or martyrdom to some other.

Although much is still a matter of conjecture and dispute concerning the terrorist attacks on the United States on September 11, 2001, what is indisputable is that Osama bin Laden was a big winner. His popularity and respectability increased among the millions of individuals all across the world who view the United States and its citizens as their enemies or as threatening to their interests (Nacos, 2007, p. 118). About 2 weeks after the attacks, when fans at a European Cup soccer game in Athens, Greece, were asked to observe a minute of silence for victims of 9/11, they jeered the United States and even tried to burn a U.S. flag (p. 121). Definitions and understandings of terrorism and its victims are thus not universal.

Some organizations (e.g., the British Broadcasting Company) refuse to use the term *terrorist* to describe any individual or group, no matter how violent or savage the actions (Jenkins, 2003, p. 18). We do not need to adopt this extreme view. Rather, we can acknowledge that reasonable people agree that certain violent incidents qualify as terrorism, while also conceding that disagreement exists over what terrorism is and what it means to different audiences. It is clear that the terms *terrorism* and *terrorist* are used nowadays by influential people in powerful organizations to further their own interests and agendas. The terms are not only used descriptively; they are also used to condemn and discredit—to deny or remove any legitimacy that a so-called terrorist might otherwise have.

The word *terrorism* is often used by some nations to describe the actions of nations they do not like, but not to describe what seem to be similar actions of nations they do like (Ross, 2013, p. 283). During the 1980s, President Ronald Reagan and other members of his administration fully supported the activities of "insurgents" (or Contras) in Nicaragua, who were fighting to overthrow the Sandinista government of Daniel Ortega. Reagan compared the Contras with the U.S. Founding Fathers, opining that if they were, in fact, counterrevolutionaries, then so was he. This praise was curious because the Contras were responsible for acts of brutal violence against civilians—men, women, and children—in order to pressure their government. According to the consensus view of terrorism and terrorist, the Contras were terrorists, but they were not viewed that way (at least officially) by key players in the Reagan administration, including Reagan himself.

Little doubt exists that nations use the terms *terrorism* and *terrorist* for political gain, taking advantage of violent incidents, typifying them in whatever way will further their own political interests (Chomsky, 1988). The "war on terror" provides the opportunity for authorities to instruct the U.S. public to be continually afraid *and* perpetually prepared for some future attack on U.S. soil. What this does is to give U.S. citizens the responsibility for protecting themselves from future attacks amid a climate of surveillance, intrusion, and suspicion (T. Monahan, 2010, p. 113). Terrorism may be uniquely susceptible to this form of distortion and exaggeration because the agencies that we rely on to provide valid and reliable information about terrorism have many reasons to not want to divulge all that they know about it (Jenkins, 2003, p. 5). Sometimes, this involves powerful groups taking advantage of terrorist attacks against themselves so that it will make any subsequent violent retaliations seem justified and reasonable (Kelman & Hamilton, 1989).

Fact and Fancy

It is difficult to separate fact from fancy in regard to what happened during the terrorist attacks on the World Trade Center and the U.S. Pentagon on September 11, 2001 (Bonn, 2010). The problem is made even more acute by the fact that the media capitalized on the attacks of 9/11 to further their own interests. Media representatives rationalized both subsequent military intervention in foreign nations and increased domestic surveillance. In the days following the attacks, new facts became harder to find, so reporters and journalists scrambled to find stories that regaled audiences with accounts that exaggerated the tragedy and pathos of events that were already filled with enough tragedy and pathos (B. A. Monahan, 2010, p. 122).

The attacks represent both a tragedy for individual Americans and families and a horrible and horrifying event for the nation as a whole. They were not just attacks on Americans and America. They were organized and deliberate assaults on a constellation of U.S. cultural icons (i.e., the World Trade Center as the embodiment of business and consumption; the Pentagon as the embodiment of the military; and, had the plane forced down in Pennsylvania reached what was probably its target, the White House, as the embodiment of U.S. politics) (Ritzer, 2006, p. 247). Although the United States is no stranger to terrorist attacks (Chomsky, 1988; Howard & Forest, 2008; Stritzke, Lewandowsky, Denemark, Clare, & Morgan, 2009), the enormity of the damage of the September 11 attacks was too much for most Americans to comprehend; certainly it was too much for them to forgive. The attacks seemed to be unprovoked and unprincipled, the taking of innocent life by a crazed and crazy terrorist group. While this is true, it is not the whole truth, and more is involved in what happened than meets the eye.

A study of the September 11 attacks by Ahmed (2002) suggests that "significant elements" in the U.S. government, the military, and the intelligence community had "extensive" warnings about them. Rather than moving vigorously to either stop them or to lessen their damage, these significant elements remained silent, expecting to benefit from what happened (p. 290). The attacks were ultimately used to justify an invasion of Afghanistan and Iraq that was being planned in advance of September 11 in order to obtain strategic and economic advantages in the region (p. 255). Although reasonable people can disagree over who or what was really responsible for the attacks of September 11, few people can disagree that they came at a good time for the Bush administration. They made it possible for Bush's presidency to end the crisis of legitimacy that had threatened to topple it and to enter the world stage with a new sense of purpose and confidence.

A few things seem true about 9/11 that demand a measure of caution in accepting the official view that the attacks came out of nowhere. First, U.S. intelligence agencies apparently knew in advance that an attack from the air on key U.S. targets was likely; they even had a fairly good idea about when it would occur.

> It is a fact that the American intelligence community received multiple authoritative warnings, both general and specific, of a terrorist attack on the U.S. using civilian airliners as bombs, targeting key buildings located in the nation's capital and New York City, and likely to occur around early to mid-September. (Ahmed, 2002, p. 290)

On July 10, 2001, an FBI agent (Kenneth Williams) sent a message to FBI headquarters to alert his superiors that Middle Eastern students were enrolled in an Arizona flight school. He feared that al-Qaeda operatives could possibly be trying to infiltrate the U.S. aviation system. However, his warnings were ignored (Franken, 2003, p. 118), even though by late June of that year, high-ranking officials in the administration (e.g., Richard Clarke) and at the CIA (e.g., George Tenet) were certain that terrorist attacks were imminent (Clarke, 2004, p. 235).

Second, it is very difficult to understand why standard operating procedures fell apart on September 11, allowing the attacks on the World Trade Center and the Pentagon to reach their deadly conclusion. Air traffic controllers followed the flights of the hijacked airliners from start to finish. They were certain that a hijacking had occurred by 8:20 AM, a full 15 minutes *before* the first plane (Flight 11) slammed into the North Tower of the World Trade Center, 43 minutes before the second plane (Flight 175) slammed into the South Tower, and 80 minutes before the third plane (Flight 77) hit the Pentagon (Ahmed, 2002, pp. 151–155).

It seems incredible that fighter planes were not dispatched in time to intercept the hijacked planes and, if necessary, shoot them from the sky. Although presidential approval is required to shoot down a civilian aircraft, it is *not* required to scramble jets to intercept one. An F-15 Strike Eagle could have left McGuire Air Force Base in New Jersey and reached the World Trade Center in less than 3 minutes. Yet this did not happen. Why were no planes dispatched until 95 minutes *after* clear evidence existed that a hijacking of commercial airlines was in progress and only after destruction of the World Trade Center and a section of the Pentagon had already occurred?

The sluggish response of the U.S. Air Force to the terrorist attacks, in violation of standard operating procedures of the FAA and 95 minutes too late, was apparently due to decisions by the president and high-ranking members of his cabinet (Ahmed, 2002, p. 171). This *does not* mean that U.S. officials staged the attacks or that hijackers were paid in U.S. dollars and told what to do by U.S. officials. This also does not mean that members of the Bush administration knew just how costly the attacks would be but were willing to sacrifice both lives and property to generate political capital. What it *does* mean—if Ahmed is right—is that "significant elements" in the United States must bear some responsibility for what happened on September 11 and its aftermath.

Faulty Intelligence

The organizations that were entrusted to protect U.S. citizens did not do so. They failed to get information to the right place at the right time, and they failed to act more courageously to eliminate, or at least reduce, the threat of a terrorist attack (Clarke, 2004, p. 235). The war on terror has made it possible to manage citizen complaints about U.S. foreign and domestic policy, while it has allowed a crackdown on civil rights, dissent, and free speech. The attacks of September 11 made it much easier for the Bush administration to justify the U.S. invasion of Iraq. The specter of international terrorists and the al-Qaeda network will continue to offer "significant elements" in the United States a golden opportunity to expand into other nations and extend U.S. military, political, strategic, and economic influence abroad (Ahmed, 2002). The war on terror is being used to justify intervention into regions of strategic and economic importance to the United States and to consolidate U.S. hegemony over them. By keeping the bona fide horrors of 9/11 and the need for increased security always in the public eye, "significant elements" in the United States are likely to reap a cornucopia of rewards in the years ahead.

When it came to foreign policy, the distinguishing feature of the presidency of George W. Bush was not so much what he would do as whom he would appoint to his war cabinet. His foreign policy advisors adopted a name for themselves, the Vulcans, based on the name of the Roman god of fire, metalwork, and the forge. This word embodied the precise image that Bush's advisors wanted to project: power, durability, and toughness (Mann, 2004). The most significant foreign policy decision of the Bush administration was the decision to invade Iraq in 2003. It resonated so well with the Vulcans' view of global events that it is unlikely it could have been averted. Members of this war cabinet had great respect for U.S. military power, believing that the United States personified what is good and right in global politics. They remained confident that America would prevail quickly and firmly in Iraq without outside help or interference.

The Vulcans' political astuteness in capitalizing on 9/11 was matched only by their political blindness in going to war in Iraq, using excessive means to accomplish limited ends. The true claim that a legitimate security threat to the United States—its interests and its values—is posed by terrorism was based on a simpleminded (and ultimately counterproductive) strategy that to stop the spread of Middle Eastern terrorism, it required a U.S. military presence that would transform the entire social fabric of the Middle East (Mann, 2004). The U.S. intervention in Iraq was, according to Abu-Lughod (2010), "extraordinarily self-serving and arrogant" (p. 213). The U.S. media's treatment of Iraq and its people was distorted by parroting the official view that it was a fight to bring freedom and democracy to a troubled land, using terms that lack any clear or universally accepted meanings. One of the U.S. media's principal failures has been its disinclination to do enough stories about the richness of Iraqi society, the intelligence and humanity of the Iraqi people, and the destructiveness caused in the region by U.S. policies and programs (p. 213).

The terrorist attacks of 9/11 should have made it clear to everyone that the United States needed to mobilize its resources to eliminate al-Qaeda, help strengthen any nation that was threatened by radical Islamic terrorists, and reduce as much as possible U.S. domestic vulnerabilities to further terrorist attacks (Clarke, 2004). Instead of using the apparatus of government and the full resources of the United States to deal with the terrorist threat in a reasoned and effective way, President George W. Bush (and his advisors) pursued a different strategy. Clarke succinctly describes what it was:

> September 11 erased memories of the unique process whereby George Bush had been selected as President a few months earlier. Now, as he stood with an arm around a New York fireman promising to get those who had destroyed the World Trade Center, he was every American's President. His polls soared. He had a unique opportunity to unite America, to bring the United States together with allies around the world to fight terrorism and hate, to eliminate al Qaeda, to eliminate our vulnerabilities, and to strengthen important nations threatened by radicalism. He did none of those things. He invaded Iraq. (p. 286)

Based on faulty intelligence, either of the country or its leader, the decision to wage war in Iraq, a country that had not sponsored much, if any, anti-U.S. terrorism, has arguably made the United States less safe and secure.

As our national debt increases at a dizzying pace to pay for the wars in Iraq and Afghanistan, so does the body count in the latter. U.S. credibility and status decrease with both friends and foes. By invading an oil-rich Arab nation that posed little threat to the United States, it made it practically impossible for other Arab nations to work alongside the United States to ferret out and eradicate the terrorist threats that do exist. U.S. retaliation for 9/11 has arguably strengthened al-Qaeda while increasing Muslim contempt for the United States. Rather than acting like a superpower, the United States acted like a super-bully, ignoring or even criticizing policies and procedures that it would later need (Clarke, 2004, p. 273).

National Insecurity

National security has always been both a curse and a blessing for U.S. presidents. It reveals the tensions and opportunities that exist between political pragmatism and lofty idealism. Presidents from Woodrow Wilson to Jimmy Carter to George W. Bush have been defined by how successfully they spread democracy and human rights throughout the world. These men faced criticism from the left and the right, as well as from idealists and pragmatists. Barack Obama campaigned in 2008 as an anti-Bush candidate in regard to foreign policy and national security, and the effort was not without success. After Bush's shoot-from-the-hip approach, Obama's more calculated, deliberative approach seemed to be a better option.

Richard Clarke and Barack Obama met on May 16, 2007, at a dilapidated apartment in northeast Washington, D.C., months before Obama would become the forty-fourth president of the United States (Klaidman, 2012, pp. 13–17). Clarke was drawn to Obama, believing he might be able to offer the kind of wisdom and inspired policy initiatives that had been lacking for so long in U.S. counterterrorism work. As Clarke listened to Obama's analysis of global events, he found that he agreed with him on every point. The strongest area of agreement, however, was on how foolish it had been to invade Iraq and how much damage had been done to U.S. interests and reputation all across the world. The two men agreed that the world must be shown that the United States was not at war with Muslims or the Islamic faith. Clarke, however, was not sure that Obama had the toughness and grit to be an effective leader in the war on terror. Could he understand that as president he would be fighting an implacable and resolute foe for whom the only option would be to capture or kill? Clarke was eventually convinced that Obama did indeed have the mettle to make the fight and would use both soft and hard power to craft a counterterrorism strategy that was both effective *and* restrained.

Clarke played a central role in Obama's preparation for a national security speech, given on August 1, 2007, at the Woodrow Wilson Center in Washington, D.C. Clarke advised the presidential hopeful that two political objectives should be his guiding principles if he were elected. First, he had to find a convincing way to show U.S. citizens that the United States was less safe due to the counterterrorist activities of the Bush administration. Second, Obama had to convey to the American people that he would be tough on terror whenever it was the prudent thing to do and that he was fully prepared to use force when it was necessary. Obama intended to use economic incentives and sanctions to interfere with whatever support might exist for extremist alternatives by doing what he could to eliminate poverty and to spread secular education in the Middle East. Coupled with this velvet glove was Obama's iron fist in which he intended to call for more troops to combat terrorism in Afghanistan, ground zero for the proselytizing efforts of al-Qaeda and the Taliban.

As president, Obama was good to his word (at least in his willingness to use force in the war on terror). Early on the morning of May 2, 2011, under orders from him, U.S. Navy SEALS charged the residence of Osama bin

Laden, in Abbottabad, Pakistan. The mastermind of the 9/11 attacks had been living there with members of his family (three wives, along with a dozen of his children and grandchildren). The sky was moonless, and the electricity in the compound had been made inoperable by the men who hunted bin Laden. The total darkness made a tense and confusing situation even more so, at least for the terrorist leader. Members of the SEAL team made their way from floor to floor, dispatching anyone who stood in their way. Their ascent required them to blast open one metal gate, but they were prepared to do whatever was necessary to reach bin Laden.

Instead of getting the weapons he kept in his bedroom (an AK-47 and a Makarov machine pistol), bin Laden opened a metal gate to his room. When he stuck his head out to gauge the progression of his pursuers, he was spotted by members of the SEAL team. Bergen (2012) reported that bin Laden then ducked behind the metal door but, surprisingly, did not lock it. Members of the SEAL team burst into bin Laden's bedroom after running down a short hallway. Amal, bin Laden's 29-year-old wife, threw herself at the foot of her husband. She was shoved aside by the first SEAL in the room, and another SEAL shot her in the calf. Bin Laden, though he was unarmed and offering no resistance, was still viewed as a threat that had to be eliminated. He was killed quickly by two shots, one through his left eye socket and the other to his chest. (A book by Owen and Maurer [2012] modified Bergen's rendition a bit. Owen, whose real name is Matt Bissonnette, was a member of the SEAL team that killed bin Laden. This book claims that bin Laden was shot immediately when he stuck his head out of his bedroom. Owen and another member of the team then finished the job.)

Bin Laden's remains were transported to the U.S.S. *Carl Vinson,* an aircraft carrier in the Arabian Sea. His corpse was prepared for burial at sea, and it was dropped overboard so that no gravesite would exist to be honored by his admirers. In February 2012, the complex in which he had lived in Pakistan was razed, and the ground on which it once stood is now the site of cricket matches played by people in the region. Modest fines ($110) and 45-day prison sentences were assessed to bin Laden's three widows and two of his daughters. Whether the killing of bin Laden furthered U.S. interests is still an open question. Martyrs' importance and influence usually increase after their deaths, so bin Laden may still reap rewards in the days ahead (though he will not be alive to enjoy them). Ritzer (2006, p. 251) concluded about the terrorist (in advance of his killing): "Destroying his body may be satisfying to some, but it may well create a greater cultural problem for the United States, one that might translate into still more American citizens killed and structures destroyed" (p. 251).

Sense and Nonsense

The genuine interests of citizens of the United States are not always the same as the political interests or corporate loyalties of those who are given the reins of governmental power. The terrorist attacks of 9/11 offered the opportunity or necessity—it is sometimes hard to know which is the principal motive—to expand counterterrorist activities, rules (e.g., USA Patriot Act), and agencies (e.g., Department of Homeland Security). The attacks of 2001 were not the first time terrorists had staged an assault on the United States on U.S. soil (an attack on the World Trade Center in 1993 killed 7 and injured 103), but 9/11 was a watershed event. U.S. responses to the attacks showed that at least two styles of counterterrorist activities exist. One is a legalistic, criminal justice approach, which remains faithful to the importance of due process and defendants' rights, civil liberties, and individual freedoms, even while it acknowledges the distinctive nature of international terrorism. The second type of counterterrorism is militaristic; it wages war against terrorists with little concern for legal restrictions, due process, or civil rights of suspected terrorists (Deflem, 2010). During the George W. Bush years, militaristic counterterrorism was the primary strategy (embodied in Bush's taunt to terrorists to "Bring it on"). Barack Obama has moved closer to embracing a law-enforcement counterterrorism (though the killing of Osama bin Laden lacked any elements that would place it in the legalistic, criminal justice approach category).

It does seem clear that a militaristic, Wild West approach to international terrorism is doomed to failure. It may accomplish the short-term goal of vengeance and seem to be just deserts to those wronged by an egregious act, but it is counterproductive in the long run if a safe, secure, sane world is our objective. Not only does it fail to eliminate terrorist organizations, but it also generates greater resistance and the counterviolence that this strategy often precipitates (Mullins & Young, 2012). In addition, it leads to the United States being viewed as an outlier nation by other countries in the world (Deflem, 2010). Bush capitalized on the confusion precipitated by 9/11 and the anger over it to encourage U.S. military intervention in Iraq. He portrayed U.S. intervention as not only necessary but heroic, designed to rescue Iraqis from a toxic leader as well as protect them from themselves because they lived in a violent, undemocratic, and repressive land (Messerschmidt, 2010). Bush's ethnocentrism alienated both friends and foes alike.

One of the more embarrassing and damaging pieces of information to emerge from the war in Iraq has been evidence of U.S. torture and other human rights violations of Iraqis at Abu Ghraib prison. This facility, located about 20 miles west of Baghdad, started receiving detainees in 2003, just months after President George W. Bush ordered missile strikes on military targets in Iraq. Photographic evidence and two visits to the prison by the International Committee of the Red Cross documented the use of forced nudity of prisoners, sensory overloads, shackles, sleep deprivation, and engineered stress to break prisoners' wills in order to obtain confessions. In particular, photos offered (or seemed to) clear evidence of torture being administered by U.S. military personnel. These photos seemed to show an attitude of smugness, or at least indifference, among the soldiers as they participated in acts of sadistic brutality and cruelty that euphemisms such as "coercive interrogations," "permissible duress," or "stress positions" could no longer mask (Carrabine, 2011, pp. 18–20).

The U.S. military's initial response to accusations that soldiers were torturing rather than detaining prisoners was filled with denials or obfuscations in regard to inhumane treatments and abuses. When these claims were no longer credible due to press investigations and formal hearings that showed that widespread abuse had occurred in Iraq (and Afghanistan), denials and obfuscations stopped. However, military spokespersons had little interest in coming clean and telling the whole and unvarnished truth about the role that torture was playing in the war on terror. They worked, instead, to make the abuses of prisoners look cleaner, more reasonable, and more necessary than they probably were, making it more likely that as a political issue, "prisoner abuse" would go away quickly (Rosso, 2011).

One population in the United States that was mightily affected by 9/11 was Arab and Muslim Americans. They were the targets of efforts at deportation, surveillance, investigations, accusations, random searches, and hate crimes. Though reactions were relative, depending on time or place, a tendency existed to view Arab Muslim men as a security threat and Arab Muslim women as a cultural threat (Cainkar, 2009). Arab men were given undue attention from governmental representatives because of race, religion, and ethnicity, and Arab women were given undue attention by the public principally because their differentness (particularly in clothing styles) was defined as a rejection of America and its values. Hate crimes against Muslims and Arabs went up following the attacks of 9/11, while hate crimes against other racial/ethnic minorities went down (Disha, Cavendish, & King, 2011). What seemed to be operating is that many Americans reached the conclusion that they were at war with a new enemy (i.e., Arabs or Muslims), which justified and normalized the hate crimes perpetrated against them (p. 40).

The "war on terror," now a permanent feature of the global landscape, has cemented the alliances between the private sector and the public war-making apparatus of the United States (Rothe, 2009). Companies (such as Halliburton) have used the war in Iraq as an opportunity for systematic and significant overcharging for services and supplies. Under rules instituted by the Bush administration, Halliburton was able to obtain no-bid contracts, even when it had a history of violating environmental, labor relation, and trade laws (p. 441). This allowed monumental war profiteering. The over-costs, overcharges, failure to provide goods and services that were charged and paid for, and kickback profits resulted principally from the cozy relationship between a handful of politicians and corporate boosters. This has created the opportunity for private corporations to amass substantial profits in a war-torn nation. Amid all the death, injury, misery, stupidity, and waste found in the U.S. war with Iraq, Halliburton was still able to make a tidy profit. By the end of 2006, this energy giant had earned $20 billion in revenues since the war's start (Klein, 2007, p. 16).

Privilege, Power, and Penalties

Sutherland's (1940, 1945, 1949, 1983) study of white-collar crime showed him that its perpetrators were able to avoid the stigma and the punishment accorded lesser offenders. The legal status of white-collar crime is more ambiguous, and laws may be more difficult to apply to the wrongdoings of the powerful (Gerber & Weeks, 1992, p. 330). Irrespective of its moral or ethical status, behavior is illegal only if laws exist to criminalize it. Laws are crafted by lawmakers, and lawmakers can be influenced in all kinds of ways by powerful people who do what they can to control the content of law and how it applies to them (Livingston, 1996, pp. 294–300).

The arrogance of power can easily prompt individuals to believe that laws are inapplicable to them. This heightened sense of importance and invincibility can motivate and rationalize many untoward activities. Richard Nixon, forced from the office of President of the United States for his role in the Watergate scandal, claimed—and probably believed—that whatever the president did, no matter how unsavory, was not against the law. Key players in the Iran-Contra scandal of the Reagan era—in which arms were sold to Iran, and monies from the sale were used to aid the Contras in Nicaragua—assumed that everything they did was legal.

> Organizations have their own versions of events and respond to accusations of deviance with accusations and assertions of their own. In the exchange of claims and counterclaims, whether an organizational action actually comes to be seen as deviant is fundamentally a matter of definition. (Ermann & Lundman, 2002, p. 27)

The confusion created by disputes over the legal status of this act or that act has great benefits for white-collar offenders who capitalize on the ambiguity and turn it to their own ends. In this project, they are often able to take advantage of organizational resources to create and disseminate ideas that are the most beneficial to them and their interests.

Even when laws are firmly in place, it may be more difficult to detect white-collar crimes, arrest and convict white-collar criminals, and then hold the organizations for which they work accountable. Because victims may be unaware that they have been intentionally hurt by some misdeed, or because an offending corporation has neither a body to kick nor a soul to damn, it is more difficult to apply to white-collar misdeeds the same legal procedures and penalties that were invented to cover one-on-one harms of individuals (Belbot, 1995, pp. 229–232). The nature of law, the size and power of the corporation, the privileged status of white-collar offenders, and the diffuse nature of white-collar victimizations all mean that penalties for white-collar crime are likely to be relatively painless and ineffective (Sutherland, 1945). What seem to be huge fines of corporations for misdeeds are seldom large enough to deter their illegal behavior (J. W. Coleman, 2006, p. 153). A fine of $3 million to a company like McDonald's, even if it had been paid, would have been little more than a slap on the wrist.

However, it would be an error to conclude that privileged and powerful people *always* fare better in a court of law than do the less powerful or prosperous. A study of accounting scandals in the United States from 1999 to 2006 (Benediktsson, 2010) reports that corporate boards of offending companies did what they could to sever all ties with the law-breaking executives, making them stand trial alone whenever their companies came under scrutiny for allegations of wrongdoing. This has the advantage for corporate managers and owners of diverting attention away from the organization itself and toward individual deviants, while reaffirming the more popular and more easily conveyed and understood "bad apple" theory of corporate wrongdoing. This meant that any assertion that it was really the apple tree itself that was defective seems less likely and more difficult to accept. What is true, however, is that legal penalties are relative, being responsive to factors other than the degree of injury produced by some untoward act. This relativity can produce an inconsistency in how sanctions are dispensed, which can benefit high-status offenders and major organizations. Sometimes, high-status individuals are treated preferentially, receiving greater leniency when compared to what happens to individuals of lower rank who are guilty of far less. At other times, however, they are treated more harshly (Rosoff et al., 2004, pp. 531–534).

What is important to remember about white-collar crime is not simply that high-status deviants can receive preferential treatment. We must also remember that some privileged and powerful individuals, usually acting through the organizations for which they work, do a great deal of harm to a society, not only in terms of the taking of other people's belongings but also in terms of the number of people killed or injured by white-collar activities. These predatory acts generate both public resentment and political outrage, mostly because they are done by persons in positions of responsibility and trust in political and economic institutions. The fact that these people who are responsible for so much wanton injury receive *any* leniency in a court of law is a bitter pill to swallow.

Conclusions

Power plays a singularly important role in the social construction of deviance, and it must play a similar role in our understanding of it. Regardless of whether we are examining the plunder of a Detroit community or the game/swindle of three-card monte, power—especially the power that is found in complex organizations—will be implicated in much of what happens. It is true that sometimes individuals will be able to take advantage of their access to positions of power or influence to break the rules so as to benefit themselves with no support from others. However, this deviance by individuals inside an organization to benefit themselves is just the tip of the iceberg.

Organizations themselves may be corrupt and a major part of the problem. It is almost always a web of relationships and the power that this allows that account for the patterns of deviance that occur. Power corrupts, and absolute power has the tendency to corrupt absolutely. Power is also a critical variable in understanding how harmful acts are viewed, defined, and described. What is considered as criminal and what penalties are prescribed for the crimes almost always reflect the power and interests of specific groups. If you are a carrier, your taking will be dealt with harshly; if you are a General Motors, your taking may not be viewed as taking at all. It may even be viewed as a valuable renovation project for the city of Detroit.

The many incidents we examined in this chapter can in one way or another be traced to power, privilege, and organizational dynamics and social networks. Regardless of whether it is the plunder of Poletown, the Carrier's case, occupational crime, corporate crime, white-collar crime, elite deviance, excessive profiteering, or international terrorism, certain groups will use the power that organizational networks give them to do things that other people cannot and then to justify and excuse them as both valuable and necessary. The icing on the cake for powerful groups is that they will be able to influence the content of law and other social norms, which legitimates and normalizes the activities and understandings based on them.

References

Abu-Lughod, R. A. (2010). Legitimacy of the war in Iraq: The role of the media in sorting fact from Fox-tion. In R. L. Bing III (Ed.), *Race, crime, and the media* (pp. 210–218). New York, NY: McGraw-Hill.

Ahmed, N. M. (2002). *The war on freedom: How and why America was attacked, September 11, 2001.* East Sussex, UK: Institute for Policy Research and Development.

Belbot, B. (1995). Corporate criminal liability. In M. Blankenship (Ed.), *Understanding corporate criminality* (pp. 211–237). New York, NY: Garland.

Benediktsson, M. O. (2010). The deviant organization and the bad apple CEO: Ideology and accountability in media coverage of corporate scandals. *Social Forces, 88,* 2189–2216.

Bergen, P. L. (2012). *Manhunt: The ten-year search for Bin Laden from 9/11 to Abbottabad.* New York, NY: Random House/Crown.

Blau, J. (1999). *Illusions of prosperity: America's working families in an age of economic insecurity.* New York, NY: Oxford University Press.

Bonn, S. A. (2010). *Mass deception: Moral panic and the US war on Iraq.* New Brunswick, NJ: Rutgers University Press.

Box, S. (1983). *Power, crime, and mystification.* London: Tavistock.

Brady, D. (2009). *Rich democracies, poor people.* New York, NY: Oxford University Press.

Cainkar, L. A. (2009). *Homeland insecurity: The Arab American and Muslim American experience after 9/11.* New York, NY: Russell Sage Foundation.

Carrabine, E. (2011). Images of torture: Culture, politics and power. *Crime, Media, Culture, 7,* 5–30.

Carroll, W. K. (2010). *The making of a transnational capitalist class: Corporate power in the 21st century.* New York, NY: Zed Books.

Cavender, G., Gray, K., & Miller, K. W. (2010). Enron's perp walk: Status degradation ceremonies as narrative. *Crime, Media, Culture, 6,* 251–266.

Cavender, G., Jurik, N., & Cohen, A. (1993). The baffling case of the smoking gun: The social ecology of political accounts in the Iran-Contra affair. *Social Problems, 40,* 152–166.

Chambliss, W., & Seidman, R. (1982). *Law, order, and power* (2nd ed.). Reading, MA: Addison-Wesley.

Charbeneau, T. (1992). Ragged individualism: America's myth of the loner. *Utne Reader, 51,* 132–133.

Chomsky, N. (1988). *The culture of terrorism.* Boston, MA: South End Press.

Clarke, R. (2004). *Against all enemies: Inside America's war on terror.* New York, NY: Free Press.

Clinard, M. B., & Quinney, R. (1973). *Criminal behavior systems: A typology* (2nd ed.). New York, NY: Holt, Rinehart & Winston.

Coleman, J. S. (1982). *The asymmetric society.* Syracuse, NY: Syracuse University Press.

Coleman, J. W. (1987). Toward an integrated theory of white-collar crime. *American Journal of Sociology, 93,* 406–439.

Coleman, J. W. (2006). *The criminal elite: Understanding white-collar crime* (6th ed.). New York, NY: Worth.

Collins, P. H. (2010). The new politics of community. 2009 Presidential Address. *American Sociological Review, 75,* 7–30.

Conklin, J. (1977). *Illegal but not criminal.* Englewood Cliffs, NJ: Prentice Hall.

Davis, N. (1980). *Sociological constructions of deviance: Perspectives and issues in the field* (2nd ed.). Dubuque, IA: W. C. Brown.

Deflem, M. (2010). *The policing of terrorism: Organizational and global perspectives.* New York, NY: Routledge.

Della Porta, D., & Piazza, G. (2008). *Voices of the valley, voices of the straits: How protest creates communities.* New York, NY: Berghahn Books.

Disha, I., Cavendish, J. C., & King, R. D. (2011). Historical events and spaces of hate: Hate crimes against Arabs and Muslims in post-9/11 America. *Social Problems, 58,* 21–46.

Dorling, D. (2010). *Injustice: Why social inequality persists.* Portland, OR: Policy Press.

Ermann, M. D., & Lundman, R. (2002). Corporate and governmental deviance: Origins, patterns, and reactions. In M. D. Ermann & R. Lundman (Eds.), *Corporate and governmental deviance: Problems of organizational behavior in contemporary society* (6th ed., pp. 3–49). New York, NY: Oxford University Press.

Feniger, Y., & Yuchtman-Yaar, E. (2010). Risk groups in exposure to terror: The case of Israel's citizens. *Social Forces, 88,* 1451–1462.

Fox, J. (2009). *The myth of the rational market: A history of risk, reward, and delusion on Wall Street.* New York, NY: HarperCollins.

Franken, A. (2003). *Lies (and the lying liars who tell them): A fair and balanced look at the right.* New York, NY: Dutton.

Freudenberg, W., & Gramling, R. (2011). *Blowout in the Gulf: The BP oil spill disaster and the future of energy in America.* Cambridge, MA: MIT Press.

Freudenberg, W., Gramling, R., Laska, S., & Erikson, K. T. (2009). *Catastrophe in the making: The engineering of Katrina and disasters of tomorrow.* Washington, DC: Island Press.

Fullerton, A. S., & Villemez, M. J. (2011). Why does the spatial agglomeration of firms benefit workers: Examining the role of organizational diversity in U.S. industries and labor markets. *Social Forces, 89,* 1145–1164.

Geis, G., & Goff, C. (1983). Introduction. In E. H. Sutherland, *White-collar crime: The uncut version* (pp. ix–xxxiii). New Haven, CT: Yale University Press.

Gerber, J., & Weeks, S. (1992). Women as victims of corporate crime: A call for research on a neglected topic. *Deviant Behavior, 13,* 325–347.

Goldsmith, G., & Blakely, E. J. (2010). *Separate societies: Poverty and inequality in U.S. cities.* Philadelphia, PA: Temple University Press.

Gosselin, P. (2009). *Highwire: The precarious financial lives of American families.* New York, NY: Basic Books.

Green, G. (1997). *Occupational crime* (2nd ed.). Chicago, IL: Nelson-Hall.

Gross, M. (1996). *The political racket: Deceit, self-interest and corruption in American politics.* New York, NY: Ballantine.

Groysberg, B. (2010). *The myth of talent and the portability of performance.* Princeton, NJ: Princeton University Press.

Hall, J. (1952). *Theft, law, and society* (2nd ed.). Indianapolis, IN: Bobbs-Merrill.

Harvey, D. (2010). *The enigma of capital: And the crises of capitalism.* New York, NY: Oxford University Press.

Hightower, J. (2003). *Thieves in high places: They've stolen our country—and it's time to take it back.* New York, NY: Viking.

Ho, K. (2009). *Liquidated: An ethnography of Wall Street.* Durham, NC: Duke University Press.

Howard, R., & Forest, J. (Eds.) (with Bahema, N.). (2008). *Weapons of mass destruction and terrorism.* New York, NY: McGraw-Hill.

Jacobsson, K. (2012). Accounts of honesty: Refuting allegations of bribery. *Deviant Behavior, 33,* 108–125.

Jenkins, P. (2003). *Images of terror: What we can and can't know about terrorism.* New York, NY: Aldine de Gruyter.

Juravich, T. (2009). *At the altar of the bottom line: The degradation of work in the 21st century.* Amherst: University of Massachusetts Press.

Kahan, A. S. (2010). *Mind vs. money: The war between intellectuals and capitalism.* New Brunswick, NJ: Transaction Publishers.

Kelman, H., & Hamilton, V. L. (1989). *Crimes of obedience: Toward a social psychology of authority and responsibility.* New Haven, CT: Yale University Press.

Kendall, D. (2008). *Members only. Elite clubs and the process of exclusion.* Lanham, MD: Rowman & Littlefield.

Keynes, J. M. (1930). *A treatise on money: Volume 1. The pure theory of money.* New York, NY: AMS Press.

King, B. G. (2011). The tactical disruptiveness of social movements: Sources of market and mediated disruptiveness in corporate boycotts. *Social Problems, 58,* 491–517.

Klaidman, D. (2012). *Kill or capture: The war on terror and the soul of the Obama presidency.* Boston, MA: Houghton Mifflin Harcourt.

Klein, N. (2007). *The shock doctrine: The rise of disaster capitalism.* New York, NY: Picador/Henry Holt.

Kramer, R., Michalowski, R., & Kauzlarich, D. (2002). The origins and development of the concept and theory of state-corporate crime. *Crime & Delinquency, 48,* 263–282.

Krippner, G. R. (2011). *Capitalizing on crisis: The political origins of the rise of finance.* Cambridge, MA: Harvard University Press.

Kristal, T. (2010). Good times, bad times: Postwar labor's share of national income in capitalist democracies. *American Sociological Review, 75,* 729–763.

Lauderdale, P., & Cruit, M. (1993). *The struggle for control: A study of law, disputes, and deviance.* Albany: State University of New York Press.

Lendman, S. (2011). *How Wall Street fleeces America: Privatized banking, government collusion and class war.* Atlanta, GA: Clarity Press.

Livingston, J. (1996). *Crime and criminology* (2nd ed.). Englewood Cliffs, NJ: Prentice Hall.

Mann, J. (2004). *Rise of the Vulcans: The history of Bush's war cabinet.* New York, NY: Penguin.

Martin, I. W. (2008). *The permanent tax revolt: How the property tax transformed American politics.* Stanford, CA: Stanford University Press.

Menard, S., Morris, R. G., Gerber, J., & Covey, H. C. (2011). Distribution and correlates of self-reported crimes of trust. *Deviant Behavior, 32,* 877–917.

Merton, R. K. (1938). Social structure and anomie. *American Sociological Review, 3,* 672–682.

Messerschmidt, J. W. (2010). *Hegemonic masculinities and camouflaged politics: Unmasking the Bush dynasty and its war against Iraq.* Boulder, CO: Paradigm.

Monahan, B. A. (2010). *The shock of the news: Media coverage and the making of 9/11.* New York: New York University Press.

Monahan, T. (2010). *Surveillance in the time of insecurity.* New Brunswick, NJ: Rutgers University Press.

Mouw, T., & Kalleberg, A. L. (2010). Occupations and the structure of wage inequality in the United States, 1980s to 2000s. *American Sociological Review, 75,* 402–431.

Mullins, C. W., & Young, J. K. (2012). Culture of violence and acts of terror: Applying a legitimation-habituation model of terrorism. *Crime & Delinquency, 58,* 28–56.

Nacos, B. (2007). Terrorism as breaking news: Attack on America. In T. Badey (Ed.), *Annual editions: Violence and terrorism 07/08* (10th ed., pp. 110–125). New York, NY: McGraw-Hill.

Nader, R., & Smith, W. (1996). *No contest: Corporate lawyers and the perversion of justice in America.* New York, NY: Random House.

O'Flynn, M. (2009). *Profitable ideas: The ideology of the individual in capitalist development.* Leiden, Netherlands: Brill.

Owen, M., & Maurer, K. (2012). *No easy day: The autobiography of a Navy SEAL.* New York, NY: Dutton.

Posner, R. A. (2010). *The crisis of capitalist democracy.* Cambridge, MA: Harvard University Press.

Poveda, T. (1994). *Rethinking white-collar crime.* New York, NY: Praeger.

Prechel, H., & Morris, T. (2010). The effects of organizational and political embeddedness on financial malfeasance in the largest U.S. corporations: Dependence, incentives, and opportunities. *American Sociological Review, 75,* 331–354.

Prus, R., & Sharper, C. R. D. (1977). *Road hustler: The career contingencies of professional card and dice hustlers.* Lexington, MA: Lexington.

Reardon, S. F., & Bischoff, K. (2011). Income inequality and income segregation. *American Journal of Sociology, 116,* 1092–1153.

Reich, R. B. (2010). *Aftershock: The next economy and America's future.* New York, NY: Knopf.

Rigney, D. (2010). *The Matthew effect: How advantage begets further advantage.* New York, NY: Columbia University Press.

Ritzer, G. (2006). September 11, 2001: Mass murder and its roots in the symbolism of American consumer culture. In G. Ritzer (Ed.), *McDonaldization: The reader* (2nd ed., pp. 240–252). Thousand Oaks, CA: Pine Forge/Sage.

Robbins, T. (2008). *The modern con man: How to get something for nothing.* New York, NY: Bloomsbury/Macmillan.

Rooney, B. (2011, January 27). Financial crisis was avoidable. *CNNMoney.* Retrieved January 23, 2013, from http://money.cnn.com/2011/01/27/news/economy/fcic_crisis_avoidable/index.htm?hpt=T2

Rosoff, S., Pontell, H., & Tillman, R. (2004). *Profit without honor: White-collar crime and the looting of America.* Upper Saddle River, NJ: Pearson/Prentice Hall.

Ross, J. (2013). Conceptualizing the criminological problem of terrorism. In A. Thio, T. Calhoun, & A. Conyers (Eds.), *Deviance today* (pp. 281–288). Upper Saddle River, NJ: Pearson.

Rosso, J. D. (2011). The textual mediation of denial: Congress, Abu Ghraib, and the construction of an isolated incident. *Social Problems, 58,* 165–188.

Rothe, D. (2009). War profiteering: Iraq and Halliburton. In P. Adler & P. Adler (Eds.), *Constructions of deviance: Social power, context, and interaction* (6th ed., pp. 433–445). Belmont, CA: Thomson/Wadsworth.

Rothkopf, D. (2012). *Power, Inc.: The epic rivalry between big business and government—and the reckoning that lies ahead.* New York, NY: Farrar, Straus & Giroux.

Routledge, P., & Cumbers, A. (2009). *Global justice networks: Geographies of transnational solidarity.* Manchester, UK: Manchester University Press.

Roy, W. (1997). *Socializing capital: The rise of the large industrial corporation in America.* Princeton, NJ: Princeton University Press.

Rugh, J. S., & Massey, D. S. (2010). Racial segregation and the American foreclosure crisis. *American Sociological Review, 75,* 629–651.

Samuel, Y. (2010). *Organizational pathology: Life and death of organizations.* New Brunswick, NJ: Transaction Publishers.

Scarne, J. (1974). *Scarne's new complete guide to gambling* (Rev. ed.). New York, NY: Simon & Schuster.

Sherwood, J. H. (2010). *Wealth, whiteness, and the matrix of privilege: The view from the country club.* Lanham, MD: Lexington Books.

Simon, D. (2008). *Elite deviance* (9th ed.). Boston, MA: Allyn & Bacon.

Smith, Y. (2010). *ECONned: How unenlightened self interest undermined democracy and corrupted capitalism.* New York, NY: Palgrave Macmillan.

Soule, S. (2009). *Contention and corporate social responsibility*. New York, NY: Cambridge University Press.

Staples, W. (2000). *Everyday surveillance: Vigilance and visibility in postmodern life*. Lanham, MD: Rowman & Littlefield.

Stiglitz, J. E. (2010). *Freefall: America, free markets, and the sinking of the world economy*. New York, NY: Norton.

Stiglitz, J. E. (2012). *The price of inequality: How today's divided society endangers our future*. New York, NY: Norton.

Stritzke, W., Lewandowsky, S., Denemark, D., Clare, J., & Morgan, F. (Eds.). (2009). *Terrorism and torture: An interdisciplinary perspective*. New York, NY: Cambridge University Press.

Sutherland, E. H. (1940). White-collar criminality. *American Sociological Review, 5,* 1–12.

Sutherland, E. H. (1945). Is "white-collar crime" crime? *American Sociological Review, 10,* 132–139.

Sutherland, E. H. (1949). *White-collar crime*. New York, NY: Dryden.

Sutherland, E. H. (1983). *White-collar crime: The uncut version*. New Haven, CT: Yale University Press.

Tavits, M. (2010). Why do people engage in corruption? The case of Estonia. *Social Forces, 88,* 1257–1280.

Thio, A. (2009). *Deviant behavior* (10th ed.). Boston, MA: Allyn & Bacon.

Tillman, R., & Pontell, H. (1995). Organizations and fraud in the savings and loan industry. *Social Forces, 73,* 1439–1463.

Tilly, C. (1998). *Durable inequality*. Berkeley: University of California Press.

Traugott, M. (2010). *The insurgent barricade*. Berkeley: University of California Press.

Tunnell, K. D. (1992). *Choosing crime: The criminal calculus of property offenders*. Chicago, IL: Nelson-Hall.

Tunnell, K. D. (2006). *Living off crime* (2nd ed.). Lanham, MD: Rowman & Littlefield.

Vela-McConnell, J. (1999). *Who is my neighbor? Social affinity in a modern world*. Albany: State University of New York Press.

Villette, M., & Vuillermot, C. (2009). *From predators to icons: Exposing the myth of the business hero* (G. Holoch, Trans.). Ithaca, NY: ILR Press.

Viner, J. (1940). The short view and the long in economic policy. *American Economic Review, 30,* 1–15.

Wacquant, L. (2009). *Punishing the poor: The neoliberal governmentality of social insecurity*. Durham, NC: Duke University Press.

Wilkinson, R., & Pickett, K. (2010). *The spirit level: Why greater equality makes societies stronger*. New York, NY: Bloomsbury Press.

Wylie, J. (1989). *Poletown: Community betrayed*. Urbana: University of Illinois Press.

4

Mental Disorders

Medicalization on 34th Street

A 1947 novel by Valentine Davies described what could have been the trial of the century: the time that Santa Claus was hauled into court and his sanity questioned. The story really begins at the Maplewood Home for the Aged in Great Neck, Long Island. An elderly and kind gentleman, at the peak of health, whose name was Kris Kringle, spent his time making toys and smoking his pipe. One November, the resident physician at Maplewood (Dr. Pierce) gave Kris the bad news that he was being evicted. The reason was that state laws and Maplewood's charter allowed only people who were in good physical *and* mental health to live there. Kris's claim that he was the one and only Santa Claus indicated that he was mentally ill, so he had to leave Maplewood Home. He collected his belongings and left to make his way in the world. Luckily for him, he had a friend who lived and worked at the Central Park Zoo, and he made room for Kris at his place. It was a good arrangement because Kris had an uncanny ability with animals, especially the reindeer.

Mr. Kringle wanted to see the Macy's Thanksgiving Day Parade. That year, the fake Santa that Macy's had hired got drunk, too drunk to carry out his duties. When Kris saw the man, he was furious. He complained directly to the personnel director and organizer of the parade, Doris Walker. She was visibly upset, dispatched the phony Santa, and asked Kris to take his place. Kris consented only because he did not want to disappoint the children. He did so well that he was offered a job at Macy's as the permanent Santa, a position he reluctantly accepted.

Kris ran afoul of entrenched beliefs of other Macy's employees, continuing to insist (at least when asked) that Santa Claus did exist and that he was the one and only. Questions arose about his sanity and his dangerousness. In fact, Ms. Walker wondered if Kris was as harmless as he appeared. She consulted Macy's resident expert on psychology and vocational guidance, Mr. Albert Sawyer. He was an arrogant, dogmatic fellow who thought he knew practically everything about practically everything. He told Doris Walker that he would be pleased to interview Kris. Sawyer concluded without much to go on that Kris had a fixed delusion and could be dangerous, and he reported this to Ms. Walker.

That December, Sawyer was scheduled to give a lecture titled "Exploding the Myth of Santa Claus." Kris attended because he believed that he had some valuable information to contribute. At the lecture, Sawyer vociferously condemned the myth of Santa Claus and insisted that any adult who believed in Santa Claus revealed himself or herself to have an incomplete and neurotic personality. Sawyer opined that the "vicious myth" of Santa Claus had done more harm in the world than had opium. Kris's presence unnerved Sawyer. His speech became incoherent, and he garbled sentences. Finally, Sawyer demanded that the old "jackanapes" be removed from the room, but Kris refused to leave. Sawyer advanced on him. Kris raised his cane in protection, Sawyer grabbed it and tugged, making Kris lose his grip so that Sawyer hit himself in the cheek. Sawyer accused Kris of attacking him. The altercation with Sawyer (along with Kris's claim that he was Santa Claus) worried others. Steps were taken to have a hearing to determine if Kris should be committed to Bellevue Psychiatric Hospital for his own good and for the safety of the people around him.

The commitment hearing was under the charge of Judge Henry X. Harper. Thomas Mara represented the state of New York, and Fred Gayley represented Kris Kringle. The first witness Mr. Mara called was the defendant, Mr. Kringle. Kris was a right sprightly old elf, and Judge Harper smiled when he saw him in spite of himself. Mara got right to the point and asked Kris if he believed that he was Santa Claus. "Of course!" was the reply. The courtroom erupted. The old gentleman didn't even try to hide his craziness! Mara rested his case and sat down, confident that he had proved that the old man was insane. Gayley was desperate as he sat in court. He was trying to prove by a preponderance of the evidence that Kris Kringle was mentally healthy, but things were not going well. It looked as if Kris might be committed to Bellevue after all. However, a fortuitous turn of events kept this from happening.

Gayley was summoned from the courtroom and was shown bundles and bundles of letters, each one addressed to Santa Claus. (Every letter addressed to Santa Claus that was in the local post office had been bundled up and delivered to Kris at the courthouse.) Struck by an idea, Gayley returned to the courtroom and reminded the court that it was a serious offense to deliver mail to the wrong party. He then produced three letters from his jacket, each one addressed simply to "Santa Claus, USA." Their delivery to Kris proved (or so Gayley claimed) that Kris was recognized by a competent authority (i.e., the U.S. Post Office) to be the one and only Santa Claus. The court was unimpressed. Three letters were hardly enough to make such a strong claim, but Gayley had further exhibits. Judge Harper insisted that they be put on his bench. Gayley complied, and the judge was eventually covered by a mountain of mail. Judge Harper ruled that if the United States government believed Kris Kringle was Santa Claus, his court would not disagree. The case was dismissed. Kris was deeply moved. Smiling happily, he rushed to the bench and wished the judge a Merry Christmas. Then Kris disappeared into the night. After all, it was Christmas Eve.

Davies's book about the *fictional* trial of Santa illustrates something factual: Mental illness is a social construction. Claiming to be Santa is no different in certain respects from claiming to be Judge Harper, Fred Gayley, or Thomas Mara. The rendering of a judgment that a mental disorder exists comes from the determination that an individual is not what he or she claims to be and that he or she should not be thinking, feeling, or doing what he or she is thinking, feeling, or doing. The dispute over the sickness or wellness of Kris's so-called delusion, or even the determination that he had one in the first place, cannot be separated from the social context in which that decision is made. A pivotal issue seems to be whether a "competent authority" will state for the record that an individual is sick or well, insane or sane, or abnormal or normal.

The Medicalization Process

Different narratives exist to describe and evaluate human conditions or experiences. Sometimes, none of the narratives is viewed as more legitimate or correct than any of the others. An intellectual division of labor exists in which each narrative has its own turf, and its supporters follow a policy of live and let live. For example, it would be possible for a killing of one human being by another to be considered a legal matter, major depression to be considered a medical matter, sin to be considered a religious matter, and poverty to be considered a social matter. At other times, however, turf wars are frequent, and skirmishes and battles to expand one's sphere of influence are ongoing. Individuals and the organizations that they represent try to expand both their power and influence, doing what they can to be viewed as the most authoritative, knowledgeable source around. In this social process of defining "deviance" and tagging "deviants," some groups are more successful than others.

> Although negotiations may occur, more powerful interests in society are better able to implement their version of reality by creating and legitimating deviance definitions that support their interests. (Conrad & Schneider, 1992, p. 25)

The outcome is that certain groups come to "own" particular problems (e.g., religion's relationship to sin; medicine's relationship to disease), and members of these groups will then be widely viewed as the only real experts on the problems in question (Gusfield, 1981). Until that happens, it can still be a highly contentious issue whether a specific attitude, behavior, or condition is best viewed as sin, sickness, crime, or something else altogether. Narratives change all the time, and new ones are invented on a continual basis.

When a physician diagnoses a patient as having measles, mumps, or chicken pox, we really don't need to spend much time trying to figure out whose interests are served or why this ailment received medical attention. Medicalization of the illness is both reasonable and helpful. Sometimes, however, the institution of medicine is used to control people, perpetuating the status quo and helping physicians to expand their power and privilege. In 1851, the physician Samuel Cartwright first diagnosed (or invented) the "illness" of *drapetomania.* It referred to the "disease" of slaves in the South running away from the plantations of their white owners (Conrad & Schneider, 1992, p. 35). It is easy enough to see that a diagnosis of drapetomania is different in fundamental ways from a diagnosis of ailments such as chicken pox, measles, or mumps. The determination that running away from a plantation qualifies as a disease is both arbitrary and political. It was a disease only because someone who had the authority and credibility to define a human condition as a medical problem said it was. In the early 1970s in the former Soviet Union, psychiatrists diagnosed political dissidents as having *sluggish schizophrenia,* a so-called medical condition characterized by symptoms of wanting to change a social system and having actual ideas regarding how to go about it. This medical diagnosis made it possible to control political dissidents by sending them to special mental hospitals that were established exclusively for them, run in conjunction with the KGB (Gosden, 2003, p. 409). There was a time in the past when masturbation was thoroughly medicalized, and things were blamed on it that seem laughable by today's standards (e.g., homosexuality). In like fashion, erectile dysfunction, attention-deficit hyperactivity disorder (ADHD), menopause, posttraumatic stress, alcoholism, withdrawal from caffeine, and the inability to do arithmetic have been medicalized as well. Things that seem to facilitate medicalization include support from the medical profession, a convincing and empirically supported theory of the origin and prognosis of the illness, the existence of profitable therapies, willingness of insurance companies to pay for treatment, and the inclination of individuals who have the condition to accept medicalization of it (Conrad, 2007, p. 7).

With increasing regularity, conditions that were once viewed as crime, sin, or bad manners are now being viewed as medical diseases in need of cure. Part of this transformation from badness to sickness can be attributed to medical crusades by physicians to expand their sphere of influence, but not all of it. In some cases, patient collectivities or even individual sufferers have been insistent that their conditions be treated as diseases. The corporate sector, especially the pharmaceutical industry and medical insurers, has been playing a more significant role in the medicalization process. Some human conditions (e.g., childbirth, senility, pregnancy, AIDS, Alzheimer's) have been thoroughly penetrated by medical interpretations. Others, such as alcoholism, menopause, baldness, or suicide, have been partly medicalized. Still others, such as hypersexuality (or hyposexuality) or compulsive gambling, have been only slightly medicalized.

The greater the economic and political benefits that come from "owning" this or that type of social deviance, the more intense will be the turf wars between different organizations for control of it. As religious interpretations of human conditions lost their influence and as the power of science increased, it led to an increase in the influence of the medical profession and the power and privilege of medical practitioners. A wider range of human conditions came to be medicalized and treated as disease rather than as sin, crime, or even voluntary action.

Although corporations play a less significant role in the medicalization process than do physicians, hospitals, and patients, times are changing. Odd as it sounds, the trend now is for pharmaceutical companies to invent and then peddle *diseases* for which they have curative drugs or to exaggerate the medical nature of conditions that had heretofore not been considered as medical problems (Watters, 2010). GlaxoSmithKline pathologized anxiety by "selling" the idea that shyness was a medical problem that could and should be cured (Conrad, 2007, pp. 16–19). Its advertising campaigns changed consumers' views of "social anxiety disorder" and "generalized anxiety disorder," which expanded the market for Paxil, its anxiety-reducing drug.

Psychiatry, as the medical profession that is granted the most authority to deal with *mental* illness, is in a unique position. It can deal with *anything* defined as an abnormality, especially if the abnormality is defined as lacking rhyme or reason. In this way, psychiatry has been able to extend its authority over a terrain that was coveted by other professionals and groups (e.g., lawyers, social workers, clinical psychologists, counselors) (Foucault, 2003). Many human conditions exist as medical diseases principally because they have powerful lobbies, consisting of physicians, politicians, and consumers, that authenticate or ratify constellations or syndromes of complaints as legitimate mental disorders (Sharkey, 1997).

Disease-mongering is clearest in psychiatry, where the focus has shifted away from the use of psychotherapy and group therapy and toward the use of genetic explanations of cause and drug-based cures. This trend has been encouraged by insurance companies, most of which will pay for drugs used for the treatment of mental illness but practically no other kind of therapy. Although it is not at all clear when "normal" psychology becomes "abnormal," it is clear that deviance has been extensively medicalized. As noted above, what was once viewed as "badness" is increasingly being viewed as "sickness" (Conrad & Schneider, 1992). Physicians' inclination to use drugs to treat disease prioritizes pharmaceutical treatments over every other possible type of treatment, which drives medicine more and more, both in its practice and in its theories of disease (Grob & Horwitz, 2010).

Increasingly, medicine is insurance driven, insurance is quick-treatment driven, and quick treatments are drug driven. If medicine is not exactly addicted to drugs, it is true that medical treatments are heavily dependent on them. Drugs give physicians both the ability to cure some disease *and* the appearance of competency, justifiably or not. In a situation that looks much like putting the cart in front of the horse (or the tail wagging the dog), it is the treatment options (e.g., drugs) that seem to determine medical diagnoses. For example, supplemental serotonin reuptake inhibitors (SSRIs) are classified as antidepressants, but they could just as correctly be classified as anti-anxiety drugs. Physicians were more likely to diagnose the diseases they treated with SSRIs as forms of depression rather than as forms of anxiety (Grob & Horwitz, 2010, p. 139).

The pharmaceutical industry, with assistance from physicians and patients, actively promotes psychotropic drugs as the best way to cure problems in living in practically any way it can. This close affinity between drug therapies and biological psychiatry is no accident, as each one gains sustenance from the other. The promotion of Miltown (meprobamate), the first U.S. minor tranquilizer, illustrates how human ailments can be constructed in the interest of the pharmaceutical industry and medical profession even when patients—some of them—can benefit, too. This drug was developed and peddled during the 1950s, an anxious time in U.S. history. The threat of nuclear war; a fear of communism; and the growth of alienation, loneliness, and insecurity were defining features of the period. Though patients wanted to find some medical relief for their anxieties, the drug industry played a central role in promoting meprobamate. It peppered newspapers and magazines of the time with favorable assessments of the drug.

Once physicians were convinced that mepobamate was a good choice to prescribe to deal with a wide range of human complaints—and Hollywood stars praised it—its success was practically ensured. This drug came to define the parameters of psychiatric treatment and physician–patient relationships in regard to mental health and illness in the years that followed. Though meprobamate eventually fell into disuse, it was followed by other drugs that were advertised as even better. Drugs came to be defined by practically everybody as the way to treat human ailments—ailments that might never have been treated chemically if not for the history of Miltown (Tone, 2009).

Manufacturing Madness

Diversity Into Disease

The medical manufacture of the idea of mental illness (or madness) spans a period of more than 2,000 years, and the development of the concept has been an uneven one, characterized by starts, stops, and side trips (Conrad & Schneider, 1992; Foucault, 1965). Social and cultural factors play a pivotal role in creating those attitudes, behaviors, and conditions that are viewed as indicators of mental illness (Schieman & Glavin, 2011). They also play a pivotal role in establishing the criteria by which a syndrome or constellation of attitudes, behaviors, and conditions is diagnosed as a mental illness instead of something else (King & Bearman, 2011).

> When a society regards highly individuals who are able to produce unusual psychological states, such persons will appear. However, the society also stipulates the boundaries within which it will accept or at least tolerate such behaviour. Cultural values serve not only to encourage or to check the experiences and acts of these individuals; they also provide the criteria by which deviant behaviour of this type is judged and differentiated from other forms. (Rosen, 1968, p. 63)

Being strange or acting strangely does not automatically qualify an individual as sick and in need of cure. No specific attitude, behavior, or condition is universally and uniformly construed as an indicator of mental illness, and mental illness varies from place to place and time to time. For example, feeble minds can be understood only in the context of a matrix of relationships in which certain pursuits become so central—material success, upward mobility, intellectual superiority—that anyone who does not display the appropriate levels of self-interest, emotional maturity, and cognitive ability will be branded as mentally defective (Trent, 1994).

For the medical approach to become ascendant among competing narratives, it was necessary for physicians of the mind to become widely viewed as a legitimate source of information about mental sickness and wellness, separate from both regular physicians and nonmedical practitioners. The development of a unitary and convincing concept of mental illness required a growth in the power and influence of the medical profession, especially psychiatry. More important was the development of medical therapies that could be used to treat mental illness. Physicians dealing with physical illnesses had recorded some successes (e.g., leprosy and the plague had been wiped out by the end of the nineteenth century, and malaria and smallpox had been brought under some control). Medical practitioners specializing in diseases of the mind hoped for a similar record of success (Scull, 1977b, pp. 344–345).

Before the Industrial Revolution in the United States, deviants—criminals, the poor, delinquents, the dependent, the insane—were cared for at the local level by family or friends or, when these significant others were unavailable, the local community. Families, friends, and communities became increasingly ineffective as the population grew, the number of deviants increased, and the forms of deviance changed so that it seemed to be more threatening (Rafter, 1997). Large-scale institutions were built for housing deviants of all types, leading eventually to the segregation of the insane into special institutions designed to hold only them (Rothman, 1974; Sutton, 1991).

Psychiatric Segregation

The first general hospital in the United States was built in Philadelphia by the Quakers (in 1756). It was the first U.S. hospital to care explicitly for the sick poor. Some of the sick who were admitted were diagnosed as mad and were the target of a great deal of prejudice and discrimination, even inside the institution. They were confined to the cellar of the hospital. Their scalps were shaved and a blister-inducing powder was administered. They were even periodically chained to the walls. Members of the community could pay money to be permitted to visit the hospital to view the mental patients, which served both to remind the patients of their stigmatized status and to celebrate the virtues of mental normality and psychic conformity (Conrad & Schneider, 1992, p. 48).

Mental health reformers of the nineteenth century were initially quite optimistic. They believed that treatment of the mentally ill inside a specialized institution (i.e., the asylum) would lead to their eventual cure and return to a normal life, free from psychic distress (Horwitz, 2002). The dominant view was that most mental patients were normal persons who had temporarily lost both their way and their reason because of exposure to social pressures, stresses, and temptations. A new therapy was invented called *moral therapy.* It consisted of companionship for patients, analyses of their difficulties by caring and compassionate therapists, and meaningful activities for them to do. Caregivers of the time hoped their patients would learn more effective ways of coping that would protect them from the corrupting influences of society once they were released from the asylum.

Moral therapy eventually fell into disfavor because the view of mental disorders changed. No longer were they viewed as the product of a stressful environment. A medical perspective was growing in power and popularity, and its supporters increasingly argued that mental disorders were the result of physical disease. The mad were conceptualized more and more as sick individuals in need of therapies based on science. The growth of capitalism in the United States (and Britain) altered in significant ways whatever sense of mutual responsibility and trust had existed between rich and poor, challenging substantially whatever lingering paternalism the poor (and powerless) might have received (Scull, 1977b, p. 340).

A formal view of mental illness developed that conceptualized abnormality as a natural occurrence that could be treated or even cured through medical intervention. Psychiatrists and the asylums within which they did their treatment work were inseparable, and each one reinforced the apparent value of the other. Separating the mad from other kinds of deviants (e.g., the bad or the lazy), as well as from the general population, came to be viewed as the only approach that would have any chance of success. Asylums developed into *total institutions* in which large numbers of individuals were confined together for long periods of time, sometimes for life, and all their activities—work, sleep, play—were organized and regulated (Goffman, 1961, pp. 5–6). Although these large, bureaucratic asylums were costly, what they provided seemed worth the investment. They authenticated the claim that mental problems were medical problems, while they allowed management and control of the mentally ill under more centralized authority.

Asylums initially received a great deal of positive press that portrayed them as an effective way to deal with abnormality. However, the rosy assessments were more rhetoric than reality. "Even a superficial acquaintance with the functioning of nineteenth century mental hospitals reveals how limited was the asylum's concern with the human problems of its inmates" (Scull, 1977b, pp. 346–347). By the end of the nineteenth century, asylums were little more than holding pens for people who either would not or could not adjust to a changing society. They became a repository for the most deranged and abnormal, and asylums were tainted terrain. Families would only send even grossly disabled members to them if no other option existed. Asylums were dreary places, bereft of optimism and characterized by huge buildings, rigid routine, and a stifling monotony.

Psychiatrists and paraprofessionals within the asylums, while still affirming the importance of treatment and rehabilitation, were little more than custodians for the wayward. They were adrift, separated in many ways and for many reasons from regular physicians and mainstream medicine. Cure had been replaced by custodialism, and a creeping hereditarianism challenged the earlier optimism that mental illness and insanity could be cured by the application of scientific principles. If disease was inborn, originating in the genes, what could any kind of talk-based therapy hope to do? In reality, psychiatrists could not cure the mentally ill because they lacked a coherent system of classification, empirically based theories of the etiology of diseases of the mind, and effective therapies.

Expanding Definitions

Psychiatrists were able to salvage psychiatry principally by finding a new population of patients to treat: the mentally sick in the general population who could be treated outside of asylums in community-based clinics. The chronic and severely disabled were abandoned whenever possible, left in asylums to be managed by those lower on the professional food chain (e.g., superintendents or hospital aides). They dropped the old term for their profession, *alienist,* in favor of *psychiatrist,* committing themselves more thoroughly to the idea of prevention instead of cure. Psychiatrists had a renewed sense of optimism and confidence, expecting to be able to find mental illness in its early stages and employ scientifically based cures. The outcome, they believed, would be a healthier, more efficient society (Rafter, 1997, pp. 169–170).

The use of asylums declined dramatically after World War II, and more and more patients were moved out of mental hospitals in a process of *decarceration* (Scull, 1977a). The community mental health movement became the new cure-all (p. 98). Its stated goals were to promote the reintegration of the patient into the home and community and to foster positive mental health (Leifer, 1969, p. 210). Small institutions replaced large ones;

professional personnel replaced custodial personnel; and mental patients were moved out of institutions and into community centers, halfway houses, or even their own homes. Community psychiatry expanded the medicalization of problems in living, which increased psychiatry's domain and influence (Dunham, 1976).

Psychiatrists formulated an ever-expanding definition of mental illness, and all types of problems in living became a target of community psychiatry (e.g., alcoholism, children's school adjustment problems, sleep disorders, bad marriages, drug addiction, impotence, excessive smoking, children's defiance of authority, caffeine withdrawal, job loss). Not only did community psychiatry medicalize an increasing number of human conditions, but its representatives also reported that they had found high rates of untreated mental disorders in U.S. communities. However, rather than showing that U.S. society was undergoing an unprecedented psychic meltdown, the findings of epidemiological studies were an artifact of how the information was collected. Community surveys exaggerated the number of mentally ill individuals because the questions were incapable of distinguishing expectable and reasonable reactions to life's troubling events from those reactions that made no sense at all (Horwitz & Wakefield, 2008).

Mental illnesses that were once said to be restricted to only adults are today being said to exist among youngsters, too. Representatives of the psych sector claim that it is possible for even infants and toddlers to be afflicted by major depression, posttraumatic stress disorder (PTSD), insomnia, social-anxiety disorder, and bereavement (Kluger, 2011). Any objections to the expansion of psychiatry into unchartered waters are dismissed by psychiatrists as unreasonable, being founded on a lack of knowledge about what signs to look for in these youthful sufferers. It may be true that the young are now being afflicted with the same maladies as the old, but it may also be true that this is one more way for therapists to do what they have done before: Find a new population of humans to treat for individual dysfunctions and personal maladjustments.

Decarceration could not have occurred without the development of psychoactive drugs, The development and availability of these drugs made it possible for therapists to control disordered behaviors of former patients outside of hospitals, starting in the 1950s (Scull, 1977a).

The discovery of tranquilizing drugs permitted the elimination of physical restraints such as the straightjacket, chloroform, and the "sick needle." Almost overnight, tranquilizers transformed the madhouse and made possible the introduction of psychotherapy and activity programs for patients who had previously been regarded as hopeless. (Sommer, 1976, pp. 155–156)

These drugs were far from a perfect solution. They did not cure. They only suppressed the more overt signs and symptoms of certain disorders, making patients easier to control in a nonhospital setting. They did not ensure the development of the kind of behaviors a former patient would need in the outside world. Most patients stopped taking their tranquilizers shortly after their release from the institution (Scull, 1977a, p. 89).

Decarceration was also made possible by the passage of state laws that mandated periodic review of a mentally ill individual's confinement in a mental hospital to determine if it was warranted (Walker, 2011, p. 186). Most former mental patients faced a rather bleak existence after their release from mental hospitals, with the more disordered faring the worst, as inadequate or nonexistent services for them were the order of the day (Klein, 2009). U.S. prisons and jails became holding pens for many of the mentally ill who had been decarcerated (Adams & Ferrandino, 2008; Lamb, Weinberger, & Gross, 2004; Torrey, 1995).

Currently, genetic explanations of mental illness are at the cutting edge of psychiatry, and genetic/biological explanations of abnormality have moved to the center of medical and public discourse about illness and health. Increasing knowledge about the body and brain has shifted the focus of attention even more away from psychotherapy, family dynamics, and social factors and toward psychopharmacology, neuroscience, and genomics. The choice today is not *whether* to use a talk-based therapy or a therapeutic drug. The choice is *which* type of drug works best and should be prescribed (Conrad, 2007, p. 15).

Psychiatry has reached an impressive level of success in its efforts to control its turf and define its subject matter. This monopoly, like all monopolies, can have a life of its own, seeming no longer to be nourished directly by the groups or organizations that it benefits most. The expanding net of definitions of mental disorder to include physical, cognitive, and emotional distress directs attention away from what might be bona fide illnesses and focuses more on the boundless (and ill-defined) category of "abnormality." According to Foucault (2003), the medicalization of abnormality allowed psychiatrists to claim for themselves the principal functions of protection of health and preservation of social order.

Psychiatry has established for itself a *causal permissiveness* that is difficult for anyone to successfully challenge (Foucault, 2003). Its claim that some errant hereditary factor is responsible for an imbalance in the brain, which produces problems in living and constellations of complaints, seems now to be beyond dispute and thus practically impossible to refute. Every new ailment is blamed on a new hereditary factor or brain pathology. The fact is that psychiatry has no valid and reliable understanding of how individual factors lead to most of the mental disorders or of what cures could possibly be used to heal a sick mind. What makes a medical intervention morally permissible to psychiatry is not that it is therapeutic, but that it is something a patient wants (Szasz, 1973, p. 78). Not all individuals with problems in living willingly accept medicalization of their issues. Former patients—they call themselves "psychiatric survivors"—regularly protest at American Psychiatric Association (APA) meetings to publicize what they believe are injuries inflicted by their treatments.

The Myth of Mental Illness

Madness and Metaphors

One of the more influential scripts for classifying human attitudes, behaviors, and conditions is the *Diagnostic and Statistical Manual of Mental Disorders (DSM)*, published by the American Psychiatric Association. The 2000 "text revision" of the fourth edition *(DSM-IV-TR)*, the current edition as of this writing, is the largest and most inclusive of all the *DSMs*. *DSM-IV-TR* is 943 pages long, has 16 major diagnostic categories, and describes almost 400 separate mental disorders. The only thing that all these different disorders have in common is that they all appear in *DSM-IV-TR;* any other similarity is purely coincidental (Caplan, 1995).

The manual is not a coherent framework for understanding and explaining mental disorder (but it does not attempt to be). It is an exhaustive list of clusters of signs and symptoms that the architects of the *DSM* think characterize one mental disorder or another. It simply provides a long (extremely so) list of things that a therapist *might* encounter at some point in his or her career. The manual is laboriously descriptive and completely atheoretical. The *DSM* represents a strange mix of cultural values, political compromise, scientific research, and human ailments or complaints that can be legitimately recorded on insurance claim forms (Kutchins & Kirk, 1997). Each new edition of the *DSM* expands the number of thinking, feeling, and behaving patterns—the constellation of complaints—that it medicalizes and defines as mental disorders.

What does it mean to lose a mind? You can lose weight, you can lose your hair, you can lose an earring, you can lose your money, and you can even lose your life. But how can you lose your mind? One of the best and most lucid accounts of "mind" was written by a social behaviorist named George Herbert Mead. *Thinking, mind,* or *reflexive intelligence*—Mead (1934) used these terms interchangeably—is an inner conversation through the use of symbols or significant gestures (p. 47). Mead concluded that mind and brain are not the same. The brain is a biological organ, and without it, the mind is impossible. However, the existence of a brain does not necessarily mean that an organism has a mind, and it is possible to have mental processes that may appear odd to others but that are not caused by any brain *dysfunction* or abnormality.

Psychiatrists conceptualize deviants as having experiences that could only be understood by proceeding *as if* their states of mind were diseased and responsible for their trespasses. Central to this project has been the sustained reconceptualization by psychiatry of disorders of the *mind* as actually disorders of the *brain* (Insel & Wang, 2010, pp. 1970–1971). Whatever the consequences of this for patients in terms of health and illness, it does allow psychiatrists to legitimate their interventions and treatments of patients as being based more on science than on moral philosophy or ethics. The utilization of explanations of mental illnesses founded on genetics, epigenomics (which specializes in the molecular effects of human experience), and neuroscience has strengthened psychiatry's efforts to be both scientific and successful.

To say that a person's mind is sick is like saying that the economy is sick or that a joke is (Szasz, 1973, p. 97). A metaphor is a figure of speech wherein two things are contrasted to present a new way of thinking about an old concept. "The moon is a ghostly galleon" and "she has abdominal muscles of steel" are both metaphors. These words paint pictures that help us understand the concepts, but we must not confuse a metaphor with a scientific description or a truth statement. The moon is not a boat, and no human can have abdominal muscles made of metal. When a metaphor is mistaken for reality, used to advance some group's interests more than others, then we have the makings of myth. The *mythical* nature of the claim that minds can be sick was eventually forgotten (Conrad & Schneider, 1992, p. 47).

Individual Dysfunction or Social Deviance?

Psychiatrists have crafted a definition of mental illness that makes "losing a mind" look entirely individualistic (i.e., no social factors need apply), objective, and uniformly debilitating. In the *DSM-IV-TR*, a lengthy definition of *mental disorder* is included (the term "mental *illness*" rarely appears), a portion of which is reproduced below:

> [Each mental disorder is conceptualized as] a clinically significant behavioral or psychological syndrome or pattern that occurs in an individual and that is associated with present distress (e.g., a painful symptom) or disability (i.e., impairment in one or more important areas of functioning) or with a significantly increased risk of suffering death, pain, disability, or an important loss of freedom. (APA, 2000, p. xxxi)

The authors of this definition emphasize that these syndromes or patterns absolutely *cannot* be an "expectable" or "culturally sanctioned" response to a particular event (p. xxxi). The disorder must be a manifestation of a *dysfunction* in an *individual* (behavioral, psychological, or biological). Neither deviant behavior (political, religious, or sexual) nor conflicts between an individual and society are mental disorders *unless* they are a symptom of some individual dysfunction (p. xxxi). This conceptualization of mental illness creates a false separation between those people whose life experiences make no sense and everybody else.

Psychiatrists' desire to separate deviance, interpersonal conflicts, and all the rest from an individual dysfunction of mental disorder is based on little more than wishful thinking. They really have no way to know an individual dysfunction when they spot one or separate it from "expectable" and "culturally sanctioned" responses (Caplan, 1995; Fernando, 1991). Mental disorder is a vague, ambiguous, and confusing term. Human behaviors, thoughts, and feelings are just too diverse to be neatly separated into the two categories of "sick" or "healthy."

It may come as a surprise to learn that psychiatry was disinclined to define mental disorder in early editions of the *DSM*. In one sense, this reluctance does make sense. It made it possible for psychiatrists to diagnose and then treat practically anything they wanted to treat. The only requirement was that this thing being treated not be entirely normal. Ultimately, it became both embarrassing and potentially injurious to the success of psychiatry to be unable to offer a definition of mental illness. So, over 135 years after the founding of the American Psychiatric Association and after going through two editions (in 1952 and 1968), *mental disorder* was finally defined in *DSM-III*, published in 1980 (Kutchins & Kirk, 1997, p. 29). The definition of mental illness really didn't do much to help clear up the mystery of exactly what mental illness is or how to separate it from related deviances. It did, however, offer a definition that could be used by the APA as one more tool in its quest to amass more and more patients (Kirk & Kutchins, 1992). (The American Psychiatric Association started in 1844 as the Association of Medical Superintendents of American Institutions for the Insane; changed its name in 1892 to the American Medico-Psychological Association; and changed its name again in 1921 to the current one.)

Individuals both inside and outside of the mental health field are skeptical that disorders can be differentiated from non-disorders or that *mental* problems can be neatly separated from problems that are physical, behavioral, social, or moral (Kirk & Kutchins, 1992, p. 226). In fact, the architects of *DSM-IV-TR*, in a moment of unusual candor, confess as much:

In *DSM-IV[-TR]*, there is no assumption that each category of mental disorder is a completely discrete entity with absolute boundaries dividing it from other mental disorders or from no mental disorder. There is also no assumption that all individuals described as having the same mental disorder are alike in all important ways. (APA, 2000, p. xxxi)

This is quite a remarkable statement! It acknowledges that mental disorders cannot be separated from each other or even from a condition called "no mental disorder." According to this excerpt, individuals who have been given the same diagnostic label are not even necessarily alike in terms of the defining features of the diagnosis, let alone in terms of other biological, psychological, or social factors. If psychiatrists, who have the strongest incentive to formulate a definition of mental disorder that is beyond reproach, can do no better than they have done, then it probably cannot *be* done.

Diagnostic Dilemmas and Difficulties

It defies common sense, logic, and all that we know about human attitudes, behaviors, and conditions to believe seriously that it is possible to distinguish the socially acceptable from the socially unacceptable in terms of some individual dysfunction. Determining mental illness is an ineradicably social process of deciding who is normal and who is not that has little to do with a diagnosed individual's physical characteristics (Turner & Edgley, 1996, p. 434). What wayward chemical or brain pathology could possibly exist to differentiate all those individuals who hear socially *acceptable* voices, such as God's or Allah's, from all those individuals who hear the socially *un*acceptable voices of space invaders or some dead relative?

What wayward chemical or brain pathology could possibly distinguish the socially *acceptable* pretending of children, adolescents, actors, magicians, defense attorneys, lovers, parents, flatterers, and inveiglers from the socially *unacceptable* pretending of people who claim to be (and may believe that they are) Napoleon, Jesus Christ, or Santa Claus? It is easy to see how a society could make clear distinctions between the sick and the well or between the acceptable and the unacceptable; it is much more difficult to see how neurochemistry could (Turner & Edgley, 1996). Any effort to define mental disorder in some objective and uniform way is doomed to failure.

When the primary diagnostic strategy of a medical specialty is to create diseases mainly through naming and proclaiming—as psychiatry is prone to do—it can produce all kinds of difficulties and dilemmas for its practitioners. This can be seen with the example of autism. This is a heterogeneous category that includes conditions that are diagnosed early in a child's life (before the age of 3) and includes difficulties in interacting or communicating with others or the presence of repetitive behaviors (e.g., throwing a wooden stick up in the air again and again to watch it bounce on the ground over and over). One of the disorders included in the category is a condition in which people have trouble interacting with others despite having normal or even high intelligence (called Asperger's disorder).

The APA is planning to narrow how autism will be diagnosed in the next edition of the *DSM*. (For example, Asperger's disorder would no longer be classified as an autistic disorder.) The problem is that families who currently have a member who has been diagnosed with autism are understandably alarmed by the proposed change. They fear that it would influence the available research monies, government funding in schools to help with troubled children, and the payments made by insurance companies. The APA claims that it is only going to make the changes to remove inconsistencies and mis-understandings (Rochman, 2012). If history is any guide, it is unlikely that greater consistency and clarity will be the outcome of the APA's diagnostic prestidigitations.

Finding and diagnosing mental illness is problematic, because mental ill-ness is not itself a *specific* type of attitude, behavior, or condition. Mental illness is a name that is attached to a constellation of signs and symptoms, a constellation that is both wide and heterogeneous (Goode, 2011). Szasz (1973) nicely illustrates the variable and relative nature of mental illness while showing the folly of searching for biological causes of it:

> If you believe that you are Jesus, or have discovered a cure for cancer (and have not), or the Communists are after you (and they are not)—then your beliefs are likely to be regarded as symptoms of schizophrenia. But if you believe that the Jews are the Chosen People, or that Jesus was the Son of God, or that Communism is the only scientifically and morally correct form of government—then your beliefs are likely to be regarded as reflections of who you are: Jew, Christian, Communist. This is why I think that we will discover the chemical cause of schizophrenia when we will discover the chemical cause of Judaism, Christianity, and Communism. No sooner and no later. (pp. 101–102)

Psychiatry has tried to calm its critics by convincing them that it is doing both good science and good medicine and that mental illnesses are really no different from physical illnesses. The factual basis of this claim is suspect. A human cadaver can have physical illnesses that are no different from what living humans can have, such as cancer, pneumonia, or a myocardial infarc-tion. However, a cadaver most certainly cannot have a mental illness (Szasz, 1973, p. 87).

Sharp lines between the normal and the abnormal cannot be drawn in the murky world of right/wrong, legal/illegal, proper/improper, healthy/sick, moral/immoral—that is, in the complex and ever-changing world of rules and rule breaking—and when lines are drawn, they have more to do with sociocultural settings, languages, meanings, and interpersonal conflicts than with an individual's body chemistry or brain structure. Any psychological disorder tells us not only about the anguish of an individual but also about patterns of interaction: what they are and how they unfold over time (Banton, Clifford, Frosh, Lousada, & Rosenthall, 1985, p. 74). Despite a multitude of uncertainties and disagreements in regard to what qualifies as mental illness and who exactly has one, it is beyond dispute that a large number of groups have a vested interest in what the *DSM* says about mental illness—how it is defined and what it covers (Kupfer & Regier, 2010). This includes physicians, patients, hospitals, drug companies, psychologists, social workers, nurses, medical insurers, and taxpayers.

Declaration that an individual has a mental illness, rather than being based on sophisticated knowledge of disease, is really a judgment about one individual's personal, social, and ethical problems in living, offered by others who do not share or subscribe to the same understandings (Szasz, 1974, p. 262; see also Szasz, 1960). The basic struggle for survival in the human kingdom is a struggle over *words:* name or be named, define or be defined (Szasz, 1973, p. 20). The only way that a judgment could be rendered that an individual who claims to be Santa Claus (or to be Jesus Christ or to be persecuted by the FBI or the communists) is mentally sick is for a definer to conclude that this claim is false by comparing it to other claims that he or she believes are healthier and happier. Mental illness is a practical accomplishment of people acting together. It cannot be understood apart from the methods and procedures that we use to make the phenomenon describable (Blum, 1970, p. 32). In order to find witches, we must already know what they are and how to identify them. The same goes for mental illness (Szasz, 1970).

Psychiatric Imperialism

Transcultural psychiatry (and global mental health) is the new growth industry for psychiatry. Its stated objective is to develop diagnoses and treatments to improve the lives of the mentally disordered, wherever they may be found (Patel & Prince, 2010). In Appendix I of the *DSM-IV-TR* the authors wrestle with a fundamental paradox of both the document and the edifice of psychiatry to the extent that it passes itself off as providing universally applicable and value-free approaches to mental disorders. It is here that a glossary of culture-bound syndromes is delineated and described, along with another remarkable statement:

> Although presentations conforming to the major DSM-IV[-TR] categories can be found throughout the world, the particular symptoms, course, and social response are very often influenced by local cultural factors. (APA, 2000, p. 898)

The APA undercuts the fundamental plank of its definition of abnormality that specifies that a mental disorder exists *only if* it is an individual dysfunction and *only if* it is not "merely" an expectable and culturally sanctioned response to a particular event. So, we are told about *amok* (a violent outburst against people and objects in response to a perceived slight or insult); *brain fag* (a term used originally in West Africa to describe a condition found among high school or university students in which they have trouble thinking, concentrating, and remembering); and *koro* (an intense anxiety in males over the fear that the penis will withdraw back into the body, causing death; in females, a fear that the vulva and nipples will recede into the body, also with lethal consequences). (Twenty-five culture-bound syndromes are listed in Appendix I, along with additional regional variations.)

Cross-cultural syndromes of mental *illness* (in Appendix I of the *DSM-IV-TR*, for the first time, the word *illness* does appear) prove by their very existence that mental illnesses vary by geographical region and cultural expectations. So, by the APA's own admission, mental illness is not necessarily an individual dysfunction with uniform and universal signs and symptoms. More and more individuals (professional and nonprofessional) are concluding that Western psychiatry (and the *DSM*) is particularly inapplicable, inappropriate, ineffective, and incomplete in cross-cultural settings. What is required is a more culturally sensitive definition of mental illness, along with therapies that can be applied cross-culturally, in order for psychiatry to have any relevance for global issues (Wedenoja, 2006, p. 1962).

The anthropological literature on cross-cultural variations in mental illness does permit a few conclusions. First, a relatively small percentage of people in societies across the globe are severely and chronically disordered due to their high levels of irrationality and their inability to fulfill even the minimal requirements of participation in social life. This is true, but it is not the whole truth. Although attitudes, behaviors, and conditions that are defined as products of mental disorders are recognized in most places and times, these disorders are conceptualized in a multitude of ways. No human characteristic has universal significance or meaning; time, place, and situation always exert an influence. *Eudysphoria* is dysphoria (i.e., anxiety or distress) that is viewed positively and as worthwhile. In the Mediterranean region, displays of suffering and misfortune are valued and valuable, being both functional and admired. Those who suffer are viewed as no different from individuals who have been divinely blessed, and the ability to experience suffering and sadness demarcates the mature personality. For Buddhists, eudysphoria occurs because thoughts of worthlessness or meaninglessness are considered to be indicative of insight and spiritual transcendence (Gaines, 2006, p. 870).

A second conclusion is that most people who act in strange ways do not do so in an extreme or chronic fashion, and the labeling of people as mentally ill is a complex matter, influenced by a wide range of regional factors (Goode, 2011, pp. 293–294). Scheff (1984) asserts that the mentally ill have actually violated a *residual rule,* a rule associated with no label other than one that indicates a mental abnormality. It is as if some of the violations of expectations prompt humans to quickly go through names for normative departures, searching for the one that fits best. If individuals break the law, they are criminals; if they drink to excess, they are drunkards; if they misuse drugs, they are addicts; if they don't use good manners when eating, they are boors. However, if individuals think they have bee hives in their stomachs or that their ideas turn into butterflies, things are different. It is clear that something is wrong, but it is not entirely clear what it might be. At this point, a residual rule has been violated, and so the residual label of "crazy," "mad," "insane," or "just plain nuts" is most likely. The label of mental illness can be called into service as a wastebasket category to cover all those distressing attitudes, behaviors, and conditions that have no specific label of their own.

The changing demographics of U.S. society pose a challenge, if not an insurmountable obstacle, to U.S. psychiatry and any clinical approach influenced by it (Garcia & Petrovich, 2011, pp. 2–3). The United States is a nation of immigrants, and the existence of so much diversity based on race, ethnicity, national origin, religion, class, sex, gender, and geography poses genuine difficulties for any therapeutic approach founded on an assumption of inherent pathology and homogeneity of experiences. According to Garcia and Petrovich, one thing that would help the psychiatric enterprise is the addition of the idea of *intersectionality,* an understanding of the ways that an individual's statuses and cultural factors affect one another, and how the intersections of various factors influence individuals and their lived experiences (pp. 4–32). The value of considering how society and culture work together to influence individuals is, of course, well understood by social scientists, but it undercuts the core requirement of psychiatry that mental illnesses be individual dysfunctions. Rather than some poorly defined notion of mental health, cultural competence and resilience may be more reasonable treatment objectives (pp. 41–48).

Mental Health Buccaneers and Social Control

At one time, the number and type of wayward events to which the label mental illness was attached were small, but things have changed.

> The variety of conditions currently regarded as mental illnesses, the large number and wide distribution of people who presumably suffer from these illnesses, and the great number of professionals who treat them are unprecedented. The reasons mental illnesses have proliferated in modern life stem from specific social and historical circumstances and from the interests of particular groups that benefit from classifying psychological conditions as states of illness. (Horwitz, 2002, p. 208)

Though many groups and professions benefit from a society-wide interest in being mentally healthy (Herman, 1995), psychiatry sits at the top of the heap (Dowbiggin, 1991). This medical specialty has a near monopoly over definitions of mental health and mental illness, and its practitioners have a disproportionate influence over the treatment and cure of mental disorders. It is impossible to talk about mental illness without discussing the structure and function of psychiatry and the central role that it plays in the definition and treatment of it.

The search for biochemical causes of mental disorders and the confidence that they will always be found is what allows psychiatrists to stay at the top of the mental health hierarchy. This is what legitimates psychiatry as a medical specialty (Breggin, 1991, p. 23). Psychiatrists are able to claim that they, just like all other physicians, specialize in the discovery and treatment of pathological body structures that just happen to cause diseased minds. When psychiatrists were unable to find structural abnormalities in the brain and trace them to particular signs and symptoms of mental illness—the usual situation—they were not discouraged. They merely *invented* mental diseases through the simple but effective strategy of proclaiming that certain specific attitudes, behaviors, and conditions were sick and in need of cure. They hoped that they would eventually find some biochemical or genetic abnormality to go along with each newly named disease (Kutchins & Kirk, 1997; Szasz, 1974, p. 12).

Critics of psychiatry deplore the arbitrary and pseudoscientific way that psychiatrists determine what is sick and what is not. Armstrong (1993) took psychiatrists to task for using what she calls the *Peter Pan method* to create and validate diagnostic categories: Clap if you believe in fairies (p. 152). In this case, the "fairies" are conditions like schizophrenia, simple phobia, and posttraumatic stress disorder. Only the hopelessly naive or extremely gullible could believe that high consensus among psychiatrists is the same thing as the scientific discovery of mental disease. Breggin (1991), himself a psychiatrist, also criticized his colleagues in the profession: "Only in psychiatry is the existence of physical disease determined by APA presidential proclamations, by committee decisions, and even, at times, by a vote of the members of APA, not to mention the courts" (p. 141). The opinions of psychiatrists are part of what they judge, and mental disorders are not separable from the language that names and interprets them (Kovel, 1988, p. 134). Modern psychiatry has achieved the enviable position in which proclamations are taken as truth, wishes can become achievements, and propaganda is taken as science (Breggin, p. 182).

Psychiatrists have tried to align themselves more closely with specialists in brain abnormalities, laboring to convince the public, health insurance companies, and the federal government that psychiatry is a bona fide medical science (Szasz, 1985, p. 712).

[Organized psychiatry] develops media relationships, hires PR firms, develops its medical image, holds press conferences to publicize its products, lobbies on behalf of its interests, and issues "scientific" reports that protect its members from malpractice suits by lending legitimacy to brain-damaging technologies. (Breggin, 1991, pp. 366–367)

Some therapists will admit that good psychiatry is an art more than a science, requiring skills not taught in medical school, such as compassion, sensitivity, insight, and intuition. This admission, true though it may be, does blur the line between psychiatry on the one hand and science, art, and religion on the other (Neill, 1995, p. 219).

What are psychiatrists? Are they brain doctors, mind doctors, body doctors, friends and confidants, sages, healers, spiritual advisers, philosophers, entrepreneurs, cops in lab coats, or overpaid social workers? Psychiatry is at a turning point. Its practitioners can abandon their traditional concern with the mind and specialize in the treatment of the brain. However, if they do this, they will be indistinguishable from neurologists. An alternate path is to start worrying more about the mind and leave the brain alone. If they choose this route, however, they will be little different from nonmedical therapists and counselors. (It practically goes without saying that many models of madness exist, and psychiatrists disagree among themselves over some fundamental issues in regard to mental illness and mental health [Gallagher, 2002].)

Psychiatric intervention is used at times to handle unruly or errant populations, such as the insane, the deranged, the idle, the ignorant, or even the deprived. The psychiatrization of more and more problems in living makes it quite likely that what are actually manifestations of *social* problems are being refurbished as individual problems of adjustment (Szasz, 1997, p. 215). Caplan (1995) provides an excellent example of this. At a clinic where she was employed early in her career as a clinical psychologist, she was told by her supervisor that her job was *not* to attempt to find better jobs or additional welfare monies for the poor families who came to the clinic for help (even though that is what Caplan believed they really needed). Her charge was to find some appropriate psychiatric label that would fit her clients' complaints and then to suggest some appropriate medical treatment—such as psychotherapy—that was an established part of traditional mental health care (p. 280).

One of the populations that psychiatry has controlled is children, almost always under the guise of helping them. The psych deck, however, has been stacked against them. Not only are they young and powerless, but they are also defined by psychiatrists as having individual dysfunctions, and they have probably alienated central figures in their families, their schools, and their communities. The claim that some children have serious mental disorders can serve as a convenient smokescreen.

> Poverty was let off the hook. Social injustices were let off the hook. Parents were let off the hook. Lousy schools and dysfunctional teachers were let off the hook. There was simply something biologically wrong with these children that accounted for all the things that teachers, parents, and Boy Scout leaders did not like about a whole panoply of childhood behaviors: not sitting still, not paying attention, not learning to read correctly (on time), butting in. (Armstrong, 1993, p. 196)

Psychiatrists cannot determine in any scientific way how many of children's problems in living are individual dysfunctions and how many are actually normal responses to abnormal situations. Psychiatrists cannot even agree on exactly *who* would benefit from psychiatric treatment. Are we talking about behavioral misfits, the emotionally ruined, the angry, the unmotivated, the irresponsible, the intractable, the socially deprived, the abused, the maladjusted, the promiscuous, the frigid, the rigid, the amoral, the immoral, the insane, the depressed, the hyperactive, all of the above, or none of the above?

What gets a child defined as mentally ill is almost always a persistent conflict or disagreement with some adult authority figure. Most of these children usually have little difficulty getting along with their peers in situations of their own making. To call a lack of fit between children and adults a mental illness of the child is at best a distortion and at worst an outright lie. Too much is blamed on the child and not enough on the people with whom he or she must cope or situations the child must handle successfully. Practically any characteristic of children that irritates, interferes with, or troubles authority figures can be medicalized and used to justify psychiatric intervention into children's lives. A child's inappropriateness may be little more than a method of adapting to what seems to the child to be an intolerable or undecipherable situation (Breggin & Breggin, 1994, p. 114).

In some cases and at some times, no rush existed to intervene in the lives of individuals, and psychiatrists used a great deal of restraint in their dealings with problem behaviors. Some parents have children who are markedly disordered, being a threat to themselves and to others. They have done all they could to understand their children's problems and correct them, but to no avail. They know something must be done to change the behaviors and attitudes of their self-destructive, violent, troubled youngsters, but they don't know what to do. The problem in these cases is not too much medicine, cognitive therapy, or psychiatric intervention; it is too little (J. Warner, 2010). One strategy employed by some adults who are suffering from problems in living is to accept (or even actively pursue) a medical diagnosis for the benefits it provides but reject any stigma that accompanies it.

Sense and Nonsense in the Psychiatric Enterprise

A script for human experience that is formal, shared, and viewed as inviolable gives the impression that certain experiences are far more reasonable, healthy, necessary, normal, and uniform than they really are. Unsurprisingly, people who have taken a great deal of time and trouble to master a particular script—learning its language, coming to believe in its importance and value, appreciating its logic—have trouble accepting that it is just one script among many. People march to a different beat because they hear a different drummer, but ideal scripts tend to make it appear that only one beat exists. Psychiatric nomenclature, along with the medicalization of problems in living that it creates and justifies, is characterized by a great deal of ethnocentrism and the imposition of standards of health and normality on people for whom they are inadequate (Bartholomew, 1997). A growing tendency exists in U.S. society to find psychological abnormality where there is only pathos and to believe that problems in living can be cured by attaching a medical diagnosis and a code number to each one (Kutchins & Kirk, 1997).

The authors of the *DSM* claim that logic, science, and well-conducted research have all worked together to tell them what is normal and what is not. However, the *DSM* has little to do with science. In fact, according to Caplan (1995), it is "shockingly unscientific" (p. 31). The contents of the manual are determined primarily by the gatekeeping efforts of the small number of influential psychiatrists who have the directive to decide which disorders will be allowed to appear and which will not (p. 185). The *DSM* was constructed primarily to benefit psychiatrists (and other mental health professionals), not their patients (Kovel, 1988). A handbook of mental disorders gives psychiatrists many benefits. It gives them a sense of competency and control, it gives them some professional respectability, and it gives them legitimacy and credibility. If psychiatrists cannot reliably and correctly diagnose a patient's mental illness, how can they treat it? It also allows them to know which diagnoses will result in compensation from health insurers (Grob & Horwitz, 2010, p. 111; Kirk & Kutchins, 1992, p. 219).

As the *DSM* has gone through its many revisions, it has expanded its list of mental disorders and lost both its sense of proportion and its utility as a guidebook that could reasonably help people to overcome some debilitating human afflictions.

> A comprehensive medically oriented diagnostic manual could be helpful for some purposes, but only if it were much narrower in scope, included only clearly distinguishable mental disorders that entail severe consequences and didn't pander to insurers, drug companies and therapists by medicalizing so many social problems. (Kirk & Kutchins, 1994, p. A17)

If architects of the *DSM* had packaged their document as what it is—a sourcebook of diagnoses based on a sampling of studies of unknown validity and reliability, as well as on ethics, values, hunches of psychiatrists (and others in the mental health field), reflecting political pressures, tradition, and economic/business decisions—it could be honestly accepted or rejected. As it stands now, it is an ailing document. Though reasonable people can disagree over what should or should not be included in a manual of mental disorders, they must agree that the definitions of terms and ailments in the *DSM* are fuzzy and that people—therapists and nontherapists—use them without much precision (Kirk & Kutchins, 1992, pp. 185–186).

Some of the fuzziness of the *DSM-IV-TR* can be appreciated by examining some of the disorders that appear on its pages. One of these is the *disorder of written expression* (APA, 2000, pp. 54–56). The essential feature of this disorder is that a person's writing skills (as measured by standardized tests) are "substantially below" those expected given the individual's chronological age, measured intelligence, and age-appropriate education. The presence of this disorder is indicated by such things as grammatical or punctuation errors within sentences, poor paragraph organization, multiple spelling errors, and excessively poor handwriting. What is wrong with this picture? Though a few students may be bad writers because they have sick minds, the manual provides no clue about how to separate them from those who are poor writers because they were poorly trained or were unresponsive to writing instruction. The *mathematics disorder* (pp. 53–54) covers individuals who are unable to learn multiplication tables, to carry numbers correctly, to decode word problems, to obey mathematical signs, or to copy numbers or figures correctly. Once again, something that can have many causes (and is really only a problem in places where math skills are necessary for daily living or success in school) is transformed into an individual pathology through the process of naming and proclaiming. Perhaps the most unclear of the lot is the *learning disorder not otherwise specified,* which covers learning disorders that *do not* meet the criteria for any other learning disorder:

> This category might include problems in all three areas (reading, mathematics, written expression) that together significantly interfere with academic achievement even though performance on tests measuring each individual skill is not substantially below that expected given the person's chronological age, measured intelligence, and age-appropriate education. (p. 56)

Practically any problems relating to learning could be pigeonholed here, regardless of test scores, any of which could be average, above average, or even far above average. The APA seems to have covered all its bases.

The *DSM-IV-TR* includes Appendix B, a list of proposed disorders that require further study (APA, 2000, pp. 759–818). Each of the proposed disorders, the authors claim, was subjected to a careful empirical review, and wide commentary was solicited from the field (p. 759). Each one apparently failed to receive the kind of support necessary to warrant making it a bona fide disorder in the body of the text. One wonders how one of these— *caffeine withdrawal*—was subjected to this "careful empirical review and wide commentary from the field." One also wonders why it is not a bona fide disorder in the body of the text. The diagnostic criteria of caffeine withdrawal are heavy caffeine use; some physical withdrawal symptoms from abrupt cessation of caffeine (headaches, marked fatigue or drowsiness, marked anxiety or depression, nausea or vomiting); and clinically significant distress or impairment in social, occupational, or other important areas of functioning. How hard can it be to find someone who fits this profile? The most baffling thing, however, is that caffeine withdrawal *does* get included in the manual, but in a sneaky way. On page 234, "caffeine-related disorder not otherwise specified" is listed, along with its own code (292.9), as one of the substance-related disorders. This diagnosis is reserved for "disorders associated with the use of caffeine that are not classifiable as Caffeine Intoxication, Caffeine-Induced Anxiety Disorder, or Caffeine-Induced Sleep Disorder" (p. 234). To illustrate this "not otherwise specified" disorder, the APA directs readers to caffeine withdrawal and its research criteria in Appendix B on page 764! As Alice said on her journey through the looking glass, "Curiouser and curiouser!"

The kind of disorders we have been examining—learning disorders or caffeine withdrawal—seem to lack enough rigor and precision to be considered serious entries in a manual of mental disorders. Still, we would expect the classic disorders, such as schizophrenia, to be the model of objectivity and scientific precision. However, research into the causes and nature of schizophrenia is both extensive and contradictory. A dazzling array of symptoms is exhibited by schizophrenics, and about 20 distinct explanations have been proposed to make sense of the disorder (Gallagher, 2002, p. 84). Heinrichs (1993) reviewed 70 years of research on schizophrenia. His principal conclusion was that very little is known or understood about it and that it suffers from a *heterogeneity problem,* a polite way of saying that the term is used in so many different ways to cover so many different things that it is losing much of its meaning. Things have changed little, according to Feldman (2009). He concludes that people diagnosed with schizophrenia show "significant differences" in their constellation of signs and symptoms, even when they are labeled with the same diagnostic category (p. 469).

Whatever schizophrenia is, it is not pure abnormality, and, if it is a disease, it is one of the most peculiar around. As Strauss (1991) commented, "Schizophrenia is very different from an illness like a broken leg. You cannot break a leg, take off the cast in order to play football, and then, after the game, put on the cast again and be an invalid" (p. 82). An individual who displays mentally disordered behaviors under some situations (e.g., stress or social isolation) may be perfectly normal or healthy under different situations (e.g., less stressful conditions or when their social support networks are strong) (Goode, 2011, p. 280). Schizophrenics can alternate back and forth between normality and abnormality on a moment-to-moment, hour-to-hour, or day-to-day basis (Strauss, 1991, p. 83). Schizophrenia has been branded as a defective, deficient, disrupted, and disorganized construct (Wiener, 1991, p. 205).

Cross-cultural data indicate that social and cultural factors have a powerful impact on the course of schizophrenia. Schizophrenia in Third World countries is neither as debilitating for sufferers nor as disruptive of their relationships as it is in the Western world (R. Warner, 2008, p. 244). In order to maximize the chances for recovery from the seriously debilitating effects of schizophrenia, the schizophrenic must be given genuine responsibilities, usually in the form of important work, that are neither too much nor too little for his or her capabilities. The schizophrenic must also not be exposed to the extremes of emotional contagion (such as either smothering or condemnation).

In countries where the hallucinations and delusions that regularly accompany schizophrenia are credited to supernatural forces and not blamed on some individual dysfunction, the mentally ill may actually experience *less* alienation, rejection, and stigma. Many times in Third World countries, the signs and symptoms of schizophrenia actually *elevate* the status of any individual who has them. "In non-industrial cultures throughout the world, the hallucinations and altered states of consciousness produced by psychosis, fasting, sleep deprivation, social isolation and contemplation, and hallucinogenic drug use are often a prerequisite for gaining shamanic power" (R. Warner, 2008, p. 249). In nonindustrial societies of the Third World, human labor power is valued for its contributions to the well-being of the community even if it is done by a mentally ill individual.

The *DSMization* of problems in living and constellations of complaints— meaning they are included in the book and defined as individual dysfunctions—practically guarantees that the mentally ill will be more isolated and alienated from the community as a whole. This can intensify the very problems complained of in the first place. Social isolation of the schizophrenic, both before and after a flare-up of the disorder, is found consistently to be one of the best predictors of poor treatment outcome for those who suffer from it. It practically goes without saying that the way that schizophrenia is treated in the West has all the elements necessary to exacerbate the problems of the mentally ill. "In the Third World, it appears, the person with a psychotic disorder is more likely to retain his or her self-esteem, a feeling of value to the community and a sense of belonging" (R. Warner, 2008, p. 251). Psychoactive drugs, shock therapy, surgery, hospitalization, MRIs, CT scans, and the rest of what is at the disposal of Western medicine fail to accomplish any of these integrative, assimilative functions often enough for us to have much confidence in their long-term efficacy.

Depressive symptoms are also influenced by sociocultural factors. The increase in depressive symptoms as individuals age is due principally to poor physical health, loss of one's spouse, and unemployment (specifically, unemployment's adverse impact on lifestyle and finances). If individuals stay married, productive, socially involved, financially well-off, and healthy, mental health improves with advancing age (Clarke, Marshall, House, & Lantz, 2011). Young adults are able to cope with disappointments in their lives, along with whatever depression they can produce, if they have sufficient levels of *adaptive resilience*, which is a willingness to try again after some failure or the inclination to find something positive in the fact that they did not accomplish all that they wanted to accomplish (Reynolds & Baird, 2010, pp. 160–166). When depression is found among the young, one critical reason is that depressed teenagers are inclined to withdraw from friends over time, meaning they have few friends to help them overcome their episodes of depression (Schaefer, Kornienko, & Fox, 2011).

Meltdown in the *DSM*

The APA has occasionally messed with the wrong group and then found itself the target of unwanted attacks. Sometimes these conflicts are little more than skirmishes, but other times they are outright wars over the validity and reliability of some of the mental disorders that psychiatrists include in the manual. For example, the gay community successfully pressed its claim that homosexuality is not a mental illness, and it was eventually omitted from psychiatric nomenclature (Bayer, 1981). No doubt, similar battles would have been fought over many more of the disorders in the manual if other offended groups had been able to muster the resources to challenge organized psychiatry's monopoly over determining what is normal and what is not. One group that the APA has consistently offended, or even outraged, is women. Women's battles with psychiatry show that tension and discord are at the heart of any effort to pigeonhole behavior and people, especially if those people prefer to be left alone and have the resources and abilities to defend themselves. When psychiatrists took on women, they had a tigress by the tail.

In the *DSM*'s third, revised edition (*DSM-III-R*; APA, 1987), an appendix appeared that included three disorders that were classified as needing further study: sadistic personality disorder, self-defeating personality disorder, and late luteal phase dysphoric disorder (LLPDD). The first two were cast out of *DSM-IV/DSM-IV-TR*, but the last was renamed premenstrual dysphoric disorder (PDD) and included in Appendix B. *Premenstrual dysphoric disorder* essentially transforms women's more extreme premenstrual experiences—anxiety, depression, irritability, despondency, anger—into a mental disorder. The APA apparently does not really consider PDD a *proposed* diagnosis that requires further study (the logic of appearing in Appendix B), because it *does* appear in the body of the text as a "depressive disorder not otherwise specified" (APA, 2000, p. 381). A disorder that is relegated to a provisional appendix can apparently be called into service as a bona fide mental disorder when the need arises.

In the 1950s, Katherine Dalton, a British physician, concluded that women's raging hormones were responsible for their mood swings and antisocial behavior that became especially prevalent during premenstrual periods. Dalton and an associate called this constellation of hormonally caused afflictions "premenstrual syndrome," or PMS (Francoeur, 1996, p. 44). PMS is a diagnosis that ratifies a nineteenth-century belief that women were uncontrollably swayed by the sex hormones produced by their ovaries. These hormones were blamed for premenstrual tension, and premenstrual tension was blamed for women's apparent inability to work and to carry out other social responsibilities (Frank, 1931; Rittenhouse, 1991, p. 419). Critics of the view that PMS is a clinical medical disorder believe that too much hoopla has been generated over far too little.

Even if significant monthly changes can be found in premenstrual women, they may have more to do with social relationships and how women interpret their physical changes than they do with raging hormones and ovarian dysfunctions. Some women do experience a debilitating syndrome of maladies on a regular basis, but this can hardly be typical for most women or even for a substantial minority of them. No consistent biological markers have been found to separate PMS women from non-PMS women, and practically all women handle what they must handle—jobs, children, households, relationships—regardless of how they feel during their menstrual periods. A woman's mood swings have a lot to do with the quality of her life. Representatives of different *social domains*—groups of people who share views, concerns, and commitments—continue to contest the status of PMS as a mental illness, and PMS continues to be a different construct to different audiences: women, health and mental health practitioners, and scientists (Figert, 1995, p. 58).

Premenstrual changes—physical, mental, emotional—may occur in women (to a greater or lesser degree), but these altered states are not necessarily mental disorders. Women who do report the most acute problems live in situations that are characterized by high levels of stress, poverty, insecurity, and abuse. The treatments that seem to help these women the most are participation in self-help groups, changes in diet, and increases in exercise (Caplan, 1995, p. 156). According to Caplan, some women may feel depressed, angry, or irritable all the time, but they may notice it more during their periods or believe that it is more legitimate for them to give expression to these feelings when they are premenstrual (p. 162).

Women's growing independence and assertiveness, as well as their anger over persistent gender inequality, can be inauthenticated or delegitimized by attributing them to PMS. This social transformation of the political into the biological helps to "cool out" interpersonal tensions. Women may be less likely to vent their fury—or to unite with others to identify mutual problems and work to eradicate them—when they define the turbulence in their lives as physical, abnormal, and transitory (Laws, 1983). Martin (1992, pp. 120–121) reported that PMS is branded as a serious individual problem at those points in time when it is necessary to keep women out of the labor force and in the home. When women were needed to assist in the war effort, little attention was paid to PMS. However, when men returned from war and needed jobs, women were nudged back into more traditional roles by the discovery (or rediscovery) of the crippling effects of PMS. When women's participation in the labor force is seen as a threat, menstruation is more likely to be construed as a liability.

Some of the same disease-mongering and diagnostic imperialism that psychiatry has shown with women and female conditions is being found increasingly with men and male conditions. Men's aging experiences, along with some features of male sexuality, have been medicalized, making them look more undesirable as they are portrayed as treatable. Many men do feel anxious over some of the physical changes they undergo, and some would like to slow them down or stop them altogether. In this medicalization of male conditions, one of the biggest winners may well be the pharmaceutical industry, which supplies the pills to make many of the promised transformations possible.

> Concerns with aging and performance are propelling men to seek medical solutions for declining signs of masculinity. The perception of these physical changes as threats to traditional characteristics of manliness is not universal, but it seems to be increasing as pharmaceutical and medical entrepreneurs seek to establish markets, amplify male anxieties, and provide solutions to the problems of aging men. The medicalization of aging male bodies requires the joint action of men who seek solutions for a perceived decline in masculinity and the medical treatments that are offered to reinvigorate significant attributes of such masculinity. The partial medicalization of andropause and hair loss and the huge success of Viagra may be only the beginning. (Conrad, 2007, p. 45)

The question really isn't whether men should be upset by the physical changes that occur as they age. The question is whether psychiatrists and other therapists are acting properly to define these changes as abnormal conditions in need of a cure. Most every male will experience unreasonable pressure to regain his youth in light of the promises and propaganda.

Three features of changing masculinity that have been targeted for medical concern and treatment are andropause or male menopause (a decline in testosterone levels that is sometimes correlated with weakness, depression, asexuality, and unhappiness); baldness; and erectile dysfunction.

When natural and often inevitable biological changes can be linked together and portrayed as a "syndrome" of unwanted but treatable conditions, it pathologizes ordinary or at least expectable human conditions. The effort to medicalize and pathologize hair loss is gaining momentum, especially as more drugs (e.g., Helsinki formula, Rogaine, Propecia) and new surgical techniques (scalp reduction, hair implants) become available. Although baldness is still not widely viewed as an illness, some male sexual problems are.

Because of the close association among virility, sexuality, and masculinity, one of the more troubling experiences for some men—and one that psychiatry has felt the best equipped to medicalize—is erectile dysfunction. Inspired by a 1992 National Institute of Health conference and a 1994 study on the condition, the diagnosis has been expanded from the rather strict criterion of inability to get an erection to the more elastic and subjective criterion of inability to get an erection adequate for "satisfactory sexual performance." Aggressive marketing of drugs, such as Viagra, Cialis, and Levitra, only adds more fuel to men's anxieties over their masculinity. This intensifies pressures to seek a "cure" in an atmosphere that is powerfully influenced by the economic interests of drug companies and medical practitioners.

The APA (2000, pp. 545–547) categorizes *male erectile disorder* (302.72) as one of the sexual and gender identity disorders. The crux of the diagnosis is a persistent inability to attain or maintain an adequate erection until completion of sexual activity, which produces marked distress or interpersonal difficulties. The authors of the *DSM* acknowledge that many things can account for erectile dysfunction, so they exclude erectile dysfunctions that are infrequent, do not cause marked distress, or that are caused by other known medical conditions or by medications (e.g., antidepressants or neuroleptic medications). As psychiatrists become more comfortable using the "marked distress" decision rule, baldness—and a lot of other things—may find itself listed on the pages of the *DSM*, too.

A *baldness dysphoric disorder* would be no stranger, no less reasonable, or no less scientific than some of the others that are now in the book or that are proposed for possible inclusion in future editions: *road rage* (i.e., unreasonable anger over things that happen while driving); *Internet addiction* (i.e., using it so much that school performance drops, jobs are lost, or relationships are impaired); *jury duty disorder* (i.e., life events made more difficult following stressful jury duty); *lottery stress disorder* (i.e., certainty that one's lottery ticket is going to win and abrupt deflation of mood when it doesn't); *premature ejaculation* (you're on your own with this one); *jet lag disorder* (i.e., being out of whack due to rapid changing of time zones during an extended plane trip); *binge eating disorder* (i.e., excessive eating bouts leading to feeling uncomfortably full or eating more than most people would eat); and *bruxism* (i.e., abnormal grinding of one's teeth while sleeping). *DSM-V* is scheduled for publication in May 2013.

Conclusions

The efforts to define mental disorders in some uniform, systematic, and objective way, though understandable, are doomed to failure. Terms such as *mental disorder* or *mental illness* are just too fuzzy and unscientific to be used in objective ways to define and to differentiate among people for what they say, think, feel, and do. So-called mental disorders are constructed within the context of a society, and they tell us more about the quality of life in that society than they do about individual dysfunctions. Sharp lines cannot be reliably drawn between the sick and the well in the complex and ever-changing world in which we live.

Whatever good a manual such as the *DSM* does is hardly justified by the great harm that it does to our understanding of human diversity. Mental illness is less an objective medical condition than something that is socially constructed and socially sustained. Representatives of organized psychiatry further their interests by crafting an ideal script to define human normality and abnormality that seems beyond dispute. The proffering of an image of inherent order and incontrovertible individual normality, as wrongheaded as it may be, is probably the major accomplishment of the *DSM*.

Mental disorders flesh out our understanding of the relativity of deviance. They show us that even private, personal experiences (such as "losing one's mind") are also public, social events. Power, conflict, and the social construction of reality all play a part in the manufacture of madness. Psychiatry, an organized and influential medical specialty, has mustered sufficient resources to craft understandings of sick and well that directly benefit it. Medicine generates meanings about the human condition that are given life through the words and deeds—the concrete actions and reactions—of people who use what they have learned to judge, evaluate, and classify certain attitudes, behaviors, and conditions as sick or abnormal.

Deviance is in the eyes of the beholders, it is true, but these beholders are not always lone moral crusaders. Each of us may be upset by what we believe are odd qualities of others: appearances, eccentricities, quirks, and attributes. However, more and more, the definitions of deviance depend on the actions, interests, outlooks, and resources of representatives of formal organizations or professions (such as psychiatry) who can draw on a vast arsenal of meanings in their dealings with troublesome and maybe troubled individuals. Institutions and formal organizations are important centers of social activity, and they provide rules and understandings about proper and improper ways of acting, thinking, feeling, and being.

References

Adams, K., & Ferrandino, J. (2008). Managing mentally ill inmates in prison. *Criminal Justice and Behavior, 35,* 913–927.

American Psychiatric Association. (1952). *Diagnostic and statistical manual of mental disorders.* Washington, DC: Author.

American Psychiatric Association. (1968). *Diagnostic and statistical manual of mental disorders* (2nd ed.). Washington, DC: Author.

American Psychiatric Association. (1980). *Diagnostic and statistical manual of mental disorders* (3rd ed.). Washington, DC: Author.

American Psychiatric Association. (1987). *Diagnostic and statistical manual of mental disorders* (3rd ed., rev.). Washington, DC: Author.

American Psychiatric Association. (1994). *Diagnostic and statistical manual of mental disorders* (4th ed.). Washington, DC: Author.

American Psychiatric Association. (2000). *Diagnostic and statistical manual of mental disorders* (4th ed., text revision). Washington, DC: Author.

Armstrong, L. (1993). *And they call it help: The psychiatric policing of America's children.* Reading, MA: Addison-Wesley.

Banton, R., Clifford, P., Frosh, S., Lousada, J., & Rosenthall, J. (1985). *The politics of mental health.* New York, NY: Macmillan.

Bartholomew, R. (1997). The medicalization of the exotic: Latah as a colonialism-bound "syndrome." *Deviant Behavior, 18,* 47–75.

Bayer, R. (1981). *Homosexuality and American psychiatry: The politics of diagnosis.* New York, NY: Basic Books.

Blum, A. (1970). The sociology of mental illness. In J. Douglas (Ed.), *Deviance and respectability: The social construction of moral meanings* (pp. 31–60). New York, NY: Basic Books.

Breggin, P. (1991). *Toxic psychiatry: Why therapy, empathy, and love must replace the drugs, electroshock, and biochemical theories of the new psychiatry.* New York, NY: St. Martin's.

Breggin, P., & Breggin, G. R. (1994). *The war against children.* New York, NY: St. Martin's.

Caplan, P. (1995). *They say you're crazy: How the world's most powerful psychiatrists decide who's normal.* Reading, MA: Addison-Wesley.

Clarke, P., Marshall, V., House, J., & Lantz, P. (2011). The social structuring of mental health over the adult life course: Advancing theory in the sociology of aging. *Social Forces, 89,* 1287–1314.

Conrad, P. (2007). *The medicalization of society: On the transformation of human conditions into treatable disorders.* Baltimore, MD: Johns Hopkins University Press.

Conrad, P., & Schneider, J. (1992). *Deviance and medicalization: From badness to sickness* (Expanded ed.). Philadelphia, PA: Temple University Press.

Davies, V. (1947). *Miracle on 34th Street.* San Diego, CA: Harcourt Brace Jovanovich.

Dowbiggin, I. (1991). *Inheriting madness: Professionalization and psychiatric knowledge in nineteenth-century France.* Berkeley: University of California Press.

Dunham, H. (1976). *Social realities and community psychiatry.* New York, NY: Human Sciences Press.

Feldman, R. (2009). *Essentials of understanding psychology* (8th ed.). New York, NY: McGraw-Hill.

Fernando, S. (1991). *Mental health, race and culture.* New York, NY: St. Martin's.

Figert, A. (1995). The three faces of PMS: The professional, gendered, and scientific structuring of a scientific disorder. *Social Problems, 42,* 56–73.

Foucault, M. (1965). *Madness and civilization: A history of insanity in the age of reason.* New York, NY: Pantheon/Random House.

Foucault, M. (2003). *Abnormal: Lectures at the Collège de France, 1974–1975* (V. Marchetti & A. Salomoni, Eds.; G. Burchell, Trans.). New York, NY: Picador/St. Martin's.

Francoeur, R. (1996). Introduction. In R. Francoeur (Ed.), *Taking sides: Clashing views on controversial issues in human sexuality* (5th ed., p. 44). Guilford, CT: Dushkin.

Frank, R. T. (1931). The hormonal causes of premenstrual tension. *Archives of Neurology and Psychiatry, 26,* 1053–1057.

Gaines, A. (2006). Eudysphoria. In H. J. Birx (Ed.), *Encyclopedia of anthropology* (pp. 870–871). Thousand Oaks, CA: Sage.

Gallagher, B. J., III. (2002). *The sociology of mental illness* (4th ed.). Upper Saddle River, NJ: Prentice Hall.

Garcia, B., & Petrovich, A. (2011). *Strengthening the* DSM: *Incorporating resilience and cultural competence.* New York, NY: Springer-Verlag.

Goffman, E. (1961). *Asylums.* Garden City, NY: Anchor/Doubleday.

Goode, E. (2011). *Deviant behavior* (9th ed.). Upper Saddle River, NJ: Pearson/Prentice Hall.

Gosden, R. (2003). The medicalisation of deviance. In D. Kelly & E. Clarke (Eds.), *Deviant behavior* (6th ed., pp. 402–409). New York, NY: Worth.

Grob, G. N., & Horwitz, A. V. (2010). *Diagnoses, therapy, and evidence: Conundrums in modern American medicine.* New Brunswick, NJ: Rutgers University Press.

Gusfield, J. (1981). *The culture of public problems.* Chicago, IL: University of Chicago Press.

Heinrichs, R. W. (1993). Schizophrenia and the brain: Conditions for a neuropsychology of madness. *American Psychologist, 48,* 221–233.

Herman, E. (1995). *The romance of American psychology: Political culture in the age of experts.* Berkeley: University of California Press.

Horwitz, A. (2002). *Creating mental illness.* Chicago, IL: University of Chicago Press.

Horwitz, A., & Wakefield, J. (2008). The epidemic in mental illness: Clinical fact or survey artifact? In J. Goodwin & J. Jasper (Eds.), *The contexts reader* (pp. 345–352). New York, NY: Norton.

Insel, T. R., & Wang, P. S. (2010). Rethinking mental illness. *Journal of the American Medical Association, 303,* 1970–1971.

King, M. D., & Bearman, P. S. (2011). Socioeconomic status and the increased prevalence of autism in California. *American Sociological Review, 76,* 320–346.

Kirk, S., & Kutchins, H. (1992). *The selling of* DSM: *The rhetoric of science in psychiatry.* New York, NY: Aldine de Gruyter.

Kirk, S., & Kutchins, H. (1994, June 20). Is bad writing a mental disorder? *New York Times,* p. A17.

Klein, G. C. (2009). *Law and the disordered: An exploration in mental health, law, and politics.* Lanham, MD: University Press of America.

Kluger, J. (2011, March 21). Small child, big worries. *Time, 177,* 38–39.

Kovel, J. (1988). A critique of *DSM-III.* In S. Spitzer & A. Scull (Eds.), *Research in law, deviance and social control* (Vol. 9, pp. 127–146). Greenwich, CT: JAI.

Kupfer, D., & Regier, D. A. (2010). Why all medicine should care about *DSM-5. Journal of the American Medical Association, 303,* 1974–1975.

Kutchins, H., & Kirk, S. (1997). *Making us crazy:* DSM, *the psychiatric bible and the creation of mental disorders.* New York, NY: Free Press.

Lamb, H. R., Weinberger, L. E., & Gross, B. H. (2004). Mentally ill persons in the criminal justice system: Some perspectives. *Psychiatric Quarterly, 75,* 107–126.

Laws, S. (1983). The sexual politics of pre-menstrual tension. *Women's Studies International Forum, 6,* 19–31.

Leifer, R. (1969). *In the name of mental health: The social functions of psychiatry.* New York, NY: Science House.

Martin, E. (1992). *The woman in the body: A cultural analysis of reproduction.* Boston, MA: Beacon.

Mead, G. H. (1934). *Mind, self, and society: From the standpoint of a social behaviorist.* Chicago, IL: University of Chicago Press.

Neill, J. (1995). "More than medical significance": LSD and American psychiatry 1953–1966. In J. Inciardi & K. McElrath (Eds.), *The American drug scene: An anthology* (pp. 214–220). Los Angeles, CA: Roxbury.

Patel, V., & Prince, M. (2010). Global mental health: A new global field comes of age. *Journal of the American Medical Association, 303,* 1976–1977.

Rafter, N. (1997). *Creating born criminals.* Urbana & Chicago: University of Illinois Press.

Reynolds, J. R., & Baird, C. L. (2010). Is there a downside to shooting for the stars? Unrealized educational expectations and symptoms of depression. *American Sociological Review, 75,* 151–172.

Rittenhouse, C. A. (1991). The emergence of premenstrual syndrome as a social problem. *Social Problems, 38,* 412–425.

Rochman, B. (2012, February 6). The end of an epidemic? Why a proposed new definition of autism has parents and advocates worried. *Time, 179,* 16.

Rosen, G. (1968). *Madness in society: Chapters in the historical sociology of mental illness.* New York, NY: Harper & Row.

Rothman, D. (1974). *The discovery of the asylum.* Boston, MA: Little, Brown.

Schaefer, D. R., Kornienko, O., & Fox, A. M. (2011). Misery does not love company: Network selection mechanisms and depression homophily. *American Sociological Review, 76,* 764–785.

Scheff, T. (1984). *Being mentally ill: A sociological theory* (2nd ed.). Chicago, IL: Aldine.

Schieman, S., & Glavin, P. (2011). Education and work–family conflict: Explanations, contingencies and mental health consequences. *Social Forces, 89,* 1341–1362.

Scull, A. (1977a). *Decarceration: Community treatment and the deviant.* Englewood Cliffs, NJ: Prentice Hall.

Scull, A. (1977b). Madness and segregative control: The rise of the insane asylum. *Social Problems, 24,* 337–351.

Sharkey, J. (1997, September 28). You're not bad, you're sick. It's in the book. *New York Times,* pp. E1, E5.

Sommer, R. (1976). *The end of imprisonment.* New York, NY: Oxford University Press.

Strauss, J. (1991). The meaning of schizophrenia: Compared to what? In W. Flack, Jr., D. Miller, & M. Wiener (Eds.), *What is schizophrenia?* (pp. 81–90). New York, NY: Springer-Verlag.

Sutton, J. (1991). The political economy of madness: The expansion of the asylum in progressive America. *American Sociological Review, 56,* 665–678.

Szasz, T. (1960). The myth of mental illness. *American Psychologist, 15,* 113–118.

Szasz, T. (1970). *The manufacture of madness.* New York, NY: Harper & Row.

Szasz, T. (1973). *The second sin.* Garden City, NY: Anchor.

Szasz, T. (1974). *The myth of mental illness* (Rev. ed.). New York, NY: Harper & Row.

Szasz, T. (1985, September 28). Psychiatry: Rhetoric and reality. *Lancet, 2,* 711–712.

Szasz, T. (1997). Idleness and lawlessness in the therapeutic state. In L. Salinger (Ed.), *Deviant behavior 97/98* (2nd ed., pp. 214–219). Guilford, CT: Dushkin/Brown.

Tone, A. (2009). *The age of anxiety: A history of America's turbulent affair with tranquilizers.* New York, NY: Basic Books.

Torrey, E. F. (1995). Jails and prisons—America's new mental hospitals. *American Journal of Public Health, 85,* 1611–1613.

Trent, J., Jr. (1994). *Inventing the feeble mind: A history of mental retardation in the United States.* Berkeley: University of California Press.

Turner, R., & Edgley, C. (1996). From witchcraft to drugcraft: Biochemistry as mythology. In H. Pontell (Ed.), *Social deviance: Readings in theory and research* (2nd ed., pp. 432–441). Englewood Cliffs, NJ: Prentice Hall.

Walker, S. (2011). *Sense and nonsense about crime, drugs, and communities* (7th ed.). Belmont, CA: Wadsworth.

Warner, J. (2010). *We've got issues: Children and parents in the age of medication.* New York, NY: Riverhead Books/Penguin.

Warner, R. (2008). Schizophrenia in the Third World. In R. Heiner (Ed.), *Deviance across cultures* (pp. 243–253). New York, NY: Oxford University Press.

Watters, E. (2010). *Crazy like us: The globalization of the American psyche.* New York, NY: Free Press.

Wedenoja, W. (2006). Psychiatry, transcultural. In H. J. Birx (Ed.), *Encyclopedia of anthropology* (pp. 1961–1964). Thousand Oaks, CA: Sage.

Wiener, M. (1991). Schizophrenia: A defective, deficient, disrupted, disorganized construct. In W. Flack, Jr., D. Miller, & M. Wiener (Eds.), *What is schizophrenia?* (pp. 199–222). New York, NY: Springer-Verlag.

5

Predatory Violence

The Social Construction of Murder and Violence

Legal and Social Definitions: Understanding Murder

One of the facts of the human condition is that people die. Some of these deaths are caused by factors that seem to be beyond the control of human beings, unrelated to human intent. These deaths are officially classified in the United States as either "accidental" or "natural." Other deaths, however, are viewed as deliberate human acts that are malicious and unnecessary. The individuals held responsible for them are subjected to punishments for what they have done. Some of these intentional killings are against the law, in which case they are called murder. *Murder* is defined by the Federal Bureau of Investigation (FBI) (2012) as the willful (nonnegligent) killing of one human being by another. Murder is the most serious, but rarest, of all the *violent crimes* (any crime that involves force or the threat of force) defined by this federal agency. Rates of violence, especially lethal violence, are high in the United States when compared to other Western, industrial nations (Winslow & Zhang, 2008); in fact, violence is a routine occurrence (Beeghley, 2003, pp. 41–77).

Killing (i.e., homicide) and murder are related, but they are not identical. It is possible for a killing to not be a murder (but not the other way around), as when a police officer shoots a felon in the line of duty or when a condemned criminal is lawfully executed for a crime. Murder and manslaughter are the two types of illegal killing identified by U.S. law. A killing in which an offender plans out the murder *(premeditation)* and then deliberately carries it out (with *malice aforethought,* which indicates that criminal intent exists) is a *first-degree murder. Second-degree murder* lacks the element of premeditation, but malice aforethought is still present. *Manslaughter* is an illegal killing that lacks both premeditation and malice aforethought (Hall, 2002, pp. 398–400). Some killings are excluded from the FBI's definition of murder because they are not considered willful. These include suicides, accidental deaths, and traffic fatalities. If a person dies of a heart attack as the result of being robbed or witnessing a crime, it is not classified as a murder either.

A psychiatric diagnosis used to explain individual violence is that of *antisocial personality disorder* (Bogg, 1994). This diagnosis describes someone who is self-centered and uncaring about others, willing to do anything that will benefit him or her, even if it involves extreme acts of violence. The ambiguity of the term "antisocial personality"—it is also called psychopathy or sociopathy—is paralleled by confusion over its meaning. Despite strenuous efforts to make the term more precise, it is still used as a catch-all to describe bad people and bad behaviors that seemingly cannot be understood in any other way. The diagnosis is a way to explain how seemingly normal people could do seemingly abnormal things: They have a mental disorder that has afflicted their moral development. The trouble is that the term is circular—individuals get labeled as having antisocial personality because they do antisocial things. The unrestrained pursuit of self-interest—the principal sign that identifies antisocial people—is too general for the diagnosis to have much value.

Persistent rule breaking or chronic incivility may be a result of life experiences in communities where violence and aggression are commonplace (Green, 1993, p. 261). If people are not taught kindness and generosity—or never experience them in their dealings with others—it is unlikely these qualities will become part of their character structure. Another thing to note is that sociopathic traits are not necessarily bad for an individual who possesses them and, kept within limits, they are not bad for others either (Regoli, Hewitt, & Delisi, 2010, p. 147).

The Elasticity of Violence

No act is universally defined as violent and then negatively sanctioned in all human societies. In one setting, people may be negatively sanctioned for too much violence; in another setting, they may be sanctioned for too little violence; and in still another setting, they may be sanctioned for committing the wrong type of violence (Edgerton, 1976, p. 46).

What audiences label as violence is not dependent on the harm that is inflicted. Instead, what observers regard as instances of violence are illegitimate, unjustified, inexcusable—or *deviant*—actions taken by one person or a set of persons against another. In other words, violence is a loaded, biased, socially constructed concept. (Goode, 2008, p. 150)

In some places, for some people, certain acts of violence are viewed as normal and reasonable—as evidence of courage and bravery—and at other times, for other people, what appear to be similar acts are viewed as serious public health emergencies (Koop & Lundberg, 1992).

The killing of one human being by another can elicit a wide range of social reactions, influenced not only by time and place, but also by characteristics of the victim and victimizer and the relationship between them (Cooney, 2009). Killers may be lynched, brutally killed by outraged mobs, executed by the government, imprisoned for life, banished from the society, fined, scorned, or even admired and rewarded for their violent acts. Different groups in a society may have very different views of the *same* killing (or killer), with some groups being outraged by the killing and others being delighted that it occurred. Some individuals in societies all across the world communicate to others how horrific or brutal they find the violence that they have witnessed or actually experienced, while others do what they can to normalize or dismiss it (Six-Hohenbalken & Weiss, 2011).

Centuries ago, Roman holidays involved the slaughter of thousands of combatants in gladiator shows. After Spartacus's uprising, the crucified bodies of 6,000 slaves lined the road from Rome to Capua like lampposts. In Christian Europe, executions replaced the Roman circuses. Criminals were beheaded publicly; they were hanged, their intestines drawn out and their bodies quartered; they were elaborately tortured and guillotined in front of enthralled crowds; their severed heads were exposed on spikes, their bodies hung in chains from gibbets (gallows). The public was amused and excited, more delighted than shocked. An execution was like a fun fair, and for the more spectacular occasions, even apprentices got the day off (Alvarez, 1972, pp. 53–54). If an Ashanti woman of West Africa calls a man a fool, it is considered a violent act, and she can be killed for it. However, if an Ashanti child dies before puberty, he or she is given no funeral rites. The body is simply ditched in the community garbage dump. In that culture, the death of a child is no big deal, nor is the killing of an insulting woman; however, insulting a man is a very serious matter indeed (Service, 1963, pp. 376–378). In slave-owning societies, if a slave kills an owner (called an "upward" killing), it is dealt with harshly. However, if a slave owner kills a slave (called a "downward" killing), it is treated leniently or may even be overlooked (Cooney, 2009).

Bad Murders and Good Murders

Wayne Wilson (1991) separated what he called "good" from "bad" murders. The distinction is based on the premise that groups of people distinguish those who deserve to die (a *good murder*) from those who do not but are killed anyway (a *bad murder*). It seems to be true that the nastier the killer, the more ghastly the killing, and the purer the victim is perceived to be, the greater the likelihood that the killing of the victim will be viewed as bad and the killing of the offender (if it occurs) as good (p. 2). In 1911, an accused rapist was bound on the stage of an opera house in Livermore, Kentucky, and tickets were sold to see him. Ticket holders were allowed to shoot at the rapist as they sat in their seats (Lane, 2003, p. 52). Some violence may reach the point where it is viewed as so good that it doesn't even look like violence anymore. Decisions about who should live and who should die are fundamentally social decisions that cannot be separated from issues of race, class, gender, geography, or organizational dynamics (Roy, 2009).

No doubt exists that some individuals are prepared to use brutality and violence to get what they want and that they produce untold misery for everybody else. Consider the following account, written by Ms. Kuzmaak, describing the anguish caused by the murder of her daughter Donna. It is an example of a "bad murder," if anything is.

> I keep searching for the right descriptive words to convey the emotional impact our daughter's murder made on us. "Devastating" just doesn't make it—"ravaged" is closer, engulfed, overwhelmed, drowning in sadness, numb, oblivious to EVERYTHING else, totally immersed in the horror, the why, the who, what she had to go through in the closing minutes of her short life, how terrified she must have been, did she scream for help and no one came, did she fight, the pain, how it felt to be strangled, what her dying thoughts were, how she must have held out hope until the last that she would be rescued, her shock and disbelief that this was happening, and as the information unfolded itself to us in bits and pieces that first day, the anguish of hearing how badly she was beaten, then a couple of hours later crying out when I heard that she had been repeatedly stabbed. Then, the ultimate horror to learn that the cause of death was strangulation. To be deprived of breath—lungs bursting—"Oh, God, oh God," I would wail, tears streaming, hands clenched and imploring.
>
> That is how I remember the day, March 21, 1979. A decade has passed, but the emotions go on, the anger, the sorrow, and the loss. (Hickey, 1997, pp. 125–126)

If the killer were ever to be caught and executed for murdering Donna, the execution would fit W. Wilson's (1991) idea of a "good murder" (though it would no longer be called murder because, as noted, murder by definition is an *illegal* killing). However, a genuine dilemma exists in applying good murder/bad murder definitions to real-world events. The unique qualities of a victim—how innocent, pure, or kind he or she is (or is considered to be)— cannot reasonably be used to determine a killer's level of criminal responsibility or what his or her penalty should be (Lesser, 1993, p. 6).

Another example of bad murder is to be found in the killing of Adam Walsh. On July 27, 1981, Revé (pronounced *Ree-vay*) Walsh and Adam, her 6-year-old son, made their way to the Sears Mall in Hollywood, Florida. Sears had some brass barrel lamps on sale, and Revé's husband, John Walsh, suggested that she go to the store to see if the lights were something the family could use. Upon entering Sears, Adam saw that the toy department had a video display with a demonstration game running. He asked his mother if he could play it, a request she approved. Revé kissed her son good-bye—for the last time as it turned out—and headed for the lamp section, expecting to return within minutes to get her son and finish the day's activities (Standiford, 2011, pp. 2–3).

While Ms. Walsh looked for the lamps—the store had not received the advertised item, so the purchase could not be made—other children entered the toy department to play. A scuffle ensued between two of the youngsters, and a store security guard, Kathy Shaffer, was summoned by store personnel. She promptly hustled all the children out of the store, including Adam Walsh, the youngest of the gamers in the toy department. Adam found himself standing alone outside the store.

Though Adam was not outside Sears for long, it gave a violent predator named Ottis Toole enough time to abduct him. Toole got Adam into his car and drove the child away. Adam soon realized that he had been taken by a strange and violent man. He yelled and screamed. In order to quiet the child, Toole hit Adam several times with powerful blows until the child was unconscious. Toole continued to drive, heading north from Hollywood on Florida's Turnpike. He spotted an unmarked service road, which he took. Soon thereafter, he stopped the car. Toole lifted the unconscious and perhaps already-dead child from the car and carried him to an opening among a tangle of brush and trees. He laid him face down in the dirt. Toole returned to his car, getting the tools he needed: a machete and a bayonet. He returned to the boy and began his grisly work.

On August 10, 1981, just about 2 weeks after Adam's abduction, Franklin Cox, Indian River County medical examiner, received a call from a sheriff in Vero Beach. A fisherman had found a child's severed head floating in a canal near the turnpike (the body has never been found). The following day, John Monahan, a friend of the Walsh family, armed with dental records, made a positive identification. It was Adam Walsh. The child had been murdered, decapitated, and his body parts strewn about the Florida countryside.

John and Revé Walsh on the day that the remains of their son were identified were in New York, doing a segment on *Good Morning America*. It was mostly about Adam's disappearance, but they also talked about other missing children and the extreme grief suffered by parents who have lost a child. At the end of the segment, the interviewer (David Hartman) asked the Walshes what they knew about the remains of the young boy found in the canal near Vero Beach. At that point, it seemed unlikely to the Walshes that the remains could have been Adam's. However, by noon of that day, John received the news that he and his wife had been dreading ever since Adam was lost at Sears. John returned to his hotel room, opened the door and joined his wife, saying simply, "Our baby's dead." Revé took her husband in her arms, telling him that she already knew (Standiford, 2011, p. 56).

The Walshes knew that nothing would bring back their murdered child, but they also knew that one way to manage their grief was to do all they could to find Adam's killer and get justice for him. Though it took almost 30 years, the family finally did get some closure. On Friday, November 20, 2008, at a meeting at the Broward County State Attorney's office, it was unanimously decided by those assembled that, pending final approval of the Broward County state's attorney, the murder of Adam would be exceptionally cleared and that the killer was Ottis Toole. Detective Sergeant Joe Mathews, a Miami Beach police officer, worked long and hard to gather enough evidence to prove that the murderer of Adam Walsh was Ottis Toole.

Had Toole still been alive—he died on September 15, 1996, from cirrhosis of the liver at age 49—he would have been arrested and prosecuted for Adam's murder. It seems probable that he would have been convicted and executed for the crime (Toole had made a deathbed confession of sorts to the murder of Adam, a rambling confession overheard by B. Gemelli, the health services administrator at the Union Correction Institution) (Standiford, 2011, p. 22).

In the Eye of the Beholder

We must be familiar with social context and cultural understandings, or it will be impossible to know what an act means or how it should be understood. Police officers use "roughness" in their jobs, and so do football players, wrestlers, and animal trainers. In Brownstein's (2000) words, "We do not have any precise or simple measure of violence in our society. We do not even have agreement on how to define violence, or when and how to identify particular acts or actions as violent" (p. 169). Most people commit acts of violence at some point in their lives—most of them more than once—and practically everyone has the opportunity to use violence in a variety of ways and for a variety of reasons. The boundary that separates violence from nonviolence is fuzzier and more permeable than most people think (Eller, 2006, p. 13). The "violency" that inheres in some act (i.e., violence in the eye of the beholder) is a matter of dispute, depending on many social and individual factors.

The relativity of violence is easy enough to see by examining something that at first blush would seem to be straightforward: figuring out how many individuals died during the terrorist attack on the World Trade Center, September 11, 2001, and then how to classify them (i.e., as accidents or something else). The number who died as a result of being on the two planes that slammed into the North and South Towers could be accurately determined from both airline records and reports from surviving family members. Figuring out how many died in the Twin Towers, however, proved to be more challenging. On September 24, 2001, the number of casualties was estimated to be 6,453. As the days passed, however, the list got shorter. Some victims had been counted multiple times, which had incorrectly inflated the number of presumed casualties; some people classified as dead (or missing) were actually found to be alive; and some people fraudulently claimed that they had lost family members, hoping to receive survivors' benefits. A year after the attack, the authoritative list of estimated deaths due to the World Trade Center attack stood at 2,801, less than half of the initial estimate (Best, 2004, pp. 109–111). The FBI's Uniform Crime Reports (UCR) for 2001, which also included in its estimate the deaths at the Pentagon and on the plane that crashed in Pennsylvania, reported the body count from 9/11 to be 3,047.

If estimating the number of individuals killed was difficult, it was even harder to know how to classify them. They fit perfectly the FBI's own definition of murder: These killings were willful; they were done *by* human beings, and they were done *to* human beings. How much clearer could it be that these killings were murders? The FBI (2001), however, decided *not* to count these approximately 3,000 deaths as murders, so the murder and non-negligent manslaughter figures for 2001 did not increase at all in spite of the thousands of killings that occurred on that day (p. 302). What is most curious is that the FBI stated that it did not know what to call the killings because so much disagreement and dispute existed over what they should be called (e.g., an act of war, a local crime, an international conspiracy, or terrorism). The FBI apparently knew enough, however, to decide not to call them murders.

Some individuals, groups, or organizations will use violence to get what they want (e.g., terrorists using violence to terrorize) (Schinkel, 2010). Individuals, groups, and organizations can also use social constructions of violence as part of their cultural (or subcultural) conflicts with others by depicting others' attitudes, behaviors, and conditions as forms of violence, justifying their condemnation and control. Having the authority to decide what and who is violent has great symbolic value (Brownstein, 2000, p. 169). The violence of professional boxing, hockey, rugby, wrestling, rodeos, or cage fighting is not defined as a social problem, but the violence of school shootings or Halloween sadism is. Some violence that was once viewed as a serious problem (e.g., wilding) has gone the way of the buggy whip, and some violence that was once ignored is now viewed more seriously (e.g., road rage or cruelty to animals). Some groups will manipulate our fears of violence to advance their interests.

Arbitrary Meanings

Definitions of deviance, violence included, develop and grow in specific locations or arenas in a society, such as government, mass media, research communities, social action groups, professional organizations (medicine and law), and religious organizations. It is at the intersections of these different arenas that notions of risk are created, massaged, and manipulated; they are also where remedies or solutions for the problems we face are constructed and presented for review (Bing, 2010; Ghatak, 2011). Best (1999, pp. 68–69) refers to media, government, experts, and activists as the *iron quadrangle,* because these four arenas are (or can be) central in promoting an interest in some troubling event in mutually reinforcing ways (even while disagreement can and does exist).

Unless influential and powerful advocates in the iron quadrangle, organizational dynamics, and institutional resources all coalesce to get some troubling event authoritatively established as a type of deviance or social problem, it will remain ambiguous; the object of competing claims; or part of some other, broader problem, lacking its own unique identity (Jenness, 1995; Loseke, 1992; Unnithan, 1994, p. 71). A lack of sustained attention is a principal reason that the "battered husband problem" did not receive the same level of attention and concern as did the "battered wife syndrome."

> Professional and mass media attention to the issue of battered wives has been instrumental in its creation and continuation as an identified social problem. Along with social movement/organizational factors, this attention has been

crucial to the construction of the social problem called "battered wives." The *lack* of these two factors has been of considerable importance to the failure of battered husbands. (Lucal, 1995, pp. 105–106)

What little media attention was directed to husband battering quickly withered on the vine once the problem's novelty wore off. One reason for its demise, however, may have been that battered husbands, on average, are not really battered very much (DeKeseredy, 2011). While some women do hit men without provocation, perhaps injuring or even killing their male partners, the bulk of violence in intimate relationships is done by men (p. 58).

A moral enterprise against violence can develop into a *moral panic* in which the social reaction is so extreme that it is wholly inappropriate and disproportionate to the threat posed (Goode & Ben-Yehuda, 1994). This is what happened when the "devil came to day care" and refused to leave for almost a decade. In the 1980s, individuals (how many is a matter of dispute) in the United States came to believe that day care centers were the site of horrendous violence against children, done by the very people entrusted to care for them (DeYoung, 2008). The new buzz words of "satanic ritual abuse" emerged as a shorthand way to describe these terrifying acts, and the McMartin Preschool in Southern California (located in the town of Manhattan Beach) was defined as the epicenter of it all.

In 1983, Judy Johnson was in a bind. She needed affordable, quality child care at the exact point in time when the societal demand was great but the supply was not. She tried to enroll her 2-year-old son at McMartin, but the center was full and no openings were anticipated. Nonetheless, one day she simply dropped off her son at the center and went to work. Employees arrived and found the child playing all alone in the center's yard. They took pity on him (and on his mother, who had recently separated from her husband) and made room for him. The rest of what happened should be placed in the "no good deed goes unpunished" file, because the staff's willingness to care for the child and assist the mother eventually led to catastrophe for the center and for all the people who owned and worked in it.

One day, after her son was back home from school, Johnson decided on the flimsiest of evidence and with little substantiation that he had been sexually assaulted by someone at the school (the child had an irritated anus). During a drawn-out process of the questioning of her son, filled with leading questions, repeated again and again, Johnson extracted the kind of information she needed to convince herself that her initial suspicions were true. Her son had been sodomized, and she knew by whom: Raymond Buckey, the only male staff member (and the grandson of the founder of the day care center). Though her son had said that Buckey had done nothing to him,

Johnson was not dissuaded. Finally, in response to her relentless questioning, the boy indicated that Buckey had taken his temperature. The mother had her smoking gun. She concluded that the "thermometer" was really Buckey's penis, which he had used to anally penetrate her child.

Johnson had her son examined by a physician (the physical was inconclusive), and she then went to the police. Other parents who had used the day care center learned of the complaint against it, and they started quizzing their children, too. Aggrieved parents were encouraged in letters from the police to take their children to the Children's International Institution (CII), a nonprofit treatment facility, to be interviewed by the resident social workers. Social workers subsequently talked to more than 400 McMartin youngsters, concluding that 369 of them had been victims of satanic ritual abuse. The way that CII social workers questioned them led the children to realize that truth statements about any conscientious and compassionate care they had received at the center were not what the social workers wanted to hear.

> And so they told . . . tales—tales about the ritualistic ingestion of feces, urine, blood, semen, and human flesh; the disinterment and mutilation of corpses; the sacrifices of infants; and the orgies with their day care providers, costumed as devils and witches, in the classrooms, in tunnels under the center, and in car washes, airplanes, mansions, cemeteries, hotels, ranches, gourmet food stores, local gyms, churches, and hot air balloons. (DeYoung, 2008, p. 73)

The greater the degree of strangeness in the children's tales, the more convinced the social workers—and practically everyone else—became that the children were telling the truth about what had happened. Due process went out the window, along with both truth and reason. The social workers played a central and powerful role in the construction of a reality that they believed they played no role in at all. In February 1984, seven of the day care center's staff were indicted on multiple charges.

Two trials were held in the McMartin Preschool case, and all charges against the seven defendants were eventually dropped. However, the damage had already been done. The accused individuals had no way to get back what they had lost. Judy Johnson had a nervous breakdown and was institutionalized for a time with a diagnosis of paranoid schizophrenia. (She told police detectives that her ex-husband had anally penetrated her son and that an unknown intruder had done the same thing to the family dog.) She died in 1986 of liver failure due to the effects of alcohol, but her legacy lived on as more and more day care centers fell under the suspicion of parents, police, prosecutors, politicians, social workers, and the media. The story was told and retold of a massive network of organized predators who victimize children in day care centers all across the United States.

> Originating in cultural anxieties about the socialization and protection of young children, triggered by the McMartin Preschool case, and spread across the country by interest, grassroots, and professional groups, the satanic day care center moral panic swept across the country. (DeYoung, 2008, p. 75)

The moral panic ended almost a decade after it started, in 1992, with the arrest and conviction of day care center owner Fran Keller (who owned Fran's Day Care in Austin, Texas) and her husband (Dan). They were both convicted of aggravated sexual assault on a child and each received a sentence of 48 years for the crime. Sadly, some abuse may have occurred—and it probably did—but moral panics do not have to be entirely unfounded or entirely false to be moral panics. They can be disproportionate to the threat posed, as seems to be true in the McMartin incident.

Once some event, group, or individual is defined as menacing, this definition and the reaction based on it become part of how the event (or group or individual) is understood and identified (Young, 2011, pp. 251–252). The process of demonization is furthered often enough by media coverage, which routinely offers distorted or even false images of, for example, crime, criminals, and victims (Bjornstrom, Kaufman, Peterson, & Slater, 2010; Covington, 2010; Farrall, Jackson, & Gray, 2009). It is difficult, if not impossible, to figure out if the "panic" is a reasonable reaction to some objective threat or if it is in actuality an exaggerated response to some earlier *reaction* to an objective threat. Moral panics have the ability to create their own reality.

Patterned Violence

Subcultures of Violence

Human aggression can occur in a variety of ways, depending on the opportunities to express it and the cultural understandings about it (Goetting, 1995, p. xxii). At certain times, violence is both normal and normative: It occurs frequently, is well-integrated with other parts of society and culture, and is defined as legitimate and reasonable. This kind of violence is legal, socially supported, and rational. It is *organized violence*. Other violence, however, does not flow from any clear or discernible social conditions or cultural issues. It is illegal, asocial, and irrational (Yablonsky, 1990, p. 154). This is *raw violence*. Raw violence is more often done by the kinds of people who are considered immoral, sick, or evil; these individuals will be labeled more often as psychopaths, sociopaths, or as having an antisocial personality. They are usually hostile toward, and suspicious of, others, and their predatory activities usually come from their aberrant or warped personalities or character structures. The distinction between "raw" and "organized" violence is not a hard and fast one. It is functional for some groups to portray the violence of other groups (or individuals) as rawer than it really is (i.e., barbaric and incomprehensible). People can disagree over the degree of rawness or organization that inheres in some violent act.

In a society characterized by diversity and heterogeneity (as is found in the United States), a number of subcultures exist. The wealthy may associate primarily with the wealthy, the poor primarily with the poor, and people from different ethnic and racial groups may interact primarily with people who share a similar identity and social history. This diversity of subcultures produces a diversity of life experiences, opportunities, and outcomes. People from some subcultures consistently do better in achieving their dreams than people from other subcultures. They have more money, more control over their lives, and better jobs. They generally feel good about what they do and what they are. In other subcultures, however, there is misery and degradation, and people who live within them are frustrated and angry much of the time (Blau & Blau, 1982). This social environment can stimulate interpersonal conflicts and individual tensions from which interpersonal violence can result (Linsky, Bachman, & Strauss, 1995).

When a tradition of neighborhood support for violence exists, along with the presence of actual groups that champion aggression, then violence is more likely (Felson, Liska, South, & McNulty, 1994, p. 170; Pinderhughes, 1993). A *subculture of violence* provides opportunities to observe, learn, and act out the kinds of violence that would shock, upset, or baffle individuals from other subcultures (Athens, 1980, 1989; Wolfgang & Ferracuti, 1967). In a subculture of violence, it is not some individual amorality or immorality that explains what happens. Rather, it is the internalization of a subculture's core values and norms that is the principal cause. Some neighborhoods are found to be more likely to generate a sense of hopelessness among their members, and these individuals have no optimism or faith that their opportunities will ever improve.

Dueling is a good example of how violence can become both normative and normalized (Kiernan, 1988). At one time, duels were disorderly gatherings, with witnesses and spectators often joining in the fight. However, duels eventually became more ritualized and formalized. Each duelist selected someone to serve as a *second,* who ensured that the rules were enforced and the duel was fair. If swords were used, they had to be the same length. If pistols were used, they had to carry the same charge or be of the same caliber. Neither duelist was supposed to be at a disadvantage by, for example, having to face the sun or to shoot into the wind. In France and England, the main weapon was the sword, whereas in the United States it was the pistol. In some places, a duel was ended at the drawing of first blood, but in other places, the dueling code required death. Though a large number of incidents, some quite petty, could precipitate a duel—personal insults, arguments over property, affronts to personal honor, or even cheating at cards—failing to respond to a challenge, no matter how ridiculous it was, meant disgrace and dishonor. Individuals who were arrested by police for dueling (it became a federal crime in the United States in 1877) almost always lacked remorse or shame because they were duty bound to duel if challenged. The participants viewed the violence as both justified and justifiable regardless of its legal status.

Social Inequality, Concentrated Disadvantage, and the Code of the Street

Anderson (1999) directed attention to a neighborhood characteristic that he believed plays a central role in patterns of African American violence: the code of the street. His *code of the street thesis* indicates that violence in African American neighborhoods is caused by a subculture (i.e., a code) that allows those who share its understandings to know how to use violence, primarily to maintain personal status and respect. The code of the street encourages both a positive evaluation of violence in the abstract ("Tough guys are to be admired") and a willingness to use it ("If someone starts trouble, I will finish it"). Kids who have spent time on the streets, away from whatever positive effects come from watching and interacting with adults as role models, show higher rates of violence (Crawford, Whitbeck, & Hoyt, 2011). Youth who adopt the code of the street think that they are more vulnerable to becoming targets of violence, though they generally express fearlessness regarding it (Baron, 2011).

The street code demands of its followers that they be ready, willing, and able to use physical violence in order to defend personal honor (or the honor of others close to them). If unwilling to do so, it could make one a "punk" in the eyes of others, inviting future attacks from them. The code is found more frequently in inner-city areas characterized by poverty, a scarcity of legitimate jobs, unemployment, a surplus of illegitimate jobs, guns, drugs, crime, violence, declining welfare payments, hopelessness, and despair (Kirk & Papachristos, 2011). The code of the street emerged from the U.S. history of slavery and the continuing prejudice and discrimination against blacks that it spawned. In some communities today, fighting to protect one's honor is a core value for both males and females (Ness, 2010).

Concentrated disadvantage—poverty, social disorganization, normlessness, lack of opportunity, disharmony—and the code of the street are usually found together. A study of over 2,500 census tracts in 13 U.S. cities over a 10-year period reported reciprocal effects between inequality and violence (Hipp, 2010, pp. 217–222). Those neighborhoods with the highest amount of poverty experienced a long-term increase in crime, and neighborhoods with higher rates of violent crime experienced a greater increase in concentrated disadvantage (p. 223). An increase in crime rates can change a neighborhood's characteristics (e.g., retail outlets are replaced by bars and liquor stores) and reduce its attractiveness as a place to live. This leads to the influx of lower-income families. "Neighborhoods with more crime tend to experience increasing levels of residential instability, more impoverished residents, a worsening retail environment, and more racial/ethnic minorities and heterogeneity" (p. 224). Some neighborhoods generate a sense of hopelessness among the people who live there, and these individuals have no optimism that their opportunities will ever improve. This sense of despair is a factor that leads to both an adoption of the code of the streets and involvement in the higher rates of violence that the code reinforces (Drummond, Bolland, & Harris, 2011). As concentrated disadvantage rises in a community, female and male participation in violence becomes more similar (Zimmerman & Messner, 2010, pp. 970–971).

Areas characterized by concentrated disadvantage in an unequal society, with subcultures of violence and a code of the street, have an additional liability: weak social capital. *Social capital* (Coleman, 1988, p. 143; Putnam, 2000) is a network of relationships that makes it possible for community members to act together to achieve common goals. They will have a sense of community spirit, along with a sense of mutual trust and responsibility. One offshoot of social capital is *collective efficacy* (Sampson & Raudenbush, 1999; Sampson, Raudenbush, & Earls, 1997). This exists when community residents are able to control the public space (e.g., streets, street corners, parks, playgrounds) within which they live and move, which makes it possible for them to maintain order. They may call police to report crimes in their communities, or they may even take responsibility themselves to patrol them. One outcome of high levels of social capital and collective efficacy is a lowering of rates of crime and delinquency. Even the rates of serious crime (e.g., homicide) go down as collective efficacy goes up (Morenoff, Sampson, & Raudenbush, 2001). Bullying between students is less likely in schools where a tradition of collective efficacy exists (Williams & Guerra, 2011).

Whites are more likely than African Americans or Latinos to abandon neighborhoods with high rates of violent crime, and they are less likely to move into neighborhoods with high and increasing rates of violent crime (Hipp, 2011, pp. 421–427). This fact is of more than passing importance. A study by Peterson and Krivo (2010) of census tracts in about 100 large U.S. cities reports that the *lowest* violent crime rates in African American neighborhoods are comparable to the *highest* rates in white neighborhoods (although greater overlap exists with the rates of property crime). Their analysis shows that the principal factor is economic inequality (with racial and ethnic segregation playing a subsidiary role). A high level of economic disadvantage in a neighborhood means that rates of violent crime will be high regardless of what race or ethnic group lives there. Most research shows that economic inequality and homicide are positively related (Bernard, Snipes, & Gerould, 2010, p. 105).

Even in a subculture of violence with a code of the street, some individual variation exists. Though interpersonal violence may be both accepted and generally acceptable, not everyone will learn the message and follow the script. Not all parents, even in a violent neighborhood, teach their kids to use violence to defend themselves and their honor. Most children who are abused by their parents do not grow up to become abusers themselves (Cochran, Sellers, Wiesbrock, & Palacios, 2011; Kaufman & Zigler, 1989; Payne, Triplett, & Higgins, 2011). Research suggests that some individuals are more susceptible to environmental influences than are others.

> Individuals at genetic risk for the highest rates of aggression in response to adverse social conditions are also genetically predisposed to show the lowest rates of aggression when they grow up in a favorable environment. Individuals most likely to develop anger, a hostile view of people, a concern with toughness, and aggression in reaction to adverse social conditions are also the most likely to develop a peaceful, sanguine orientation in response to a favorable social environment. (Simons et al., 2011, p. 906)

What is unknown, but which seems likely, is whether critical periods exist in an individual's developmental life regarding susceptibility to violence, and whether this susceptibility cannot then be undone if the environment changes to become one of peace and harmony.

Dehumanizing Others

The enactment of violence usually depends on the social construction of an "other"—an individual or group that is defined as a legitimate target of aggression and deserving of injury. The "other" is dehumanized, transforming a "person" into an "inferior object." This helps to neutralize any lingering moral inhibitions against violence that might still exist among aggressors, which makes it possible for rather ordinary people to commit acts of extraordinary evil (F. Katz, 1994). They may even develop justifications and excuses for violence that become part of the cultural tradition, being internalized by members of the group or society. This makes certain kinds of violence seem more necessary, more reasonable, and less in need of correction than other kinds of violence done by other kinds of people. If these excuses and justifications are persuasive enough, some individuals will be able to commit acts of extreme cruelty with very little social prompting, even when they are given clear opportunities to renege without penalty or embarrassment (Browning, 1992, pp. 169–183). The "other" may even be blamed for things over which he or she could have had no control whatsoever. In 1923, thousands of Koreans were massacred by the Japanese in Tokyo because they were held responsible for the earthquake that had occurred that year (Baudrillard, 2002, p. 99).

Zimbardo (2007) explored how seemingly good people can do seemingly bad things. The *Lucifer effect*—the transformation of ordinary men and women into beings who are capable of committing reprehensible atrocities against their fellows—is something that can occur practically anywhere if the situation is right. Zimbardo concluded that evil is something of which we are all capable, depending on the time and circumstances (p. 7). (By evil, Zimbardo [p. 5] means intentionally behaving in ways that harm, abuse, demean, dehumanize, or destroy innocent people—or using one's authority and systemic power to encourage or permit others to do so on one's behalf.) He may have overstated his case: Some people would forfeit their own lives before they would do anything to hurt another living thing, nonhuman animals included. However, he is on firm ground when he argues that the dividing line between good and bad, between evil and honor, is nebulous and permeable (p. 3). The cause of the Lucifer effect is found mainly in systems of power and how authorities use propaganda to scapegoat outsiders so that insiders dehumanize them, making them legitimate targets of aggression. Insiders can reach the point where they will not only willingly victimize the dehumanized others; they are happy to do so.

Goldhagen (1996) uncovered from his study of Hitler's executioners that the Holocaust was only possible because enough ordinary citizens believed that Jews were subhuman, inferior, and desperately in need of extermination. The killing of innocent men, women, and children was an outgrowth of the anti-Semitism that had developed and spread throughout Germany and other Central European countries long before the atrocities of the Third Reich occurred. Ordinary Germans might have quibbled over exactly how much violence was required to deal with the "Jewish problem" or to rid the planet of the "Jewish menace," but very few of them doubted that this matter deserved direct and immediate governmental intervention.

The extermination of so many Jews did not emanate exclusively from the requests or demands of higher authority in the German state. It was not a crime of obedience (Kelman & Hamilton, 1989). It was precipitated by the intimate, voluntary, and purposeful acts of thousands of ordinary Germans who shared a belief that Jews were a threat that needed to be removed (Goldhagen, 1996). It is difficult to understand in any other way the personal pleasure and sense of accomplishment that so many ordinary Germans apparently derived from their sadistic cruelty. It seemed that one objective was for them to humble and humiliate Jewish citizens before the mass killings occurred. It is a historical fact that most of those responsible for these atrocities experienced little or no guilt over what they did (Browning, 1992; Goldhagen, 1996).

A study of more than 900 lynchings of black males, between 1882 and 1929 in 10 southern U.S. states, showed that the victims had been at the margins of the social and economic currents of the communities that lynched them. They were targeted because of their marginality and separation, not because of their occupational, social, or educational accomplishments (e.g., literacy). Being an "uppity" or successful black man was far less important to lynch mobs than the fact that he was an outsider (Bailey, Tolnay, Beck, & Laird, 2011, pp. 422–428). Lynching became a method of social control of blacks by whites at a point in time when other methods of control were weakening or disappearing altogether. Southern whites were fearful about their economic future, anxious over the fate of southern women in the climate of emancipation, and concerned about the consequences of increasing social equality between whites and blacks. These multiple sentiments found expression in a lynch culture that targeted blacks more than it did whites (prior to the defeat of the South in the Civil War, lynchings were more often of whites than of blacks) (I. Evans, 2011).

Groups will use violence to get what they want, but they develop—or try to—ideologies that legitimate their violent activities as necessary and reasonable, while branding the violence of other people as dangerous and unreasonable. Sometimes, one particular group's *ideology of violence* will be internalized by a majority of people in the society; at other times, support for this ideology will be very limited. It is even possible for members of a group to be seduced by their own ideology about the value of violence, coming to believe what it says without question. If an ideology of violence is firmly in place, the violence of the group that adheres to it will appear more normal, more legitimate, more necessary, and less in need of correction than other groups' violence.

The *thugs* were a group of violent criminals who once lived in India, beginning in the late 1600s. They murdered and robbed their victims in honor of Kali, the Hindu goddess of destruction. Her followers believed that if they worshipped her and carried out her bidding, she would bestow great power and great riches upon them (Hutton, 1981, p. 15). The weapons the thugs used in their murders were represented as parts of Kali herself: The pickaxe was imaged as one of her teeth, the knife was imaged as one of her ribs, and the cloth that thugs used to strangle their victims (called a *roomal*) was imaged as a piece of her garment. The thugs believed that their robberies and murders were not only moral, but also admirable and completely justified (Hollick, 1840, p. 11).

The favorite victims of the thugs were native soldiers on leave, men of nobility and bearing, and treasure carriers (Ahmad, 1992, pp. 94–95). Sometimes, the thugs brought along their children, partly so that they could learn how to kill, and partly to help disguise the thugs' true mission. The thugs would journey along with their intended victim until the time was ripe for the killing. One member of the gang would throw a rope or cloth around the victim's neck and hold one end tightly, and a second thug would hold the other end. The rope or cloth would be crossed behind the victim's neck and drawn very tight. The two thugs would push the victim's head forward to guarantee that suffocation occurred quickly. To make certain that the job was rightly done, the thugs would kick and hit the immobile victim to damage vital organs (Thornton, 1837, pp. 6–8). Victims were sometimes dispatched with weapons other than a rope or cloth: A pickaxe could be used to bludgeon and disembowel a victim, or a knife could be used to stab and cut. Sometimes, the thugs would travel several days with their intended victim to allay any suspicions.

The thugs believed that if they carefully followed the wishes of Kali, they would receive great riches and earn supernatural points that could pay off in a subsequent life. This is one reason that they showed so little guilt or remorse over their violence. Murder was defined by them as good and necessary, and thugs who did it in the proper way were thought of by their associates as heroes. Their killings were acts of worship and reverence that would allow them one day to attain a state of grace and a close affinity with Kali. However, their murderous ways were not at all acceptable to the British, who began a drive in 1831 to end the practice of what was called thuggee. However, what if the thugs had been more successful at spreading their religious beliefs and violent customs to others? What then?

Righteous Slaughter and Violentization

Jack Katz's (1988) attention to the meanings of crime, its moral and sensual attractions, provides a valuable contribution to our understanding of it. One central feature of the typical murder, which Katz calls *nonpredatory,* is that the killer views the killing as a reasonable and meaningful act, and the victim is usually a family member, friend, or acquaintance. The killer usually feels comfortable in the setting in which the murder takes place. Nonpredatory murders are not carefully planned, coldly executed acts of violence, such as political assassinations, public executions, serial murders, murders that occur during the commission of some other felony (e.g., during a robbery), or terrorist attacks. Casual life, Saturday nights out drinking and cruising Main Street, day-to-day activities with family members and friends, and the search for escape from the routines of ordinary life are the cradle for the occurrence of nonpredatory homicidal violence.

Rather than being the incomprehensible behavior of a deranged or insane individual, the average nonpredatory killing is done by someone who thinks the killing actually *supports* widely held values, such as obedience, self-respect, bravery, and honor. Even though the murder can appear irrational or foolish to everyone else—and may even appear that way to the killer at its conclusion—it does not seem that way to the killer during its commission or in the events leading up to it. Most nonpredatory killers lack premeditation or even a well-developed motive; they really don't plan on becoming killers until the murder actually occurs.

Nonpredatory killers do not murder until they reach the point where they decide that the only way to defend themselves and their rights is to kill the individual they think has done them wrong. Once done, in the killer's view, a *righteous slaughter* has occurred. Most homicides and aggravated assaults in modern societies, Black (1983, p. 36) informs us, are really attempts by individuals to maintain or regain control of perplexing situations and to help themselves. What may appear to be irrational and meaningless violent acts to an outsider may be very reasonable and meaningful to the people committing them (and perhaps even to their associates, friends, or relatives) (Black, 1993; Heimer, 1997, p. 806).

Some killings, however, are cold-blooded *predatory murders.* An example is the one that occurred in Tucson, Arizona, on January 8, 2011, when Jared Loughner, wearing sunglasses and a hoodie, took a taxi to a Safeway grocery store. He went inside to get change to pay the cab driver, and then he calmly proceeded to a parking lot where he used his Glock 19 pistol to kill 6 people and wound 13 (one of whom was Gabrielle Giffords, Democratic representative, who survived the attack). Another example is the mass murder by

James Holmes. On July 20, 2012, he entered a movie theater in Aurora, Colorado, and used an AR-15-type semiautomatic assault rifle to open fire in the crowded theater. When the smoke had cleared, 12 were dead and another 70 wounded. On December 14, 2012, Adam Lanza killed his mother in her home and then went to Sandy Hook Elementary School (in Newtown, Connecticut). He was heavily armed. Over the span of about 15 minutes, he killed 20 children and 6 adults before taking his own life with a shot to the head. It is easy to understand why an immediate response to horrific violence like this is that the perpetrator is insane or mentally ill (or the embodiment of evil). It seems to have been done without rhyme or reason, bringing the killer no advantage. This, however, is almost always an incorrect assessment of most predatory murders (Declercq & Audenaert, 2011; J. Katz, 1988, pp. 274–309; Leyton, 1986).

Multiple murderers are those who kill others in order to make a statement through the fundamental insult of killing the innocent. In this sense, Leyton (1986, p. 16) concludes, their motives are obvious and their gratifications are intense.

> Multiple murderers are not "insane" and they are very much products of their time. Far from being a randomly occurring freakish event, the arrival of the multiple murderer is dictated by specific stresses and alterations in the human community. . . . He is thus a creature and creation of his age. (p. 269)

Multiple murderers are almost always individuals who have no interest in continuing the dull lives that they see no way of escaping. The killings alleviate both their alienation and their boredom by giving them a cornucopia of rewards: revenge on what they define as an uncaring society, celebrity status, a new identity, and maybe even a measure of sexual excitement and pleasure. The killings have meaning because they give meaning to the killer's life. They are a way for the killer to get the attention of others while transforming the killer into something that he or she desperately wants to be (pp. 26–27).

There are important predisposing factors to mass murder: having a personal history of committing violence; having been the victim of bullying (if the killer is an adolescent) or having been rejected by female intimate partners, family members, or people at work (if the killer is an adult); preoccupation with firearms and war; and a fantasy life revolving around violence and revenge. Adolescent mass murderers turn "hot shame into cold anger" (Meloy et al., 2004, p. 297). The bullying and accompanying humiliation that they experienced lies dormant as these killers-to-be try to manage the intolerable shame and loss of self-respect by withdrawing into a fantasy world. Adult mass murderers embody a compensatory fantasy that culminates in a "warrior mentality," which promotes an inflated sense of power and superiority (p. 297). These inner feelings eventually crystallize into feelings of anger and vengeance that find their expression in mass murder. Rarely does this kind of violence erupt in an act of excited, agitated fury. It is almost always an unemotional, intentional, premeditated act that is methodically executed. The principal emotions of the killer are relief and exhilaration, and the principal outcome is a sense of peace or calm (Declercq & Audenaert, 2011).

Gary Gilmore was the first individual to be executed in the United States after the U.S. Supreme Court ended a 4-year moratorium on executions. (He was executed by firing squad on January 17, 1977, in Utah.) In 1976, Gilmore robbed a filling station attendant by the name of Max Jensen in Orem, Utah. After robbing Jensen, he shot the man twice in the head at close range, killing him. A day later, he entered a motel lobby and murdered Bennie Bushnell, the manager. He ordered Bushnell to lie down on the floor, and he then fired two bullets into the back of Bushnell's head, execution style. Then he stole the money from the hotel safe and fled. During the Bushnell murder, Gilmore accidentally shot himself in the hand, and the dripping blood was noticed by a man at a service garage when Gilmore returned to get his truck. The witness jotted down its license plate number—he'd heard about the robbery and murder on a police scanner—and notified police. Gilmore was arrested shortly thereafter without incident.

Although authorities eventually decided that Gilmore killed his victims to eliminate witnesses to his crimes, this conclusion hides a more complicated reality. Gilmore could have worn a mask so that he was difficult to identify, making any murders unnecessary, or he could have been more careful in the commission of his robberies. He did commit murder and robbery together, but J. Katz (1988, p. 275) concludes that Gilmore used the robbery to cover his murderous rage, not the other way around. To predatory murderers like Gilmore, conformity is the problem, especially what they view as a numbing conformity, and extreme and aberrant deviance is their road to salvation and moral transcendence. Cold-blooded killing gives the killer an edge. According to Katz, "As the deviant increasingly appreciates the moral dangers of conformity to conventional rules and reasons, he may simultaneously appreciate the transcendent power he might attain through a 'senseless' killing" (p. 297). A principal anxiety of cold-blooded killers is that they are—or will be viewed by others as—individuals who go straight mainly because they are afraid to be deviant. Cold-blooded killings establish killers as individuals who are like no others, people who are so much in control of their lives and so powerful that it is unnecessary for them to follow even rudimentary principles of human decency.

Some seriously violent people do look at the world differently from how more peaceful individuals do. Athens (1980) theorizes that some violent men and women have gone through a developmental process of *violentization* in childhood during which they were brutalized by adults in their families, and so were their siblings (and even their friends). They learned that violence is a way for humans to deal with interpersonal difficulties that they may encounter during their lives. At some point, the individual decides to stop being a victim and takes command of situations whenever possible, both violently and definitively. The individual passes from being a victim to being a victimizer. All that remains is for the individual to become more comfortable using violence with others in different situations in the real world to get what he or she wants (e.g., using a weapon to intimidate others). If successes come from using violence, the individual's self-image has now changed. He or she is now defined by others and also by himself or herself as a violent person. As the individual performs this role more and more, he or she becomes increasingly engulfed by the new identity and comfortable with it. When the point is reached that the individual has a reputation as a "badass," a significant change has occurred. He or she knows that violence is now expected. The individual then uses violence for all kinds of reasons and in all kinds of situations: as protection, to defend the person's honor, to get something of value, or to punish someone defined as deserving it. (Only a minority of violent people experience the violentization process described by Athens; it is a relatively rare occurrence.)

Social Encounters

Motives of the participants are a central part of every social encounter, violent or not. They are sometimes viewed as inner factors that cause individuals to act in certain ways. "He hit his brother because he was angry" identifies anger as the motive for the assault. *Motives,* however, are more than this. They are vocabularies or verbal statements used by people in a social encounter to explain, define, and interpret social action as it unfolds and develops (Mills, 1940). They are provided in response to the question, "Why did you do that?" (p. 907). People use motives to understand and sometimes to explain what they do; they also use motives to interpret and make sense of what others do. Motives are themselves part of a social scene, and they can determine how social relationships unfold and how they are viewed and evaluated by others (p. 904).

Just as individuals learn the proper ways of acting, they also learn a finite number of proper motives *for* acting. In some instances, individuals will abandon entirely what they plan to do, or they will choose a different course of action, if they are unable to find appropriate motives for their planned activities (or motives that others will accept). Individuals can disagree over which motives are operating in a particular situation, and they can be confused over what motivated others just as they can be unsure over their own motives (Mills, 1940, pp. 911–912). People may offer motives for their actions that are disbelieved by others, or people may negotiate with each other until an appropriate motive is found that almost everybody will accept. A corrupt politician may insist that he or she was forced to go above the written law for the good of the country. Others may believe it was the politician's greed, arrogance, or stupidity—not the good of the country—that was the real motivating factor. Self-defense is a motive for violence that is easier for most people to accept than is the claim that violence is being used to serve the goddess Kali. If the motives seem reasonable enough, the activity may not even be defined as a form of violence in the first place.

How does it help us to know that motives are social constructions that are situationally specific? Let us consider an example. Professional killers—individuals who are paid money to kill other people—have a vocabulary of motive that makes it possible for them to kill people with neither guilt nor regret. They organize their murders in such a way that the violence appears routine and necessary and the victims appear deserving of whatever happens to them. "Routine kill of targets for money" is a motive that allows professional killers to ignore the fact that they are ruthlessly killing real human beings; this motive helps them to maintain the degree of coldness, detachment, and daring required by their professional activities (Levi, 1989).

Accounts (see Chapter 2) are interjected into social relationships by individuals who want to influence perceptions about their intent or motive. If an individual who did a violent act successfully uses an account, he or she has been able to convince others that the violence that occurred is excusable (unintentional) or justified (necessary and unavoidable). Accounts are sometimes so standardized within specific cultures or subcultures that they are routinely expected when conduct departs too much from what is supposed to happen. For example, a police officer may handcuff an arrested suspect without offering any account. Handcuffing is part of the job, and it is expected. However, if a suspect is brought to the police station bruised and battered, some account will have to be offered by the arresting officer. He or she might give the "standardized account" that the suspect was "resisting arrest." If this account is believed by others, it will convince them that the police officer did not really want to hurt the suspect but was forced to by the suspect's failure to comply with the officer's commands.

A study of 73 incarcerated felons (in 11 different correctional facilities in Colorado) who were found guilty of gun-related crimes that produced either death or injury for their victims reveals the power of accounts (Pogrebin, Stretesky, & Unnithan, 2009, pp. 23–50). These inmates offered either excuses to deflect responsibility for the violence from themselves (e.g., by blaming external factors) or justifications (in which responsibility was accepted for the crime but its deviancy was discounted by insisting that it was necessary that they use violence). The most common *excuse* used by members of the sample was that they were not completely free at the time they used their guns, embodied in the claim that they were not thinking clearly or were forced to act violently by others (pp. 38–39). The most common *justification* used by members of the sample was denial of a victim, embodied in their claim that the victims deserved to be shot (p. 27). These prisoners used many different excuses or justifications, some of them simultaneously, to account for their gun violence.

Research indicates that, in cases of domestic violence, "intimacy repels law" (i.e., familiarity between offender and offended leads to some confusion for police about what to do) (Black, 1980). The likelihood of an offender being arrested for assaulting another individual is lower if the victim and victimizer are romantically involved or related by family ties than if they are acquaintances or strangers. Factors that operate to change this association between intimacy and the low likelihood of arrest are drug use by the perpetrator (alcohol or other drugs), a perpetrator's use of a weapon, or physical injury to a victim. Males who assault females, regardless of relational distance (i.e., stranger, acquaintance, or family/intimate) are more likely to be arrested than are males who assault males (or than females who assault others). What seems to be operating is that the closer the relationship, the greater is the inclination of police to conclude that other mechanisms of informal control and regulation will kick in and start working. They believe they do not have to arrest an assaulter in incidents of intimate partner violence unless clear indicators are present that show the situation might get worse rather than better (e.g., a weapon, drugs, or physical injury to a victim). The "amount of formal control, in this case enforcement, applied in any given situation is inversely proportional to the amount of informal control perceived present" (Lally & DeMaris, 2012, p. 116).

Peralta and Cruz (2006) were interested in how a sample of university students viewed and interpreted (i.e., attached meanings to) alcohol-related violence. It is clear from their study that drinking a lot and often is viewed as both an indicator of masculinity and as a way to justify and excuse some of the violent things that drinking men are inclined to do.

> [T]he general belief some males "naturally" become violent after drinking helps to shape and inform the gendered world of drinking behavior within the context of college culture. What is more, these common expectations may reduce a student's ability to recognize harmful behavior as damaging and undesirable if these behaviors are assumed to be natural byproducts of gender. (p. 117)

From their interviews with 78 respondents, the authors found that these individuals were inclined to believe that alcohol plays a major role in patterns of violence, especially for young males, and that alcohol-related violence represents a form of "macho" behavior ("beer muscles"). These definitions and understandings normalize violent behavior while they motivate it.

A study by Faris and Felmlee (2011) of high school students' violent behavior shows that violence is not necessarily the province of marginal, psychologically deranged, out-of-control individuals. In fact, these researchers uncovered a link between relatively high levels of status in a social hierarchy and aggressive behaviors. Moving up in status in the school hierarchy and being able to maintain it require a willingness to use violence when necessary. Students at the very bottom of the status hierarchy lack a capacity for using violence to increase their status and those at the very top refrain from using it because they have no reason to do so. However, "for the vast majority of adolescents, increases in status are, over time, accompanied by increases in aggression toward their peers" (p. 67). The researchers also found evidence of an expressive use of violence, especially with same-sex aggression. Some individuals torment others only because they find it pleasurable to hurt them and think that they can get away with it.

In the world outside the school, defined more by occupational status than by grade point average, athletic prowess, or dating success, the relationship between status and aggression is different. Individuals at *both* the top and bottom of the occupational status hierarchy are found to be the angriest—that is, angrier than individuals in intervening positions (Collett & Lizardo, 2010). Those at the top, however, have a different relationship to aggression than do those at the bottom. The individuals at the top are better able than those at the bottom to exercise control of their angry outbursts in their dealings with others because they are able to follow feeling rules that mandate the suppression of negative feelings (pp. 2083–2085). It is the *expression* of violence that is variable and relative, not the feelings of being angry.

The Curious Case of Jack the Ripper

Murder Most Foul

In 1888, a killer who came to be known as Jack the Ripper prowled the streets of London's East End. Although the identity of this killer was never uncovered in a court of law—it is one of Scotland Yard's most famous unsolved crimes—a consensus view evolved that the killer was a male who acted alone to murder five women (known as the "canonical five"), all of whom were prostitutes, from the end of August until the beginning of November. He killed his victims through asphyxiation and/or cutting and stabbing. The loss of blood was extensive. Robbery or theft did not seem to be a primary motive, and body cavities had been cut open and body parts removed for some specific reason by the killer. All but the last known victim (Mary Jane Kelly) were killed and mutilated on the street, probably close to where they met their killer. Except for the one killing that occurred in the City of London (Catherine Eddowes), the rest were confined to districts in the East End known as Whitechapel or Spitalfields, which lay just outside the city's northeastern boundary. The identity of the killer was a matter of speculation and dispute in 1888 and still is to this very day.

Douglas and Olshaker (2000, p. 1) claim that, when it comes to serial killers, Jack the Ripper is ground zero, the point at which both history and discussion begin. In fact, interest in the killings, the killer, and the victims has not lessened with the passage of time.

> Interest in the Jack the Ripper murders is probably greater today than at any time since the killer himself actually stalked the streets of London's East End. In recent years we have been all but deluged in a swelling tide of books, articles, films, plays and comics inspired by the case, and aficionados can now debate their theories and exchange views via Internet sites, at annual conferences and in the columns of specialist magazines. (Sugden, 2002, p. xi)

The murders and murderer continue to be the object of investigative reports, board games, computer games, wax museum exhibits, trading cards, songs, operas, comic books, movies, television shows, baseball caps, and even alcoholic drinks (e.g., the Ripper Tipple, containing blood-red spirits). One of the most interesting features of the Ripper's killings is their longevity in the face of so much uncertainty and disagreement.

We must be cautious in what we say and believe about the Ripper and the murders. Although a place like the East End had all the elements necessary to produce a Jack the Ripper—and most every other human aberration—it also had all the elements necessary to produce biased accounts and incorrect statements about what was happening.

> Any comparison of the books about Jack the Ripper will reveal contradictions and a wealth of deceptive, unsupported, and in some cases utterly false detail. The names of witnesses have been incorrectly given, some important witness testimony has been omitted or given insufficient attention, relevant documents have been misunderstood or misinterpreted, sources have not been cross-checked and errors have not been corrected. (Begg, 1988, p. 11)

Sugden (2002, p. 105), who would certainly agree, was astonished at the large number of errors made in supposedly factual accounts of the case and how long these errors have persisted. He concluded that few of the authors who have written about the case bothered to adequately research the facts. Some of the books are so misleading that they should be placed on shelves containing only works of fiction.

It is not hard to accept as truth some of what contemporaries of the killer believed. He had physical strength, both daring and coolness, and perhaps special knowledge and skill to be able to do what he did (though some medical experts testified at inquests that they believed the killer had no special knowledge at all). These hunches, however, did not limit the field enough to do much good. The number of suspects remains large, and nobody is widely accepted as *the* killer. Russo's (2004) examination of 71 possible suspects led him to conclude that we are no wiser about the true identity of Jack the Ripper than we ever were. Even Lewis Carroll (also known as Charles Dodgson), famous author of children's books, was included on the list, supposedly killing in tandem with a lifelong friend from Oxford, Thomas Bayne (Wallace, 1996). Other suspects who were suggested at the time of the murders are a sunstroked physician, a cattle drover, a Malay, a slaughterhouse employee, a Frenchman who dabbled in the supernatural, and an American anatomist (Fisher, 1997, p. 213). Eddie Victor (the Duke of Clarence), grandson of Queen Victoria, has also been identified as possibly being the infamous killer (Abrahamsen, 1992; Russo, 2004, pp. 144–151).

Folk Devils and Moral Panics

Jack the Ripper has become bigger than life, a concrete example of a folk devil (a principal reason for the case's longevity). *Folk devils* embody evil, and they symbolize in a clear and consistent way, free from distractions and ambiguities, something despicable and ugly (S. Cohen, 1972, pp. 10–11). They are "unambiguously unfavorable symbols," stripped of any positive qualities and imbued with the ultimate evil (p. 41). Importantly, in such a symbolization process, "images are made much sharper than reality" (p. 43).

> London has been, in its time, the largest city in the world. It is well over two thousand years old, and has stood at the heart of an empire that spanned the globe. Of all the blood that has been shed, the violence and the secrecy, the rise and fall of dynasties, five murders in the autumn of 1888 have cut more deeply into the memory of horror than any others. (Perry, 2006, p. 182)

Newspapers (of which there were hundreds in the area) did what they could to promote or even inflame residents' fears and anxieties. The media either improvised rumors or manipulated and massaged the available ones to make each murder seem more sensational and barbaric than the previous one. Because fear sold more newspapers, editors and reporters had a vested interest in making the crimes look as horrific as possible and the theories as outlandish as they could (Fisher, 1997, p. 209). Simply put, violence and sex sold newspapers, and Jack the Ripper seemed to exemplify both.

Moral panics—and the public reaction in 1888 to the Ripper's killings is a good example of one—by their very nature identify, condemn, and work to eliminate folk devils (Goode & Ben-Yehuda, 1994, pp. 28–30). A moral panic involves predictions of catastrophe; heightened sensitivity to, and selective perception of, signs of danger; coping mechanisms and exaggerated reactions; rumors about present threats and future possibilities; false alarms; and sometimes even mass delusions (pp. 144–148). As Fisher (1997) says,

> A community will attempt to contain the threat by attributing it to an outsider or someone from another part of society, or by ultimately finding the victims themselves responsible for their own misfortune. Social distancing, finding fault, and laying blame are a community's classic defense. (pp. 217–218)

The Ripper's killings chipped away at the structure of the community, at least temporarily, weakening whatever bonds existed and intensifying ethnic and religious animosities. Residents became less trusting and more suspicious of one another. With each murder, the level of police patrol went up and citizen presence on the streets of the East End went down. Sporadic violence broke out in which groups of vigilantes would beat up any man walking the streets of Whitechapel who brought suspicion upon himself.

A roaming, brutal, relentless murderer, killing at will and with impunity, was perfectly fit to demonstrate to residents of the East End in 1888—and people elsewhere forevermore—the dangers of public life and the risks of trusting others. "The blacker the villain," A. Cohen (1974) instructs, "the more useful he is to the ordinary man, who might otherwise be hard put to produce the desired contrast effect" (p. 17). The tale of Jack the Ripper was spread by newspapers and word of mouth, and given substance by letters to authorities, supposedly from the killer himself. Rather than having a generalized sense that something was wrong, with its natural correlate of diffused anxiety, a tangible threat like the Ripper made it possible to deal with the anxiety and for the East End inhabitants to respond in some deliberate and meaningful way (Kerckhoff & Back, 1968, pp. 159–160).

The East End was regularly portrayed in both the press and in the oral tradition as a grimy, sordid, degenerate place, populated by both the morally and physically unclean, who were thoroughly committed to idleness instead of work. It was widely defined as a strange and foreign land, a locale beyond the reach of both morality and law (Marriott, 2008). The East End became a synonym for pestilence, poverty, danger, and social decay. Without the East End, the Ripper is just another slasher story (Bloom, 2008, p. 248). So, the East End was demonized, too. It became known by the fall of 1888 as the "abyss," "murderland," "plague spot," or "evil quarter-mile" (Ross, 2008, p. 181). In short, it was conceptualized as "outcast London" (Rumbelow, 1988). News stories, editorials, and even cartoons in the popular press nudged Victorians in the direction of defining the East End, and especially Whitechapel, as a site of both political unrest and inherent pathology (Gray, 2011). To many Victorians, the streets of the East End themselves were the real Ripper (Ackroyd, 2008, p. 29).

It was not long before a quest ensued to find an "other" to blame for the crimes. Jack Pizer, a Jew, was the first one arrested. Whether fomenting anti-Semitic feelings among the populace was one objective of the Ripper, it can never be known. It is clear, however, that the Ripper murders did become entwined with the treatment of Jews in the East End. The words on the wall at Goulston Street (*The Juwes are the men that will not be Blamed for nothing*), thought to be written by the killer after he killed Eddowes, were deemed both anti-Semitic and inflammatory by police (and erased before they could be photographed). Ackroyd (2008, p. 26) insists that the words on the wall were simply a Cockney way of saying that Jews will not take responsibility for anything, the work of an unhappy or prejudiced Brit. One thing is clear: If the words on the wall were written by the killer, he was not Jewish. A Jew in that era would have used the word "Yid" or "Yiddish," and no Jew in England would have written "Juwes" (Fisher, 1997, p. 213). In their haste to remove the message, police may have confused what they thought was on the wall—*Juwes*—with what was actually there: *Juives*, the French spelling of "Jews" (p. 213). What seems most likely is that the writing had nothing to do with the murders.

Constructing Jack

The social construction of the Ripper as a folk devil and demonization of the murders rests on three "planks." None of them is necessarily true, and each one is open to dispute. If any one of them were to be proven false, it would change substantially how this classic example of predatory violence is understood.

1. *One man was responsible for the series of murders in the East End in 1888.* The belief that one individual was responsible for each and every murder of the "canonical five" (Nichols, Chapman, Stride, Eddowes, and Kelly) is the core of the social construction of the Ripper. However, this may just be smoke and mirrors, a belief generated more by official responses and media attention than by any characteristics of the killings themselves. Street thugs and ruffians prowled the East End in search of cash and valuables. Some of the victims blamed on the Ripper could just as easily have been killed by these marauding gangs. These ruffians used violence both to make prostitutes pay extortion money and to punish them if they refused. This sent a clear message to any others who might have been inclined to keep the money they had earned for themselves (Cornwell, 2002, p. 126; Fido, 1993; Rumbelow, 1988). Stride, mainly because her murder was different from that of the other victims (i.e., no mutilations and no parallel incision in the throat), is a good candidate for someone who was killed by a gang. In fact, one police view, eventually rejected for reasons that are unclear, was that a gang of blackmailing ruffians was responsible for the string of murders (Jackson, 2008, p. 122).

During their lives, the canonical five had a great deal of interpersonal difficulties with husbands, ex-husbands, boyfriends, adult children, bosses, apartment owners, acquaintances, and friends. Where life is miserable, nasty, solitary, and brutish, little reluctance exists to act violently toward others. Even the fear of arrest and incarceration is an insufficient deterrent to override the brutalizing impact of horrid social conditions. Florence Fenwick Miller, in a letter to the *Daily News* during the time of the murders (October 1, 1888), refers to the fact that women at the time were regularly kicked, beaten, jumped on till they were crushed, chopped, stabbed, steamed with vitriol, bitten, eviscerated with red-hot pokers, and deliberately set on fire. If the woman died, it was called manslaughter; if she lived, it was called common assault. Cutting throats was not an unusual way to murder people in 1888, especially in cases of domestic violence (Cornwell, 2002, p. 126). Furthermore, it is almost an article of faith among criminal profilers that stabbing a person multiple times in the region of the face is a very personal act. When it is found, it is taken as strong circumstantial evidence by police and medical examiners that victim and victimizer knew each other (Cornwell, 2002, p. 32). More than one killer could have been operating in the area, and the canonical five could have been slain by other than a canonical one Jack the Ripper.

2. *The Ripper killed many women.* Estimates of the number of Ripper victims fluctuate over time and from writer to writer, going as low as 2 and as high as 11 (or higher if the Whitehall Mystery victim or the unidentified woman murdered in December 1887 with an iron stake is added to the count). These are widely divergent estimates and produce very different images of this nineteenth-century murderer. In fact, if it were to be true that the Ripper killed but two women—the consensus definition of serial killing requires that three or more people be killed, with a lengthy cooling-off period between each murder (Homant & Kennedy, 2006, p. 190)—it would mean that Jack the Ripper, the most famous serial killer in the annals of crime, was not a serial killer at all.

S. Evans and Rumbelow (2006) consider but then reject the prevailing view that Jack the Ripper killed five and only five women (i.e., the "canonical five"). They note that there is very little hard evidence and no certainty available about which killings were done by whom. Because no murderer was arrested and convicted for the crimes, they concluded that it is impossible to know which victims fell to the Ripper. They whittle the list down to three on the basis of how the killings were done by the murderer (*modus operandi*): Nichols (victim #1), Chapman (victim #2), and Eddowes (victim # 4) were victims of the same killer. It is less likely that Stride (victim #3) and Kelly (victim #5) were (p. 260). This probably should have been the end of the discussion, but it was not. On page 268, in the "Authors' Epilogues," Rumbelow states the following: "Here I find myself agreeing with Superintendent Arnold that there were only four victims."

The press at the time of the killings concluded that a series of murders was occurring when it was no series at all. Two women had been killed in the general vicinity of Whitechapel, Emma Smith in April and Martha Tabram in August. When Mary Ann Nichols was slain in August, the three deaths were lumped together and blamed on the same person. "The three Whitechapel murders were immediately identified as a 'series' and the press proclaimed that a homicidal maniac was on the loose" (S. Evans & Skinner, 2001, pp. 2–3). This conclusion was reached in spite of the fact that very few people in the area actually believed that the three victims were killed by the same hand. The seriality was established on the flimsiest of evidence: All three women had been cut and stabbed, and murder was not common in the district. It seems that when the need arises, the number of victims credited to Jack the Ripper is easily fudged in the upward direction.

The Federal Bureau of Investigation coined the term *linkage blindness* to describe the *failure* of members of the public to recognize that the same killer is responsible for multiple murders occurring at different places and times (Jenkins, 1994, p. 6). This is a legitimate concern with killers like Theodore Robert Bundy, executed in Florida by electric chair on January 24, 1989, for killing a preteen female by the name of Kimberly Diane Leach. When the killer is mobile and the victims are many—Bundy killed women in many different states—linkage blindness may impede both efforts to nab the killer and efforts to understand all that happened. With Jack the Ripper, however, we may have a mirror image of this phenomenon, a *linkage quest*. This term describes the inclination to link murders together that are neither connected nor done by the same individual. This usually leads to a perception that a surge has occurred in the actual rate of serial murder rather than what it really is: an artifact of how the data are being reported and understood.

3. *The Ripper was a sexually sadistic killer.* If these murders were, in fact, sexually motivated, they were unusual. Not a lot of evidence of sexual muti-lation existed in the 1888 murders, as most of the damage was done to the throat, abdomen, and internal organs. C. Wilson's (1988) proof for his claim that Jack the Ripper inaugurated the age of sex crime is no proof at all. The only objective indicator he offers for classifying the killings the way he does is that "nightmarish mutilations" were inflicted upon the victims on their genital areas (p. 2). It seems just as accurate to assert that the Ripper had a sexual attraction to stomachs (called *alvinolagnia*) as it does to decide that because he stabbed people in body parts that can be used for reproduction it means that he was a sex criminal. Curiously, the possible Ripper victim who comes closest to having been assaulted by a sexually sadistic killer is Emma Smith. She was assaulted with a blunt object that was inserted into her vaginal vault, and she died a day later in the London Hospital. She has been discounted, however, as a Ripper victim.

Medical specialists in 1888 could find no evidence of any sexual contact between the killer and the killed when they autopsied the victims. For exam-ple, Dr. Frederick Gordon Brown, the surgeon for the City of London police, reported at the inquest to determine the cause of death of Catherine Eddowes that no secretions of any kind were on the deceased's thighs, leading him to conclude that no traces of recent "connection" existed. Fido (1993, p. 47) finds this conclusion significant. It indicates that nineteenth-century medical men were well aware that a serial murderer like Jack the Ripper might cop-ulate with his victims (or masturbate on or near the body). The medical examiner looked for evidence of this but could find none. It is true that forensic science in 1888 was in its infancy and had not yet developed tests for crime scene investigators to determine the presence of semen in or on a victim's body. It is *not* true, however, that they were ignorant about the possibility that murders were sometimes done for sexual reasons.

None of the indicators used by Warren, Hazelwood, and Dietz (1996) in their study of 20 sexually sadistic serial killers was found in *any* of the Ripper murders. These researchers found binding, blindfolding, or gagging in 100 percent of the 20 murders studied; none of these occurred in the Ripper murders. They found intended torture in 100 percent of the 20 murders; no torture occurred in the Ripper murders. They found careful planning of the offenses in 95 percent of the 20 murders. The murders in the East End in 1888 were more a product of luck or opportunity than of careful planning. These researchers found sexual bondage in 95 percent of the 20 murders; no sexual bondage was found in the Ripper murders. They found evidence of penile penetration in 95 percent of the 20 murders; no evidence of sexual connection was uncovered by medical examiners in any of the Ripper murders. They found evidence of sodomy (e.g., anal or oral sex) or object penetration in 90 percent of the 20 murders; nothing like this occurred in the Ripper murders.

It is true—or seems to be—that lust murders (i.e., killings in which murderers obtain sexual excitement from their brutal acts, also known as *erotophonophilia*) are associated with *piquerism*, a proclivity to use a knife to stab, cut, or wound another person, usually in the genital region and/or on the breasts. The repeated stabbings and penetrations are exciting to the killer (Purcell & Arrigo, 2006, p. 6; Vronsky, 2004, p. 65). However, the fact that repeated stabbings *can* be titillating for a killer does not mean that they were for Jack the Ripper. Lust murders are also, according to Purcell and Arrigo, associated with *flagellationism* (the intense desire to beat, whip, or club a person, which can be carried out in acts of torture); *anthropophagy* (the intense desire to eat the flesh or body parts of another person); and *necrosadism* (sexual contact with a dead body) (p. 6). Little to no evidence exists that any of these were found in any of the Ripper murders. (One letter to authorities, supposedly from the Ripper, did claim that part of a victim's kidney was eaten, but the factual basis of this letter and the anthropophagy it described are highly suspect.)

Some evidence—or more than was found—should have been present at the crime scenes or uncovered at the autopsies if Jack the Ripper was, in fact, a sexually sadistic serial killer. The Ripper may simply have wanted to generate as much fear and outrage as possible in the general public and concluded that brutal murders and horrific mutilations were the way to do it. It would probably be wise to err on the side of caution and not assert confidently that Jack the Ripper was a sexually sadistic serial killer. One thing certainly is true: Not all serial murderers are lust murderers (Holmes & Holmes, 2010, p. 11; Ioannou, 2010, p. 302). Serial murderers are motivated by things other than, or in addition to, sex, such as attention-seeking, anger, thrills, or even financial gain (U.S. Department of Justice, 2008). They search for victims who are vulnerable and thus easier to isolate and control (Alvarez & Bachman, 2008, p. 109).

The Ripper's Legacy

If some doubt exists that the Victorians actually gave us the first sexually sadistic serial killer, no doubt should exist that an important legacy originated in the fog-shrouded streets of the East End. The Victorians did give concrete meaning to the idea of *seriality*. These five killings (related or not) gave sustenance and nourishment to the developing view that separate crimes could be linked together. "Serial" came to mean something other than *repeated*. It indicated sinister characteristics of an offender, such as irrationality, compulsiveness, and extreme violence. Actual killers could draw inspiration from the idea of seriality and pattern their murders on the idea of stalking and repetition. Some individuals in the United States during the time of the murders devoured reports from abroad about the killings (Larson, 2003, p. 70). A Whitechapel Club formed in Chicago. The club's president held the title of "The Ripper," and members, mostly journalists, both revered and sensationalized murder and mayhem. The meetings consisted of a sharing of tales about actual murders that had occurred on the streets of Chicago. Weapons used in actual murders, supplied by the police, adorned the walls of the clubhouse. Skulls supplied by a nearby asylum did, too (pp. 31–32).

The Ripper murders seemed to show that serial killers' level of violence escalates over time. Sugden (2002) shows this way of thinking when he describes the murder of Mary Jane Kelly, generally believed to be the last victim of the series, as "certainly his [the Ripper's] most extensively mutilated victim" (p. 112). The only way, however, that escalating violence could be confirmed in the East End killings is *if* they were all done by the same individual, and if the slow, methodical, private killing of Mary Kelly could be scientifically proven to be more violent than the savage blitz attack and frenzied mutilations, done in the open, of Catherine Eddowes. The claims about how many women Jack the Ripper killed, still a matter of dispute, get hopelessly confused with claims about whether the violence went up, went down, or stayed about the same.

Variable Violence

Killing the Young

The prevailing standards in the United States today with regard to when life begins and when it can be taken away, though ambiguous, are clear in one respect: It is totally unacceptable for anybody to intentionally kill or abuse an infant or child. Even the most adamant proabortionist believes that once a child is born, he or she is a person and has the right to live and grow, and antiabortionists would no doubt agree. The killing or abuse of an infant or child is viewed as inexcusable—a monstrous act by either a very sick or a very sadistic individual (Kantrowitz, 1998, p. 53). However, *infanticide*—killing of babies and small children—has not always been considered a heinous act.

Infanticide occurs among nonhuman primates (Rees, 2009), and it was once a fairly common human practice (deMause, 1974). Childhood was considered a brief period of development during which children were expected to acquire adult skills and capabilities as quickly as possible, and they were viewed as ungrateful dependents or even as parasites (McCoy, 1992). Middle- and upper-class parents believed that having too many children interfered with their lifestyles and their pursuit of pleasure. Working- and lower-class families also had their reasons for not wanting too many children. A new child meant another mouth to feed and another person to care for in a family where resources were limited. Time spent in the birth and care of a child pulled the mother away from important duties that contributed to the survival of the entire family. If the mother were to die in childbirth—a distinct possibility given the low level of medical knowledge and skill—an important and valuable family member would be gone. Illegitimate children, deformed children, babies born to parents who did not want them, and infants born to families who were too poor to afford them were regularly killed outright or simply allowed to die through abandonment or neglect.

Improvement in economic conditions, new civil liberties for all people, healthier living conditions, and better medical care served to change attitudes about children and childhood. Children came to be seen as more valuable. By the late 1600s and early 1700s, child-rearing practices were already starting to change throughout the world. The Puritans, for example, elevated the status of children to new heights. They believed strongly in the value of the family, especially family cohesion and integration. The corporal punishment of children was acceptable only if it was authorized by community leaders and done to strengthen the family unit (Pleck, 1987). By the late

1700s, more women had access to birth control techniques, allowing some choice in regard to pregnancy. Because having a child was more voluntary, it meant that more parents had children because they wanted them. Children came to be defined more as rewards than as burdens, and a new closeness developed between parents and their children. Parents were more affectionate toward children and more indulgent of them than they had ever been (Zelizer, 1994).

Children came to be increasingly viewed as persons who needed to be protected from risks and hazards of life. Child labor laws were passed in most Western nations to ensure that youngsters were no longer economically exploited by adults. (Massachusetts passed the first state child labor law in the United States in 1836.) During the twentieth century in the United States, children came to be viewed less as economic assets and more as priceless human beings. Their principal value came to be found in the pleasure that they brought to others and their capacity for learning and future success. Children had attained a sentimental value in the Western world that was unheard of and unimagined at other times and places (Zelizer, 1994).

At times, in some places, infanticide has been viewed as both necessary and reasonable, an expression of parental duty and love, not a retreat from it. The Netsilik Eskimo (Inuit) are a native group who live on the Arctic coast of North America. They hunt seals, caribou, and salmon with harpoons and spears. They were once nomadic and lived in tents in the summer and snowhouses (igloos) in the winter that were heated by soapstone lamps. Up to the 1930s, they were well-known for their custom of infanticide, and girl babies were usually killed more frequently than boy babies (Balikci, 1970/1989, p. 147).

> Once when there was a famine Nagtok gave birth to a child, while people lay around about her dying of hunger. What did that child want here? How could it live, when its mother, who should give it life, was herself dried up and starving? So she strangled it and allowed it to freeze and later on ate it. (Rasmussen, quoted in Balikci, p. 151)

The Netsilik considered infanticide as a way to increase their chances of survival in a harsh environment. They were hunters and gatherers, so they could not grow crops to feed themselves or control the movements of the animals on which their survival depended. Sometimes, little was available to gather or hunt, prospects became very bleak, and starvation was imminent. Under these harsh conditions, infanticide was a rational but desperate act.

Female children were also killed under more normal conditions of life when adults were neither angry and frustrated nor terribly hungry. Why kill girls instead of boys? The Netsilik defined females as both poor hunters and big eaters, so their loss from society was considered less objectionable than the loss of males. They believed that female infanticide increased the entire community's chances for survival by reducing the number of people who ate food but were deemed less able to hunt for it (Balikci, 1970/1989, p. 151). If a woman gave birth to a daughter and cared for her, it was considered time poorly spent; the mother could have given birth to a son and raised him in an equal amount of time. Thus, a daughter might be killed to make it possible for the family to bring forth a son.

Patterns of authority in a Netsilik household were not rigid, and it was possible for an individual with a strong personality to have a significant impact. An older woman might speak with enough strength and conviction that she was able to determine the fate of a newborn. Infanticide was a flexible custom, not a rigid cultural rule, and alternatives to it existed. In the usual case of female infanticide, however, the biological father made the final decision, and the mother carried out the killing. Infants were killed in several ways. If a birth occurred during the winter, the newborn was placed at the entrance to the igloo. The child's screams only lasted a few minutes because the infant froze to death. In summer, a newborn was placed in a small grave, dug near the family's dwelling. The infant usually cried several hours before dying. A third method was used for all seasons: A furry skin was placed over the infant's face until the baby suffocated.

The Netsilik were either unconcerned with, or unaware of, the grave dangers that female infanticide posed to community survival. The custom produced powerful tensions and a great deal of disharmony. It produced an imbalance in the sex ratio, thereby reducing the number of marriageable females. This increased the pressure on men to find and hold mates. The community divided itself into many small, mutually suspicious groups. Sometimes, husbands were murdered. They were simply stabbed in the back by envious men who wanted to marry their wives. In 1936, a Catholic missionary established a mission near the Netsilik. As a result of his preaching and ongoing personal involvement with them, he was able to suppress the practice of female infanticide. This eventually caused a much greater balance in the sex ratio. Men were able to find wives more easily, and they were less likely to murder each other to obtain mates. Monogamy became the rule, and other marital arrangements (such as polygyny or polyandry) fell into disfavor. Very quickly, according to Balikci (1970/1989), the Netsilik started acting like "good Christians" (p. 250).

Killing the Not-So-Young

In some places, killing a person who is legally determined to "deserve it" because of some injury he or she has visited on the community receives great support. The killing by the government—called *capital punishment* or the *death penalty*—may not even be viewed as a violent act because of its legitimacy in the eyes of the beholders. Unlike dueling violence, which skirted the official apparatus of control, the killings produced by capital punishment occur according to strict rules and formalized procedures, carried out by representatives of the government itself. Specific due-process requirements must be followed for an individual to be sentenced to death and then executed, and the convict is legally permitted to appeal the sentence many times in the usual case. Amnesty International (2012) reports that in 2011, a total of 20 nations executed condemned criminals, a decrease from a decade earlier when 31 countries carried out executions. The trend worldwide is toward abolition of use of the death penalty with over two-thirds of the world's countries terminating the use of capital punishment in law, in practice, or in both.

Not all states in the United States have the death penalty, and different people have different opinions about its propriety, especially with subpopulations, such as juveniles, those with mental retardations, the insane, or the mentally ill (Kubiak & Allen, 2011). Attitudes about capital punishment in the United States are volatile, having shifted during the last 45 years or so from weak support (42 percent favored it as a punishment for murder in 1966) to the strong support of the 1980s and 1990s (71 percent favored it in 1996) (Maguire & Pastore, 1998, p. 141). Support for capital punishment declined a bit as the United States moved into the twenty-first century (61 percent favored it as a punishment for murder in 2011 [Bureau of Justice Statistics, 2011, Table 2.52]). However, a survey of college freshmen shows they have become more supportive of the death penalty with the passage of time. In 1969, a total of 56 percent of them agreed ("strongly" or "somewhat") that the death penalty should be abolished; in 2006, only 35 percent of them felt the same way (Bureau of Justice Statistics, 2006, Table 2.93).

Ancient executions were savage affairs, characterized by a great deal of community rage and anger, in which the offender was expected to die slowly and in great misery. All members of the community participated, either as executioners or as witnesses (Johnson, 1990, p. 6). The bodily organs of some offenders were mutilated to increase their punishment even more. Intestines, hearts, and kidneys have been ripped out of condemned criminals by angry crowds, sometimes while the condemned was still alive, and their hands, noses, tongues, and ears have been either cut off or mutilated. In some cases, it was done because the body parts were viewed as the organs responsible for the crimes. Other times, offenders were mutilated simply to prolong their suffering or to humiliate them further (Newman, 1978, pp. 47–50).

The identifying features of modern, government executions are their bureaucratic nature and their isolation from the community. Community feelings of rage are supposed to be absent or at least suppressed. What was once an act by a community on its own behalf has become the special province of prison officials, who are expected to approach executions with professionalism and detachment. The last government-sponsored *public* execution in the United States occurred in Owensboro, Kentucky, in 1937, where a young black man (named Rainey Bethea) was hanged for assaulting a 70-year-old woman. Twenty thousand people attended, and they were a coarse, unruly crowd (Prejean, 1989, p. 101).

Murderers not only take lives needlessly and ravage the families and friends of the victim, but also violate the sentiments of trust and affiliation that serve as the foundation of social life. The anger, the hurt, and the desire for revenge are easy enough to understand (Berns, 1982, pp. 334–335). However, not everyone who has had a family member murdered is in favor of the death penalty.

> I was eight years old when my father was murdered. It is almost impossible to describe the pain of losing a parent to a senseless murder. And in the aftermath, it is similarly impossible to quiet the confusion: "Why him? Why this? Why me?" But even as a child one thing was clear to me: I didn't want the killer, in turn, to be killed. . . . I saw nothing that could be accomplished in the loss of one life being answered with the loss of another. And I knew, far too vividly, the anguish that would spread through another family—another set of parents, children, brothers, and sisters thrown into grief. (M. K. Kennedy, 1989, p. 1)

The author of this quotation is M. Kerry Kennedy, the daughter of Robert F. Kennedy. Her father was gunned down in Los Angeles in June 1968 during his bid for the Democratic nomination for the presidency of the United States. Why was Ms. Kennedy so strongly opposed to capital punishment, even as a child, and even after the murder of her father, when other people, whose lives have not been as dramatically changed by a violent crime, are not? Do they have greater concern for the victims of violence than does Ms. Kennedy, or is something else operating?

Elements can be found in an execution of a convicted felon to suggest that it is—or could be interpreted as—a premeditated, violent act. Johnson (1990) describes an execution he witnessed of a felon named Jones. The man was strapped into the electric chair, electrodes were attached to his head and leg, and a tight mask was placed over his face. Only his nose was visible. At the legally designated time, the electric switch was thrown, and 2,500 volts of electricity, at 5 to 7 amps, passed through Jones's body, starting at his head and ending at the electrode on his ankle. The following describes the grisly details:

> Jones sat perfectly still for what seemed an eternity but was in fact no more than thirty seconds. Finally, the electricity hit him. His body stiffened spasmodically, though only briefly. A thin swirl of smoke trailed away from his head, then dissipated quickly. (People outside the witness room could hear crackling and burning; a faint smell of burned flesh lingered in the air, mildly nauseating some people.) The body remained taut, with the right foot raised slightly at the heel, seemingly frozen there. A brief pause, then another minute of shock. When it was over, the body was inert. (p. 111)

An execution is characterized by harm (death of the convicted felon), intent to kill (the execution is meticulously planned and carefully rehearsed to ensure a smooth and successful killing), and a deliberate taking of an individual's life by state representatives. In those characteristics, a murder and an execution are identical (M. C. Kennedy, 1976, pp. 59–62). M. C. Kennedy argues that it is one group's superior power that creates and sustains the belief that punishment and crime are different from one another, belonging to mutually exclusive categories (p. 62). It is peculiar, he thinks, that some groups will go to great lengths to stop the violence of murder but will allow, or even encourage, the violence of capital punishment.

Most people view executions as less violent than the killings that offenders committed that got them sent to the death chamber in the first place. Executions seem to be activated by proper motives, such as retribution and protection of innocent victims. Executioners are able to portray their acts as necessary and beneficial for protection of social order, both a professional duty and a legal obligation. It is widely believed that individuals who cannot live peacefully in an open, free, and prosperous society, such as the United States, deserve what they get, even if it is the death penalty. The heightened fear of violent crime, coupled with media coverage of criminal violence, no doubt plays a role when people's support for capital punishment increases (Mandery, 2012; Rankin, 1979, p. 197). The U.S. Supreme Court, along with a majority of state legislatures, reformed the death penalty in the 1970s so that it seemed moral enough to justify its continued use—less arbitrary, less racist, and less brutal (because lethal injections replaced electrocutions and gassings) (Garland, 2005, p. 350).

One thing that has made some difference in how executions are viewed is that the U.S. Supreme Court rendered decisions that restricted their use with certain categories of people. In *Atkins v. Virginia* (2002), the Court declared that individuals with mental retardations could no longer be executed (due primarily to the diminished capacity that can accompany mental retardations). In *Roper v. Simmons* (2005), which extended similar logic about capacity to the young, the Court ruled by a vote of 5 to 4 that executing individuals who at the time of their offenses were juveniles (anyone under the age of 18) was in violation of the Eighth and Fourteenth Amendments. Executions of juveniles were declared to be cruel and unusual punishments. Research has shown that the repeal of the death penalty for juveniles has had no impact on rates of murder committed by them, because its existence had no deterrent effect on murder for offenders under age 18 (Flexon, Stolzenberg, & D'Alessio, 2011, pp. 942–943).

Supporters of the death penalty are traditionally more conservative than liberal, more concerned with public safety than with individual rights, and more focused on the malevolence of humans than on their benevolence or possibility for redemption (Garland, 2005, p. 359). Curiously, some *extreme* supporters of the death penalty express their rage over violent crime by wanting murderers killed—as painfully as possible—along with anyone who *opposes* the death penalty (and the opponents' families, too) (Vandiver, Giacopassi, & Gathje, 2002). For individuals who see an execution as a reasonable or even necessary retribution for serious crimes, the desirability of the death penalty is a core value, and core values are unlikely to change much, if at all (Mandery, 2012).

Public attitudes about the death penalty do change, however. Just as many factors work together to determine the likelihood of an individual being executed (Petrie & Coverdill, 2010), so do many factors work together to determine public opinions about the death penalty. Evidence of the conviction and execution of innocent individuals, political decisions to commute sentences, examples that the penalty is racist and discriminatory, and growing awareness that the United States is out of step with other countries in the global environment—all of these can intensify pressures to change the law to abolish the practice. Public support for the death penalty seems to rise when the public is convinced that it is administered fairly, free from prejudice and discrimination, and where innocent individuals are unlikely to be executed (Mandery, 2012, pp. xxvii–xxxiv).

Changes in the actual use of capital punishment, as well as public attitudes about it, are influenced by changing views of its morality, constitutionality, reliability, irrevocability, and fairness (Mbionwu, 2010, p. 182; Walker, 2011, p. 130). However, one other influence is how executions are described and portrayed by the media. Important in this regard has been the role played by the media in the development of an *innocence frame,* as more and more people have learned that innocent individuals are arrested, convicted, and executed for crimes that they did not commit (Mbionwu, pp. 182–184). Capital punishment is a penalty with a negligible impact on crime, but one that comes with high costs. No necessary reason exists to believe that the death penalty *must* continue, and the United States is now on the same abolitionist trajectory as were other nations that have already abolished it (Garland, 2005).

Conclusions

Violence—or social acts called violence—is a regular feature of most societies, and much of it is done by ordinary people who view their use of violence as practical and necessary, a form of self-help when legal authorities either will not or cannot help. These individuals seek their own brand of justice, and they seem to care little that they might be arrested and imprisoned for what they have done. Some of the individuals who commit murder may even wait for police to arrive or report the crime themselves. Important factors in the relativity of violence are the ability to offer appropriate motives for what one has done and to offer accounts if one's violence is called into question.

Infanticide, capital punishment, dueling, thuggee, mass murder, nonpredatory violence, and serial murder are not simply random events, precipitated by stress and frustration. They almost always reflect patterns of social organization. What are the differences among the deaths caused by capital punishment, dueling, thuggee, predatory murder, nonpredatory murder, or infanticide and other violent happenings in some society? Are there any objective, intrinsic, or inherent qualities of killings *themselves* that would allow a dispassionate observer to know which deaths are legitimate and which are not? Even serious deviances, like the different kinds of violence described in this chapter, vary a great deal from place to place, time to time, and situation to situation. Individual motives and intent are important to know about to understand predatory violence, but so are social dynamics and cultural meanings.

References

Abrahamsen, D. (1992). *Murder and madness: The secret life of Jack the Ripper.* New York, NY: Donald Fine.

Ackroyd, P. (2008). Jack the Ripper and the East End. In A. Werner (Ed.), *Jack the Ripper and the East End* (pp. 7–29). London, UK: Chatto & Windus.

Ahmad, I. (1992). *Thugs, dacoits, and the world-system in nineteenth century India.* Unpublished doctoral dissertation, State University of New York at Binghamton.

Alvarez, A. (1972). *The savage god: A study of suicide.* New York, NY: Random House.

Alvarez, A., & Bachman, R. (2008). *Violence: The enduring problem.* Thousand Oaks, CA: Sage.

Amnesty International. (2012). *The world moves towards abolition.* Retrieved January 27, 2013, from http://www.amnestyusa.org/our-work/issues/death-penalty/international-death-penalty

Anderson, E. (1999). *Code of the street: Decency, violence, and the moral life of the inner city.* New York, NY: Norton.

Athens, L. (1980). *Violent criminal acts and actors: A symbolic interactionist study.* Boston, MA: Routledge/Kegan Paul.

Athens, L. (1989). *The creation of dangerous violent criminals.* New York, NY: Routledge.

Atkins v. Virginia, 536 U.S. 304 (2002).

Bailey, A. K., Tolnay, S. E., Beck, E. M., & Laird, J. D. (2011). Targeting lynch victims: Social marginality or status transgressions? *American Sociological Review, 76,* 412–436.

Balikci, A. (1989). *The Netsilik Eskimo.* Prospect Heights, IL: Waveland. (Original work published 1970)

Baron, S. W. (2011). Street youths' fear of violent crime. *Deviant Behavior, 32,* 475–502.

Baudrillard, J. (2002). *The spirit of terrorism and other essays* (C. Turner, Trans.). London, UK: Verso.

Beeghley, L. (2003). *Homicide: A sociological explanation.* Lanham, MD: Rowman & Littlefield.

Begg, P. (1988). *Jack the Ripper: The uncensored facts. A documented history of the Whitechapel murders of 1888.* London, UK: Robson Books.

Bernard, T. J., Snipes, J. B., & Gerould, A. L. (2010). *Vold's theoretical criminology* (6th ed.). New York, NY: Oxford University Press.

Berns, W. (1982). The morality of anger. In H. A. Bedau (Ed.), *The death penalty in America* (3rd ed., pp. 331–341). New York, NY: Oxford University Press.

Best, J. (1999). *Random violence: How we talk about new crimes and new victims.* Berkeley: University of California Press.

Best, J. (2004). *More damned lies and statistics: How numbers confuse public issues.* Berkeley: University of California Press.

Bing, R. L., III (Ed.). (2010). *Race, crime, and the media.* New York, NY: McGraw-Hill.

Bjornstrom, E., Kaufman, R. L., Peterson, R. D., & Slater, M. D. (2010). Race and ethnic representations of lawbreakers and victims in crime news: A national study of television coverage. *Social Problems, 57,* 269–293.

Black, D. (1980). *The manners and customs of police.* New York, NY: Academic Press.

Black, D. (1983). Crime as social control. *American Sociological Review, 48,* 34–45.

Black, D. (1993). *The social structure of right and wrong*. San Diego, CA: Academic Press.

Blau, J., & Blau, P. (1982). The cost of inequality: Metropolitan structure and violent crime. *American Sociological Review, 47*, 114–129.

Bloom, C. (2008). Jack the Ripper: A legacy in pictures. In A. Werner (Ed.), *Jack the Ripper and the East End* (pp. 229–267). London, UK: Chatto & Windus.

Bogg, R. (1994). Psychopathic behavior as perpetual gaming: A synthesis of forensic accounts. *Deviant Behavior, 15*, 357–374.

Browning, C. (1992). *The path to genocide: Essays on launching the final solution.* New York, NY: Cambridge University Press.

Brownstein, H. (2000). *The social reality of violence and violent crime*. Boston, MA: Allyn & Bacon.

Bureau of Justice Statistics. (2006). *Sourcebook of criminal justice statistics online.* Retrieved August 16, 2012, from http://www.albany.edu/sourcebook/pdf/t2932006.pdf

Bureau of Justice Statistics. (2011). *Sourcebook of criminal justice statistics online.* Retrieved August 16, 2012, from http://www.albany.edu/sourcebook/pdf/t2522011.pdf

Cochran, J. K., Sellers, C. S., Wiesbrock, V., & Palacios, W. R. (2011). Repetitive partner victimization: An exploratory application of social learning theory. *Deviant Behavior, 32*, 790–817.

Cohen, A. (1974). *The elasticity of evil: Changes in the social definition of deviance.* Oxford, UK: Oxford University Penal Research Unit.

Cohen, S. (1972). *Folk devils and moral panics: The creation of the mods and rockers.* London, UK: MacGibbon & Kee.

Coleman, J. (1988). Social capital in the creation of human capital. *American Journal of Sociology, 94*, 95–120.

Collett, J., & Lizardo, O. (2010). Occupational status and the experience of anger. *Social Forces, 88*, 2079–2104.

Cooney, M. (2009). *Is killing wrong? A study in pure sociology.* Charlottesville: University of Virginia Press.

Cornwell, P. (2002). *Portrait of a killer: Jack the Ripper—case closed.* New York, NY: Putnam.

Covington, J. (2010). *Crime and racial constructions: Cultural misinformation about African Americans in media and academia.* Lanham, MD: Lexington Books.

Crawford, D. M., Whitbeck, L. B., & Hoyt, D. R. (2011). Propensity for violence among homeless and runaway adolescents: An event history analysis. *Crime & Delinquency, 57*, 950–968.

Declercq, F., & Audenaert, K. (2011). Predatory violence aiming at relief in a case of mass murder: Meloy's criteria for applied forensic practice. *Behavioral Sciences and the Law, 29*, 578–591.

DeKeseredy, W. W. (2011). *Violence against women: Myths, facts, controversies.* Toronto, Ontario, Canada: University of Toronto Press.

DeMause, L. (Ed.). (1974). The evolution of childhood. In L. DeMause (Ed.), *The history of childhood* (pp. 1–74). New York, NY: Psychohistory Press.

DeYoung, M. (2008). The devil goes to day care. In R. Heiner (Ed.), *Deviance across cultures* (pp. 68–79). New York, NY: Oxford University Press.

Douglas, J., & Olshaker, M. (2001). *The cases that haunt us.* New York, NY: Simon & Schuster.

Drummond, H., Bolland, J. M., & Harris, W. A. (2011). Becoming violent: Evaluating the mediating effect of hopelessness on the code of the street thesis. *Deviant Behavior, 32,* 191–223.

Edgerton, R. (1976). *Deviance: A cross-cultural perspective.* Menlo Park, CA: Cummings.

Eller, J. (2006). *Violence and culture: A cross-cultural and interdisciplinary approach.* Belmont, CA: Thomson/Wadsworth.

Evans, I. (2011). *Cultures of violence: Racial violence and the origins of segregation in South Africa and the American South.* Manchester, UK: Manchester University Press.

Evans, S., & Rumbelow, D. (2006). *Jack the Ripper: Scotland Yard investigates.* London, UK: Sutton.

Evans, S., & Skinner, K. (2001). *Jack the Ripper: Letters from hell.* London, UK: Sutton.

Faris, R., & Felmlee, D. (2011). Status struggles: Network centrality and gender segregation in same- and cross-gender aggression. *American Sociological Review, 76,* 48–73.

Farrall, S., Jackson, J., & Gray, E. (2009). *Social order and the fear of crime in contemporary times.* New York, NY: Oxford University Press.

Federal Bureau of Investigation. (2001). Special report: The terrorist attacks of September 11, 2001: A compilation of data. In *Crime in the United States, 2001* (pp. 302–313). Washington, DC: Government Printing Office.

Federal Bureau of Investigation. (2012). *Crime in the United States, 2011.* Retrieved November 4, 2012, from http://www.FBI.gov

Felson, R. B., Liska, A. E., South, S., & McNulty, T. L. (1994). The subculture of violence and delinquency: Individual vs. school context effects. *Social Forces, 73,* 155–173.

Fido, M. (1993). *The crimes, detection, and death of Jack the Ripper.* New York, NY: Barnes & Noble.

Fisher, J. (1997). *Killer among us: Public reactions to serial murder.* Westport, CT: Praeger.

Flexon, J. L., Stolzenberg, L., & D'Alessio, S. J. (2011). Cheating the hangman: The effect of the *Roper v. Simmons* decision on homicides committed by juveniles. *Crime & Delinquency, 57,* 928–949.

Garland, D. (2005). Capital punishment and American culture. *Punishment & Society, 7,* 347–376.

Ghatak, S. (2011). *Threat perceptions: The policing of dangers from eugenics to the war on terrorism.* Lanham, MD: Lexington Books.

Goetting, A. (1995). *Homicide in families and other special populations.* New York, NY: Springer-Verlag.

Goldhagen, D. (1996). *Hitler's willing executioners: Ordinary Germans and the Holocaust.* New York, NY: Knopf/Random House.

Goode, E. (2008). *Deviant behavior* (8th ed.). Upper Saddle River, NJ: Pearson/Prentice Hall.

Goode, E., & Ben-Yehuda, N. (1994). *Moral panics: The social construction of deviance.* Oxford, UK: Basil Blackwell.

Gray, D. (2011). *Contextualizing the Ripper murders: Poverty, crime and unrest in the East End of London, 1888.* A paper presented at Jack the Ripper Through a Wider Lens: An Interdisciplinary Conference, Drexel University, Philadelphia, PA, October 28–29.

Green, E. (1993). *The intent to kill: Making sense of murder.* Baltimore, MD: Clevedon.

Hall, K. (Ed.). (2002). *The Oxford guide to American law.* New York, NY: Oxford University Press.

Heimer, K. (1997). Socioeconomic status, subcultural definitions, and violent delinquency. *Social Forces, 75,* 799–833.

Hickey, E. (1997). *Serial murderers and their victims* (2nd ed.). Belmont, CA: Wadsworth.

Hipp, J. R. (2010). A dynamic view of neighborhoods: The reciprocal relationships between crime and neighborhood structural characteristics. *Social Problems, 57,* 205–230.

Hipp, J. R. (2011). Violent crime, mobility decisions, and neighborhood racial/ethnic transition. *Social Problems, 58,* 410–432.

Hollick, F. (1840). *Murder made moral.* Manchester, UK: A. Heywood.

Holmes, R., & Holmes, S. (2010). *Serial murder* (3rd ed.). Thousand Oaks, CA: Sage.

Homant, R., & Kennedy, D. (2006). Serial murder: A biopsychosocial approach. In W. Petherick (Ed.), *Serial crime* (pp. 189–223). Burlington, MA: Academic Press/Elsevier.

Hutton, J. (1981). *Thugs and dacoits of India.* New Delhi, India: Gian.

Ioannou, M. (2010). Serial murder. In C. Ferguson (Ed.), *Violent crime: Clinical and social implications* (pp. 300–326). Thousand Oaks, CA: Sage.

Jackson, L. (2008). Law, order, and violence. In A. Werner (Ed.), *Jack the Ripper and the East End* (pp. 99–139). London, UK: Chatto & Windus.

Jenkins, P. (1994). *Using murder: The social construction of serial homicide.* New York, NY: Aldine de Gruyter.

Jenness, V. (1995). Social movement growth, domain expansion, and framing processes: The gay/lesbian movement and violence against gays and lesbians as a social problem. *Social Problems, 42,* 145–170.

Johnson, R. (1990). *Death work: A study of the modern execution process.* Pacific Grove, CA: Brooks/Cole.

Kantrowitz, B. (1998). Cradles to coffins. In L. Salinger (Ed.), *Deviant behavior 98/99* (3rd ed., pp. 53–54). Guilford, CT: Dushkin.

Katz, F. (1994). *Ordinary people and extraordinary evil: A report on the beguilings of evil.* Albany: State University of New York Press.

Katz, J. (1988). *Seductions of crime: Moral and sensual attractions of doing evil.* New York, NY: Basic Books.

Kaufman, J., & Zigler, E. (1989). The intergenerational transmission of child abuse. In D. Cicchetti & V. Carlson (Eds.), *Child maltreatment: Theories of research on the causes and consequences of child abuse and neglect* (pp. 95–128). New York, NY: Cambridge University Press.

Kelman, H., & Hamilton, V. L. (1989). *Crimes of obedience: Toward a social psychology of authority and responsibility.* New Haven, CT: Yale University Press.

Kennedy, M. C. (1976). Beyond incrimination: Some neglected facets of the theory of punishment. In W. Chambliss & M. Mankoff (Eds.), *Whose law? What order?* (pp. 34–65). New York, NY: Wiley.

Kennedy, M. K. (1989). Foreword. In I. Gray & M. Stanley (Eds.), *A punishment in search of a crime: Americans speak out against the death penalty* (pp. 1–3). New York, NY: Avon.

Kerckhoff, A., & Back, K. (1968). *The June bug.* New York, NY: Appleton-Century-Crofts.

Kiernan, V. G. (1988). *The duel in European history: Honor and the reign of aristocracy.* New York, NY: Oxford University Press.

Kirk, D., & Papachristos, A. V. (2011). Cultural mechanisms and the persistence of neighborhood violence. *American Journal of Sociology, 116,* 1190–1233.

Koop, C. E., & Lundberg, G. D. (1992). Violence in America: A public health emergency. *Journal of the American Medical Association, 267,* 3075–3076.

Kubiak, S. P., & Allen, T. (2011). Public opinion regarding juvenile life without parole in consecutive statewide surveys. *Crime & Delinquency, 57,* 495–515.

Lally, W., & DeMaris, A. (2012). Gender and relational-distance effects in arrests for domestic violence. *Crime & Delinquency, 58,* 103–123.

Lane, R. (2003). Murder in America: 1865–1917. In M. Silberman (Ed.), *Violence and society: A reader* (pp. 49–57). Upper Saddle River, NJ: Prentice Hall.

Larson, E. (2003). *The devil in the White City: Murder, magic, and madness at the fair that changed America.* New York, NY: Crown.

Lesser, W. (1993). *Pictures at an execution.* Cambridge, MA: Harvard University Press.

Levi, K. (1989). Becoming a hit man: Neutralization in a very deviant career. In D. Kelly (Ed.), *Deviant behavior* (3rd ed., pp. 447–458). New York, NY: St. Martin's.

Leyton, E. (1986). *Compulsive killers: The story of modern multiple murder.* New York: New York University Press.

Linsky, A., Bachman, R., & Strauss, M. (1995). *Stress, culture, and aggression.* New Haven, CT: Yale University Press.

Loseke, D. (1992). *The battered woman and shelters: The social construction of wife abuse.* Albany: State University of New York Press.

Lucal, B. (1995). The problem with "battered husbands." *Deviant Behavior, 16,* 95–112.

Maguire, K., & Pastore, A. (Eds.). (1998). *Sourcebook of criminal justice statistics 1997*. Washington, DC: Government Printing Office.

Mandery, E. (2012). *Capital punishment in America: A balanced examination* (2nd ed.). Sudbury, MA: Jones & Bartlett.

Marriott, J. (2008). The imaginative geography of the Whitechapel murders. In A. Werner (Ed.), *Jack the Ripper and the East End* (pp. 31–64). London, UK: Chatto & Windus.

Mbionwu, L. E. S. (2010). Media frames: The impact of public opinion on the death penalty. In R. L. Bing III (Ed.), *Race, crime, and the media* (pp. 177–186). New York, NY: McGraw-Hill.

McCoy, E. (1992). Childhood through the ages. In K. Finsterbusch (Ed.), *Sociology 92/93* (21st ed., pp. 46–49). Guilford, CT: Dushkin.

Meloy, J. R., Hempel, A. G., Gray, G. T., Mohandie, K., Shiva, A., & Richards, T. C. (2004). A comparative analysis of North American adolescent and adult mass murderers. *Behavioral Sciences and the Law, 22*, 291–309.

Mills, C. W. (1940). Situated actions and vocabularies of motive. *American Sociological Review, 5*, 904–913.

Morenoff, J. D., Sampson, R. J., & Raudenbush, S. W. (2001). Neighborhood inequality, collective efficacy, and the spatial dynamics of urban violence. *Criminology, 39*, 517–559.

Ness, C. D. (2010). *Why girls fight: Female youth violence in the inner city*. New York: New York University Press.

Newman, G. (1978). *The punishment response*. Philadelphia, PA: J. B. Lippincott.

Payne, B. K., Triplett, R. A., & Higgins, G. E. (2011). The relationship between self-control, witnessing domestic violence, and subsequent violence. *Deviant Behavior, 32*, 769–789.

Peralta, R., & Cruz, J. (2006). Conferring meaning onto alcohol-related violence: An analysis of alcohol use and gender in a sample of college youth. *Journal of Men's Studies, 14*, 109–125.

Perry, A. (2006). Why we will never forget Jack the Ripper. In P. Begg (Ed.), *Ripperology* (pp. 182–183). New York, NY: Barnes & Noble.

Peterson, R. D., & Krivo, L. J. (2010). *Divergent social worlds: Neighborhood crime and the racial–spatial divide*. New York, NY: Russell Sage Foundation.

Petrie, M. A., & Coverdill, J. E. (2010). Who lives and dies on death row? Race, ethnicity, and post-sentence outcomes in Texas. *Social Problems, 57*, 630–652.

Pinderhughes, H. (1993). The anatomy of racially motivated violence in New York City: A case study of youth in southern Brooklyn. *Social Problems, 40*, 478–492.

Pleck, E. (1987). *Domestic tyranny: The making of American social policy against family violence from colonial times to the present*. New York, NY: Oxford University Press.

Pogrebin, P. B., Stretesky, & Unnithan, N. P. (2009). *Guns, violence, and criminal behavior: The offender's perspective*. Boulder, CO: Lynne Rienner.

Prejean, Sister H. (1989). A pilgrim's progress. In I. Gray & M. Stanley (Eds.), *A punishment in search of a crime: Americans speak out against the death penalty* (pp. 93–101). New York, NY: Avon.

Purcell, C. E., & Arrigo, B. A. (2006). *The psychology of lust murder: Paraphilia, sexual killing, and sexual homicide.* Boston, MA: Academic Press.

Putnam, R. (2000). *Bowling alone: The collapse and revival of American community.* New York, NY: Simon & Schuster.

Rankin, J. (1979). Changing attitudes toward capital punishment. *Social Forces, 58,* 194–211.

Rees, A. (2009). *The infanticide controversy: Primatology and the art of field science.* Chicago, IL: University of Chicago Press.

Regoli, R. M., Hewitt, J. D., & Delisis, M. (2010). *Delinquency in society* (8th ed.). Sudbury, MA: Jones & Bartlett.

Roper v. Simmons, 543 U.S. 551 (2005).

Ross, E. (2008). "Deeds of heroism": Whitechapel's ladies. In A. Werner (Ed.), *Jack the Ripper and the East End* (pp. 81–217). London, UK: Chatto & Windus.

Roy, B. (2009). *41 shots . . . and counting: What Amadou Diallo's story teaches us about policing, race, and justice.* Syracuse, NY: Syracuse University Press.

Rumbelow, D. (1988). *Jack the Ripper: The complete casebook.* New York, NY: Berkley Books.

Russo, S. (2004). *The Jack the Ripper suspects: Persons cited by investigators and theorists.* Jefferson, NC: McFarland.

Sampson, R. J., & Raudenbush, S. W. (1999). Systematic observation of public spaces. *American Journal of Sociology, 105,* 603–651.

Sampson, R. J., Raudenbush, S. W., & Earls, F. (1997). Neighborhoods and violent crime: A multilevel study of collective efficacy. *Science, 277,* 918–924.

Schinkel, W. (2010). *Aspects of violence: A critical theory.* New York, NY: Palgrave Macmillan.

Service, E. (1963). *Profiles in ethnology.* New York, NY: Harper & Row.

Simons, R., Lei, M., Beach, S., Brody, G., Philibert, R., & Gibbons, F. (2011). Social environment, genes, and aggression: Evidence supporting the differential susceptibility perspective. *American Sociological Review, 76,* 883–912.

Six-Hohenbalken, M., & Weiss, N. (2011). *Violence expressed: An anthropological approach.* Burlington, VT: Ashgate.

Standiford, L. (with Detective Sergeant J. Matthews). (2011). *Bringing Adam home: The abduction that changed America.* New York, NY: HarperCollins.

Sugden, P. (2002). *The complete history of Jack the Ripper.* New York, NY: Carroll & Graf.

Thornton, E. (1837). *Illustrations of the history and practices of the thugs.* London, UK: W. H. Allen.

Unnithan, N. P. (1994). Children as victims of homicide: Making claims, formulating categories, and constructing social problems. *Deviant Behavior, 15,* 63–83.

U.S. Department of Justice. (2008). *Serial murder: Multi-disciplinary perspectives for investigators.* Washington, DC: Behavioral Analysis Unit, National Center for the Analysis of Violent Crime.

Vandiver, M., Giacopassi, D., & Gathje, P. (2002). I hope someone murders your mother! An exploration of extreme support for the death penalty. *Deviant Behavior, 23,* 385–415.

Vronsky, P. (2004). *Serial killers: The method and madness of monsters.* New York, NY: Berkley Books.

Walker, S. (2011). *Sense and nonsense about crime, drugs, and communities* (7th ed.). Belmont, CA: Wadsworth.

Wallace, R. (1996). *Jack the Ripper: Light-hearted friend.* Melrose, MA: Gemini Press.

Warren, J., Hazelwood, R., & Dietz, P. (1996). The sexually sadistic serial killer. *Journal of Forensic Science, 41,* 970–974.

Williams, K. R., & Guerra, N. G. (2011). Perceptions of collective efficacy and bullying perpetration in schools. *Social Problems, 58,* 126–143.

Wilson, C. (1988). Introduction. In D. Rumbelow, *Jack the Ripper: The complete casebook* (pp. 1–17). New York, NY: Berkley Books.

Wilson, W. (1991). *Good murders and bad murders.* Lanham, MD: University Press of America.

Winslow, R., & Zhang, S. (2008). *Criminology: A global perspective.* Upper Saddle River, NJ: Pearson/Prentice Hall.

Wolfgang, M., & Ferracuti, F. (1967). *The subculture of violence.* London, UK: Tavistock.

Yablonsky, L. (1990). *Criminology* (4th ed.). New York, NY: Harper & Row.

Young, J. (2011). Moral panics and the transgressive other. *Crime, Media, Culture, 7,* 245–258.

Zelizer, V. (1994). *Pricing the priceless child: The changing social value of children.* Princeton, NJ: Princeton University Press.

Zimbardo, P. (2007). *The Lucifer effect: Understanding how good people turn evil.* New York, NY: Random House.

Zimmerman, G. M., & Messner, S. F. (2010). Neighborhood context and the gender gap in adolescent violent crime. *American Sociological Review, 75,* 958–980.

6

Sexual Violence

Cultural Scripts and Forcible Rape

Most everything that was discussed in Chapter 5 can be used to help make sense of sexual violence, too. So, why have a chapter about *sexual* violence when no separate chapters are included in this book about racial violence, ethnic violence, youth violence, environmental violence, domestic violence, and so on? The answer is that females are frequent victims of violence, almost always at the hands of males; females may be becoming more violent, starting at a young age (Garbarino, 2006); and a multitude of social and cultural supports exist, some of which are institutionalized and formalized, to both create violence toward females and to justify and excuse it after it occurs (DeKeseredy, 2011; Faris & Felmlee, 2011, pp. 67–68). Female victims of sexual violence may even fail to realize or acknowledge that they are indeed victims of sexual violence. Sexual violence is such a good example of the relativity of predatory violence that it deserves its own separate analysis (Chesney-Lind & Jones, 2010).

Rape is the term that is used to refer to acts of sexual violence or coercive sexuality. The term originates from the Latin word *rapere,* a verb meaning to seize or obtain by force. Initially, the word had no sexual meaning at all, and it can still be used in a more generalized sense as in the "rape" of the land or the environment. When the term came to be used to refer to a type of violent crime, its meaning was restricted so that the legal definition meant only one thing: the vaginal penetration of a female by a male through the use of force. Today, the word does (or can) cover a broader range of violent sexual behaviors, such as forced oral sex, forced anal penetration, forcible fondling, or forcible object penetration. In this broader interpretation or understanding of rape, not only can men rape women, but men can also rape men, women can rape women, and women can rape men.

The Federal Bureau of Investigation historically has used a restricted definition of *forcible rape,* defining it as the carnal knowledge (vaginal intercourse) of a female, forcibly and against her will. Though this definition seems clear and direct, it is not applied clearly and directly. In actuality, legal authorities may think of rape in an even more selective way: "It is deemed a rape only if the assailant is a violent stranger, if the victim reports the rape immediately after it occurred, and if she can provide evidence of the attack and of her active resistance" (Weis & Borges, 1973, p. 71). The determination that rape has occurred is really an outgrowth of the give-and-take among individuals who have different interests, resources, and understandings about what happened and why (Allison & Wrightsman, 1993, p. 3; Meadows & Kuehnel, 2005, pp. 25–35).

Rape is not a set of concrete actions that can be objectively and uniformly identified no matter what. Its definition—the construction or interpretation of it—varies from one observer, audience, or party to another; from one society to another; and from one historical time period to another (Gilmartin, 1994, p. 16). Simply put, different audiences define rape in different ways, and it matters a great deal exactly *who* is doing the defining (Goode, 1996). Rape is both interpersonal conduct *and* a legal/social category with shades of meaning.

In 2012, a firestorm of controversy raged among U.S. politicians over the meaning of rape, principally because of disagreements over right-to-choice and right-to-life issues. Richard Mourdock (Republican), during his bid to be elected as an Indiana state senator, expressed his view that abortions should not be allowed in cases where a rape leads to a pregnancy (unless the mother's life is in jeopardy). His rationale was that he believes that in these cases it was "something that God intended to happen" (Madison, 2012, n.p.). Mourdock, in response to the criticism he received, clarified (with the help of Rick Santorum, former GOP presidential candidate) that the "something" to which he was referring was the human life in the woman's womb, not the rape itself. In August 2012, Todd Akin (a Republican from Missouri) opined that "legitimate rape" was unlikely to result in pregnancy. His poorly chosen words (which indicate a profound ignorance of both human biology and human sexuality) generated the reaction from more informed individuals that no rape is legitimate and that sperm and egg can get together regardless of whether a rape is deemed by politicians as legitimate or illegitimate. Even Republican vice presidential candidate Paul Ryan, who had coauthored an antiabortion bill with Akin, felt compelled to distance himself from Akin's words by stating that "rape is rape. Period. End of story." President Obama responded to a question from Jay Leno when Obama appeared as a guest on NBC's *Tonight Show* by declaring that "rape is rape and rape is a crime." If the president's or Ryan's tautological statements were designed to clarify matters, they didn't help much. However, all this political wrangling (and verbal miscues) does show that different understandings of rape exist. Law in action, as Roscoe Pound (1910) observed, is different from law on the books.

On January 6, 2012, Attorney General Eric Holder announced that the definition of rape was being modified to allow for a more comprehensive national reporting of the crime. The new definition of rape describes it in the following way: "The penetration, no matter how slight, of the vagina or anus with any body part or object, or oral penetration by a sex organ of another person, without the consent of the victim" (FBI, 2012). This revision is a welcome one in that it will give a better understanding of rape by providing a more valid picture of it. The revision is based on an evolving understanding of rape that acknowledges that both males and females can be raped; that both males and females can be rapists; and that rape is an attack on a person's identity, not specifically on a female's vaginal vault. By shifting more attention to lack of consent and away from the use of force, it lessens the obligation of victims to prove beyond a shadow of a doubt that they have actively resisted. Only time and data will tell us if the change is a good one.

Another type of coercive sexuality is *sexual harassment,* because it, like rape, objectifies and depersonalizes victims, while it controls and hurts them (Fitzgerald, 1993, p. 1072; MacKinnon, 2003, p. 261; McKinney, 1994). Unsurprisingly, men and women may not agree on exactly what qualifies as harassment. Where females may see harassing behavior directed toward them, men may see the same behavior as complimentary, harmless seduction, or horseplay (i.e., clowning around). Men who believe strongly in a sexual double standard and who have received a traditional masculine upbringing are more likely to see sexual harassment as both normal and normative (Quinn, 2003, p. 274).

Some states already use a definition of rape that includes acts in addition to vaginal penetration (e.g., forced oral sex, object penetration), and they have replaced "rape" with terms such as *sexual assault, sexual battery,* or *criminal sexual conduct* to emphasize that sexual violence is more about violence than sex. They have removed requirements that a victim must corroborate her charge of rape with some objective proof before she is believed. They have removed requirements that a woman must offer the utmost resistance to her attacker and be able to prove in a court of law that she did. They have adopted rape shield laws that have made evidence of the woman's past sexual behavior inadmissible in court.

Rape law reforms are in a constant state of flux, and considerable variation exists from jurisdiction to jurisdiction in the United States (Epstein & Langenbahn, 1994, p. 7). Some states have moved quickly to make extensive reforms, but others have moved slowly and sluggishly (Spohn & Horney, 1992, pp. 159–175). The legal changes, if they have accomplished nothing else, highlight the importance of reform, and they help to clarify the nature of rape, along with what is true and false about it. Only by an outmoded and unrealistic standard could the rape law reform movement be considered a failure, and evidence exists that traditional beliefs about rape and its victims are changing, especially as more and more victims' voices are heard (Cuklanz, 1996, p. 116). Little doubt exists that the FBI's new definition of rape will pressure states that have not already done so to adopt a similar definition of this crime.

Forcible rape is no longer a capital crime in the United States, although it had been for much of U.S. history (Ronald Wolfe was the last man executed in the United States for the crime of forcible rape, in 1964). The U.S. Supreme Court decided in 1977 in *Coker v. Georgia* that the raping of an adult female was no longer serious enough to warrant a penalty of death (although in Coker's case, the "adult female" was only 16 years old). An execution was deemed to be a grossly disproportionate and excessive penalty, representing a form of cruel and unusual punishment (Bedau, 1982, p. 299; Mandery, 2012). Think how the 455 men who have been executed for rape in the United States (Barlow, 1996, p. 395) would feel if they learned that it was not so much what they did, who they were, or the region of the country in which they raped that got them executed; it was mainly *when* they did it. And think how rape victims must *now* feel. Many—perhaps most—rape survivors view rape as much more than an assault on their bodies. They view it as a death of the self (Carosella, 1995, p. xx). These women must find it incomprehensible that an experience so harmful to them is no longer considered serious enough to warrant the ultimate penalty.

Sexual violence is a principal cause of anxiety, fear, injury, and sometimes even death for women, especially for those who become direct victims of it (Ferraro, 1996, p. 675; Goodman, Koss, Fitzgerald, Russo, & Keita, 1993, p. 1054; Koss, 1993, p. 1062). This "female fear" is a special burden that women carry that is not shared with men who have not themselves been raped. Some of the fear exists because women believe—incorrectly, as it turns out—that a substantial number of rape victims are murdered by their assailants (Gordon & Riger, 1989). In those murders in which circumstances were known (between 1976 and 1994), 1.5 percent involved rape or some other sex offense (Greenfeld, 1997, p. 3). Rape does have a *shadow effect* in that women, especially young ones, are apprehensive about *any* victimization because they always fear that it could lead to a rape (Ferraro, 1996, p. 669).

The Symbolic Organization of Sexual Violence

Some individuals enhance their own feelings of power and control, release feelings of anger, and satisfy sadistic urges by persuading, manipulating, or actually forcing other people to engage in unwanted sexual acts (Groth, 1979; Pelka, 1995, pp. 251–252). Few nonhuman animals can accomplish a mating without the cooperation of *both* partners (Gregersen, 1983, p. 54), but both the human female and the human male are susceptible to rape. *Every* rape fuses together elements of manipulation, power, control, anger, and sadism into one brutal sexual act, even while the extent of these can vary from rape to rape. Even though *all* rapes are sadistic to a degree, some are far more so than others.

Holmes and Holmes (2009) give an example of a sadistic rapist in their description of the "Four-Poster Rapist." Like all sadistic rapists, he eroticized violence and aggression. After gaining entrance to an unsuspecting victim's home (and subtly determining that she had needle and thread in the house), he would become violent. He would force her into a bedroom and then tear off her clothing, while using vile and humiliating words. He would hit and slap her while committing acts of anal, oral, and vaginal rape. He would bite and scratch his victim. He would even rip out clumps of her hair. As a final degradation, he would force his victim at gunpoint to stand so that a bedpost was between her breasts. He then used the needle and thread to sew the woman's nipples together so they encircled the bedpost (pp. 163–164).

The kinds of acts that qualify as sexual violence and how they are interpreted are variable, and the determination that sexual violence has occurred is conditioned by a large number of social and cultural factors (Palmer, 1989). No society has yet developed a purely objective way to measure the amount of force or the degree of consent that is present during an act of sex, nor has any society developed a purely objective way to determine at what point sex becomes coercive enough to qualify as rape. "The act must be interpreted as rape by the female actee, and her interpretation must be similarly evaluated by a number of officials and agencies before the official designation of 'rape' can be legitimately applied" (Svalastoga, 1962, p. 48). A female who reports to police that she has been raped will find that her account of what happened will be scrutinized for consistency and believability by criminal justice personnel, and so will her character and reputation. If she is a woman who is deemed to be of low social standing, and therefore not a "good witness," she may find that she is sent packing (Frohmann, 2005). Cross-cultural comparisons of rape rates are practically useless because nations use different definitions of rape and have differential or varying abilities to find and measure it. Even within the same society or community, the study of rape is filled with difficulties and complications (Chappell, 1976, p. 296).

Bourque (1989) interviewed a sample of 126 white and 125 black Los Angeles County residents during the summer and fall of 1979 to determine how they defined rape (p. 61). Her respondents used information about the assailant's degree of force and the victim's degree of resistance to decide if a rape had occurred, but they did not all reach the same conclusion. Some respondents focused on what the female victim did and were prone to blame her for what happened. They believed that rape could be avoided if a woman resisted strenuously enough. If a rape occurred, it was because a woman did something to make it happen. These respondents tended to view rape in sexual terms. Other respondents, by contrast, looked primarily at the assailant. If he used any force to achieve his sexual goals, they believed that a rape had indeed occurred. These respondents tended to view rape as a form of predatory violence. The rest of Bourque's sample used information about force and resistance, but also about location, acquaintanceship, ethnicity, prior sexual history, and socioeconomic status of the participants in deciding what had really happened (p. 204). Bourque found a great deal of variation in definitions of rape. White females were the most likely to use information on the degree of force as their principal cue and were the ones most likely to define a sexual encounter as rape; black males were the most likely to use information on resistance, and they were the least likely to label sexual encounters as rape.

More recently, Buddie and Miller (2000) report that rape victims are more likely to be blamed for their own victimizations if they are raped by acquaintances in a dating situation rather than by a stranger and if they fail to quickly resist the sexual advances of their partners. Women with sexual experience are also more likely than those without to be held responsible for what happens to them (p. 140).

What kinds of decision rules do women use to decide that they have been raped? A study by Williams (1984) of 246 female rape victims who had obtained help from a Seattle rape relief center uncovered a number of reasons why some victims report their rapes to police. Reporting, of course, is different from defining, but this study does give valuable information about how women understand rape. The women who were most likely to report their rapes were those who had endured what Williams called *classic rapes:* They had been forcibly raped in their own homes, cars, or public places by strangers, and the rapes caused them a great deal of serious injury. Women who were sexually assaulted in a social situation (e.g., at a party or on a date) by people whom they knew (acquaintances, friends, or relatives) were much less likely to report the incidents to police. Part of the reason was that a prior relationship between the rapist and his victim meant that the rape was usually less violent, causing less physical damage to the victim and requiring less immediate medical aid. However, even if a woman was severely injured during a rape, she was still less likely to report the crime if she had been raped by someone she knew. Williams concluded that when the elements of a classic rape are present, they provide the victim with the evidence that she needs to convince herself that she is indeed a true rape victim (p. 464).

We cannot know for sure if Williams's interpretation is the correct one. All women who are raped may know it regardless of how classic it is, but they may feel confident that police authorities will believe their accusations *only* if their rapes show the classic elements. Victims of *unclassic rapes—* forced sex by a man who has some prior relationship to them and who does not beat them or use a weapon—may see themselves as true victims, but they may not see themselves as legitimate crime victims who can get justice in a court of law. Prior-relationship rapes are more likely to be viewed by others (e.g., police and prosecutors) as private matters, the rapist is more likely to be viewed as less blameworthy, and the victim is more likely to be held responsible (Buddie & Miller, 2000; Estrich, 1987).

A study of 40 intimate partner rapes (Tellis, 2010) that were reported to authorities (Miami, Florida, in 1997) shows that the majority of them were both violent and coercive. The rapists used both physical force (victims received physical injuries in 88 percent of the assaults) and verbal threats (in 80 percent of the assaults) to accomplish their objectives. Relational distance between victim and offender does have an influence on the probability of arrest (at least in cases of domestic violence where physical battery occurs). As the relationship between offender and victim gets closer, the chances of arrest go down (Lally & DeMaris, 2012). Rape victims themselves report that when they do not tell police about their victimizations, the main reason is that they view them as private or personal matters (Bureau of Justice Statistics, 2008, Table 102). In the absence of the elements of a classic rape, some women will decide that they have not been raped at all. Studies of spousal rape find that wives are reluctant to use the word *rape* to describe their sexual experiences with their husbands even if a great deal of force is present (Bergen, 1996, p. 48).

Rape-revenge films (e.g., *Lipstick, Extremities, I Spit on Your Grave, Sudden Impact*) highlight some of the elements of changing images of men, women, and rape. Films like these both contribute ideas to popular culture and mirror it. Though different in both setting and savagery, these films share a set of focal concerns or unifying premises that are reflective of changing social and sexual attitudes of the twentieth century: Rape requires a certain and severe retaliation, itself of a savage nature; the victim, usually a female, must become the aggressor, serving as her own redeemer and avenger; and we live in a rape culture where every man is implicated in the rape of any given woman (Clover, 1992, pp. 138–139).

Despite the differences among the films in this genre, the common element is a graphic depiction of excessive violence visited upon the female, leading to her pain and humiliation. She is proxy for *every* woman who has ever been harassed, humiliated, or sexually victimized by men. The female victims in rape-revenge films turn to vigilantism, going so far as to provoke specific men into initiating violence against them. Retaliation for a specific act of sexual violence against a specific female victim spills over into sweeping violence against all men, sometimes of the most extreme and savage kind. Rape-revenge films are a concrete example of the *spillover hypothesis* of interpersonal violence. Spillover exists when violence to an individual causes him or her to become more violent in return. For example, domestic violence by a husband against his wife could interfere with her parental skills, increasing the likelihood that she will abuse her own children (Haskett, Portwood, & Lewis, 2010, p. 213).

Rape-revenge films, like academic and popular discussions of rape in the closing decades of the twentieth century, moved away from viewing rape as personal and pathological and toward viewing it as social and political, an *intentional* act of violence and domination. On the silver screen, rape was portrayed more and more as a deliberate act designed to pleasure a man while it degraded and subjugated a woman, making her fearful of leading the life she had once led successfully. The sexual violence did not kill her physical body, but it did something worse: It killed her spirit, quashing her self-confidence, along with her sense of potency and purpose. Rape rendered her life far less meaningful and rewarding than it had once been. Rape-revenge films offer a primitive insight into the dangers to women that can come from both sexual inequality and male dominance.

The relationships between rape and popular culture are complex and dynamic. During the colonial period in the United States, narratives and stories alleged widespread Native American savagery in the kidnapping of, and sexual attacks on, Anglo females. These captivity narratives were both distorted and inaccurate, leaving little room for exploration of Anglo attacks on Native American women or the existence of positive relationships across the ethnic divide. Rape was regularly portrayed as one of the weapons that the uncivilized used against white colonists. White men's anxieties were enflamed by their fear that they could not protect their wives and daughters from sexual attacks (Bailey, 2010, p. 11).

During the days of U.S. slavery, the narratives changed but the themes did not. Though some awareness existed that whites did sexually exploit blacks, it was little more than dust in the wind. Racial stereotypes capitalized on the popular view that African women were either asexual ("Mammies") or seductive and wanton "Jezebels," especially in regard to white men. White men were able to rape black women with impunity by claiming either that the woman was a seductress and wanted the rape to happen or that someone with a lascivious nature cannot be harmed by sex no matter what type it is. Female slaves were property with no rights of their own. Male slaves, of course, were also stereotyped by the white population. They could be traditional and loyal to white slave owners ("Uncle Toms"); lazy but uncomplaining field hands ("Sambos"); or both violent and sexual, willing to do anything for freedom while lusting after white women ("Nats") (Bailey, 2010, pp. 11–12).

Rape and Social Conflict

Power, Rape, and Social Control

Sexual inequalities exist in most human societies, which produce power differences between males and females (Iversen & Rosenbluth, 2010; Scott, Crompton, & Lyonette, 2010). These power differentials can lead to tensions and antagonisms in male–female relationships (Jackson, 1995, p. 24). These sexual antagonisms can breed contempt, and males can come to hate females (and vice versa). Some men are in a position to express their contempt for women through forcible rape (Smith & Bennett, 1985, p. 303). The research is clear in showing that the lower the status of females in comparison to males, the higher the rate of forcible rape (Baron & Straus, 1987, p. 481; Schwendinger & Schwendinger, 1983). Where men are both dominant and dominating, rape is one indicator of females' low status, and it is one way that women's low status is maintained and reinforced (Baron & Straus, 1987, p. 481; Baron & Straus, 1989; Eller, 2006, pp. 120–125; Funk, 1993, p. 27; Higgins & Silver, 1991, pp. 1–2; Sanday, 1981). MacKinnon (1982) concludes that rape is more likely in any society where sexuality is a form of power and where domination is given concrete expression through sexuality (p. 533). Reiss's (1986) research on rape in many countries found that a belief in female inferiority tends to be positively correlated with the occurrence of rape (pp. 191–192).

Social and cultural factors channel and direct sexual urges, and sometimes these factors make it more likely that some men will physically and emotionally terrorize some women (Buchwald, Fletcher, & Roth, 1993). Brownmiller (1975) concluded that rape is a deliberate (she uses the word *conscious*) process of intimidation that *all* men use to keep *all* women in a state of fear and intimidation. In her analysis, *every man* is either a rapist or beneficiary of rape, and *every woman* is vulnerable, living her life in fear of being raped (p. 15). Though her conclusions are arguable, what is beyond dispute is that cultural understandings about the nature of rape can actually help to produce it.

The belief that an impetuous male sex drive causes men to lose control is partly responsible for the maintenance of male dominance and the occurrence of rape (Sanday, 1996b, p. 26). This belief allows rapists to neutralize forces of social control by disclaiming personal responsibility for what they have done (Jackson, 1995, p. 19). It also makes it possible for observers to excuse more readily a rapist's violence. Not all cultures view rape as a naturally impulsive sex act (MacKellar, 1975, p. 18). The Minangkabau peoples of West Sumatra have a fairly rape-free society that is partly due to their cultural belief that rape is neither impulsive nor uncontrollable (Sanday, 1990, p. 193). Because humans are capable of exerting conscious control over many impelling bodily urges or drives—hunger, thirst, defecation, urination—it is probable that they can control their violent sexuality as well.

Defining women as property and as seductive can foster a sense of entitlement. *Entitlement* in this context is a cultural belief that men are within their rights to demand goods and services from women *as a class* (Bart & O'Brien, 1985, pp. 100–101). Some men rape women because they believe that sex is something to which they are entitled whenever they want it. If it is not given freely, then they believe it is entirely proper for them to take it.

[Sexual] violence has deep roots in sociocultural constructions of gender and heterosexuality, constructions that promote male entitlement and social and political inequality for women. Cultural norms and myths, sexual scripts and social roles link various forms of violence and deny assistance to its victims. (Koss et al., 1994, p. 17)

A study of the sexual violence experienced by street prostitutes traced it directly to cultural beliefs about them. According to prostitutes themselves, the men who raped them were acting out core beliefs: Women who are sexually experienced cannot be harmed by sexual violence, all prostitutes are alike, and prostitutes deserve whatever happens to them (Miller & Schwartz, 1995, pp. 9–16).

Any woman can become a target of sexual violence if a rapist defines her as belonging to a class of individuals whose members are promiscuous and valueless. In order for a man to sexually assault a woman, he must not only think that he will get things of value from the attack. He must also be able to overcome or neutralize any inhibitions he might have that would prevent the rape from occurring (Felson, 2003, p. 200). Neutralizations are easier for a man to muster if a potential rape victim belongs to a class that he dislikes and depersonalizes (Scully, 1990).

Rape itself may be used as a form of social control, because it can transform a female into a powerless victim, an individual who has no control over what is being done to her (Collins, 2010, p. 90). It may also be a way to punish a woman who is perceived to have deviated from important norms of her gender. Consider the Cheyenne Indians, one of the important tribes of the Great American Plains. The Cheyenne were famous for their chastity, and they took marriage very seriously. At puberty, a female donned a chastity belt, a thin piece of rope that was knotted around her waist and then passed between her thighs. It was always worn at night and during the day when the woman was away from home. If a male trifled with a woman's belt, it was considered a very serious matter. He could be beaten or even killed by female or male relatives of the offended woman. His goods would be destroyed and his horses killed. Even his parents could have their property ravaged (Llewellyn & Hoebel, 1941, pp. 176–177).

If a female Cheyenne yielded to a man, allowing him to seduce her, she was permanently disgraced. Her trespass would never be forgotten, and she would be scorned wherever she went. It would be almost impossible for her to marry because no man would have her (unless she were to be ritually purified by a shaman). If a wife was unfaithful to her husband, it was proper for him to administer what was called the *free woman penalty* or *on the prairie*. The husband would invite all of the unmarried men in his soldier band and all of his male cousins (except for his wife's relatives) to a spot on the prairie for a "feast." He would then turn his wife over to them, and she would be raped by 40 to 50 men. From then on, she was a woman apart who lived in permanent shame and embarrassment. Some disagreement existed among the Cheyenne over the propriety of using a gang rape to punish an unfaithful wife, but the custom persisted and continued to be defined, at least officially, as a right of a husband to use against an unfaithful wife (Llewellyn & Hoebel, 1941, p. 209).

In some cultures, rape is used to punish women for things other than participation in extramarital sexual relationships. The Mehinaku of central Brazil strictly segregate the sexes, and women are forbidden to enter the sacred and private communal house of men. If women spy on the men or their sacred rituals or artifacts, they can be punished with a gang rape (Gregor, 1982). Even in the United States, rape can be one of the possible consequences for women for doing things that are defined by some men as too unconventional, untraditional, or unfeminine (e.g., staying out too late, hitchhiking, being out alone, dressing and acting provocatively, being stoned or drunk, or running away from home). In the nineteenth-century United States, women were able to get protection from violent husbands only if these women fit the Victorian image of a proper woman: respectful, dependent, and obedient. Those women who refused to follow expected feminine standards were more vulnerable to sexual attack, and they had few avenues for obtaining redress if they were raped (Pleck, 1979).

Rape and War

Rape has played a role in all wars and most revolutions, ethnic conflicts, and geographic expansions (Brownmiller, 1975). Close connections exist between violence against females and world processes. Sexual violence is a way for some men as a *gender collective* to demonstrate their power and dominance over both women and other men (Bahun-Radunović & Rajan, 2008, p. 1; Collins, 2010, p. 87). During the American Revolution, British troops raped colonial women. In the 1830s, Mormon women were raped by Missouri men in order to get them to leave the state. Southern black female slaves were raped throughout the slave era, and free black women were raped during Reconstruction. Native American women were raped during the white expansion westward.

> Sexual violence in warfare is among the darkest legacies of the twentieth century, and it continues to ravage societies in the new millennium. Instances of widespread use of sexual violence include: the 1915 Armenian genocide by Ottoman Turkey; the Japanese assault on the Chinese in Nanking during World War II, and in the Chinese civil war; the partition of India and creation of Pakistan; and Bangladesh's 1971 war of liberation. Sexual violence has been prevalent in many other conflicts during the Cold War and after, including the Korean War, Vietnam War, and Cambodia; in the wars and conflicts in Central and Latin America, and in Haiti; and in many African conflicts, such as Angola, Djibouti, Liberia, Mozambique, Sierra Leone, Somalia, and Sudan. In Asia, war rapes are found in East Timor, Sri Lanka, Burma, Kashmir (India),

Papua New Guinea; and in wars and conflicts in Central Europe and Eurasia, including Afghanistan, Turkey, Kuwait, Georgia, Bosnia, and Kosovo. No part of the world has been unaffected by wartime sexual violence. (Leatherman, 2011, p. 2)

Soldiers use rape to show their enemies the contempt with which they are held. It demoralizes the defeated side because these men can no longer protect wives and daughters, while it punishes the women for being in the wrong place at the wrong time (or simply for being at all). Rape has other benefits during war for a rapist: It demonstrates the rapist's masculinity to himself and to his peers; it is a reward for having fought hard and long; it demonstrates the impotence (political and sexual) of the vanquished; and it is a tangible way to show who has won and who has lost the war. Throughout human history, soldiers have viewed forced sexual intercourse with the wives and daughters of their enemies as one of the spoils of war (Winslow & Zhang, 2008, p. 223).

During the "ethnic cleansing" in Bosnia in 1992, Serbian soldiers sexually victimized and terrorized Muslim women. The women were herded together like cattle into concentration camps where they were tortured, raped, and sodomized by a multitude of attackers. For those women who survived the sexual torture, the ordeal did not end. Their victimization was viewed as unbearably shameful by their husbands, and these women were treated as damaged goods, lacking both value and purpose. Some were barred by their husbands from what were once their homes or even were killed by them (Farr, 2009, p. 6).

During wars, more men than women die, but more women than men are raped and sexually tortured (Alvarez & Bachman, 2008, pp. 194–197). However, men can be sexually victimized by their captors during wartime, too. Usually, male sexual assaults are hidden, unknown to all but a few. Occasionally, news reports and photographs (e.g., the sexual violence against Iraqi males at Abu Ghraib prison or male rape in the Congo) surface with disturbing effects because they show that male prisoners have been victims of anal rape and other forms of sodomy (Carlson, 2006). Males are raped during war for many of the same reasons that females are raped: to frighten, intimidate, control, traumatize, and silence a marginalized population (Stemple, 2009, pp. 611–615).

Wartime rapes are no longer—if they ever were—the sole province of a few sexually sadistic males who raped women because they enjoyed it and could get away with it. More and more, rape is strategic and used in order to advance the military goals of sovereign nations. Rape is, quite literally, a weapon of war: "In today's wars, rape is . . . often a strategy of warfare, intended at the least to terrorize, disrupt and uproot civilian communities thought to be aligned with an enemy group" (Farr, 2009, p. 4). Rape is now officially designated as a war crime, and violence against women, both nationally and internationally, is viewed more than ever before as a crime against humanity.

Rape is being used more and more as a strategy of war, used purposefully to humiliate families and destroy communities by ravaging women's bodies and destroying their spirits. Wartime rape is a way to take possession of an enemy population's resources and to make it necessary for them to leave their homes and all that they have. The sexual violence perpetrated against women in armed conflicts in today's world is the most vicious ever witnessed (Farr, 2009, p. 2). It devastates women, their families, and communities—even nations—not only while the sexual violence is occurring but also long after it has stopped (Jayaraman, 2008, p. 76). Extreme war rape is systematic and systemic, not unfortunate collateral damage as much as a central tactic of modern conflicts (*PLoS Medicine* Editors, 2009).

Wartime rape is a central part of genocidal programs, and sperm, quite literally, is used as a biological weapon. Orchestrated and systematic rapes, of the same women, carried out over an extended period of time, along with the enforced pregnancy that this often entails, can destroy the morale and will to fight of an entire region. This strategy of wartime rape may hasten a people's departure from a geographical region, and it may lead to the birth of a generation of children that is unwelcome and unloved. These children are the responsibility of a community and parents who do not want to be burdened with them (Card, 2008, pp. 185–188). A generation such as this, born in terror and trauma, unwanted and disliked, a burden that can neither be wished away nor ignored, may make women never want to have children again. In this way, rape during war is not only a way to "ethnically cleanse" an area. It is also a way to intentionally destroy a population by symbolically polluting its next generation.

Rape Scenes

Some violence can be initiated by the individual who ultimately ends up as its victim. Wolfgang (1958) classified a homicide as *victim precipitated* if an individual initiated through word or deed the fight that caused his or her own death (p. 252). Can there be victim-precipitated *rape?* Amir (1971) certainly thought so. He classified a rape as victim precipitated if in his opinion a woman said or did something to cause her own rape (or *failed* to do or say something that might have prevented it).

> The term "victim precipitation" describes those rape situations in which the victim actually, or so it was deemed, agreed to sexual relations but retracted before the actual act or did not react strongly enough when the suggestion was made by the offender(s). The term applies also to cases in risky situations marred with sexuality, especially when she uses what could be interpreted as indecency in language and gestures, or constitutes what could be taken as an invitation to sexual relations. (p. 266)

Amir concluded that 19 percent of the 646 rapes he studied were victim precipitated. However, *any* estimate of the number of victim-precipitated rapes is open to dispute, and the higher the estimate, the less credible it is. We have neither consistent definitions of rape nor incontrovertible ways to determine a rape has occurred. How can we know how many (or *if* any) are victim precipitated?

The term *victim precipitated*, though it has some value in heightening our understanding of certain types of predatory violence (e.g., murder), is woefully inadequate, or even dangerous, when it comes to forcible rape (Meadows, 2004, p. 24). It can serve as a self-fulfilling prophecy (Meloy & Miller, 2011). The belief that rape can be victim precipitated can *itself* be a precipitant of rape. Some rapes are motivated and then rationalized by rapists through the technique of neutralization that blames the victim for all that happened (Gilmartin-Zena, 1988, p. 289). When a victim of rape is blamed for her victimization, it can reduce whatever sympathy or charity she might otherwise have received (Dunn, 2010).

Blaming the victim lets both actual rapists and potential rapists off the hook (Tieger, 1981). Men who rape are more likely than men who do not rape to blame women for what has happened, even if the sexual encounter was openly violent (Garrett-Gooding & Senter, 1987). The belief in victim-precipitated rape can motivate sexual aggression toward women and then make it possible for rapists to excuse or justify to themselves and others what they have done (Berkowitz, Burkhart, & Bourg, 1994, p. 8; Scully & Marolla, 1984, pp. 533–537). Victim blaming also makes the kinds of changes that would be necessary to prevent rape (e.g., sociocultural changes or treatment/punishment of rapists) more difficult to achieve.

"Victim-precipitated rape" is a notion that has another damaging effect: It makes it easier to confuse cause and blame. Some victims of rape do things that are risky, making them more susceptible to victimization by others. However, this does not mean that they should be blamed for their own victimization. Golda Meir, former Israeli prime minister, had to respond to an outbreak of nighttime sexual assaults on women. One of the ministers asserted that the way to stop the assaults was to impose a curfew on women, forbidding them to be out after dark. Prime Minister Meir declined. Because it was men who were doing all the attacking, she concluded, it is men who should be restricted after dark, not women (Medea & Thompson, 1974, p. 59). Meir would certainly have admitted that women's travel in public places after dark was part of the *cause* of what happened. She just was not going to *blame* them for something that men were responsible for doing.

It is of some value to have terms that allow us to consider that certain victims of violent crimes do things that facilitate (or cause) some of what happens to them without blaming them for it. Terms like *victim vulnerability* (Geis, 1977, p. 21) or *victim contribution* (Kanin, 1984), though not perfect, are closer to what is needed. They make it easier to separate cause from blame, while allowing that some victims of rape do risky things while other rape victims do not.

Scully and Marolla (1984) studied the accounts of 114 incarcerated rapists in a Virginia prison who had been convicted of rape or attempted rape. Most men in the sample accounted for their rapes by discrediting their female victims and blaming them for what happened. They claimed that the women were promiscuous, seductive, or sexually aroused, and they portrayed the encounter as a consensual sex act. Even those rapists who did confess to a rape still tried to make themselves look better by blaming what had happened on their use of alcohol or other drugs—a temporary relapse—or on a simple misunderstanding of the women's wishes. Practically everybody offered some account for what he had done. Even a rapist who had raped five women at gunpoint and then stabbed each one to death attempted to make himself look good (or at least better).

> Physically they enjoyed the sex [rape]. Once they got involved, it would be difficult to resist. I was always gentle and kind until I started to kill them. And the killing was always sudden, so they wouldn't know it was coming. (p. 541)

The length to which some rapists will go to account for what they have done is truly amazing!

An adolescent male may initially have great ambivalence about the propriety of sexually coercive behavior. In time, however, he may acquire group-based vocabularies of motive and techniques of neutralization that are sufficient for him to overcome any victim resistance he may encounter.

> In a rape-supportive culture, attitudes and values that degrade women and make rape possible are in existence and learned at some level by all men. . . . Some men choose to accept these values, integrating them into their own, and create neutralizations that allow them both to maintain their self-image as law-abiding citizens and also to victimize women. (Miller & Schwartz, 1995, p. 17)

Some males may devalue and depersonalize women, reducing them to sex objects by defining them as "loose," "teases," or "sexually experienced." This is clear in the case of Fred (Lowney, Winslow, & Winslow, 1981, p. 337). He was standing at a bus stop in Arizona when a woman, age 35, picked him up in her car, which by that very fact indicated to him that she was "asking for it." He pulled a knife on her, forced her to drive 30 miles out into the desert, raped her forcibly, stole her car and clothes, and abandoned her in the 120-degree sun, all without guilt or remorse. In fact, he reported that he enjoyed the whole experience quite a lot. A while later, he saw the woman out in public. He approached her, telling her that he could not change what had happened and that she should never see him again. For some reason, their relationship grew, and Fred was able to report that "[e]ver since then I've sent her a Christmas card, she sends me one too, and now we're good friends." These *Cinderella rapes* (rapes with a happy ending), even if they do occur, should not cloud the facts. Rapes are violent acts that brutalize and humiliate the victims. Even if Christmas cards are exchanged afterward, it does not change this fact.

Peer group support for sexual violence against women may make coercive sexuality even more likely (Kanin, 1967b, pp. 501–503). We must remember, however, that some men who are not tightly integrated into male peer groups still can come to believe that some women can be legitimately raped (Gebhard, Gagnon, Pomeroy, & Christiansen, 1965). These men may cobble together their own vocabularies of motive and rationalization from parts of culture or may simply create them on their own from personal experiences they have had. In some cases, rape is simply a way for men who lack sufficient levels of personal control to achieve immediate gratification of their own sexual desires (Larragoite, 1994, p. 167). An individual who is prepared to rape ignores some clear social cues, while making other cues far more significant than they actually are. Rape can move a rapist away from boredom and toward a more involved, more exciting phase of existence (Katz, 1988, p. 4). Each successful rape or sexual assault that a man commits reinforces the original definition of the situation that some women can be legitimately raped.

Normalizing Sexual Violence

At certain times, in certain places, sexual violence against women is expected, encouraged, or even trendy. Consider Ingham, a small town in the countryside of Australia. In the 1970s, Schultz (1978) identified three characteristics of this community that made sexual violence against women a common occurrence. First, women were viewed as men's possessions. Every woman was expected to lead a virtuous life under the roof of her father until she married, whereupon she was expected to assume the duties of faithful wife and devoted mother under the roof of her husband. Second, women were never supposed to do or say anything that might bring shame on their families. Third, women were devalued. They were placed into one of two mutually exclusive categories, virgin or whore, depending almost entirely on how sexually experienced they were perceived to be. The virgin received some grudging respect for her chastity, but she was still resented because she spurned the sexual advances of men. The whore—a woman perceived to be sexually promiscuous—was considered contemptible by both the men and women of the town.

Factors worked in concert in Ingham to make it likely that women would be raped by men. Because women were viewed as men's possession and devalued, men had little reason *not* to treat them as sex objects. This depersonalization was especially likely with any woman who was defined as a whore. Because women were expected to protect their families from any kind of humiliation, any woman who was raped was under strong pressure to keep it to herself and suffer in silence. Rape victims were unlikely to tell even their closest friends or members of their families, and they were even less likely to tell police. The women of Ingham were in an extremely difficult situation. Their upbringing encouraged them to blame themselves and to handle the shame and guilt alone if they were raped.

Victim selection usually took place at weekly cabarets, the center of social life in Ingham. At these parties, attended by hundreds of men and women, one member of the all-male "rape squad" would select a victim and pump his arm up and down (as if he were pulling the cord on a bus or streetcar). This motion would then be copied by other men who wanted to participate. Once the selection had been made, the men waited until their intended victim left the cabaret and followed her to some convenient location; then all of them would rape her in turn. Sometimes the "rape squad" would follow a man and a woman to a secluded place. A member of the squad would tell the man that they wanted to "train his woman." If the man refused to cooperate, he was criticized for being unmanly and threatened with rejection in a town where manliness was highly prized and where acceptance by other males was very important. In this small town, the pressures on men to share women were almost as great as the pressures on women to be uncomplaining victims.

Rape on Campus

The Ingham case suggests that when men are strongly integrated into a cohesive, all-male group, both devaluation of women and sexual violence against them are more likely. However, we do not have to travel all the way to Australia to see these processes in operation. Consider the fraternity gang rape described by Sanday (1990, pp. 19–20). It occurred in February 1983, at a large university in the eastern United States, at the end of one of the weekly parties of a Greek organization identified as Fraternity XYZ. (In the second edition of Sanday's book on the incident, published in 2007, she revealed the location of the gang rape to be a fraternity house at the University of Pennsylvania, and a reviewer of the 1990 book identified the fraternity as Alpha Tau Omega [see http://www.nytimes.com/1991/04/28/books/in-short-nonfiction-871291.html].)

A woman named Laurel, inebriated and semiconscious in one of the bedrooms in the fraternity house, was viewed by some of the fraternity brothers as a legitimate sexual target. She was vaginally penetrated by at least five of them while others stood by and watched and cheered. It was not until 5 days later that Laurel told a university administrator that she had been raped by several men at the XYZ house. She claimed that she had not reported the rape immediately because she believed she could handle the matter alone. However, she found that she could not. This delay in reporting was taken by some people on campus to mean that she did not really believe that she had been wronged and that nothing really serious had happened.

The brothers of Fraternity XYZ thought Laurel was being cruel and vindictive in an effort to get them into trouble. They defined themselves as the injured party, and most of them thought that they had done nothing wrong. They were astounded anyone would consider what happened as a rape, and most of the brothers refused to believe anything out of the ordinary had occurred with Laurel. They branded her as the one who was really at fault because she drank too much, wanted the sex to happen, and offered no resistance to their sexual advances. She was vilified as a "nympho," "fish," and "red meat." This attack on Laurel, coupled with the fraternity brothers' legitimation of what they had done to her, renewed the bonds of brother-hood among those men who directly participated in the rape, as well as among those who derived some vicarious enjoyment from it (Sanday, 1990, p. 109). Most of the members of the fraternity continued to believe that what had happened was all Laurel's fault and that all the participants were too drunk to know any better (pp. 68–69). Members of the fraternity who voiced an objection to the victimization of Laurel ran the risk of being called "wimps," "gays," or "faggots."

How was this incident viewed outside the fraternity? Did anyone believe a rape had occurred? Laurel certainly did. She sued the state, the university, the fraternity, and the sorority she had been pledging at the time for $2.5 million. A year after the rape, the fraternity's charter was revoked by its national organization. Feminists on campus who learned of the incident also believed that a rape had occurred. Their definition of the situation was sup-ported by the local district attorney of the Sex Crimes Unit. Sanday (2007), an expert on the case, also believed a rape had occurred. If the incident had been officially branded as a rape, it would have had serious repercussions. The men responsible could have been prosecuted and imprisoned for many years, and the university would have had to take strong measures against the fraternity and the entire Greek system. In the end, the university administra-tion took the path of least disruption. The offending members of the frater-nity were required to take a reading course to increase their understanding of feminist issues; they also were required to perform several hours of com-munity service. The fraternity house itself was closed for one semester (Sanday, 1990, p. 62).

Females who attend universities and colleges are at a greater risk of rape and other forms of sexual assault than are women of comparable ages in the wider population (Alvarez & Bachman, 2008, p. 188). Kanin (1967a) con-cluded from his study of coercive sexuality on a university campus that fraternities attracted sexually aggressive males and then supported or even championed a conquest mentality toward women. The fraternities contained a social dynamic that encouraged their members to accumulate as many sex a-ts with females as possible with less concern shown for how they were accomplished. If persuasion failed, males felt comfortable in using force to get what they wanted. They did not have trouble finding sexual outlets; they had trouble finding authentic sexual fulfillment, principally because their sexual desires and wishes always outstripped their actual sexual achieve-ments (Kanin, 1967a, pp. 429–430).

Date rapists usually suffer from *sexual relative deprivation*. They are dissatisfied with their sexual accomplishments, because they are swayed by definitions of their peers who put such a high value on sexual accomplishment and confer high prestige for sexual success (Kanin, 2003, p. 213). The more females that a male can brag about having sexually "snagged," the higher is his status (Sanday, 2007, p. 7). In this atmosphere, men's inclination for their sexual reach to exceed their grasp is group-based and something that puts their dates at risk of being the target of sexual violence. Date rapists are *somewhat* predatory but very *opportunistic*. Fraternities create a climate in which the use of coercion to reach sexual goals is normative, and few restraints exist to curb this exploitation of women for sexual purposes (Yancey & Hummer, 1989).

Some of the same social factors that cause sexual violence to occur in the fraternity setting are—or can be—found in the colleges and universities of which they are a part. Sanday (1996a) concluded that some colleges and universities are more "rape-prone" than others. *Rape-prone campuses* have both ideational and relational elements that make male sexual violence toward women more likely. A rigid inequality and institutionalized double standard are coupled with the encouragement (or at least tolerance) of heavy drinking in males. The males view females in highly stereotypical ways (as sex objects and boosters for male interests and needs), and males are encouraged to be both hypermasculine and hypersexual. These social structural elements spill over to create rigid norms of male dominance that make some men prepared to take sexual advantage of women, especially those who are intoxicated. An intolerance of sexual minorities (e.g., gays) also characterizes rape-prone campuses, and the penalties for sexual violence against women are mild or even nonexistent.

Sometimes, sexual assaults occur more frequently on campuses because of negligence on the part of college and university administrators (Bohmer & Parrot, 1993, pp. 10–11). They find it easier—and better public relations—to stick their heads in the sand than to deal directly with sexual violence on campus. One practical piece of advice for campus administrators from Sanday's assembled works is that creating a rape-free campus will require the setting in motion of social dynamics that can transform the social structural elements that make up the foundation for sexual violence toward women. A *rape-free campus* will have a culture that both reflects and contributes to sexual equality between males and females and between straights and gays, no double standard so that women are viewed by men as equals, abolition of heavy drinking, and direct and immediate punishment at the institutional level of sexual assaults whenever they occur. If it is warranted, evidence of sexual assaults on campus should be turned over to criminal justice system representatives for review and punishment of offenders.

Acquaintance rapes are the bulk of all rapes, and date rape is a type of acquaintance rape that can grow out of a social or romantic situation (Hall,

1995, p. 83). Kirkpatrick and Kanin (1957) sampled 291 college females at a midwestern university in the 1950s, and they found that over half of them (55.7 percent) reported that they had been sexually offended at some point during the academic year (by being the target of unwanted kissing, fondling, or vaginal penetration). A follow-up study by Kanin and Parcell (1981), done approximately 20 years later, found similar results (though the data were collected at a different large midwestern state university, and U.S. society had gone through both a sexual revolution and a women's liberation movement in the intervening years). In the follow-up study, 50.7 percent of the 282 university females who participated reported that they had been offended at some level of erotic intimacy during the academic year.

A recent study via questionnaire, translated into different languages to accommodate the particular locale, of 13,877 students, in 32 countries, attending 68 universities, reported that *both* males and females used violence to obtain sex from their dating partners, though males used it more often (Gámez-Guadix, Straus, & Herschberger, 2011). The use of verbal coercion to achieve sexual goals was reported by 26.7 percent of male students and 19.6 percent of female students, while the use of physical force to obtain sex was reported by 2.4 percent of males and 1.8 percent of females. One cause of the coercive sexuality that was found in this international sample was that these students had themselves been victimized as children, reporting that they had been neglected, spanked, slapped, or sexually abused.

The search for both fun and status in the campus setting can work to the disadvantage of females and to the advantage of predatory males. At fraternity parties, where alcohol flows freely and the situation is controlled strongly by the men who give the party, elements are present that can lead to sexual violence. Much of what happens takes place behind closed doors and with little accountability to outside agents of social control. Norms exist at parties that structure them in such a way that everyone is supposed to have a good time (or at least act like it), and partygoers are supposed to like and trust one another. Hosts, especially, are to be trusted, and they, in turn, are expected to treat their guests with courtesy and respect. The real situation at parties, however, can depart from the ideal. What may actually exist is a *shadow sexual culture* that makes it possible for some men to ensnare an inebriated, vulnerable female who is unable to control herself well enough to avoid being sexually victimized (Sanday, 2007, p. 3).

Women may find themselves in a highly gendered situation in which they are objectified and depersonalized. They may find that by fulfilling the expectations of what a "proper" partygoer is supposed to do, they put themselves in a situation that can be risky, making them more vulnerable to sexual violence. Vulnerability, however, is not a crime, and it only becomes sexual violence if men are willing to take advantage of a woman's dependent situation.

> Party rape is accomplished without the use of guns, knives, or fists. It is carried out through the combination of low level forms of coercion—a lot of liquor and persuasion, manipulation of situations so that women cannot leave, and sometimes force (e.g., by blocking a door, or using body weight to make it difficult for a woman to get up). These forms of coercion are made more effective by organizational arrangements that provide men with control over how partying happens and by expectations that women let loose and trust their party-mates. This systematic and effective method of extracting non-consensual sex is largely invisible, which makes it difficult for victims to convince anyone—even themselves—that a crime occurred. Men engage in this behavior with little risk of consequences. (Armstrong, Hamilton, & Sweeney, 2009, p. 495)

Alcohol (or some other drug) can be used as a weapon by some men to sexually assault women, and it is an effective one. It undermines a woman's capacity to resist, her clarity and recollection about what actually happened, and her inclination to report any sexual victimization that took place. Excessive alcohol consumption could make a female uncertain about whether she was victimized and, if she was, who exactly was responsible (Armstrong et al., p. 494). Alcohol is used as a weapon against women's sexual reluctance, and it is an important tool that fraternity males (and others) use to control females (Martin & Hummer, 2003, pp. 219–220).

Date rape—disputes over what it is, how many occur, and how it should be handled—reflects some of the normal ambiguity that can characterize dating relationships (Ward, Dziuba-Leatherman, Stapleton, & Yodanis, 1994). "Sexuality is messy, passionate, unclear, tentative, anxiety-producing, liberating, frightening, embarrassing, consoling, appetitive, and cerebral. In other words, sexuality is contradictory, it is different for different people, and it is even different for the same person at different times" (Schwartz, 1995, p. 35). The ambiguity of human sexuality is one of the principal justifications for the formulation of what came to be called the *Antioch policy* (at Antioch College in Yellow Springs, Ohio), adopted in 1993. (Since then, many other colleges and universities have adopted the language and procedures of Antioch College in order to deal with sexual violence on their campuses.)

The Antioch policy required that each new level of intimacy be verbally consented to by a partner. Without this consent, any subsequent sex was viewable as forced, and it could be penalized through one of several sanctions, such as expulsion, suspension, mandatory therapy, or restrictions on class scheduling (Antioch College Community, 1995). More than ever before, males were expected to take steps to be certain that they were not forcing themselves on their sexual partners and that the sexual encounters in which they were involved were mutually rewarding (Pineau, 1996, pp. 17–18). Active verbal consent was the foundation of the establishment of a sexual culture that was designed to be less exploitative and dangerous for dating partners. (Antioch College closed its doors on June 30, 2008, due to financial reasons, but it reopened in October 2011.)

Does a rape crisis currently exist at colleges and universities? It all depends on what is meant by rape. Some researchers use such a broad definition of sexual violence that the real difference between the brutality of rape and the disappointment of bad sex gets lost in the shuffle.

> We all agree that rape is a terrible thing, but we no longer agree on what rape is. Today's definition has stretched beyond bruises and knives, threats of death or violence to include emotional pressure and the influence of alcohol. (Roiphe, 1995, p. 75)

The belief that a rape epidemic exists on college and university campuses may be caused more by a new way of interpreting ambiguous data than it is by actual changes in the rate of rape. Broadening the definition of rape to include any bad or regretted sex—Cathy Young (1992) calls this *definitional shenanigans*—may actually lead to the unintended and unwanted outcome of trivializing severe forms of sexual violence.

Dworkin explored the sexed world of dominance and submission in her book entitled *Intercourse* (1987). Practically *every* instance of heterosexual intercourse is portrayed in the book as just one more example of the sexual violence perpetrated by the class of men against the class of women (pp. 122–143). According to Dworkin, the only real difference between rape and heterosexual intercourse is that the latter occurs so often that few people are able to see it for the sexual violence it really is. Dworkin concludes that in this dance of dominance and submission between men and women, women are at a distinct disadvantage. They have been controlled by men for so long that they actually aid in their own objectification and inferiorization. In a new preface to the 1987 book, Dworkin (1995) claimed years after *Intercourse* was published that she did not say that all men are rapists or that all intercourse is rape (p. x). However, if Dworkin believed a distinction exists between sexual intercourse and rape, it is difficult from reading her book to know what that might be. (Dworkin died on April 9, 2005.)

Research has found that most males who commit date rape do not define it as rape (Capraro, 1994, p. 22). Male college students and males in general tend to believe that a woman's refusal to engage in sex is usually nothing more than a required part of the dating ritual (Celes, 1991). They rarely view a "no" from their dates as being as definite or as firm as it is. A "no" is even more likely to be meaningless to an individual who truly believes that sex should be the outcome of any male–female relationship. Females may not be viewed by their dates as equal sexual partners with the same right as anybody else to say "no" to sex when they don't want it (Sanday, 2007, p. 19).

An asymmetry may exist in how interactants view the same relationship. A study of 41 women who had been followed by males indicated that the victims and their stalkers did not agree on the dynamics of what was happening. The women believed that little or no relationship existed between them and their stalkers; the stalkers, however, believed (or said that they did) that a strong, close relationship existed (or would one day) between them and the individuals they were following. What was most alarming to the victims was not that they were being stalked, but that the stalkers wanted them to know how vulnerable and susceptible they actually were (Emerson, Ferris, & Brooks, 1998, p. 296).

New(er) technologies in regard to communication and information storage have made it possible for stalkers to intrude into the lives of their victims by using e-mail, texting, tweets, and instant messaging. These technologies also make it possible for stalkers to gather information online about people they intend to stalk that at one time would have been impossible to obtain (e.g., e-mail addresses). The electronic culture not only makes *cyberstalking* possible, but it also makes it possible for cyberstalkers to repeatedly victimize others without fear of either punishment or retribution. Even though most cyberstalkers know their victims at some level, they are more likely to be strangers to them when compared to stalkers who track their victims in more traditional ways (i.e., directly or physically, without the use of electronic gadgets) (Reyns, Henson, & Fisher, 2012).

Sex and Violence in Gusiiland

It is possible to have a great deal of sexual violence in a relationship without the encounter automatically being defined as forcible rape. LeVine (1959) studied sexual relationships between the men and women of Gusii, a small agricultural community in the highlands of southwestern Kenya. Every relationship between males and females in this community was filled with hostility, and even marriage brought no relief from sexual antagonisms. All it did was bring together a man and a woman from different and probably warring clans and unite them in a continually stormy relationship. Women were especially ambivalent about marriage. They needed to marry because marriage and the birthing of sons were the only ways that women could gain status and respect. However, marriage forced them to sever ties with their own families and to live with a clan that might be cruel and mean-spirited. Practically every Gusii bride was fearful of what would happen to her when she left the protection of her own home and family.

Even though a woman's parents had granted permission for the marriage to proceed, and the woman herself had adjusted to the prospect, the bride-to-be strongly resisted when her husband-to-be sent escorts to get her. Part of the resistance was obligatory. She could not look too willing, or she might be considered a whore. However, much of it was genuine and born out of anxiety over just what would become of her in her future husband's clan. She might run away and hide. Her parents might have to find her and convince her to go. She might have to be dragged out of her house by her friends and relatives, all the while kicking and screaming. She might even go to her new home in tears, with her hands on top of her head in a gesture that combined sorrow, regret, and a fear of the unknown.

The wedding night sexual encounter was an ordeal for both husband and wife, and it displayed the kinds of sexual conflicts that plague all Gusii marriages. The bride put her new husband's sexual abilities to the test. She did everything that she could to ensure his impotence and to guarantee his failure at intercourse. She might use magical charms. These included such things as chewing a small piece of charcoal, placing a piece of knotted grass under the marriage bed, or twisting the phallic flower of the banana tree. She might tie her pubic hairs together so that they covered the opening of her vagina. She might constrict her vaginal muscles so tightly that any penetration by her husband would be impossible. She might even refuse to get onto the bed at all. Her resistance to his advances persisted throughout the entire wedding night, and wives took great enjoyment in being able to keep their husbands from achieving intercourse for an indefinite period of time.

The new husband, however, did all he could to guarantee his own success and to overcome his wife's resistance. He made certain that he was well fed by eating special herbs as well as large quantities of coffee beans, valued as an aphrodisiac. He was cheered on by his brothers and male cousins, who stayed close to the wedding-night dwelling and sang and danced while the events unfolded. The man's relatives might become more than onlookers. If the new groom was young (under 25) and his new bride was particularly uncooperative, some of these men might come to the rescue. They would grab the woman, undress her, throw her on the bed, and hold her down until her husband could penetrate her. The husband wanted to cause his new bride as much physical pain as possible. In fact, his status was greatly enhanced if she were unable to walk the next day. "Legitimate heterosexual encounters among the Gusii are aggressive contests, involving force and pain-inflicting behavior which under circumstances that are not legitimate could be termed 'rape'" (LeVine, 1959, p. 971). Even though husbands obtained sex from their wives through force and wives strenuously resisted, the sex was not defined as rape.

The Rape of Males

The multiple ways that society and culture impact both rape and our understandings of it—normalizing it by suppressing some things and exaggerating others—are clear with a relatively neglected topic: the rape of males.

> Men have been abused and sexually humiliated during situations of armed conflict, such as the highly publicized Abu Ghraib scandal in Iraq. Childhood sexual abuse of boys is alarmingly common; in fact, the vast majority of those abused at the hands of Roman Catholic clergy in the United States were boys. And sexual assault against gay men remains unchecked due to assumptions that, as was once commonly assumed about women, gay men who have been raped must have "asked for it." (Stemple, 2009, p. 605)

Males are raped both inside and outside of prisons and jails. In fact, male-on-male rape *inside* of penal institutions is more frequent than is male-on-female rape *outside* of penal institutions, even though far more women than men are raped in a given society (Gilligan, 1996, pp. 175–176; Thio, 2010, p. 103). Stemple concludes that not only is inmate-on-inmate rape a serious human rights abuse, but it is also a major public health problem (p. 609).

The first-ever National Former Prisoner Survey provides information on sexual victimization of incarcerated individuals (both male and female). It reports that approximately 10 percent of former state prisoners claimed they had been victims of one or more incidents of sexual victimization during their most recent period of incarceration (Beck & Johnson, 2012). About half were victimized by another inmate, and about half by a member of the facility's staff. The rate of inmate-on-inmate sexual victimization was higher for females than it was for males. The majority (72 percent) of the victims of inmate-on-inmate victimizations reported feelings of shame or humiliation, and over half (56 percent) reported experiencing some guilt.

When males are raped, it is usually done by other males, even when the rape occurs outside of penal institutions. The rape usually occurs in social situations that are similar to the situations in which females are raped: The men are alone, isolated, and vulnerable. Male-on-male rape has a strong symbolic message in that it tells the victim that he is an object or thing. In this sense, *all* victims of rape have a shared plight: "[N]ot women, but the weak, become the second sex, subordinate, submissive, subject to rape" (Janeway, 1975, p. 10). Sex can be a way to show who has power and who does not.

Some of the dynamics and identifying features of the rape of males can be seen in what is called the "Penn State child sex abuse scandal" or the "sex scandal at Penn State." The epicenter of this scandal is Jerry Sandusky, a former defensive coordinator under Joe Paterno, one-time head football coach at the university. (Paterno died January 22, 2012, at the age of 84.) Sandusky was arrested in November 2011 for sexually abusing and raping boys in sexual encounters that went back to the 1970s and 1980s. An investigation conducted by Louis Freeh, former director of the FBI, concluded that university administrators were aware of Sandusky's sexually predatory activities but failed to acknowledge their severity or take effective steps to stop them. Sandusky founded The Second Mile (in 1977), a nonprofit charity to assist and encourage at-risk and underprivileged youth. Whether this was a genuine effort to help the young or simply Sandusky's way to find youngsters to groom and then sexually victimize is impossible to know with any certainty. The jury, however, concluded that Sandusky planned to sexually exploit the boys in his care.

Sandusky was charged with 52 counts of sexual abuse of 10 boys extending over a 15-year-period. Four of the charges were eventually dropped (bringing the total to 48). In June 2012, Sandusky was found guilty of 45 of the charges. His victims testified—they ranged in age at the time of the trial from 18 to 28—that the coercive sexuality included kissing, fondling, joint showering, oral sex, and anal sex. Sandusky did not restrict his sexual encounters to the university's shower room; they also occurred in hotel rooms and even in his own home. Mike McQueary, a former graduate assistant coach, testified that he had witnessed Sandusky sodomizing a boy in a shower at the university. Even one of Sandusky's adopted children claimed that he, too, was sexually abused by the man. (The son was prepared to testify in court if his father had testified in his own defense.) Sandusky was sentenced to 30 to 60 years in prison for his crimes.

This scandal had a ripple effect the size of a tsunami. Paterno was fired as head football coach, and Graham Spanier, Penn State's president at the time, was also fired. (Paterno did bring the abuse to the attention of his superiors, but he did not contact police, which is what led to his dismissal.) Charges were also brought against Vice President Gary Schultz and former Athletic Director Tim Curley for failing to report the abuse and lying under oath. Along with all the injury Sandusky caused for his victims (and their families and friends) and everything that Sandusky himself lost—his reputation, his freedom, his financial standing—one other thing can be chalked up to his predatory acts: his image. His likeness was removed from a painted mural of Penn State greats. All that remains is an empty chair.

In July 2012, the other shoe dropped for the Penn State Lions, and it was a heavy shoe indeed. A 900-pound bronze statue of Paterno was removed from the sidewalk outside Beaver Stadium and secluded somewhere inside the building. A day later (July 23, 2012), the president of the NCAA (Mark Emmert) announced the details of a consent decree that had been reached with the university: no postseason play for four years; the loss of several scholarships; removal of 111 of Paterno's 409 coaching victories, dropping him to twelfth on the all-time wins list (vacated because they were earned during the 14 years since it was known that Sandusky was preying on youngsters); and a $60 million fine (to serve as an endowment to help victims of child sexual abuse). The Big Ten (football conference division) levied additional punishments. The National Collegiate Athletic Association (NCAA) placed the university's athletic department on probation for 5 years (Wolff, 2012).

Though Sandusky cannot be excused for his crimes—without him and his sexual predations, no scandal would have occurred—the fact is that the culture at Penn State, if not a cause of what happened, certainly played a pivotal role in its cover-up. The intense sense of loyalty found in the football program, both to the game and to Paterno, coupled with the incredible wealth that big-time football generates, led to an arrogance of power in which Paterno pulled the strings and most others danced. (The Freeh Report branded it a "culture of reverence.") In this climate, a disinterest and disinclination existed to scrutinize Sandusky's behavior and allegations against him very closely for fear that it would hurt the university, the football program, and the coaches.

Males who rape males are more likely than males who rape females to be strangers to their victims and to use a great deal of force and violence to overpower and sexually assault their victims. However, the motives for the rape of males are not so different from the motives for the rape of females: power, control, anger, sadism. Rape, regardless of whether the victim is female or male, is better viewed as the sexual expression of violence than as the violent expression of sexuality. If sexual release were the primary motive, a more convenient and ordinary way—less stigmatizing and less fraught with danger for the offender—would be masturbation (Thio, 2010, p. 104).

A difference exists in how men and women view their experience of being the victim of sexual violence. Men are more likely to report that they think they are less of a *man*, whereas women are more inclined to think that they are less of a *person* (Groth, 1979, p. 139). A male rape victim may become hypersexual with women after his own sexual victimization, viewing the sexual victimization of women as a way to reestablish his fractured masculinity (p. 140).

It is possible for a female to rape a male because rape's essential feature is its forcible, nonconsensual nature. Violent women could use physical objects to sodomize male victims anally, or males could be forced in one way or another (e.g., at gunpoint) to perform oral sex on a female whom they would rather avoid altogether. A woman could threaten, coerce, cajole, plead with, cry for, or beg an unwilling male to engage in sexual acts with her. If the male is overpowered physically or psychologically, being forced to consummate a sexual act he would rather not, it qualifies as a rape sociologically but not legally according to the FBI's traditional definition of forcible rape. (As noted earlier, the FBI historically defined forcible rape as something that could only happen to females.)

Humans are not all alike when it comes to sexual response and sexual capacity. A woman might experience an orgasm even though she is being forcibly raped, because she is being physically and psychologically overwhelmed, not because she is "turned on" by a rapist and enjoying the whole experience (Medea & Thompson, 1974). Likewise, it is possible for a man to have an erection during a sexual assault, even though he is anxious and under duress (Rumney, 2008, p. 76; Thio, 2010, p. 105).

The tendency of *female* victims of rape to suffer in silence, either refusing to tell anyone of their victimization or denying that it was rape at all, is even more likely with men who are raped (Rumney, 2008). This inclination to suffer in silence is especially likely if a man is raped by a woman. He is more likely to report increased levels of shame and decreased levels of self-esteem, questioning his own masculinity (Terry, Giotakos, Tsiliakou, & Ackerman, 2010, pp. 243–244).

A male who reports to police that he has been sexually victimized faces a strong possibility of encountering both scorn and suspicion (Davies & Rogers, 2006). This is especially true if he is perceived by police to be a gay man. Police are more inclined to view gay men as untrustworthy in reporting being raped unless so much force and violence have been used during the sexual assault that it is beyond dispute that a forcible rape occurred. Gay men are generally viewed by police as individuals for whom sexual assaults by other men are likely and thus not something about which they should complain. When it comes to blame, gay men and straight women are held more responsible for their own sexual victimizations than are gay women and straight men (Wakelin & Long, 2003). Whatever institutionalized sexism still exists in the criminal justice system, which extends some sympathy to male *defendants* who are charged with raping women, does not carry over to sympathetic treatment of male rape *victims* (Rumney, 2008, p. 81). This insensitivity or indifference of police toward male rape victims is particularly disturbing in light of the fact that victims of male-on-male sexual violence are likely to have faced a stranger and to have been the victims of a great deal of physical injury.

Conclusions

Rape is primarily a way for certain individuals to enhance and reaffirm their sense of power, potency, and control by hurting and overpowering others. What qualifies as rape in one place and time may be treated very differently in another place and time, regardless of how injurious the assault may be to its victim. Some of the factors used to define rapes are the amount of force used and how much resistance a victim offers.

Patterns of sexual violence and attitudes about it are powerfully influenced by social and cultural factors, gender-based associations, the structure of sexual inequality, and interpersonal dynamics. Structured inequality between males and females often leads to conflicts. Sex may come to be viewed by some men as something that they have a right to receive from women. If it is not freely given, they have no reservations about using force to get what they want. They may then attempt to excuse and justify their actions to others or even to themselves.

A classic rape, which is sexual violence done by a stranger, almost always in a public place, against strong victim resistance, causing the victim serious injury, is the type of coercive sexuality that is easiest for most people to define as rape, victims included. It seems that wherever and whenever sexual conflicts increase, forcible rape becomes more likely. The victim herself may even be blamed for her own victimization, which makes it look normal and normative. Most social conflicts, such as war, entail some men raping some women. Men are also raped, sometimes by women, but mostly by other men. The rape of males is a problem that criminal justice system representatives do not always handle sensitively or effectively.

References

Allison, J., & Wrightsman, L. (1993). *Rape, the misunderstood crime.* Newbury Park, CA: Sage.

Alvarez, A., & Bachman, R. (2008). *Violence: The enduring problem.* Thousand Oaks, CA: Sage.

Amir, M. (1971). *Patterns in forcible rape.* Chicago, IL: University of Chicago Press.

Antioch College Community. (1995). Antioch College: A sexual consent policy. In B. Leone & K. Koster (Eds.), *Rape on campus* (pp. 10–22). San Diego, CA: Greenhaven Press.

Armstrong, E., Hamilton, L., & Sweeney, B. (2009). Sexual assault on campus. In P. Adler & P. Adler (Eds.), *Constructions of deviance: Social power, context, and interaction* (6th ed., pp. 485–501). Belmont, CA: Thomson/Wadsworth.

Bahun-Radunović, S., & Rajan, V. G. J. (2008). Introduction. In S. Bahun-Radunović & V. G. J. Rajan (Eds.), *Violence and gender in the globalized world: The intimate and extimate* (pp. 1–7). Burlington, VT: Ashgate.

Bailey, F. Y. (2010). Rape, race, and the media. In R. L. Bing III (Ed.), *Race, crime, and the media* (pp. 10–27). New York, NY: McGraw-Hill.

Barlow, H. (1996). *Introduction to criminology* (7th ed.). New York, NY: HarperCollins.

Baron, L., & Straus, M. (1987). Four theories of rape: A macrosociological analysis. *Social Problems, 34,* 467–489.

Baron, L., & Straus, M. (1989). *Four theories of rape in American society: A state-level analysis.* New Haven, CT: Yale University Press.

Bart, P., & O'Brien, P. H. (1985). *Stopping rape: Successful survival strategies.* New York, NY: Pergamon.

Beck, A. J., & Johnson, C. (2012, May). *National Former Prisoner Survey, 2008: Sexual victimization reported by former state prisoners, 2008.* NCJ 237363. Washington, DC: Bureau of Justice Statistics, U.S. Department of Justice.

Bedau, H. A. (1982). The death penalty for rape: *Coker v. Georgia* (1977). In H. A. Bedau (Ed.), *The death penalty in America* (3rd ed., pp. 299–304). New York, NY: Oxford University Press.

Bergen, R. K. (1996). *Wife rape: Understanding the response of survivors and service providers.* Thousand Oaks, CA: Sage.

Berkowitz, A., Burkhart, B., & Bourg, S. (1994). Research on college men and rape. In A. Berkowitz (Ed.), *Men and rape: Theory, research, and prevention programs in higher education* (pp. 3–19). San Francisco, CA: Jossey-Bass.

Bohmer, C., & Parrot, A. (1993). *Sexual assault on campus: The problem and the solution.* New York, NY: Lexington.

Bourque, L. B. (1989). *Defining rape.* Durham, NC: Duke University Press.

Brownmiller, S. (1975). *Against our will: Men, women, and rape.* New York, NY: Simon & Schuster.

Buchwald, E., Fletcher, P., & Roth, M. (1993). *Transforming a rape culture.* Minneapolis, MN: Milkweed.

Buddie, A. M., & Miller, A. G. (2000). Beyond rape myths: A more complex view of perceptions of rape victims. *Sex Roles, 45,* 139–160.

Bureau of Justice Statistics. (2008). *Criminal victimization in the United States—statistical tables index, May 12, 2011, Table 102.* NCJ 231173. Retrieved January 30, 2013, from http://bjs.ojp.usdoj.gov/content/pub/pdf/cvus08.pdf

Capraro, R. (1994). Disconnected lives: Men, masculinity, and rape prevention. In A. Berkowitz (Ed.), *Men and rape* (pp. 21–33). San Francisco, CA: Jossey-Bass.

Card, C. (2008). The paradox of genocidal rape aimed at enforced pregnancy. *Southern Journal of Philosophy, 46,* 176–189.

Carlson, E. (2006). The hidden prevalence of male sexual assault during war: Observations on blunt trauma to the male genitals. *British Journal of Criminology, 46,* 16–25.

Carosella, C. (1995). Introduction. In C. Carosella (Ed.), *Who's afraid of the dark? A forum of truth, support, and assurance for those affected by rape* (pp. xiii–xxiv). New York, NY: HarperPerennial.

Celes, W. (1991, January 2). Students trying to draw line between sex and assault. *New York Times,* p. Al.

Chappell, D. (1976). Cross-cultural research on forcible rape. *International Journal of Criminology and Penology, 4,* 295–304.

Chesney-Lind, M., & Jones, N. (Eds.). (2010). *Fighting for girls: New perspectives on gender and violence.* Albany: State University of New York Press.

Clover, C. (1992). *Men, women, and chainsaws: Gender in the modern horror film.* Princeton, NJ: Princeton University Press.

Coker v. Georgia, 433 U.S. 485 (1977).

Collins, P. H. (2010). Assume the position: The changing contours of sexual violence. In L. J. Moore & M. Kosut (Eds.), *The body reader: Essential social and cultural readings* (pp. 80–107). New York: New York University Press.

Cuklanz, L. (1996). *Rape on trial: How the mass media construct legal reform and social change.* Philadelphia: University of Pennsylvania Press.

Davies, M., & Rogers, P. (2006). Perceptions of male victims in depicted sexual assaults: A review of the literature. *Aggression and Violent Behavior, 11,* 367–377.

DeKeseredy, W. S. (2011). *Violence against women: Myths, facts, controversies.* Toronto, Ontario, Canada: University of Toronto Press.

Dunn, J. L. (2010). *Judging victims: Why we stigmatize survivors and how they reclaim respect.* Boulder, CO: Lynn Rienner.

Dworkin, A. (1987). *Intercourse.* New York, NY: Free Press/Simon & Schuster.

Dworkin, A. (1995). Preface. In A. Dworkin, *Intercourse* (pp. vii–xi). New York, NY: Free Press/Simon & Schuster.

Eller, J. (2006). *Violence and culture: A cross-cultural and interdisciplinary approach.* Belmont, CA: Thomson/Wadsworth.

Emerson, R., Ferris, K., & Brooks, C. (1998). On being stalked. *Social Problems, 43,* 289–314.

Epstein, J., & Langenbahn, S. (1994). *The criminal justice and community response to rape.* Washington, DC: Government Printing Office.

Estrich, S. (1987). *Real rape.* Cambridge, MA: Harvard University Press.

Faris, R., & Felmlee, D. (2011). Status struggles: Network centrality and gender segregation in same- and cross-gender aggression. *American Sociological Review, 76,* 48–73.

Farr, K. (2009). Extreme war rape in today's civil-war-torn states: A contextual and comparative analysis. *Gender Issues, 26,* 1–41.

Federal Bureau of Investigation (FBI). (2012). *Attorney General Eric Holder announces revisions to the Uniform Crime Report's definition of rape.* National press release. Retrieved May 1, 2012, from http://www.fbi.gov/news/pressrel/ press-releases/attorney-general-eric-holder-announces-revisions-to-the-uniform-crime-reports-definition-of-rape

Felson, R. (2003). Motives for sexual coercion. In M. Silberman (Ed.), *Violence and society: A reader* (pp. 194–206). Upper Saddle River, NJ: Prentice Hall.

Ferraro, K. (1996). Women's fear of victimization: Shadow of sexual assault? *Social Forces, 75,* 667–690.

Fitzgerald, L. (1993). Sexual harassment: Violence against women in the workplace. *American Psychologist, 48,* 1070–1076.

Frohmann, L. (2005). Sexual assault. In E. Rubington & M. Weinberg (Eds.), *Deviance: The interactionist perspective* (9th ed., pp. 188–200). Boston, MA: Pearson/Allyn & Bacon.

Funk, R. (1993). *Stopping rape: A challenge for men.* Philadelphia, PA: New Society.

Gámez-Guadix, M., Straus, M. A., & Hershberger, S. L. (2011). Childhood and adolescent victimization and perpetuation of sexual coercion by male and female university students. *Deviant Behavior, 32,* 712–714.

Garbarino, J. (2006). *See Jane hit: Why girls are growing more violent and what we can do about it.* New York, NY: Penguin.

Garrett-Gooding, J., & Senter, R., Jr. (1987). Attitudes and acts of sexual aggression on a university campus. *Sociological Inquiry, 57,* 348–371.

Gebhard, P., Gagnon, J., Pomeroy, P., & Christiansen, C. (1965). *Sex offenders: An analysis of types.* New York, NY: Harper & Row.

Geis, G. (1977). Forcible rape: An introduction. In D. Chappell, R. Geis, & G. Geis (Eds.), *Forcible rape: The crime, the victim, and the offender* (pp. 1–44). New York, NY: Columbia University Press.

Gilligan, J. (1996). *Violence: Reflections on a national epidemic.* New York, NY: Vintage/Random House.

Gilmartin, P. (1994). *Rape, incest, and child sexual abuse.* New York, NY: Garland.

Gilmartin-Zena, P. (1988). Gender differences in students' attitudes toward rape. *Sociological Focus, 21,* 279–292.

Goode, E. (1996). Rape. In E. Goode (Ed.), *Social deviance* (pp. 284–287). Boston, MA: Allyn & Bacon.

Goodman, L., Koss, M., Fitzgerald, L., Russo, N., & Keita, G. (1993). Male violence against women: Current research and future directions. *American Psychologist, 48,* 1054–1058.

Gordon, M., & Riger, S. (1989). *The female fear.* New York, NY: Free Press.

Greenfeld, L. (1997). *Sex offenses and offenders.* Washington, DC: Government Printing Office.

Gregersen, E. (1983). *Sexual practices: The story of human sexuality.* New York, NY: Watts.

Gregor, T. (1982). No girls allowed. *Science Magazine, 3,* 26–31.

Groth, N. (1979). *Men who rape.* New York, NY: Plenum.

Hall, R. (1995). *Rape in America*. Santa Barbara, CA: ABC-CLIO.

Haskett, M., Portwood, S., & Lewis, K. (2010). Physical child abuse. In C. Ferguson (Ed.), *Violent crime: Clinical and social implications* (pp. 207–228). Thousand Oaks, CA: Sage.

Higgins, L., & Silver, B. (1991). Introduction: Rereading rape. In L. Higgins & B. Silver (Eds.), *Rape and representation* (pp. 1–11). New York, NY: Columbia University Press.

Holmes, R., & Holmes, S. (2009). *Profiling violent crimes: An investigative tool* (4th ed.). Thousand Oaks, CA: Sage.

Iversen, T., & Rosenbluth, F. (2010). *Women, work, & politics: The political economy of gender inequality*. New Haven, CT: Yale University Press.

Jackson, S. (1995). The social context of rape: Sexual scripts and motivation. In P. Searles & R. Berger (Eds.), *Rape and society* (pp. 16–27). Boulder, CO: Westview.

Janeway, E. (1975). The weak are the second sex. In U. West (Ed.), *Women in a changing world* (pp. 5–24). New York, NY: McGraw-Hill.

Jayaraman, T. V. (2008). Rape as a war crime. *UN Chronicle, 45,* 76–77.

Kanin, E. (1967a). An examination of sexual aggression as a response to sexual frustration. *Journal of Marriage and the Family, 29,* 428–433.

Kanin, E. (1967b). Reference groups and sex conduct norm violations. *Sociology Quarterly, 8,* 495–504.

Kanin, E. (1984). Date rape: Unofficial criminals and victims. *Victimology: An International Journal, 9,* 95–108.

Kanin, E. (2003). Date rapists: Differential sexual socialization and relative deprivation. In M. Silberman (Ed.), *Violence and society: A reader* (pp. 207–214). Upper Saddle River, NJ: Prentice Hall.

Kanin, E., & Parcell, S. (1981). Sexual aggression: A second look at the offended female. In L. H. Bowker (Ed.), *Women and crime in America* (pp. 223–233). New York, NY: Macmillan.

Katz, J. (1988). *Seductions of crime: Moral and sensual attractions of doing evil*. New York, NY: Basic Books.

Kirkpatrick, C., & Kanin, E. (1957). Male sex aggression on a university campus. *American Sociological Review, 22,* 52–58.

Koss, M. (1993). Rape: Scope, impact, interventions, and public policy responses. *American Psychologist, 48,* 1062–1069.

Koss, M., Goodman, L., Browne, A., Fitzgerald, L., Keita, G. P., & Russo, N. P. (1994). *No safe haven: Male violence against women at home, at work, and in the community*. Washington, DC: American Psychological Association.

Lally, W., & DeMaris, A. (2012). Gender and relational-distance effects in arrests for domestic violence. *Crime & Delinquency, 58,* 103–123.

Larragoite, V. (1994). Rape. In T. Hirschi & M. Gottfredson (Eds.), *The generality of deviance* (pp. 159–172). New Brunswick, NJ: Transaction Publishers.

Leatherman, J. L. (2011). *Sexual violence and armed conflict*. Cambridge, UK: Polity Press.

LeVine, R. (1959). Gusii sex offenses: A study in social control. *American Anthropologist, 61,* 965–990.

Llewellyn, K. N., & Hoebel, E. A. (1941). *The Cheyenne way: Conflict and case law in primitive jurisprudence*. Norman: University of Oklahoma Press.

Lowney, J., Winslow, R., & Winslow, V. (1981). *Deviant reality* (2nd ed.). Boston, MA: Allyn & Bacon.

MacKellar, J. (1975). *Rape: The bait and the trap*. New York, NY: Crown.

MacKinnon, C. (1982). Feminism, Marxism, method, and the state: An agenda for theory. *Signs, 7,* 515–544.

MacKinnon, C. (2003). The legal regulation of sexual harassment: From tort to sex discrimination. In M. Silberman (Ed.), *Violence and society: A reader* (pp. 259–270). Upper Saddle River, NJ: Prentice Hall.

Madison, L. (2012, October 23). Richard Mourdock: Even pregnancy from rape something "God intended." *CBSNews.com*.

Mandery, E. (2012). *Capital punishment in America: A balanced examination* (2nd ed.). Sudbury, MA: Jones & Bartlett.

Martin, P., & Hummer, R. (2003). Fraternities and rape on campus. In M. Silberman (Ed.), *Violence and society: A reader* (pp. 215–225). Upper Saddle River, NJ: Prentice Hall.

McKinney, K. (1994). Sexual harassment and college faculty members. *Deviant Behavior, 15,* 171–191.

Meadows, R. (2004). *Understanding violence and victimization* (3rd ed.). Upper Saddle River, NJ: Pearson/Prentice Hall.

Meadows, R., & Kuehnel, J. (2005). *Evil minds: Understanding and responding to violent predators*. Upper Saddle River, NJ: Pearson/Prentice Hall.

Medea, A., & Thompson, K. (1974). *Against rape*. New York, NY: Farrar, Straus & Giroux.

Meloy, M. L., & Miller, S. L. (2011). *The victimization of women: Law, policies, and politics*. New York, NY: Oxford University Press.

Miller, J., & Schwartz, M. (1995). Rape myths and violence against street prostitutes. *Deviant Behavior, 16,* 1–23.

Palmer, C. (1989). Is rape a cultural universal? A re-examination of the ethnographic data. *Ethnology, 28,* 1–16.

Pelka, F. (1995). Raped: A male survivor breaks his silence. In P. Searles & R. Berger (Eds.), *Rape and society* (pp. 250–256). Boulder, CO: Westview.

Pineau, L. (1996). Date rape: A feminist analysis. In L. Francis (Ed.), *Date rape* (pp. 1–26). University Park: Pennsylvania State University Press.

Pleck, E. (1979). Wife beating in nineteenth-century America. *Victimology, 4,* 60–74.

PLoS Medicine Editors. (2009). Rape in war is common, devastating, and too often ignored. *PLoS Medicine, 6,* 1–3.

Pound, R. (1910). Law in books and law in action. *American Law Review, 44,* 12–36.

Quinn, B. (2003). Sexual harassment—adult workplace. In M. Silberman (Ed.), *Violence and society: A reader* (pp. 271–277). Upper Saddle River, NJ: Prentice Hall.

Reiss, I. L. (1986). *Journey into sexuality*. Englewood Cliffs, NJ: Prentice Hall.

Reyns, B. W., Henson, B., & Fisher, B. S. (2012). Stalking in the twilight zone: Extent of cyberstalking victimization and offending among college students. *Deviant Behavior, 33,* 1–25.

Roiphe, K. (1995). A critique of "rape-crisis" feminists. In B. Leone & K. Koster (Eds.), *Rape on campus* (pp. 74–83). San Diego, CA: Greenhaven Press.

Rumney, P. (2008). Policing male rape and sexual assault. *Journal of Criminal Law, 72,* 67–86.

Sanday, P. R. (1981). The socio-cultural context of rape. A cross-cultural study. *Journal of Social Issues, 37,* 5–27.

Sanday, P. R. (1990). *Fraternity gang rape: Sex, brotherhood, and privilege on campus.* New York: New York University Press.

Sanday, P. R. (1996a). Rape-prone versus rape-free campus cultures. *Violence Against Women, 2,* 191–208.

Sanday, P. R. (1996b). *A woman scorned: Acquaintance rape on trial.* New York, NY: Doubleday.

Sanday, P. R. (2007). *Fraternity gang rape: Sex, brotherhood, and privilege on campus* (2nd ed.). New York: New York University Press.

Schultz, J. (1978). Appendix 1: The Ingham case. In P. Wilson (Ed.), *The other side of rape* (pp. 112–125). Brisbane, Queensland, Australia: University of Queensland Press.

Schwartz, P. (1995). A negative view of the Antioch Plan. In B. Leone & K. Koster (Eds.), *Rape on campus* (pp. 33–38). San Diego, CA: Greenhaven Press.

Schwendinger, H., & Schwendinger, J. (1983). *Rape and inequality.* Beverly Hills, CA: Sage.

Scott, J., Crompton, R., & Lyonette, C. (Eds.). (2010). *Gender inequalities in the 21st century: New barriers and continuing constraints.* Cheltenham, UK: Edward Elgar Publishing.

Scully, D. (1990). *Understanding sexual violence: A study of convicted rapists.* Boston, MA: Unwin Hyman.

Scully, D., & Marolla, J. (1984). Convicted rapists' vocabulary of motive: Excuses and justifications. *Social Problems, 31,* 530–544.

Smith, M. D., & Bennett, N. (1985). Poverty, inequality, and theories of forcible rape. *Crime & Delinquency, 31,* 295–305.

Spohn, C., & Horney, J. (1992). *Rape law reform: A grassroots revolution and its impact.* New York, NY: Plenum.

Stemple, L. (2009). Male rape and human rights. *Hastings Law Journal, 60,* 605–647.

Svalastoga, K. (1962). Rape and social structure. *Pacific Sociological Review, 5,* 48–53.

Tellis, K. (2010). *Rape as a part of domestic violence: A qualitative analysis of case narratives and official reports.* El Paso, TX: LFB Scholarly Publishing.

Terry, K., Giotakos, O., Tsiliakou, M., & Ackerman, A. (2010). Sex offenders: Rape and child sexual abuse. In C. Ferguson (Ed.), *Violent crime: Clinical and social implications* (pp. 229–256). Thousand Oaks, CA: Sage.

Thio, A. (2010). *Deviant behavior* (10th ed.). Boston, MA: Allyn & Bacon.

Tieger, T. (1981). Self-rated likelihood of raping and the social perception of rape. *Journal of Research in Personality, 15,* 147–158.

Wakelin, K., & Long, K. M. (2003). Effects of victim gender and sexuality on attributions of blame to rape victims. *Sex Roles, 49,* 477–487.

Ward, S., Dziuba-Leatherman, J., Stapleton, J. G., & Yodanis, C. (1994). *Acquaintance and date rape: An annotated bibliography.* Westport, CT: Greenwood.

Weis, K., & Borges, S. (1973). Victimology and rape: The case of the legitimate victim. *Issues in Criminology, 8,* 71–115.

Williams, L. (1984). The classic rape: When do victims report? *Social Problems, 31,* 459–467.

Winslow, R., & Zhang, S. (2008). *Criminology: A global perspective.* Upper Saddle River, NJ: Pearson/Prentice Hall.

Wolff, A. (2012, July 30). Is this the end for Penn State? *Sports Illustrated, 117,* 38–41.

Wolfgang, M. (1958). *Patterns in criminal homicide.* Philadelphia: University of Pennsylvania Press.

Yancey, P., & Hummer, R. (1989). Fraternities and rape on campus. *Gender and Society, 3,* 457–473.

Young, C. (1992, May 31). Women, sex and rape: Have some feminists exaggerated the problem? *Washington Post,* p. Cl.

7

Suicide

Social Frames and Definitions of the Situation

Understanding Suicide

Suicide refers to an intentional killing of oneself, by oneself, for the sole purpose of ending one's life and existence. The term is based on the Latin pronoun *sui,* meaning "self," and the Latin verb *cide,* "to kill" (Farberow, 1975, p. 1). According to the *Oxford English Dictionary,* the term was first used in English in 1651, but it actually appeared a bit earlier in a work by Sir Thomas Browne, published in 1642 (Alvarez, 1972, pp. 50–51). Before the mid-1600s, self-killings were treated as murders rather than placed in a category all their own. In some places, at some times, a suicide is viewed as a tragedy, a diminishing of the entire social fabric. It is a time of sadness, and survivors feel responsible for the death. In other places, at other times, a suicide is viewed as a trivial matter because death itself is unimportant. What matters is how one lives—how completely and how productively—not how one dies (Fedden, 1938/1980, p. 13).

Why did the term *suicide* appear when it did? Throughout the Middle Ages (approximately AD 476 to 1450), practically everyone believed, completely and without question, in the influence and power of supernatural forces and spiritual beings. Heaven and hell were real places, and their existence exerted a shadow over practically everything that everybody did. With this worldview, it was impossible for anyone—certainly for anyone with even a hint of religious belief—to believe that a self-inflicted killing would end all existence and send one into a state of nothingness. A self-inflicted death, it was believed, would simply move one to a different realm of existence—perhaps better, perhaps worse, but an existence nonetheless. The secularization of human experience that occurred in the years following the Middle Ages promoted a worldview that had less room for spiritual matters. Perhaps heaven and hell did not exist; maybe humans were physical beings without souls; and, just possibly, death might mean a permanent state of nothingness, totally devoid of any sensation or cognition. For the first time, suicide—choosing to end it all—became a real possibility (Shneidman, 1985, pp. 9–10).

Discourses about suicide have been overly influenced by reductionist models coming from medicine or psychology, making it more difficult to recognize just how much suicide is a collective experience (Gaines, 1990). It is characterized by a diversity of motives, methods, forms, rationalizations, and circumstances; the principal factor that suicidal deaths have in common is that they have all been called suicides by somebody. The classification of a death as a suicide is a social process—as is the process of dying itself—and it must be understood in its own right. Suicide is not an automatic classification that naturally flows from a death scene.

People can die in many ways (e.g., naturally, accidentally, or through murders or suicides), and the determination that a death is a suicide hinges on judgments or speculations about the inner experiences of the deceased. The problem is that the deceased is unable to tell us anything directly about his or her reasons for dying. Even when a suicide note is present—and it usually is not—it is not irrefutable proof that a suicide has occurred. A clever murderer could certainly leave a suicide note if he or she wanted to muddy the waters and make it more difficult for authorities to know what really happened. Suicide notes are usually too sketchy to give the kind of information that would be necessary in order to really know why an individual killed himself or herself.

Framing Deaths

Goffman (1974) explored the value of a "frame analysis" for understanding human behavior. For him, *frames* were definitions of social situations that individuals develop in order to give some meaning and organization to their collective experiences. Framing is a process of constructing images that help people to interpret events and then passing these images on to others. It always involves selection, presentation, and accentuation, and frames always package social experiences for *both* producers and users of them (Papke, 1987, p. xvii). Frames help people who are confronting some hard-to-understand or ambiguous event to make some sense of it (Goffman, 1974, p. 30).

Framing a death as a suicide is not a straightforward process. Reluctance may be found among the living to frame a death as a suicide if another option exists. Alvarez (1972, p. 87) offers an instructive example of how this can work. A West of Ireland coroner decided that a man who had apparently shot himself in the head with his gun had actually died accidentally. How could this seemingly clear example of a suicide be framed as an accident? The coroner concluded that the gun had discharged inadvertently as the man cleaned the barrel with his tongue.

Sometimes, disagreement exists over how a death should be framed, and the final decision shows a convoluted and contentious history. On November 14, 1997, Moshe Pergament, due to his sideswiping of several cars on the Long Island Expressway, was pulled over by a police officer (Anthony Sica). Pergament exited his automobile and advanced toward the officer's patrol car with a gun drawn. The officer ordered the man to drop the gun, but he refused. The officer drew his own revolver and killed Pergament. Although this is a clear case of self-defense by an officer in the line of duty, it is also something more. Subsequent investigation found that the gun that Pergament carried was actually made of plastic (which, of course, was unknown to the officer at the time). On the front seat of Pergament's automobile was a note that was addressed "To the officer who shot me." In it, Pergament exonerated the officer in the death, apologized to the officer, and assumed full responsibility for what happened.

The medical examiner classified this death as "homicide caused by gunshots," and the police report classified it as "justifiable homicide." Lindsay and Lester (2004) claim that it was really "suicide-by-cop" (p. 3). Other writers (e.g., Hutson et al., 1998) think that deaths like these are best classified as "law enforcement–forced assisted suicides" because an officer is left little choice in the matter. Little uniformity exists in how deaths like these are classified, with some medical examiners and coroners calling them homicides and others calling them suicides. It is unknown (and unknowable) how many times individuals who want to die provoke police officers to shoot them but fail to leave a suicide note.

Individuals who kill themselves may do it for many reasons—both personal and social—and the presence of a self-inflicted death is not a perfect indicator of suicidal intent. Some people who do not wish to die still do very dangerous and risky things, and not all suicidal deaths can reasonably be viewed as intended (Canetto & Lester, 1995, p. 4). The spark that leads to a suicide is usually transient, and a large number of people who commit suicide are actually ambivalent about it (Hendin, 1995b, p. 237). They do something in an agitated and perturbed state that commits them to a plan of action that is irreversible and deadly. We need a term to describe those acts that are self-inflicted, self-destructive, and suicide-like, but that do not result in the deaths of individuals who commit them. Instead of using the more common term of *attempted suicide,* a more fitting one is *parasuicide* (Shneidman, 1985, p. 19). Parasuicide covers things such as the use of excessive dosages of drugs or dangerous mutilations of self. The term can also extend to cover episodes in which an individual "attempts" suicide—or seems to—but it is done in a way that makes death an unlikely occurrence.

According to Brown (1996), a 28-year-old male was once brought to an emergency room (ER) at a hospital in Ashland, Virginia. He was badly bruised on the upper part of his body. What caused his injuries? Hours earlier, he had tried to kill himself (or that's how paramedics framed it) by drinking a bottle of vodka and swallowing several nitroglycerin tablets. He then forcibly rammed himself into a wall many times in order to make the nitroglycerin *explode* and end his life in a flash (p. 8). The parasuicide of a young man who walked into an emergency room in Akron, Ohio, seems different from the one just described. Days before his arrival at the ER, he had decided to take his own life. He downed a bottle of Valium tablets and drank a bottle of vodka, intending never to regain consciousness. He did awake, however, 36 hours later and with a huge hangover. He subsequently made another attempt to kill himself. He filled his bathtub with water and got in. He used a razor blade to slit both wrists, expecting to die in a bathtub full of water. However, he had cut only veins, not arteries, so the blood clotted quickly and the flow stopped. He was left sitting in a lukewarm bath of pinkish water and still alive. He then made another attempt. He got his belt and used it to hang himself from his dining room light fixture. The light fixture was not up to the task, however, and it tore from the ceiling, sending the man crashing to the floor with such force that the floor broke. He fell through and ended up in the basement. The fall did not kill him either. He searched around to find something that might finish the job where the drugs, the razor, the belt, and the fall had not. He found a bullet (.22 caliber) but no gun. He also found a pair of pliers and a ball-peen hammer. Holding the single bullet as best he could against his sternum with the pliers, he hit the compression end of the bullet several times with the hammer. On the third try, the bullet fired, knocking him to the ground. However, pliers apparently are not as good as pistols when it comes to suicide, because the bullet pierced the left side of his chest where it harmlessly bounced off a rib to lodge in subcutaneous tissue. He drove himself to the hospital (pp. 82–83).

The two incidents show us something of value about the social process of framing deaths as suicides. Both men tried to kill themselves and failed (making each one an example of a parasuicide). Sometimes, people live through an attempt because their methods are really not deadly enough to kill them (e.g., running into a wall, hoping to explode); sometimes they live because the methods they have chosen are lethal enough to kill them, but they just do not die (e.g., the shooter from Ohio). The concept of *inchoate suicide* can be used to cover those parasuicidal incidents where methods, motives, and intents are lethal enough to do the job, but death still does not result. We will find that inchoate suicides have more in common with completed suicides than they do with other kinds of parasuicide. Muddying the waters even more is the fact that a parasuicide can evolve into a completed suicide, as when an overdose of drugs, taken only to get high, leads to the accidental death of the user. It may be impossible for an outside observer to know enough details of an individual's death to be able to place it in the "right" category. Inherent difficulties exist in any naming process, and the determination of cause of death is no exception (Douglas, 1967).

It is true that most people who eventually commit suicide have spoken to others about it, just as it is true that suicidal individuals usually give some warnings about their plan to die (e.g., verbal statements; putting finances in order; withdrawing from social relationships) (Granello & Granello, 2007, pp. 9–10). However, a distinction must be drawn between those who successfully commit suicide (completed suicide) and those who only commit parasuicides, because they are separate events in many important ways. Completed suicides are done by suicidal individuals, and parasuicides are done by parasuicidal individuals. Maris (1981) reports that about 75 percent of the people who successfully kill themselves only made one attempt, and it was the one that killed them. Furthermore, only a small percentage of those people who commit parasuicides will successfully kill themselves (p. 267). All deaths should be identified as *intentional*, *subintentional* (where the deceased played an unconscious or latent role in producing his or her death), or *unintentional* (Shneidman, 1985, pp. 52–53).

Nonhuman Animals and Suicide

Difficulties in framing deaths in one way or another are compounded when we look at nonhuman animals. Huge obstacles exist in deciding if suicides are found among other members of the animal kingdom. We do not have enough examples of self-destructive acts in natural settings to speak about them with any confidence, and those examples we do have are of an indeterminate status. It is impossible to know that an animal intentionally killed itself, being fully aware of the consequences. Lemmings march into the waters off the Norwegian coast in what seems to be a clear example of a group suicide, and thousands drown. However, the deaths may be due to an error in judgment rather than to a death wish. If lemmings come to a modest body of water, they seem to be able to cross it with little trouble. However, if the body of water is too large to cross, then they drown. What looks like group suicide probably is not.

Knowing the inner state of an organism that commits a self-destructive act is difficult, regardless of which species it is. Consider the case of the male Australian redback spider (Andrade, 1996). After copulating with a female spider, he wiggles his abdomen in front of her and then positions it directly over her mouthparts. She then eats him alive. Why would he go out of his way to be devoured by his sexual partner? It seems that this "male copulatory suicide" is actually adaptive from the standpoint of reproductive success. While she is busy consuming him, his sperm are busy impregnating her. His act of self-sacrifice maximizes the chances that his genes and his alone will be passed on to future generations (pp. 70–71).

Clearly, life-threatening behaviors do occur among nonhuman animals, some of them leading directly to death (de Catanzaro, 1981). However, most of these deaths either are incidental to other necessary activities, such as eating, reproduction, or protection, or actually contribute to the overall fitness of the group. A percentage dies (usually the weakest, oldest, or sickest) so that the rest may live better lives and develop healthier offspring. When a death of a nonhuman animal is a direct response to stress or isolation, it almost always is a response to living in a captive environment around humans, and the death is a poor basis for deciding if nonhuman animals commit suicide (or even can) (p. 44).

At this point in time, the data are still too sparse to be able to decide beyond a shadow of a doubt that nonhuman animals commit suicide. What is clear is that most, if not all, of the factors responsible for changing suicide rates—increases in depression, increases in the use of chemical substances by the young, lowering of the age of puberty, an abundance of social stressors, greater tolerance for suicidal behaviors, increases in suicidal role models (Diekstra & Garnefski, 1995)—are really found only among humans. Durkheim's (1897/1951) view may still be the correct one. He believed that only humans have the intelligence to formulate an anticipatory understanding of their own death, and only humans encounter the kinds of social conditions that cause suicide (pp. 44–45).

The Meanings of Suicide

A definition of suicide—one that has stood the test of time—was offered over 100 years ago by Émile Durkheim (1897/1951) in his book *Suicide:* "Suicide is applied to all cases of death resulting directly or indirectly from a positive or negative act of the victim himself, which he knows will produce this result" (p. 44). Durkheim was confident that his definition of suicide would allow all objective observers to recognize the suicides they saw and to differentiate them from other forms of death. He rejected motive and intent as a way to explain and classify suicides, because he believed these two inner states were not objective enough to be measured. The defining feature of suicide for Durkheim was the renunciation of existence and the purposeful sacrifice of life.

Durkheim's aim to construct a purely objective definition of suicide was laudable but unrealistic (Pope, 1976, pp. 10–11). It is impossible to clearly and uniformly separate every suicidal death from all other kinds of death. Suicidal phenomena do not exist independently from human thoughts about suicide, and a great deal of subjectivity enters into the classification of a death as a suicide (S. Taylor, 1990). The difference in suicide rates of Catholics and Protestants in the Netherlands during the years 1905 to 1910 was directly related to a classification bias. A large proportion of the deaths of Catholics that had been recorded as "death from ill-defined or unspecified cause" or "sudden death" would have been recorded as suicides if the deceased had been Protestants (Poppel & Day, 1996, pp. 505–506).

As noted previously, Durkheim rejected the variables of motivation (the reasons people kill themselves) and intent (a knowledge or awareness of possible outcomes or consequences), but motive and intent worked their way into his analysis of suicide. He apparently never considered that the instances of suicide that he was objectively studying were determined by coroners, medical examiners, police, judges, and other authorities, who undoubtedly based their decisions on all those subjective variables that Durkheim wanted to discard (Pope, 1976, p. 11). The *intrinsic ambiguity* of suicide recognized by Douglas (1967, p. 251) exists because human actions and reactions are contextual, and the meaning of any social event requires observers to infer a great many details about what happened.

Suicide holds distinctive meanings for an individual contemplating it (Douglas, 1967, pp. 284–319). It offers the prospect of starting over again as a new being, in a different realm of existence. It offers the hope that changes will occur in how one is viewed by others. It offers the possibility of changes in human relationships. (If the suicide is successful, it produces an immediate *re*interpretation of the deceased's life and relationships by surviving family members, friends, and acquaintances.) Suicide also offers an opportunity to avenge some actual or imagined injustice. ("This will serve them right for treating me so badly.") These social meanings exert a powerful influence over the course and the interpretation of self-destructive acts.

Suicide attempts (i.e., parasuicides) can be rational, a way for an individual in desperate straits to do something that will significantly improve his or her life (Duhigg, 2007). On the island of Tikopia, in the western Pacific, individuals take *suicide swims* out into the ocean. These swims are one legitimate way for them to handle life's problems. The swimmers have time alone in a watery world to think, and these swims actually enhance their standing in the community. Community ties are reaffirmed because the swimmers allow themselves to be rescued and returned to shore (Littlewood & Lipsedge, 1987, p. 292).

People can change their views of suicide in light of events such as the suicides of others or perhaps even their own suicide attempts. Consider Alvarez's (1972) own effort to kill himself. He took 45 barbiturates and waited for death, but his wife discovered him and called an ambulance. He was in a deep coma, and he had a rapid pulse, vomit in his mouth, and blue skin (cyanosed). Medical technicians pumped his stomach and got him breathing again. He was unconscious for 3 days but finally recovered. He had the following to say about his experience:

> I thought death would be like that: a synoptic vision of life, crisis by crisis, all suddenly explained, justified, redeemed, a Last Judgment in the coils and circuits of the brain. Instead, all I got was a hole in the head, a round zero, nothing. I'd been swindled. (p. 282)

As a result of his experience with suicide, he concluded that when his death finally came, it would be nastier than suicide and a lot less convenient (p. 284).

The Curious Case of Autoerotic Asphyxiation

The ambiguity that exists in framing a death as a suicide can be seen with a curious—and arguably risky—form of human activity called *autoerotic asphyxiation,* which can lead to autoerotic fatalities. *Autoerotic fatalities* are deaths that occur from oxygen deprivation during solitary sexual activity. (The technical name for restriction of airflow for the purpose of sexual arousal is *hypoxyphilia.*) Typically, the deceased is found alone, wearing physical restraints such as handcuffs, gags, or blindfolds, behind a locked door, with a rope or other ligature around his or her neck. Oxygen deprivation can also have been achieved through the use of plastic bags, chemicals, chest compression, or a tub of water in which the face was immersed (R. Holmes & Holmes, 2009, pp. 190–195). Evidence of masturbatory activities usually can be found, and one goal in autoerotic asphyxiation is to heighten the pleasure of orgasm (Evans & Farberow, 1988). Erotic asphyxiates tend to have rich fantasy lives (Turvey, 2009). An escape mechanism is usually found in the individual's hand or within reaching distance (e.g., a knife to cut the rope once the "game" is over). The decedent is usually completely or partially naked, and erotic materials may be present at the death scene, although many documented cases of autoerotic fatalities are not characterized by nudity (p. 458). Hypoxyphilia is most often practiced by young, white, middle- or upper-middle-class males (Lowery & Wetli, 1982). Data collected from England, the United States, Canada, and Australia show that 1 to 2 erotic asphyxiations per million population are detected and reported each year (American Psychiatric Association, 2000, p. 573).

The reason that some people engage in erotic asphyxiation is that it is supposed to be sexually stimulating. The carotid arteries (on either side of the neck) carry oxygen-rich blood from the heart to the brain. When these are compressed, as in strangulation or hanging, the sudden loss of oxygen to the brain and the accumulation of carbon dioxide can increase feelings of giddiness, lightheadedness, and pleasure, all of which will heighten masturbatory sensations. Autoerotic asphyxia was described in writing as far back as the 1600s, where it was proclaimed to be a cure for male impotence. The basis of this belief may well have been the observation that men who were executed by hanging attained an erection. Men in Victorian England could visit "Hanged Men's Clubs," where prostitutes would administer enough asphyxiation for these men to be sexually satisfied but not so much that they would be in any danger (Uva, 1995, p. 575).

Turvey (2009) insists that autoerotic fatalities are accidental deaths, not suicides, because autoerotic asphyxiates restrict airflow to the brain to heighten their sexual pleasures, not to intentionally die (p. 461). It is hard to believe, however, that erotic asphyxiates are unaware of the riskiness of their chosen sexual practice. The carotid arteries are sensitive, and even a minor miscalculation can lead to unconsciousness and death (R. Holmes & Holmes, 2009). Even if death does not occur, brain damage still can take place if the oxygen supply stops for too long (p. 187). Though the precise details of what can happen may be unknown to practitioners of erotic asphyxia, they must at least know something about the risks involved. Autoerotic asphyxia is called "terminal sex" in the adult bondage subculture (Uva, 1995, p. 578), but it could just as easily be called sexual termination. The distinction between "intends to die" and "knows death could easily occur" is a fine line.

A suicide note, if present, is usually taken by authorities as proof that the death is a suicide. However, a suicide note itself may be part of an autoerotic game—a prop to aid the decedent's fantasy that it is possible to "die" and then be "reborn" (Hazelwood, Dietz, & Burgess, 1982, pp. 766–767). Another possibility is that a murder will be disguised as an autoerotic fatality. In fact, Wright and Davis (1976) reported just such an occurrence. A 31-year-old single male was found hanging by his neck from a necktie tied to a shower curtain rod in his apartment. His feet touched the floor. He was blindfolded with another necktie, a belt was around his neck, and his hands had been tied behind his back. He was fully clothed except that he wore no shoes. Some of his personal possessions were missing, and two females had been seen leaving his apartment. The death scene and subsequent autopsy provided enough evidence to indicate that the death was an autoerotic asphyxiation. It was ultimately decided, however, that the two females had actually robbed and murdered the man. An important clue was the fact that the victim's hands were tied behind his back, a seeming impossibility if the autoerotic activities had been completely solitary. However, even here we must be cautious. Because some people practice hypoxyphilia with others around, the man's hands could have been tied by a sexual partner.

In 2009, the actor David Carradine (best known for his role as the wandering spiritual advisor and martial arts expert in the *Kung Fu* television series, as well as for his role in the *Kill Bill* films), age 72, was found dead in his hotel room in Thailand. He was hanging by a rope in the closet, and a shoelace was wrapped around his neck and another around his genitals. His hands were also tightly bound and reported initially to be behind his back. (It was, however, subsequently reported that the hands were actually tied over his head.) The death appeared to be a clear case of suicide, but this is not what was eventually decided.

The official classification was accidental death during solitary sexual activity. This would be unlikely if his hands were tied behind his back— making it either a murder or a suicide—but possible if his hands were over his head in a position that would allow them to be freed when he tired of the sexual game. (Because he was believed to have been alone at the time of his death, murder was ruled out.) Carradine's two ex-wives both reported to authorities that the actor did have unusual sexual interests, including self-bondage. On *Larry King Live*, however, the family lawyer disputed the official interpretation, suggesting that the death could have been a murder, because Carradine was in Thailand to unmask groups that were operating in the martial arts underworld. The assessment of one of the investigating officers may be closest to the mark: death by masturbation.

Sociocultural Variations in Suicide: Motive, Intent, and Interpretation

Historical Meanings

Purposeful self-killings are not unusual, and they have been found at various times in history and in most places (R. Holmes & Holmes, 2005). Some of these self-inflicted lethal acts reflect an individual's isolation from social groups, and they are a response to loneliness and the absence of meaningful relationships. These are called *egoistic suicide,* and they occur when social integration becomes too low and the feelings of separation and despair become too high for an individual to manage (Durkheim, 1897/1951). If an individual who is isolated and separate from others (i.e., experiences too-low levels of social integration) is exposed to deeply frustrating experiences, suicide becomes more likely because the only available target of the individual's aggression is himself or herself (Henry & Short, 1954; Unnithan, Huff-Corzine, Corzine, & Whitt, 1994, pp. 96–98). Egoistic suicides are characterized by *encore anxiety,* in which individuals believe that they cannot repeat their past accomplishments, and a *fraud complex,* in which individuals believe that even if they were to be successful in life, it would be undeserved (or fraudulent). Urbanization and modernity are positively correlated with higher rates of suicide, because they lead to increases in individualism and autonomy, which means that instances of aggression will more frequently be directed toward the self (Whitt, 2010, pp. 173–174).

Depending on the time and place, attitudes toward suicide can range from strong opposition to spirited support if the suicide is done in the proper way and for all the right reasons. In some communities, the living were threatened with harsh penalties if they took their own lives. The corpse of anyone who committed suicide was abused, and the family name of the decedent was dishonored. In other places, the decedent was highly admired for committing suicide, and it was a death that he or she freely chose because of the benefits that it offered. The many forms of suicide, the many reasons it occurs, the many methods people use to self-destruct, the wide array in social meanings of suicide, and the multifaceted nature of social reactions to suicide all make for a great deal of relativity in regard to self-inflicted lethal acts.

Death in ancient Egypt was considered to be a passage from one type of existence to another. The living and the dead were viewed as not too different from one another, and they were believed to have some of the same needs and interests. Because death was seen as no big deal, it really did not matter to anyone exactly what caused it. However, if an Egyptian who committed suicide were somehow magically transported to another culture just as the last breath left the body, attitudes of indifference would not be found there.

> If [an] ancient Egyptian had killed himself in pre-Christian Scandinavia, for example, he would have been guaranteed a place in Viking paradise. If he had taken his life during the Roman Empire, his death would have been honored as a glorious demonstration of his wisdom. If he had cut open his stomach in feudal Japan, he would have been praised as a man of principle. If he had killed himself in fifteenth-century Metz, however, his corpse would have been crammed into a barrel and floated down the Moselle, sending the tainted body beyond city limits. In seventeenth-century France his corpse would have been dragged through the streets, hanged upside down, then thrown on the public garbage heap. In seventeenth-century England his estate would have been forfeited to the crown and his body buried at a cross-roads with a stake through the heart. (Colt, 1991, p. 131)

Some groups fervently believe that suicide is a good and noble way to die, whereas other groups, with equal enthusiasm, view it as a sign of biological dysfunction, immorality, or psychological abnormality. These meanings are not without consequence for the cause, course, and outcome of self-inflicted deaths and how deaths are categorized and interpreted.

The Vikings of pre-Christian Scandinavia viewed suicide as a good way to die because it was a ticket into Valhalla, the eternal home of all heroes who had died violently. The surest way to get into Viking heaven was to die heroically in battle, but a self-inflicted violent death came in a close second. The Vikings believed that people who entered Valhalla would fight mock battles and then feast for all time, drinking from the skulls of their dead enemies. The founder of the feast was none other than Odin, the Scandinavian god of war, who was supposed to have committed suicide himself. Self-respecting Vikings who saw no prospect of dying in battle often killed themselves with their swords or jumped to their deaths. This sanctification of a violent death helped to encourage and justify a violent life. Being encouraged to die by the sword usually means that you will live by the sword, an important requirement in a warrior society like that of the Vikings, which required a proper fighting spirit for its survival (Colt, 1991, pp. 134–135).

The best term to describe the attitudes of inhabitants of the Greco-Roman world toward suicide would be ambivalence or even confusion. Greek culture condemned suicide, but Greeks were not particularly intolerant of it. Homer himself regarded suicide, if it were done voluntarily and for good reasons, as both natural and heroic (Droge & Tabor, 1992, pp. 17–18). Whatever disapproval of suicide existed in the ancient world was almost entirely dependent on the motives for it. Self-killings done out of honor, devotion, or duty; to avoid dishonor; or as a response to unbearable grief were likely to be viewed as good and noble deaths. Only when self-killings evidenced signs of weakness, cowardice, or irresponsibility were they viewed as disgraceful. To the Romans, the reasons that one died were of fundamental importance in how the death was judged (Plass, 1995, p. 83). Suicides to avoid dishonor or as a response to the unbearable pain of the death of a loved one or of a love affair gone sour were not considered at all unreasonable (Farberow, 1988, pp. xi–xiii).

Christians were ultimately responsible for changing the ambivalence of the Greco-Roman world into condemnation, but initially they were not particularly intolerant of suicide. The Apostles did not moralize against it, and neither the Old nor the New Testaments directly forbade it. In fact, in the early days of Christianity, suicide was viewed as a way to achieve martyrdom and to enter the kingdom of heaven. Everybody who wanted to get to heaven (and who didn't?) could get there in a direct and expeditious way by committing suicide. The icing on the cake was that Church members took care of the surviving family members of someone who committed suicide, which significantly eased the conscience of anyone who was planning to self-destruct (Farberow, 1988).

Suicide became a too-attractive option for Christians, so around the sixth century, the Church began working to harden attitudes toward it and to redefine it as an offense against God. The moral justification for the Christian condemnation of suicide was found in the sixth commandment, "Thou shalt not kill." Life was declared to be a gift from God, and it was asserted that only God could determine when life was to end. People who took their own lives were assured by Church doctrine that they would be harshly dealt with in the hereafter. The threat of eternal damnation gave the ban on suicide a supreme moral authority and increased its ability to deter the act (Barry, 1994, pp. 91–163). Though most Christians still wanted to get into heaven and viewed life on earth as transitory and unimportant, the surest route to paradise had been taken away. However, even here, the prohibitions against suicide were not absolute. When done for the right reasons—as a response to a loss of faith, personally disgraceful behavior, being captured by an enemy, or unbearable torture—suicide was still viewed as an honorable death (Farberow, 1977).

The Victorians tended to sensationalize murder and to dread and fear suicide (Gates, 1988). The suicide was treated as the lowest of the low, so surviving family members did all they could to hide one. The Crown could take all the property of a suicide, and the only way to avert this catastrophe was to convince authorities that the deceased was actually insane, and thus unaware of the consequences of his or her action. Clerics were enlisted to aid in the deception, because people who had intentionally killed themselves were not allowed to be buried on church property (a ban that ended in the 1880s). It was customary for the corpse of a suicide to be buried at a crossroads with a stake through the heart and a heavy stone over the face so that it could not return to harm the living. The last official record of a degradation of the corpse of a suicide in England was made in 1823, but the degradation did not stop then. Bodies of suicides who had been poor during their lives or that were unclaimed were sent to medical schools for dissection and study for 50 years after that (Alvarez, 1972, pp. 46–47).

During the twentieth century, attitudes toward suicide continued to fluctuate. Some tolerance could be found among the educated, but the Christian Church remained steadfast in its opposition. Industrialization made it possible for some people to attain great prosperity, while others became dismal failures. Poverty was equated with badness, and prosperity was equated with goodness. The normlessness produced by a drastic and dramatic change in one's economic standing—especially from prosperity to poverty—was conducive to suicide (Durkheim, 1897/1951; Lehmann, 1995, p. 917). This type, called *anomic suicide* by Durkheim, was caused by too-low levels of social regulation.

The rapid change in one's social situation and living conditions produced an absence of direction and focus that spilled over into a suicidal act by a desperate individual. The growth of a middle class meant that more and more families had a stake in conformity and in maintaining their status and prominence in their community. When they could do this no longer, suicide seemed to be the only option. The stigma of suicide was only partly lessened by the predilection of authorities to define suicide as an irrational act of an individual who was suffering from severe psychological problems. The medical and the sociological emerged as the two principal paradigms for making sense of suicide.

Suicide in Different Places

People in non-Western, nonindustrial societies tend to have a generalized horror of the wandering spirits of dead people anyway, but the fear is all that much greater if the deceased died violently (Colt, 1991, p. 132). Whereas the spirit of a murdered individual is believed to have it in for only his or her killer, the spirit of a suicide is more likely—or so it is believed—to blame the entire group and to be bent on revenge of the worst kind toward the living (Fedden, 1938/1980, p. 35). A person who commits suicide is generally seen as having shown an alarming indifference to others. He or she probably has put surviving family members, friends, and acquaintances in the position of shouldering the additional and difficult responsibilities that the decedent was unwilling or unable to manage when alive. It is not hard to understand how some of the anger, regret, and sorrow that the living experience in response to the suicide of one of their own could get translated into a generalized fear of the deceased.

Some groups go to great efforts to keep the wandering spirit of a suicide from causing any mischief among the living. It was customary among a central African tribe called the Baganda to take the corpse of a suicide to a crossroads and burn it. When females passed the spot of cremation, they would hurl grass or sticks on it as a way to keep the spirit from entering their living bodies to be reborn. The Bannaus of Cambodia took the corpses of suicides far away to a corner of the forest to be buried, and the corpses of suicides in Dahomey were abandoned in the fields so that they would be eaten by wild animals. The Alabama Indians unceremoniously pitched the corpses of suicides into a river, and the Wajagga of East Africa would hang a goat in the same noose that the human had used to commit suicide, hoping that it would placate the deceased's wandering spirit. In cultures all across the world, a suicide's spirit is blamed for a host of catastrophes, such as diseases, plagues, storms, famines, droughts, and bad harvests (Colt, 1991, p. 132).

According to Balikci (1970/1989), one non-Western group with a high rate of suicide is the Netsilik Eskimo (Inuit). Like the Vikings, the Netsilik believed that the souls of individuals who died violently (and suicide qualifies) went to a paradise, one of the three afterworlds they recognized. However, this is not the entire story because, if it were, practically everybody would have committed suicide to get to paradise. A more important factor in causing the high suicide rate was the deterioration of interpersonal relationships and the disappearance of traditional sources of mutual help and support, beginning in the 1920s. Families had left the region or been torn apart by the departure of family members, and kinship bonds had become tenuous. The availability of rifles in the 1920s made it easier for a lone hunter to kill a caribou or seal without the help of others, but the new technology produced further isolation from traditional sources of support and security. Men were also very jealous over their wives, and considerable tension and insecurity characterized the marital relationship.

When a Netsilik suffered a personal misfortune—sickness, injury, loss of a loved or valuable friend, depression, despair, marital discord, divorce—too few people were available to offer relief. Suicide was culturally defined as a quick road to a better existence, and people in the community rarely had the interest or inclination to stop a suicide or to help a suicidal individual find reasons to live. In the usual case, a desperate individual faced an uncertain future without the effective support of friends and family (Bergman & Dunn, 1990). Most suicidal individuals hanged themselves using animal skins; about one-third used guns, usually fired into the head; and a small number drowned or suffocated themselves. The primary reason for a suicide was an injury to, or a loss of, a loved one, followed by personal problems, such as injury, illness, or marital discord. Males killed themselves more often than did females (Balikci, 1970/1989, pp. 163–166).

A breakdown in cohesion, intimacy, and traditional sources of group support seems to be conducive to an increase in suicide, and these disrupting forces can occur anywhere. The rate of suicide can also increase significantly as a response to stresses and strains caused by outside intervention (e.g., the slave trade in Africa or the confinement of Native Americans on U.S. reservations) or by migration to a new territory. Different ethnic and racial groups adjust to new cultures and to new groups of people in different ways. The accommodation to patterns of prejudice and discrimination in a host culture can cause an increase in suicide among members of an oppressed or exploited minority group (Group for the Advancement of Psychiatry, 1989, p. 101). It is also true, however, that claims about high rates of suicide in some out-group may reflect ethnocentrism and faulty reasoning among members of the defining group (Webb & Willard, 1975, p. 17).

An exploration of the attitudes in the African American community toward self-destruction shows how subcultural meanings and suicide are related (Early, 1992; Early & Akers, 1993). Other-directed violence, alcohol abuse, and drug use are understandable responses, albeit unfortunate, to the racism of U.S. society. However, these same experiences have promoted the development of a culture of resilience to factors that would otherwise result in an increase in suicide. "Suicide is the ultimate, unforgivable, and unredeemable offense. Abuse of alcohol and drugs, participation in the drug trade, and even violence, although strongly condemned, are not viewed as inexplicable, unforgivable, or unredeemable" (Early & Akers, 1993, p. 291). These social meanings of suicide make it not only unacceptable but practically unthinkable for most members of the African American community (p. 292).

Obligatory Suicide

One of Durkheim's (1897/1951) more provocative observations is that suicide can occur when social integration is high and the group becomes more important than any individual in it (p. 217). An example of this type— Durkheim called it *altruistic suicide*—is the death of a soldier who jumps voluntarily on a live grenade to protect other members of the platoon. In some places, altruistic suicide ceases to be optional, and certain individuals are put under great pressure to kill themselves or be scorned by other members of the group (pp. 221–222). These obligatory suicides are interesting in their own right, but they also show the importance of definitions and social constructions. One might ask, is not an obligatory suicide actually a murder?

A good example of obligatory suicide is the custom of *suttee* or *sati,* in which a widowed woman threw herself upon the flames of her deceased husband's funeral pyre, forfeiting her own life. It was named in honor of a heroine from Hindu mythology who committed suicide to prove her wifely devotion. The options confronting a widowed woman in some parts of Asia were very few, and none of them were particularly attractive from her standpoint. She could choose not to commit suicide and lead a miserable and unrewarding life for her remaining days, or she could leap onto the flames and receive the honor and respect of all who knew her (Roy, 1987, p. 75). A widowed woman in Hindu society had no identity apart from her husband (Sharma, 1988). Marriage to a second husband was rare, and it usually meant that the woman was rejected by her own family. She might even have been blamed for her husband's death in the first place (Saxena, 1975, pp. 66–76). (Suttee was banned by the British in its territories in 1829, but it has never been completely eliminated.)

The rewards of committing suicide, coupled with the punishments for refusing, were sufficient to propel most widowed women, in those places that followed the custom of suttee, in the direction of self-immolation (Rao, 1983). Even those women who were reluctant to follow their husbands into death were easy enough to manipulate. The average widow was young—in some cases no older than 10—grief stricken, and suggestible. To guarantee that she joined her husband, the bereaved widow might have been given opium, marijuana, or some other drug that would make it even more likely that she would do what she was told without complaint (Datta, 1988, pp. 207–221). By taking her own life upon the death of her husband, it proved both her devotion to him and her respect for tradition. It kept her from having to live the rest of her days as an outcast, scorned for her unmarried status, though it was no fault of her own (Eller, 2006, pp. 125–129). If the deceased was well-to-do, he would be followed in death by *several* wives, slaves, and servants. Others who felt the pinch of bereavement might also have committed suicide to be with the decedent: mother, sisters, sisters-in-law, minister, and even nurses (Thakur, 1963, pp. 142–143).

Death before dishonor was the rule to live by in "the Orient," at least among samurai warriors. The Japanese institutionalized suicide in what was called *hara-kiri* (belly slitting) or the more elegant term of *seppuku.* For centuries, it was a privilege reserved by law for the samurai (though it was outlawed in 1868). A ritualized suicide such as hara-kiri was the only way for a dishonored warrior to reclaim his honor, by forfeiting his life. Sometimes, it was done to display allegiance to a fallen leader or to avoid the dishonor of a public execution (Evans & Farberow, 1988, pp. 175–176). Hara-kiri was usually done according to a precise ritual, in special surroundings, in front of a group of invited guests.

> The samurai knelt on a white hassock on a white-edged *tatami* (reed mat), facing a small white table on which lay a short sword with its blade wrapped in white paper. Taking the blade by its middle in his right hand, the samurai made an incision in the left side of his abdomen, drew the blade to the right, and then made an upward cut. It was meritorious then to make another incision in the chest and a downward cut, allowing the entrails to spill out. (O'Neill, 1981, pp. 12–13)

Because dying could take several hours, a friend was usually close at hand to end the warrior's suffering by beheading him with a sword. The samurai's wife might choose to die with her husband by stabbing herself in the throat with a short dagger known as a *jigai,* a wedding present given to her explicitly for this purpose.

The kamikaze pilots of World War II were the heirs apparent to the samurai warriors. In a last-ditch effort to win the war, Japanese pilots flew their planes into ships of their enemy, killing themselves in the process (O'Neill, 1981, p. 140). The young men who volunteered for the suicide missions were motivated by strong feelings of loyalty and patriotism. Doggedly pursuing victory, regardless of the chances of winning, was a Japanese tradition. The greater the prospects of defeat, the more committed the Japanese became to continuing the fight. The emperor was divine and so was his word. Any war that he authorized automatically became a holy war, and losing it was unacceptable. Japanese soldiers believed that if they died heroically, they would become gods themselves and join the guardian spirits of the country at Yasukuni Shrine on Kudan Hill. The kamikazes were willing to die for the sake of their families and their emperor in the fervent belief that by sacrificing their lives, they would make a difference in the world (Naito, 1989). Put simply, a suicide mission was viewed as "a glorious way to die" (Spurr, 1981).

Revenge Suicide

Why would individuals kill themselves to get revenge on someone else? Here Durkheim (1897/1951) helps us again. He thought that *fatalism*—a condition of overregulation and excessive discipline—produced feelings of unhappiness and hopelessness in the regulated individuals to such an extent that death was the only way out for them (p. 276). For example, the rate of suicide for married women in rural China is higher than it is for single women. Though many things account for this difference (e.g., mental problems, poor relationships with parents and low levels of social support from them, increases in role conflicts and social strains), one important factor is that marriages are excessively regulated by the government, generating a fatalism that is experienced most acutely by wives (Zhang, 2010, p. 324).

What Durkheim did not seem to imagine is that suicide could be carried out to hurt or get even with the source of one's misery or pain. Fedden (1938/1980) offers a bizarre example of a *revenge suicide*. A nineteenth-century Frenchman had been betrayed by his mistress. He was so upset over her unfaithfulness that he killed himself. He had instructed his servant to get his corpse and fashion a candle from its fat, light it, and carry it to his ex-lover. The servant did so, and it was accompanied by a letter in the suicide's own hand that stated that as he had burned for her in life, he now burned for her in death. She read these words by the light given off by his burning flesh (p. 45)! Douglas (1967) claimed that committing suicide as a way to get revenge on someone and to blame him or her (or them) for the death is one of the distinctive meanings of suicide in the Western world (p. 311). However, Douglas was too restrictive; revenge suicide is found all across the planet.

In many non-Western societies, suicide is viewed as a good way for some people to get back at others who have wronged them. Malinowski (1926) described revenge suicides among the Trobriand Islanders of the New Guinea coast. They would shinny up a palm tree, loudly name their tormenters, and then jump to their deaths. The rule was a suicide for a suicide, so the marked individual had to respond in kind (or take some effort to placate the spirit of the decedent or to compensate the decedent's family). The Tshi-speaking people of Africa believe that one person can drive another person to suicide. If a person commits suicide and blames the death on another, the named party is required by native custom to commit suicide, too (Counts, 1990, p. 95).

Revenge suicide is socially patterned (Counts, 1990, p. 95). It occurs in cultures that recognize the possibility that a living individual can be held responsible for the suicidal death. This requires some ethic of shared or collective responsibility, where, for example, a husband can be blamed for his wife's misery and subsequent suicide. The culture must also provide definite mechanisms whereby the individual who kills himself or herself can clearly show who is responsible for the suicide and make the living willing to punish the responsible party. In some cases, the living come to believe that if they fail to avenge the death, they themselves will be haunted by the angry spirit of the deceased.

A revenge suicide is most likely to be successful, and the living are most likely to administer some punishment to the guilty party, if the individual commits the suicide in a public place, forewarns others of the upcoming suicide, and clearly identifies whomever is being held responsible for the death. Revenge suicides are usually done by powerless individuals, often females, who have been used and abused by people in their lives. The only way for these individuals to retaliate against those people who have hurt them is to kill themselves in a public way. Their hope is that they will shame their tormentors enough that these people will also want to kill themselves for all the injury that they have caused.

Suicide Bombers

The fact that some humans are *suicide bombers*—individuals who kill themselves violently so as to kill others and destroy property to strike a blow at an enemy—would probably come as a surprise to Durkheim. The complexity of suicide in today's world is far greater than it was in nineteenth-century France, transcending any straightforward placement in Durkheim's typology based on variations in the level of social integration and regulation. The typical suicide bomber is male, young, single, and middle class. He considers himself to be a freedom fighter or a martyr, not a terrorist, and he has decided that a suicide bombing is the only way for him to fight an enemy that possesses superior military power. The most important element of suicide bombings is to be found in their militaristic function (Kelsay, 2008, p. 228).

Suicide bombing or suicide terrorism is not a singular phenomenon (Abufarha, 2009). One type involves waging a campaign against military targets in which no possibility exists of surviving the battle. Death is a certainty, and the combatant knows it. You embark on a mission knowing *for certain* you will be killed by your enemy. An example would be the well-known banzai charge of Japanese soldiers during World War II. Another type of suicide terrorism involves an individual using suicide to attack military targets, but death is at his or her own hand (e.g., Japanese kamikazes). One other form of suicide terrorism involves death by the suicide's own hand, but the targets are civilians and not military installations (e.g., the September 11, 2001, attack on the U.S. World Trade Center).

Suicide bombers embody the *Sampson complex,* in which individuals want to kill themselves in order to bring everyone else down with them. Suicide bombing reflects "the power of the powerless" to wage war against even the most fearsome adversary (Reuter, 2008, p. 78). If it is possible for 19 terrorists, armed with little more than box cutters and a seething hatred, to produce the death and destruction that they did on September 11, 2001, on U.S. soil, it is easy to see why suicide bombing is attractive to any powerless group involved in an asymmetrical war. Suicide bombers have strong ties to groups, and they are influenced by what relatives, friends, and religious leaders think about both suicide bombers and bombings in general (Atran, 2007; Reuter, 2008, p. 83). Human bombs engage in voluntary acts of self-sacrifice that have (or at least *can* have) dramatic consequences (Abufarha, 2009, p. 235).

It is a suicide bomber's sense of righteousness, coupled with the power that a total absence of fear of death gives to an individual, that allows us to understand why suicide bombing is being used in struggles in Chechnya, Kashmir, Kurdistan, Iran, Iraq, Pakistan, Israel, Afghanistan, Turkey, Sri Lanka, Lebanon, Indonesia, Morocco, Tunisia, Mombasa, and the United States. Parents of suicide bombers tend to share the sentiments of their suicidal children. They are proud of them and the sacrifice they have made, and they view their children as martyrs for a just and noble cause. They would be as proud if all their children did the same thing, and their main regret may be that they have no more offspring to sacrifice to the struggle (Reuter, 2008, p. 82).

Suicide bombers consider themselves to be warriors or soldiers, a belief that both motivates and justifies their suicide missions. It is the willingness to die for a cause greater than oneself that shows in a very clear and public way that no personal interest or stake is involved (S. Holmes, 2005, pp. 146–149). Suicide bombers consider their acts to be both altruistic and moral. Female suicide bombers, though rarer than their male counterparts, interpret their suicides as a way to strike a blow against a despised enemy while at the same time empowering themselves in the face of the humiliation and disgrace that they and their families have had to endure (Bloom, 2007, 2009; Patkin, 2007, p. 173). Female suicide bombers' other motives are to avenge some personal loss, to redeem the family name, or to escape a dreary life.

Not only must individuals be socially supported in their willingness to die for a cause, but an enemy must also exist that is defined as the embodiment of evil (Patkin, 2007). What this does is to make the suicide bomber into someone to model and copy. He or she is a warrior for freedom, someone whose sacrifice is even more heroic and enviable because it is against such great odds and targets such a powerful and diabolical enemy. The *Werther effect* describes the case where one person's suicide triggers other people's suicides; it is suicide by imitation. This term is based on a 1774 novel by

Goethe about a spurned lover named Werther. One fateful evening, Werther sits down, writes a letter to his beloved, and then shoots himself in the head. After publication of the novel, men copied the character in the book by dressing like him (blue waistcoat and yellow vest), opening books in front of them, and shooting themselves. The novel was banned in Denmark, Germany, and Italy.

Durkheim (1897/1951) gave little attention to the influence of imitation on suicide, primarily because he viewed imitation as a psychological process that was incapable of explaining the social fact of suicide (p. 140). However, suicide is at times a fad in which some individuals take their own lives because it seems like the thing to do; those who die in clusters probably would not have killed themselves if they had been isolated from others (Grigoriadis, 2007). Some suicide bombings seem to have this suicide-by-imitation quality.

The ability to define and then attach labels to disliked groups is a form of political power, making it possible for powerful groups to manufacture new realities out of old rubble. On April 12, 2002, Ari Fleischer, then–White House press secretary, offered a new term to the Washington Press Corps. It was designed to further the political agenda of the George W. Bush administration and to reconstruct the prevailing view of Palestinian suicide bombers, demonizing them even more. The new term was *homicide bombers*. Fleischer's contribution to the propaganda war was just one more piece of ammunition in the ongoing battles between Israel and Palestine. The Palestinians, wanting to glamorize suicide bombings, prefer to call suicide *bombers* by the name of "martyrs" and suicide *bombings* by the name "martyrdom operations." Arabs prefer to use the phrase "human bomb" to describe suicide bombers. Israelis, however, prefer to call them "homicide bombers" because it emphasizes their criminal, antisocial nature. The term *homicide bomber* never caught on with the U.S. public or the pundits. First of all, it is redundant (of course a bomber kills people). Second, it was not really inflammatory enough to show the disdain with which terrorist bombings are held in the West. (A term such as *exploding excrement* or *scatological suicide* would have been better in this regard but too offensive to too many people to become popular.)

Suicide, Stigma, and Responsibility

Suicidal deaths offer fertile ground for feelings of social discomfort and embarrassment among relatives and friends of the deceased. Individuals who must cope with the suicidal death of a family member or friend may find that outsiders make the healing process more difficult. Many people continue to hold negative views of suicide, and they may blame relatives or even friends of the decedent for what happened. The general social context is far less supportive when the death is a suicide than when it results from a murder, accident, or natural causes; even those people who wish to offer aid and comfort to surviving family members may find themselves paralyzed by a lack of clarity over just what should be done or said (Calhoun & Selby, 1990, pp. 222–223).

Compared to other kinds of death, suicides precipitate more guilt, a greater search for what caused the death, and lower levels of social support (Sudak, Maxim, & Carpenter, 2008, p. 137). Although public attitudes—some, at any rate—have become more accepting of suicide with the passage of time, attitudes have not changed so much that suicide is generally or widely viewed as a good and noble way to die (Clinard & Meier, 2008, p. 340). Suicide continues to be viewed as either undesirable or unfortunate, and attitudes toward suicide tend to be generally negative, although the strength of the condemnation is conditioned by characteristics of the suicide itself.

People who attempt but do not complete suicides (i.e., who commit parasuicides) may be condemned because they are considered to be responsible for self-centered attempts at attention getting. People who successfully complete suicides may be stigmatized because what they did seems cowardly. The decedent may be viewed as an individual who expected others to bear the burden that he or she could not or would not bear, while being indifferent to the pain for survivors of losing a loved one. Even though suicide is believed to be painless, this is rarely true, and certainly not true for the surviving family and friends, whose pain may be acute.

Sadness over the loss of a loved one may be the principal emotion experienced by surviving family and friends, even while many additional emotions can be present, such as anger, shock, denial, disbelief, grief, guilt, depression, anxiety, self-blame, and confusion. Survivors may automatically assume that people who attempt or complete a suicide are mentally ill or insane. Some suicidal individuals do have a history of mental illness or substance abuse, but this is not the primary reason for most suicidal deaths (Granello & Granello, 2007, p. 9; Sudak et al., 2008, p. 138). Suicide is an act, not a disease, so what might work to cure a physical illness (e.g., drugs) is woefully inadequate when it comes to a complex happening like suicide (Szasz, 2007).

Efforts to understand what happened, to fit the death into some comprehensible whole or pattern of meaning, are particularly difficult with suicide. The problem is that it is not easy to convince oneself that the suicide of a family member or friend was inevitable or that the individual was unaware of what he or she was doing. Surviving family and friends may be inclined to believe that the death could have been prevented and that the suicidal person could have been helped if only he or she had gone to a therapist for counseling. If the death had been from an accident or natural causes, it could more easily have been defined by surviving individuals as unavoidable or inevitable (Henslin, 1970, p. 199). If it is viewed as having been caused by the individual's own deliberate act and as something that did not have to happen (and was therefore preventable), surviving individuals may be more inclined to feel guilty and responsible for the death.

Jacobs's (1967) analysis of suicide notes shows that some of the same processes that survivors go through in trying to understand and deal with the suicide of one of their own are also found among those individuals who are on a pathway to the commission of suicide. Suicidal individuals, too, must come to attach some positive meaning to the suicidal act and neutralize conventional forces of social control that strongly forbid suicide. They must reconcile their views of themselves as good and decent persons—trustworthy—with the fact that they are planning with full intent to violate the sacred trust of life that suicide represents (p. 64).

The way that individuals who are contemplating suicide typically structure it is to convince themselves that their problems in living are not of their own making, attaching blame to others or to external situations over which they have no control. They conclude that their problems are unsolvable but not from any lack of effort on their part. Finally, they convince themselves that death is the only option for them, a view that is more likely if these individuals have character structures marked by rigidity and inflexibility. They transform a *choice* to die into a *commandment* to die, removing all voluntariness or deliberation from it, reaching the point where non-suicidal possibilities are viewed as impossibilities. After convincing themselves that no reason exists to feel guilty or embarrassed about a self-inflicted death, they are prepared to die (Rodgers, 1995, p. 120). A discussion of adolescent suicide reaffirms Jacobs's suggestion that rigid cognitive structures and poor coping skills make suicide a more likely event. Adolescents who are unable to come up with practical solutions for their problems are more likely to fixate on suicide as the only option (Granello & Granello, 2007, pp. 44–45).

Stigma is a double-edged sword. The shame that attaches to a suicide can be an additional burden for surviving family members and friends to carry. The shame can deter, and the absence of it can make suicide more likely. Gladwell (2000) observes that suicide among young males in Micronesia has become ordinary and commonplace, a ritual of adolescence to which no stigma or shame attaches. One teenager killed himself because his father yelled at him, and another took his own life because his parents refused to buy him a graduation gown. Another hanged himself because his brother criticized him for making too much noise. Some adolescent males committed suicide because they saw their girlfriends chatting with other males or because their parents would not give them enough money to buy beer (pp. 216–233).

Whatever religious proscriptions exist in regard to suicide are easily neutralized by an individual who is serious about it. The individual simply convinces himself or herself that no sin has occurred because no choice exists, the suicide being an act of necessity (Jacobs, 1970, p. 234). If this belief is coupled with the individual's certainty that he or she will finally be rid of life's problems, it is easy enough to understand how religion and suicide can go together. The prospect of a hell complicates the picture, but not too much. The suicidal individual can simply conclude that hell promises fewer problems than does life on earth. In one fell swoop, religion makes it possible for an individual contemplating suicide to be able to convince himself or herself that the present troubles will be gone and that things will be better for all eternity in an afterlife.

The issues of blame and stigma are the bedrock of the controversy in the United States over assisted suicide. In 2008, a representative national sample indicated that 62 percent of people in the United States believed physician-assisted suicide should be allowed in cases where an incurable disease is causing severe pain for a patient and the patient asks to die (Bureau of Justice Statistics, 2008). An important event in the battle over assisted suicide was the involvement of Dr. Jack Kevorkian in the death of Janet Adkins. Ms. Adkins was a happily married, 54-year-old mother of three grown sons, who was afflicted with Alzheimer's disease. She wanted to end her own life before the degenerative disease made it impossible for her to take care of herself. She had tried to get help from physicians in Portland, Oregon—the city where she lived—but all of those she asked refused to help her die.

Adkins learned of Kevorkian in 1989, and she even saw him explain his procedures for assisted suicide on a national television show. Her objective was to die with dignity and without pain, and Kevorkian seemed to be the only professional who could help her. She sent him records of her medical history, and he wanted to know more. She and her husband flew from Portland to Royal Oak, Michigan. After talking to Ms. Adkins, Kevorkian was convinced that she was rational and that she was suffering from an irreversible physical condition. He decided to help her die. Her final exit came on June 4, 1990, in a rather unceremonious setting: the back of Kevorkian's Volkswagen van, parked in a Michigan campsite. When she was ready, Adkins pushed a button, and Kevorkian's suicide machine did the rest: One drug put her to sleep, and another drug killed her. Ms. Adkins's husband awaited news of her death at a nearby hotel because his wife would not allow him to be present at the actual death scene (Humphry, 1991, pp. 131–141).

How assisted suicide is framed is critical in determining the levels of support for it. Successful presentation of an assisted suicide as self-deliverance from an irreversible terminal illness, as a dignified death, or as a simple medical procedure makes it much more likely that it will be viewed favorably than if it is called suicide, lethal injection, or euthanasia (Worsnop, 1995, p. 398). Support rises if safeguards exist—clear and consistent ones that make assisted suicides fully voluntary and fully informed on the part of those choosing to die—and if the people are truly suffering from an incurable, irreversible, painful disease (Cosculluela, 1995).

Because of the secrecy and mystery that now surround physician-assisted suicide, a great fear exists that this type of suicide could be carried out for an individual who was merely tired of living or depressed, rather than a person who was terminally ill. Adkins had played tennis with one of her sons a few days before her death (although she was too mentally incapacitated to keep the score). Some critics of assisted suicide are fearful that a *right* to die could easily evolve into an *obligation* to die (Hendin, 1995a). How do we know or recognize an incurable disease when we see one? Once active euthanasia is firmly in place in society, it may become more likely that it will be called into service to get rid of people who are not terminally ill and who have not given their full and informed consent. It might be used to get rid of the friendless or despised.

Most patients who seek physician assistance in the termination of life (which is legal in the states of Oregon, Washington, and Montana through their right-to-die laws) typically do not do it to avoid unbearable pain. (The U.S. medical profession is skilled at pain control.) The principal reasons are constant nausea, discomfort, difficulty breathing, incontinence, or increasing dependence on others. Those who seek a self-assisted death are individuals who do not want to be a burden to their family and friends, who want to remain independent and self-reliant up until the end of life. They want to control how they die as much as possible, just as they control how they live (M. Taylor, 2007, p. 138).

On December 3, 1990, Kevorkian was charged with the murder of Janet Adkins. A few weeks later, all charges were dismissed because of lack of evidence that Kevorkian had planned her death and intentionally caused it. An additional factor was that Michigan had no law directly forbidding an individual from helping another to commit suicide. In 1992, the Michigan legislature passed a bill that banned assisted suicide, and the Michigan Supreme Court decided that assisted suicides could be prosecuted as felonies. However, Michigan prosecutors still found it difficult to get Kevorkian convicted of a crime. Five times they tried, and five times they failed. The trials ended either in acquittals or, in one instance, a mistrial.

On April 13, 1999, however, Kevorkian was sentenced to 10 to 25 years in prison for the murder (second degree) of 52-year-old Thomas Wouk, who had suffered from Lou Gehrig's disease (amyotrophic lateral sclerosis). Kevorkian had not only supplied the drugs used to kill Wouk, but he had also injected the drugs himself into the man. What's more, he had recorded the whole thing on film. With all this evidence, prosecutors were able to charge Kevorkian with murder and make it stick. He was released from prison on June 1, 2007, after serving about 8 years of his sentence, vowing never to assist or advise on any more suicides. Battles over assisted suicide show that the core of the controversy is not really over how or when an individual should die, but about who should decide. (Kevorkian died on June 3, 2011, at the age of 83, in a hospital in Royal Oak, Michigan. His death was painless, and no artificial attempts were made to prolong his life.)

Conclusions

At some times, in some places, suicide has been admired and has received widespread social support. At other times, in other places, suicide has been condemned and treated as evidence of immorality, disease, or antisocial tendencies. Suicides are one possible outcome of interpersonal relationships and social situations, and they reflect different patterns of social organization, ethnic and racial concentrations, and cultural beliefs. These social factors can have direct and important influences on suicide that are separate from an individual's levels of hopelessness, helplessness, or depression.

Death is symbolized in many different ways, and death of the physical body does not always denote death of the soul or spirit. Historical and cross-cultural variations in the symbolization of suicide show that contradictions exist regarding death and what it means. Before people frame a death as a suicide, they must put together what can be ambiguous bits of information into some consistent whole that will satisfactorily explain what happened, why, and who is responsible.

Suicide may be a response to normlessness, social isolation, and low levels of integration, or it may be a cultural prescription (e.g., suttee or hara-kiri). Durkheim identified four types of suicide that were correlated with changes in two social factors: social integration and regulation. When integration gets too low, egoistic suicide becomes more likely, and when it gets too high, altruistic suicide becomes more likely. When social regulation gets too low, anomic suicide is more likely, and when it gets too high, fatalistic suicide is more likely.

Suicide may be a way for a powerless individual to get revenge on some disliked individual or group. It may also be used as a military strategy in an asymmetrical war, the function it provides for suicide bombers. Because of the stigma that still attaches to suicide in U.S. culture, an individual contemplating it will do whatever it takes to convince himself or herself it is both necessary and unavoidable so as to diminish, or remove entirely, whatever stigma is attached. Controversies over assisted suicide are founded on determinations over how necessary it is and who should have the power to decide when and how an individual should die.

References

Abufarha, N. (2009). *The making of a human bomb: Ethnography of Palestinian resistance*. Durham, NC: Duke University Press.

Alvarez, A. (1972). *The savage god: A study of suicide*. New York, NY: Random House.

American Psychiatric Association. (2000). *Diagnostic and statistical manual of mental disorders* (4th ed., text revision). Washington, DC: Author.

Andrade, M. C. B. (1996). Sexual selection for male sacrifice in the Australian redback spider. *Science, 271,* 70–71.

Atran, S. (2007). The moral logic and growth of suicide terrorism. In T. Badey (Ed.), *Violence and terrorism 07/08* (10th ed., pp. 26–35). Dubuque, IA: McGraw-Hill.

Balikci, A. (1989). *The Netsilik Eskimo*. Prospect Heights, IL: Waveland. (Original work published 1970)

Barry, R. (1994). *Breaking the thread of life: On rational suicide*. New Brunswick, NJ: Transaction Publishers.

Bergman, B., & Dunn, J. (1990, June 4). Northern agony. *Maclean's,* p. 14.

Bloom, M. (2007). Many women suicide bombers are sexual abuse victims. In P. Connors (Ed.), *Suicide* (pp. 102–111). Detroit, MI: Greenhaven Press.

Bloom, M. (2009). Female suicide bombers: A global trend. In T. Badey (Ed.), *Violence and terrorism 08/09* (11th ed., pp. 144–149). New York, NY: McGraw-Hill.

Brown, M. (1996). *Emergency! True stories from the nation's ERs*. New York, NY: Villard.

Bureau of Justice Statistics (BJS). (2008). *Sourcebook of criminal justice statistics Online*. Retrieved August 18, 2012, from http://www.albany.edu/sourcebook/pdf/t2962008.pdf

Calhoun, L., & Selby, J. W. (1990). The social aftermath of a suicide in the family: Some empirical findings. In D. Lester (Ed.), *Current concepts of suicide* (pp. 214–224). Philadelphia, PA: Charles Press.

Canetto, S. S., & Lester, D. (1995). Women and suicidal behavior: Issues and dilemmas. In S. S. Canetto & D. Lester (Eds.), *Women and suicidal behavior* (pp. 3–8). New York, NY: Springer-Verlag.

Clinard, M., & Meier, R. (2008). *Sociology of deviant behavior* (13th ed.). Belmont, CA: Thomson/Wadsworth.

Colt, G. H. (1991). *The enigma of suicide.* New York, NY: Summit.

Cosculluela, V. (1995). *The ethics of suicide.* New York, NY: Garland.

Counts, D. A. (1990). Abused women and revenge suicide: Anthropological contributions to understanding suicide. In D. Lester (Ed.), *Current concepts of suicide* (pp. 95–106). Philadelphia, PA: Charles Press.

Datta, V. N. (1988). *Sati: A historical, social and philosophical enquiry into the Hindu rite of widow burning.* Riverdale, MD: Riverdale.

De Catanzaro, D. (1981). *Suicide and self-damaging behavior: A sociobiological perspective.* New York, NY: Academic Press.

Diekstra, R., & Garnefski, N. (1995). On the nature, magnitude, and causality of suicidal behaviors: An international perspective. In M. Silverman & R. Maris (Eds.), *Suicide prevention toward the year 2000* (pp. 36–57). New York, NY: Guilford.

Douglas, J. (1967). *The social meanings of suicide.* Princeton, NJ: Princeton University Press.

Droge, A. J., & Tabor, J. D. (1992). *A noble death: Suicide and martyrdom among Christians and Jews in antiquity.* San Francisco, CA: HarperSanFrancisco.

Duhigg, C. (2007). Attempted suicide can be a lucrative economic decision. In P. Connors (Ed.), *Suicide* (pp. 68–71). Detroit, MI: Greenhaven Press.

Durkheim, E. (1951). *Suicide: A study in sociology* (J. Spaulding & G. Simpson, Trans.). New York, NY: Free Press. (Original work published 1897)

Early, K. (1992). *Religion and suicide in the African-American community.* Westport, CT: Greenwood.

Early, K., & Akers, R. (1993). "It's a white thing": An exploration of beliefs about suicide in the African-American community. *Deviant Behavior, 14,* 277–296.

Eller, J. (2006). *Violence and culture: A cross-cultural and interdisciplinary approach.* Belmont, CA: Thomson/Wadsworth.

Evans, G., & Farberow, N. (Eds.). (1988). *The encyclopedia of suicide.* New York, NY: Facts on File.

Farberow, N. (1975). Cultural history of suicide. In N. Farberow (Ed.), *Suicide in different cultures* (pp. 1–15). Baltimore, MD: University Park Press.

Farberow, N. (1977). Suicide. In E. Sagarin & F. Montenino (Eds.), *Deviants: Voluntary actors in a hostile world* (pp. 503–570). Morristown, NJ: General Learning Press.

Farberow, N. (1988). Introduction: The history of suicide. In G. Evans & N. Farberow (Eds.), *The encyclopedia of suicide* (pp. vii–xxvii). New York, NY: Facts on File.

Fedden, H. R. (1980). *Suicide: A social and historical study.* New York, NY: Arno. (Original work published 1938)

Gaines, D. (1990). *Teenage wasteland.* New York, NY: Random House.

Gates, B. T. (1988). *Victorian suicide: Mad crimes and sad histories.* Princeton, NJ: Princeton University Press.

Gladwell, M. (2000). *The tipping point: How little things can make a big difference.* Boston, MA: Little, Brown.

Goffman, E. (1974). *Frame analysis: An essay on the organization of experience.* New York, NY: Harper & Row.

Granello, D., & Granello, P. (2007). *Suicide: An essential guide for helping professionals and educators.* Boston, MA: Pearson/Allyn & Bacon.

Grigoriadis, V. (2007). Suicide can be a fad among teenagers. In P. Connors (Ed.), *Suicide* (pp. 87–91). Detroit, MI: Greenhaven Press.

Group for the Advancement of Psychiatry. (1989). *Suicide and ethnicity in the United States.* New York, NY: Brunner/Mazel.

Hazelwood, R., Dietz, P. E., & Burgess, A. W. (1982). Sexual fatalities: Behavioral reconstruction in equivocal cases. *Journal of Forensic Science, 27,* 763–773.

Hendin, H. (1995a). Assisted suicide, euthanasia, and suicide prevention: The implications of the Dutch experience. In M. Silverman & R. Maris (Eds.), *Suicide prevention: Toward the year 2000* (pp. 193–204). New York, NY: Guilford.

Hendin, H. (1995b). *Suicide in America* (Expanded ed.). New York, NY: Norton.

Henry, J., & Short, A. (1954). *Suicide and homicide.* New York, NY: Free Press.

Henslin, J. (1970). Guilt and guilt neutralization: Response and adjustment to suicide. In J. Douglas (Ed.), *Deviance and respectability: The social construction of moral meanings* (pp. 192–228). New York, NY: Basic Books.

Holmes, R., & Holmes, S. (2005). *Suicide: Theory, practice, and investigation.* Thousand Oaks, CA: Sage.

Holmes, R., & Holmes, S. (2009). *Profiling violent crimes: An investigative tool* (4th ed.). Thousand Oaks, CA: Sage.

Holmes, S. (2005). Al-Qaeda, September 11, 2001. In D. Gambetta (Ed.), *Making sense of suicide missions* (pp. 131–172). New York, NY: Oxford University Press.

Humphry, D. (1991). *Final exit: The practicalities of self-deliverance and assisted suicide for the dying.* Eugene, OR: Hemlock Society.

Hutson, H., Anglin, D., Yarbrough, J., Hardaway, K., Russell, M., Strote, J., . . . Blum, B. (1998). Suicide by cop. *Annals of Emergency Medicine, 32,* 665–669.

Jacobs, J. (1967). A phenomenological study of suicide notes. *Social Problems, 15,* 60–72.

Jacobs, J. (1970). The use of religion in constructing the moral justification of suicide. In J. D. Douglas (Ed.), *Deviance and respectability: The social construction of moral meanings* (pp. 229–251). New York, NY: Basic Books.

Kelsay, J. (2008). The "just war" debate, Islamic style. In R. Heiner (Ed.), *Deviance across cultures* (pp. 227–231). New York, NY: Oxford University Press.

Lehmann, J. (1995). Durkheim's theories of deviance and suicide: A feminist reconsideration. *American Journal of Sociology, 100,* 904–930.

Lindsay, M., & Lester, D. (2004). *Suicide-by-cop: Committing suicide by provoking police to shoot you.* New York, NY: Baywood.

Littlewood, R., & Lipsedge, M. (1987). The butterfly and the serpent: Culture, psychopathology and biomedicine. *Culture, Medicine, and Psychiatry, 11,* 289–335.

Lowery, S., & Wetli, G. (1982). Sexual asphyxia: A neglected area of study. *Deviant Behavior, 4,* 19–39.

Malinowski, B. (1926). *Crime and custom in savage society.* London, UK: Routledge/ Kegan Paul.

Maris, R. (1981). *Pathways to suicide: A survey of self-destructive behavior.* Baltimore, MD: Johns Hopkins University Press.

Naito, H. (1989). *Thunder gods: The kamikaze pilots tell their story.* Tokyo, Japan: Kodansha.

O'Neill, R. (1981). *Suicide squads.* London, UK: Salamander.

Papke, D. R. (1987). *Framing the criminal.* Hamden, CT: Archon.

Patkin, T. (2007). Explosive baggage: Female Palestinian suicide bombers and the rhetoric of emotion. In T. Badey (Ed.), *Violence and terrorism 07/08* (10th ed., pp. 170–179). Dubuque, IA: McGraw-Hill.

Plass, P. (1995). *The game of death in ancient Rome: Arena sport and political suicide.* Madison: University of Wisconsin Press.

Pope, W. (1976). *Durkheim's Suicide: A classic analyzed.* Chicago, IL: University of Chicago Press.

Poppel, F. van, & Day, L. H. (1996). A test of Durkheim's theory of suicide—without committing the ecological fallacy. *American Sociological Review, 61,* 500–507.

Rao, A. V. (1983). India. In L. Headley (Ed.), *Suicide in Asia and the Near East* (pp. 210–237). Berkeley: University of California Press.

Reuter, C. (2008). Suicide bombing: The power of the powerless. In A. Thio, T. Calhoun, & A. Conyers (Eds.), *Readings in deviant behavior* (5th ed., pp. 77–86). Boston, MA: Pearson/Allyn & Bacon.

Rodgers, L. (1995). Prison suicide: Suggestions from phenomenology. *Deviant Behavior, 16,* 113–126.

Roy, B. B. (1987). *Socioeconomic impact of sati in Bengal and the role of Raja Rammohun Roy.* Calcutta, India: Naya Prokash.

Saxena, R. K. (1975). *Social reforms: Infanticide and sati.* New Delhi, India: Trimurti.

Sharma, A. (1988). *Sati: Historical and phenomenological essays.* New Delhi, India: Motilala Banarsidass.

Shneidman, E. (1985). *Definition of suicide.* New York, NY: Wiley.

Spurr, R. (1981). *A glorious way to die.* New York, NY: Newmarket.

Sudak, H., Maxim, K., & Carpenter, M. (2008). Suicide and stigma: A review of the literature and personal reflections. *Academic Psychiatry, 32,* 136–142.

Szasz, T. (2007). Collegiate suicide prevention programs may increase the number of suicides. In P. Connors (Ed.), *Suicide* (pp. 207–211). Detroit, MI: Greenhaven Press.

Taylor, M. (2007). The legality of Oregon's physician-assisted suicide law is a victory for patients and doctors. In P. Connors (Ed.), *Suicide* (pp. 133–138). Detroit, MI: Greenhaven Press.

Taylor, S. (1990). Suicide, Durkheim, and sociology. In D. Lester (Ed.), *Current concepts of suicide* (pp. 225–236). Philadelphia, PA: Charles Press.

Thakur, U. (1963). *The history of suicide in India: An introduction.* New Delhi, India: Munshi Ram Manohar Lal Oriental Publishers.

Turvey, B. (2009). Autoerotic sexual asphyxia. In P. Adler & P. Adler (Eds.), *Constructions of deviance: Social power, context, and interaction* (6th ed., pp. 451–462). Belmont, CA: Thomson/Wadsworth.

Unnithan, N. P., Huff-Corzine, L., Corzine, J., & Whitt, H. P. (1994). *The currents of lethal violence: An integrated model of suicide and homicide.* New York: State University of New York Press.

Uva, J. (1995). Review: Autoerotic asphyxiation in the United States. *Journal of Forensic Sciences, 40,* 574–581.

Webb, J., & Willard, W. (1975). Six American Indian patterns of suicide. In N. Farberow (Ed.), *Suicide in different cultures* (pp. 17–33). Baltimore, MD: University Park Press.

Whitt, H. P. (2010). The civilizing process and its discontents: Suicide and crimes against persons in France, 1825–1830. *American Journal of Sociology, 116,* 130–186.

Worsnop, R. (1995, May 5). Assisted suicide controversy. *CQ Researcher, 5,* 393–416.

Wright, R. K., & Davis, J. (1976). Homicidal hanging masquerading as sexual asphyxia. *Journal of Forensic Sciences, 21,* 387–389.

Zhang, J. (2010). Marriage and suicide among Chinese rural young women. *Social Forces, 89,* 311–326.

8

Sexual Diversity

Sex, Gender, and Sexuality

Because so little is known about what people around the world actually do (or have done) in bed (or in a hut, tent, igloo, cave, or the big outdoors), most statements about human sexual diversity are speculative and contentious. Studies that purport to tell us what really happens in our sexual lives really do not. They offer little more than biased information, coupled with a few anecdotes, about those sexual experiences that some people were willing to share with researchers (Carter & Sokol, 1989). These pictures or portraits of human sexuality are ripped from the social context that defines them, so they are stripped of much of what makes them sexual in the first place. For example, a special report was issued by the Gallup organization (Gates & Newport, 2012) on the number of U.S. adults who define themselves as lesbians, gays, bisexuals, or transgenderists. To date, it is the largest single study of its kind (with a sample that contained 121,290 individuals). Sexual identity, however, was tapped with but a single question: "Do you, personally, identify as lesbian, gay, bisexual, or transgender?" (asked in a phone interview between June 1 and September 30, 2012). The researchers reported that 3.4 percent of U.S. adults said that they are lesbian, gay, bisexual, or transgender, with more females (3.6 percent) than males (3.3 percent) so identifying.

Even if all the respondents were being honest on the survey, which seems unlikely given the way the data were collected and the personal nature of the question, the data are still not representative enough to give anything close to a satisfactory picture of the nature of human sexual experiences or sexual identities. As the authors of the report honestly confess, their results can only be understood as responses by adult Americans who were willing to publicly identify themselves as part of the LGBT community when asked about it on a survey.

While *sex* is principally about biological placement as male or female, *gender* is about attitudes and feelings in regard to masculine and feminine (Moon, 1995, p. 496; Tewksbury, 1994). Sex reflects the operation of chromosomes and body chemicals (testosterone or estrogen) on the development of anatomical structures (e.g., ovaries, testes, uterus, scrotum, vagina, clitoris), along with the development of secondary sex characteristics (e.g., body hair, breasts, voice pitch, menstruation). Gender, however, refers to the *psychological aspects* of being masculine or feminine, as well as the social statuses, roles, and cultural prescriptions and proscriptions for acting, thinking, and feeling in sex-appropriate ways. Alcohol consumption, smoking, wage differences, and wearing panty hose are more about gender than sex.

Sex and gender, of course, are not separate from one another, and interactions exist between them. An infusion of testosterone may produce increased levels of masculinity, and exercise can change the degree of muscularity and hormone levels. Sexuality, though related to both sex and gender, is separable from them both. *Sexuality* refers to those experiences that lead to erotic arousal and a genital response. *Erotic arousal* is the state of feeling "turned on," which produces a wish to continue with the relationship and its central activity, and *genital response* is a physiological reaction to some stimulus that is defined as sexual (e.g., erection, ejaculation, or vaginal lubrication) (Reiss, 1986, p. 21).

Gender is continually constructed and reconstructed, made and transformed, in the context of our relationships to others (West & Zimmerman, 2000, p. 139; Wijngaard, 1997). Gender is not a "thing" a human has as much as it is a constellation of actions that one *does* in anticipation of the actual or imagined reactions of others. When we "do" gender, we do it in front of other people. Our gender displays are regularly evaluated by our significant others, who are in a position to encourage or discourage them (Kimmel, 2000, p. 106). A crucial part of an individual's gender is the gender composition of the interactive unit or group within which he or she is interacting and functioning at any particular time. The gendered feature of an individual's identity develops and is presented in response to the gender displays of others (Maccoby, 1998).

More similarities than differences exist between boys and girls, and males and females are more like close neighbors than they are residents of different planets (Kimmel, 2000, p. 16). The belief that males and females are very different—and should be—may initiate a host of social processes to keep males and females different from each other (Martin, 1998, p. 509). We all become gendered in a gendered society, and as societies and cultures change, gender does, too.

Sexuality: A Sociocultural Understanding

Body, Brain, and Sexuality

One view of the relationship among evolution, sexual identity, and sexuality gives genes *the* preeminent position. According to this approach—going by names such as *evolutionary biology, evolutionary psychology,* or *sociobiology*—practically all sexuality, human and nonhuman, is designed to increase the reproductive success of an individual creature. Anything that makes reproductive success more likely will succeed at the expense of anything that does not (Ridley, 1993, p. 20). This approach generates a rather dismal appraisal of human sexual experience. Men, the story goes, try to acquire power and resources and then use them to attract women who will bear them offspring, to ensure that their male genes are passed on to future generations. Simply put, wealth and power are the means to attaining women, and women are the road to genetic immortality. The story continues that women search for good husbands with abundant resources who will be able to support and protect them and their children. Women are portrayed as genetically determined to be more selective and choosy in picking mates, as well as more faithful to them, and men are portrayed as preferring to spread their genes around (Buss, 1994, pp. 19–48).

Human sexual customs are related to human biological characteristics, but exactly how is a matter of dispute. It is customary to assert that biological factors are the cause and that social and sexual relationships are the effect, but this interpretation of the direction of causality is too one-sided (Fine, 2010; Jordan-Young, 2010). Sexual relationships and human experiences change the human body in all kinds of ways. When men are actively involved in sexual relationships, their testosterone levels increase dramatically, much more than if they achieve sexual pleasure through solitary acts of masturbation (Kemper, 1990). Men may actually have higher sperm counts in response to the possibility that their female mates are being unfaithful (Small, 1995, p. 118). When heterosexual men's female sexual partners have close ties with the men's friends, spending more time with them than they do with the men themselves—called *partner betweenness*—it threatens or interferes with the relationship. The men's sense of control, independence, and potency is threatened, and in the relationships in which partner betweenness is highest, men are much more likely to report erectile dysfunction (Cornwell & Laumann, 2011, pp. 192–199). The human brain may actually be the dependent structure and social relationships the independent one. The human brain, Ridley (1993) concluded, has changed and expanded because what we humans find sexually appealing in our permanent mates are wit, virtuosity, inventiveness, and individuality. These were selected for over time (p. 344).

Theories that suggest that differences in gender are caused by differences in the brain are almost always based on the idea that the left and right hemispheres develop differently in males and females. It is usually hypothesized that the male brain is more *lateralized* (the hemispheres are specialized in their abilities), whereas the female brain is more *symmetrical* because her corpus callosum (the part of the brain that joins its two sides) is larger and contains more fibers. So, the story goes, because women have more and better interconnections between brain hemispheres than men do, women excel in talk, feelings, intuition, and quick judgments. Wolf (2012) even goes so far as to insist that the neurology of the vagina and the biochemical processes in the brain are "virtually inseparable," forming one network or one whole system (p. 5). It may be true that males and females have different brains and that these account for male–female differences. However, the research on brain differences between males and females is often of limited value, because it reaches questionable conclusions based on small samples. Sometimes it does little more than reaffirm preexisting stereotypes about sexual differences.

Jordan-Young's (2010) analysis of more than 300 studies, published between 1967 and 2008, led her to conclude that the evidence for masculine and feminine brains—known collectively as *brain organization theory*—is mostly smoke and mirrors.

> [E]vidence that human brains are hormonally organized to be either masculine or feminine turns out to be surprisingly disjointed, and even contradictory— and the stakes involved in prematurely promoting the theory to a "fact" of human development are high. (p. 3)

Our sexual behaviors and our personal outlooks are far more complex than the simple distinction between right brain and left brain would allow (Tavris, 1992). The range of differences *within* a sexual category (i.e., male or female) is always greater than the range of differences *between* the "average" male and the "average" female (Kimmel, 2000). The claim that prenatal hormone differences are responsible for sex and gender differences is based on data that are contradictory and, according to Jordan-Young

(2010), "breathtakingly overblown" (p. 236). The expedition to find brain differences as the root cause of every sex and gender difference misses (or refuses to consider) the interactive effects, overlaps, and blurred or nonexistent boundaries that exist between males and females.

The interest in possible brain differences between males and females has spilled over into the study of brain differences between heterosexuals and homosexuals. Is there a homosexual brain? LeVay (1993) conducted some research that suggests there is. He autopsied hypothalamuses from 19 homosexual men who had died from AIDS and 16 heterosexual men, 6 of whom had died from AIDS. Brains from six women were also autopsied, but the women's sexual orientation was unknown. LeVay reported that his male specimens had a thickening in brain cells not found in females, and that heterosexual men had thicker brain cells than did homosexual men. LeVay concluded that sexual orientation is directly related to brain structure. However, the differences in brain structure that he found, if valid and reliable, may simply have been caused by the impact of the AIDS virus on brain chemistry and not the impact of brain structure on sexual orientation (Byne, 1994, p. 53).

More recently, researchers at the Karolinska Institute in Sweden conducted brain scans of 90 gay and straight males and females. They started with the familiar premise that heterosexual males have brain hemispheres that are lateralized and heterosexual females have brain hemispheres that are symmetrical. They reported from their research that the two hemispheres of the brains of gay *men* resembled the brains of straight *women* more than they did the brains of straight men; the brains of gay *women* looked more like the brains of straight *men* than those of straight women (Park, 2008). Much like LeVay, the researchers concluded that it is the anatomy of the brain that determines sexual orientation. This is the twenty-first-century version of the claim, which has survived long beyond its shelf life, that gays are trapped in the body of the wrong sex, which explains why they are sexually aroused by same-sex individuals.

Problems galore may be found in the claim that gays and straights have different brain structures that account for their sexual orientations beyond its oversimplification of a complex human experience. The most fundamental problem, however, is that it doesn't fit enough of the facts of human sexuality to be of much value. Some humans do conclude that they are trapped in the body of the wrong sex and may wish to change their anatomy (i.e., their sex) to be consistent with their gender. However, these individuals—called *transsexuals*—strongly resist any suggestion that they are homosexual. Homosexuals are individuals who are attracted to members of the same sex; they are not (in the case of males) feminine beings trapped in masculine bodies or (in the case of females) masculine beings trapped in feminine bodies.

The most charitable—and scientifically defensible—view of research on brains and sexual orientation is that the role of the brain in sexual orientation is a complex one, far more so than implied by the male brain–female brain distinction. We really don't know much about why *heterosexuals* are aroused by members of the *opposite* sex, and, likewise, despite the voluminous writings and research, the issue of gay sexuality is also a mystery. Nobody has yet provided a convincing explanation for how something as complex and dynamic as sexual orientation could be determined by brain structure or any other innate characteristic (Fine, 2010; Jordan-Young, 2010; Lewontin, 2000; Lewontin, Rose, & Kamin, 1984). Though certain biological markers must be present for an individual to be sexual, social factors are also implicated in the making of sexual orientation and gender. Sexual orientation has prenatal and postnatal causes that work together to produce an orientation that gets more stable over time (Money, 1988, p. 4).

Sexual Variance and Sexual Scripts

Regardless of the biological or psychological roots of sexual impulses—and these certainly do exist—the additional dimension of society and culture cannot be ignored. Even if we did have a comprehensive and thoroughly satisfying explanation of why some humans are heterosexual and some are not, this would still not tell us why human sexuality is so relative. Homosexuality at one time and place is condemned and homosexuals are persecuted; at another time and place it is deviant for *only* the "passive" partner; at still another time and place, it is a *required* act for both partners (i.e., males), ensuring that they will both develop appropriate levels of masculinity (Carrier, 2007).

The terms homosexual and homosexuality, like heterosexual and heterosexuality, are culture-bound and historically specific, and they can mean different things to different groups and at different points in time. Most certainly they are not homogeneous categories of human experience, and it is unlikely that they include humans who are all alike in attitudes, behaviors, and conditions (Jordan-Young, 2010, p. 168). Whatever makes heterosexuality more "normal" than homosexuality—if it is—is not intrinsic to any kind of sex act. It has to do with who does it, when, where, why, and how; it also matters a great deal who knows about it and what they think and do about it.

Because most societies are so strongly committed to encouraging heterosexuality, exclusive homosexuality is usually strongly discouraged for both males and females. However, a wide range of alternative forms of sexuality do exist at most times and places, homosexuality included. When we consider the wide range in persons, experiences, and objects that humans have found sexually arousing, it should come as no surprise that some people in every society have found members of the same sex more attractive and sexually stimulating than they have members of the opposite sex (Shneer & Aviv, 2006). Gays are continually in a process of constructing and reconstructing their collective identity, both in terms of what it is (or should be) and its relationships to the dominant or majority group(s) (Taylor, Kimport, Van Dyke, & Andersen, 2009). Scheitle and Hahn (2011) report that U.S. states with the highest levels of religious fundamentalism (e.g., evangelical Protestantism) are the most antagonistic to homosexuals and their interests.

No important and enduring human act or social relationship (e.g., dating, marriage, child rearing, eating) is going to be ignored by human beings and left entirely either to biology or chance. It will be scripted by human groups, and these scripts will be incorporated into human culture, passing from generation to generation. This is certainly true with human sexuality. *Sexual scripts* have been constructed to tell individuals the appropriate and inappropriate ways of acting, thinking, and feeling in regard to things sexual. Each social group will usually have a main sexual script that is known to most of its members (Gagnon & Simon, 1973, p. 19), along with additional sexual scripts that are known to only a relative few (Laumann, Gagnon, Michael, & Michaels, 1994, p. 6). With sexual deviance, as with perhaps no other form of social activity, we see that people go beyond the prevailing cultural and subcultural scripts and invent their own (Tewksbury, 1996, p. 4). Practically any act that brings pleasure—no matter what it is and regardless of whether it is done all alone or with others—can be influenced by sexual scripts.

As valuable as the idea of sexual script is in helping us understand the social construction of sexuality, it is clearly not enough. People construct their actions on the basis of the consequences of those actions, using their definitions of situations (which are strongly influenced by their relationships to others). Human sexuality always involves interplay, the expectation and experience of compromise, as well as competition and cooperation (Laumann et al., 1994, p. 51). Increases in sexual freedom can mean that a great deal of confusion exists over just what sexual behaviors should be enjoyed and to what degree (Kelly, 2011).

Some of the dominant themes in U.S. culture and society—practicality, competitiveness, individualism, consumerism—can interpenetrate the American way of sex and set the foundation for too great a degree of emotional emptiness in our most intimate relationships (Schur, 1988, p. 10).

According to Schur, the American way of sex has become too impersonal, coercive, and self-centered (p. xii). Casual sex is defined as a problem by its critics because it seems to be too irresponsible and self-indulgent. It is also defined as a problem because it is correlated with other things that are viewed as troubling: illegitimacy, teenage pregnancy, AIDS, sexually transmitted diseases, marital instability, divorce, and drug use. A letter sent to Dear Abby from a 23-year-old woman indicates how casual intimate relationships can become. She tells the advice columnist that she has been on a birth control pill for 2 years. The expense of the drug has gone up, and she thinks her boyfriend should share in the cost. However, she tells the columnist what the real problem is: "I don't know him well enough to discuss money with him" (Van Buren, 1981, p. 242).

Adolescents who have sexual intercourse prior to marriage (or who say they have) are little different from abstainers (or those who say that they abstain) on most measures of educational success *if* the sexual intercourse is part of a romantic, committed relationship. Adolescents, however, who have sexual intercourse in the context of relationships that are casual and superficial fare much worse than do abstainers on several educational outcomes. They are found to have lower grade point averages and weaker attachments to school, while having more truancies, problems in schools, and negative school sanctions (McCarthy & Grodsky, 2011, pp. 223–224).

At some point in the history of most societies, state representatives (and other moral entrepreneurs) will embark on formal and systematic efforts to define and regulate sexual desires, passions, interests, attitudes, and behaviors of others with whom they have little in common and of whom they have little understanding (Haney, 2010). Narrow-mindedness or lack of empathy is what usually dooms efforts by adults to regulate and control adolescent sexuality. Sex education classes usually accomplish little because they use a single-minded (and often simpleminded) framework in which the principal component is an "abstinence only" message.

Fields's (2008) study of sex education classes in three North Carolina schools (one private and two public) indicates that these classes—and others by implication—are irrelevant to students' sexual lives. They are too long on discussions of human anatomy and sexual techniques and too short on examinations of the sociocultural factors that so powerfully impact and interpenetrate humans' sexual lives. Classrooms, Fields insists, should be organized in such a way that an atmosphere exists in which teachers and students can and do listen to one another so that students better understand personal sexual desire, cultural sex-role expectations, interpersonal power, and sexual inequalities. In the absence of a more comprehensive understanding of social and cultural dimensions of human sexuality, knowledge of how to put on a condom or check for sexually transmitted diseases will be of little value.

The Curious Case of the Berdache

Some Native American groups had a sex/gender status in addition to male or female, called *berdache*. Almost always, a berdache was an anatomical male who combined parts of the masculine and feminine gender into a unique role (Williams, 1986, p. 142). Berdaches moved freely between men's and women's groups because of their unique status, and berdachism was not always permanent. Some men were berdaches for a while but eventually changed and acted like regular men. Transgender statuses, like that of the berdache, show us quite clearly that the division of the human race into two mutually exclusive categories of male and female or masculine and feminine fails to convey adequately the full range of possibilities with regard to sex, gender, and sexuality. (Societies in many parts of the globe— Oceania, Africa, India, Siberia, Asia, Australia—have a gender category comparable to the berdache.)

Attitudes toward the berdache went beyond mere recognition and acceptance to feelings of reverence or even awe. Berdaches were respected because they had the double vision that can flow from occupying a position that was between the male and female, between the masculine and feminine.

> American Indian cultures have taken what Western culture calls negative, and made it a positive; they have successfully utilized the different skills and insights of a class of people that Western culture has stigmatized and whose spiritual powers have been wasted. (Williams, 1986, p. 3)

Berdaches were able to transcend the confines of a one-gender worldview, and they were respected for it. Their secure position in the social life of the community practically ensured that they would enjoy both personal and social success.

Early Native American groups were some of the most egalitarian on earth. This sexual equality meant that females were seen as being of great importance to the life of the community and that their contributions—social, economic, political—were every bit as valuable as males' contributions.

> Because women had high status, there was no shame in a male taking on feminine characteristics. He was not giving up male privilege or "debasing" himself to become like a woman, simply because the position of women was not inferior. (Williams, 1986, p. 66)

Where women have high status, no loss of esteem accrues to a male who moves in a feminine direction. If anything, he may be viewed as the possessor of exceptional qualities.

It would be incorrect to conclude that the berdache status was universally respected or that berdaches were uniformly honored. However, some of the hostility directed at berdaches by their fellows reflected the impact of Europeans and their Christian ideals on Native Americans. These early Europeans tended to be intolerant and inflexible when confronted with any sexual practices or gender roles that were different from their own. The persecution of homosexuals and "sodomites" made a great deal of sense to these visitors to the New World. It gave them one way to establish—in their own minds at any rate—their superiority over other people, while convincing themselves that their way was the only natural and proper way. By the thirteenth century in Europe, the suppression of homosexuality was well under way, and by the fourteenth century, male sodomy was viewed throughout Europe as a capital crime. Sodomites, homosexuals, and pederasts were lumped together with heretics, Jews, and lepers, all of whom were branded as extreme threats to Christianity and Christians. The "abominable sin" of sodomy was suppressed wherever it was found (Moore, 1987, pp. 93–94).

A clear—and fascinating—illustration of the challenges that gender benders must deal with when their society has no institutionalized third gender role for them to occupy is found in the life of a jazz musician named Billy Tipton. This musician was born as a female, in Oklahoma City, December 29, 1914. Her birth name was Dorothy Lucille Tipton, but in 1933, she changed her name to Billy and began dressing as a man, portraying herself as a *male* jazz musician (Middlebrook, 1998). Although a few close family members knew about Billy Tipton's gender bending, most of the people he met did not.

In January 1989, Billy Tipton's health had deteriorated so much that he was too weak to do much of anything for himself, but he refused to go to a hospital. One of his adopted sons (William), who had been caring for his father, phoned his mother (Kitty) to ask for assistance when Billy collapsed. By then, she and Billy had been divorced for almost 10 years, and she had remarried. Kitty instructed William to call 9-1-1 and have Billy taken to a hospital. When the paramedics arrived, they placed the unconscious Billy on the floor of his trailer so that they could search him for a heartbeat. It was then that they—and a very shocked son—learned that Billy Tipton was, indeed, a biological woman. Billy Tipton died in the emergency room of Valley General Hospital, in Spokane, Washington, on the day of his collapse without regaining consciousness. Tipton had lived as a man from the age of

19 until his death at the age of 74, having been a successful cross-dresser, gender bender, and jazz musician for over 50 years.

The brutal economic conditions of the 1930s and the sexism of the U.S. music industry worked together to demand a dramatic response from Dorothy Tipton. Playing music required much more from her than the ability to play the scales on an instrument. It required that she wear trousers and play music as a man. Billy eventually developed all the social and personal fronts—the accoutrements—that were needed to present a façade of heterosexual masculinity, and he was considered to be a sharp-dressing, warm-hearted, good-humored individual. He was good enough as a musician to form his own trio (the Billy Tipton Trio) and good enough as a gender bender to be married to several different women, as well as being a father to three adopted sons.

Dorothy Tipton passed as Billy for most of her life in order to do something that she loved to do in an unequal, sexist society, sacrificing a great deal in order to be able to do it. Sometimes, however, things happen to humans that make it problematic for them to be placed into either one of the two dominant sex categories. One possibility is that they lack the "normal" anatomy that is used as a primary cue for classifying individuals as male or female. The usual term for individuals such as this is *hermaphrodite* or *intersexed,* an individual who possesses identifiable characteristics of *both* male and female. In the United States, the usual way this sexual ambiguity is resolved is that representatives of the medical profession determine which sex category fits the child best (i.e., male or female) based on what kind of genitals the newborn is deemed to possess (i.e., vulva/clitoris or scrotum/penis).

Usually, things are routine. A newborn is inspected shortly after birth and easily and confidently placed into one of the two available sex/gender categories. A phallus that is long enough to be called a penis, along with the presence of a scrotum, signifies that a little boy has entered the world, and a phallus that is small enough to be called a clitoris, along with a vagina, signifies that a little girl has. (The penis and the clitoris develop from the same body tissues, as do the scrotum and vagina.) However, in a relatively small number of births, inspection of the newborn's genitals leads to the conclusion that the phallus is indeterminate (i.e., too large for a girl but too small for a boy). The child then exists in a limbo world, and is defined as a hermaphrodite or an intersexed individual. A newborn could also have external genitals of one sex (e.g., penis/scrotum) but the internal sexual structures of the opposite sex (e.g., ovaries). These individuals, more difficult to classify from a quick physical examination, are also deemed to be hermaphrodites. If a newborn's sex/gender is impossible to determine from an external examination, more extensive tests can be done if the society has the technology (e.g., chromosomal analysis or hormonal evaluation).

Most of the medical personnel who regularly deal with intersexuality are inclined to define it as a liability that can and should be corrected to make the child "normal" and to make the child's development less difficult. This usually requires them to determine which sex best fits the child and then to reconstruct the child's body and indeterminate genitals through surgery and/or drugs. Sometimes this medical strategy has the desired effect, but sometimes it does not. Some hermaphrodites have been irreparably damaged by being assigned to a sex category to which they never adjust. The possibility of mistakes like this occurring justifies a different strategy in dealing with the intersexed. This alternate approach *absolutely* rejects the claim that hermaphroditism is a disorder that should be "fixed" through medical intervention, and it also rejects the idea that the two-sex, binary model of sex describes a natural and necessary division of the human race (Weinberg, Williams, & Laurent, 2005, p. 473). Advocates of this approach are inclined to view any effort to surgically reconstruct the genitals of an intersexed child as a form of genital mutilation and a human rights abuse.

Humans are wired but not programmed for gender in the same way that they are wired but not programmed for language (Money & Tucker, 1975, p. 89). Gender development reflects the joint influence of both innate factors and environmental learning. Money and Tucker hold that a *gender identity gate* is open during the early days of life and stays that way for a time. As long as the "gate" is open, gender is flexible and open to change, even though gender identity will become more rigid with the passage of time (p. 90). They relate the case of twin boys in the 1960s, one of whom experienced a bizarre and ultimately tragic event, to demonstrate the nature of gender.

> A young farm couple took their sturdy, normal, identical twin boys to a physician in a nearby hospital to be circumcised when the boys were seven months old. The physician elected to use an electric cauterizing needle instead of a scalpel to remove the foreskin of the twin who chanced to be brought into the operating room first. When this baby's foreskin didn't give on the first try, or on the second, the doctor stepped up the current. On the third try, the surge of heat from the electricity literally cooked the baby's penis. (pp. 91–92)

After the botched circumcision of the boy (whose name was Bruce Reimer), he was taken to the burn ward. His parents, Ron and Janet Reimer, were summoned to the hospital. When they arrived, Dr. Huot, the physician who had injured their son, told them about the "accident," a rather charitable and self-serving way to describe what he had done to their child. When Ron and Janet were allowed to see their son, what they saw was unforgettable. They were almost as shocked as their hapless child had been. The child's penis was blackened like a piece of charcoal. Over the next couple of days, the penis dried up and then broke away in pieces. It was not long before nothing remained of the organ (Colapinto, 2000).

The Reimers found a glimmer of hope after seeing a television interview with Dr. John Money of Johns Hopkins, one of the country's leading sexologists. The Reimers arranged to meet with Dr. Money early in 1967, and he quickly developed an interest in the case. He was interested in part because he cared about the Reimers and what had happened to their son, but he also saw the case as a test of his theories of sex, gender, and the gender identity gate. Here was a child with an identical twin brother (to serve as a comparison), who was normal at birth but who had been irreparably damaged through physician error. Money's career could benefit enormously from his involvement with a case like that of the Reimers. He laid out the options for the parents, nudging them toward the conclusion that it would be best to change their "son-without-a-penis" into their "daughter-with-a-vagina." Money assured the parents that Bruce's young age meant that he would accept the new gender and pattern his erotic interests and activities accordingly. Money emphasized that gender reassignment for their son would work best if it were started immediately.

Ron and Janet Reimer decided to follow Money's advice. Shortly after their return to their home in Winnipeg, Canada, they came up with a new name for the child—Brenda Lee Reimer—and they started treating Brenda like a girl and as if she had always been one. Her hair was allowed to grow long, and she was dressed in feminine clothing. Brenda was given toys appropriate for girls, and in all ways possible she was encouraged to be feminine. At 22 months, she was taken back to Johns Hopkins where she was surgically castrated. Both of the testicles were removed (bilateral orchidectomy), the ducts that would have carried sperm to the urethra were tied off, and the scrotal tissue was used to make external genital structures. More extensive surgery would be needed to construct a vaginal opening and canal. Hormone treatments would promote breast development, create a widening of the pelvis, and suppress both hair growth and a masculine voice. Intensive therapy sessions by trained professionals would add to the efforts of her family to erase any memories of the child's life as a boy and to get her to live as a female. At the appropriate time, additional surgery would be done to enhance Brenda's feminine appearance. No one could know, of course, how things would turn out for this family. Any predictions would have to be guarded because the case was so unique.

Brenda Lee Reimer, according to photographs, certainly looked the part of a pretty, brown-eyed, brown-haired girl. However, according to those who knew her, that's as far as her femininity went. When participating in the activities of childhood, she acted like a typical boy. The toys she preferred were those of her brother, and she used her girl toys to play boys' games. She used her jump rope to tie up people or to whip them; the sewing machine that she was given as a present was totally ignored. Brenda even insisted on standing to urinate, a position that meant the urine would shoot directly out and get all over the toilet seat. She went as far as to sneak out into an alley so she could urinate in a standing position. Despite the family's intensive efforts, Brenda never felt she was a girl. Even her regular visits with John Money at Johns Hopkins did little to change her mind. She was not a girl and never would be, no matter what anyone said. She found the physical changes produced by the feminizing drug that she was forced to take very embarrassing (i.e., her developing breasts and the accumulation of fat on her hips).

On the afternoon of March 14, 1980, when Brenda was 14 years old, her father picked her up from school and drove her home. In the family's driveway, he broke down in tears as he told her the details of the botched circumcision. Brenda's primary feeling was one of relief. She finally understood why she felt the way she did. Brenda decided that she would no longer live as a female. The first thing she did was select a new name. Thinking her birth name, Bruce, a name for "geeks and nerds," she came up with two possibilities, Joe or David, and let her parents make the final decision. "Brenda" became "David." Second on the agenda was to go public with the news. In August, a week after he turned 15, David told his extended family that he was no longer Brenda (and never had been). Next, he had to get his female form changed. After receiving injections of testosterone, he sported peach fuzz on his face, a few hairs over an inch in length. He later had a painful double mastectomy. A month before his sixteenth birthday (July 2, 1981), David had surgery to construct male genitals. A penis was crafted from tissue and muscles on the inside of his thighs, and an artificial urethra and testicles were fashioned out of plastic and placed in his reconstructed scrotum. David was very pleased with the results.

In 1988, David's brother introduced him to Jane Fontane, a divorced woman and mother of three. The two hit it off, and they started to date regularly. On September 22, 1990, approximately 2 years after they were introduced, David and Jane were married at Regents Park United Church in Winnipeg. David continued to struggle, unsuccessfully, with what had happened to him. He eventually lost his job and separated from his wife. He lost most of his life savings in a questionable golf shop investment. After three unsuccessful attempts at suicide, David Reimer finally put an end to his suffering. On May 4, 2004, at the age of 38, David Reimer sat alone in a car and shot himself in the head. (His twin brother had also killed himself, in 2002.)

Despite the way that life turned out (and ended) for David Reimer, the case should not be taken as indisputable proof that sexuoerotic identity is formed in the womb. As Brenda, David's sexual interests and outlooks were continually explored and relentlessly examined by adults who were bent on uncovering any hint or trace of lingering masculinity and eliminating it. Brenda was repeatedly given physical exams and questioned incessantly about her sexual interests and outlooks. She was even forced to simulate sexual intercourse ("dry humping") with her brother, supposedly to help her develop a female role and overcome her sexual inhibitions (Jordan-Young, 2010, pp. 293–294). Though Brenda was fully clothed during the simulated sexual intercourse, it might very well have been traumatic enough for her that it failed to achieve its intended objective of making Brenda embrace femininity. The trauma for the child of this unrelenting effort to feminize her as "all girl" might be what best explains Brenda's distaste for femininity.

One routine complaint by the intersexed themselves is that they believe that too much significance is given to the "power of the penis" to determine how decisions are made about sex assignment and surgical reconstruction (Kessler, 1998). The prevailing belief among most sexologists and medical personnel is that a lack of male genitals means that an individual will be better off being raised as a female (Weinberg & Williams, 1994). Yet, the situation of the intersexed is not understood adequately by focusing on what anatomical structures they have and which ones they lack. It is their feeling of not fitting in, of not being like everyone else, that leads them to seek medical assistance to change their anatomy. What counts as a disease and how it is to be cured are not only questions of chemistry and biology. They are directly related to social understandings about what bodies are and what they should be in relationship to other bodies (Plemons, 2010, p. 326).

Intersexed individuals are critical of the separation of the world into two mutually exclusive, non-overlapping categories of male–female or masculine–feminine (M. Holmes, 2009). They both resent and challenge the medicalization of their condition, and they refuse to look at intersexuality as a disease to be "cured" or "corrected" through surgery and gender reassignment. Kessler's (1998) intersexed respondents defined *their* happiness in terms of increased societal acceptance of themselves as individuals and their genital anomalies. The position of the Intersexed Society of North America (ISNA) is that intersexed children should be allowed to wait until they are both old enough and mature enough to make an informed decision about gender reassignment that will be best for them. This may mean that these intersexed persons will live their entire lives completely free from *any* surgical alteration. A central objective of the ISNA is to make it possible for the intersexed to live physically unaltered in a society that is understanding and accepting of them (Weinberg, Williams, & Laurent, 2005).

Sexual Differentiation and Sexual Asymmetry

Double Standards

Sexologists and physicians in the United States in the early twentieth century took it for granted that the world was naturally divided into two, mutually exclusive categories of masculine and feminine or of male and female, and that heterosexuality was more normal than homosexuality. They did what they could to convince everyone that what they believed was true (Birken, 1988). This rigid view of sexual differentiation offered sexologists and physicians abundant riches. It allowed them to seize control of the sex-gender-sexuality complex, deciding what was normal and what was not. The icing on the cake was that they then had the opportunity and power to offer "fixes" or "cures" for the sex-related problems that they had had a central role in constructing. This approach, with its appeal to innateness and naturalness, offered advantages to these early sexologists and physicians that a more dynamic, relativistic view of sex, gender, and sexuality never could have offered (Irvine, 1990, p. 285).

Any system of sexual differentiation that divides the world into two categories that are construed as mutually exclusive is almost always coupled with the tendency to prize some characteristics and condemn others. This socially constructed asymmetry is then used by the superordinate group to maintain its dominance by continuing to suppress and subdue members of the opposite group and what they are and do (Kimmel, 1996; Spain, 1992). One of the more enduring double standards or asymmetries is between males and females, with things "female" almost always being considered not as valuable as things "male." Simply put, female gender is regarded as a birth defect in much of the world (Epstein, 2012, p. 39).

In some places on earth, every female child undergoes an extreme and traumatizing mutilation of her genitals. It is known as circumcision, genital alteration, genital cutting, or—the most accurate term—*female genital mutilation*. This procedure is usually done to a child between infancy and adolescence, most often on a girl between ages 2 and 9, but in some places (e.g., Ethiopia or the Sudan), it has been done to females no more than a few days old (Dorkenoo & Elworthy, 2007). The young girl is grabbed and held down by several adults until the cutting is complete. She is then sewn together and bound for several weeks. Beyond the violence and betrayal this evidences to the child is the possibility of infection, infertility, and even death (p. 425). Sometimes, the only body part that is amputated is the clitoris in a procedure called *clitoridectomy,* usually done by untrained and perhaps unskilled individuals (Saadawi, 1982, pp. 7–11). At other times, the procedure is more radical. All the genital organs—clitoris and portions of the labia—are cut away with a knife, a razor, a pair of scissors, or even a sharp rock. The remaining flesh is then sewn together with a sharp needle, and the female's legs are bound together for many weeks to allow the skin to heal. A small hole for the passage of urine and menstrual blood is all that remains (Burstyn, 1997, p. 21). Africa is the region where the custom is most frequent, but it is also found in parts of South America, Southeast Asia, and the Middle East (Ziv, 1997, p. 10).

The custom of female genital mutilation is kept alive principally by cultural beliefs that terrible consequences will befall a female who does not undergo the procedure. One belief is that an uncircumcised clitoris will grow so large that it will drag on the ground. Another is that uncircumcised females will be unruly, oversexed, unclean, childless, and unmarriageable (Burstyn, 1997, p. 20). The Bambara of Mali believe that a man will die if his penis comes in contact with the clitoris during sexual intercourse, and in Nigeria, some groups believe that a child will die if his or her head brushes against the mother's clitoris during delivery. All of these beliefs are, of course, not based on reality, but the people who practice genital mutilation are caught in a *belief trap:* No one is brave enough to risk the costs of what might happen if the procedure is not performed (Mackie, 1996, p. 1009).

A study at Harborview Medical Center (Seattle, WA) of female genital cutting of Somali patients (in Somalia, 98 percent of women undergo infibulation) indicates how a practice that seems dangerous and unnecessary can still be a battleground of competing worldviews and power differentials (Wade, 2011). Physicians at Harborview, wanting to show respect for cultural traditions and cultural differences, developed a surgical procedure that included some cutting but as little as possible. This procedure, called a *prepotomy*, involved making a one-centimeter incision in the foreskin of the clitoris under a topically applied local anesthetic. Physicians' expectation, filtered through their own cultural understandings and medical frame of reference, was that Somalis would opt for the prepotomy initially—not wishing to abandon the custom of their homeland—but would eventually abandon it entirely.

What physicians viewed as both a humane and reasonable alternative to infibulation (i.e., the prepotomy) was not viewed that way by everyone. The disagreement rested mainly on whether the substitution of a small incision for infibulation was an expression of cultural continuity or cultural discontinuity. Opponents of the procedure, using a different understanding of culture, insisted that the prepotomy was actually no change at all. They concluded that *any* cutting whatsoever was testimony to the inability or unwillingness of Somali women to cast off the patriarchal double standard to which they were enslaved. Permanent abandonment of *all* cutting of *any* type was the only alternative that they would accept. They saw the physicians' proposal not as a compromise but as a capitulation to patriarchy and reverence for a cultural tradition that should have been abandoned long ago.

In some societies across the world, male genitals may be mutilated, too, through piercing, cutting, or inserting foreign objects into them in one way or another. Gregersen (1983) claims that mutilation of *male* genitals is both more frequent and more varied than is mutilation of female genitals. The most frequently occurring *male genital alteration* is *circumcision,* a custom that may have started during the Stone Age (p. 102). In circumcision, the removal of the foreskin of the penis is almost always justified as a way to improve men's personal hygiene and wholesomeness. However, rarely (or never) will a male be circumcised in order to make him more attractive to a woman or in order to make him more marriageable.

Castration is another form of male genital alteration (in which one or both testicles are removed). According to legend, Semiramis, the Assyrian queen in about 800 BCE and the founder of Babylon, had all her male lovers castrated after she spent the night with them. The reasons were to prevent them from opposing her female rule as well as to prevent them from giving pleasure to any other women (Simons, 1982, p. 158). Sometimes, castration was self-inflicted as a form of religious devotion, or it was done to "desexualize" a male so that he could be safely put in charge of a ruler's harem. The Khoi, a native people of southwestern Africa, used to remove one testicle from all males (called *hemicastration* or *semicastration*) to prevent the birth of twins, which was considered a very bad omen (Gregersen, 1983, p. 104). Male genital alteration and female genital alteration, however, are different social events, principally because of differences in the cultural justifications for them.

Sexual Identities and Social Inequalities

Sexual asymmetry is not confined to male and female categories. It is found almost always anytime and anywhere that mutually exclusive categories are created. A study of the imaging of prostitution in nineteenth-century Canada shows the relational and asymmetric nature of the social construction of deviance (Ball, 2012). The images of the prostitute varied from time period to time period, but each new image of Prostitute was a reflection of her opposite, Ideal Woman. Each time the image of Ideal Woman changed, an accompanying change in the image of her opposite— Prostitute—was not far behind.

In nineteenth-century Canada, man was economic and woman was domestic, a situation paralleled in the United States (Gregersen, 1983). While woman was not considered the equal of man, one type of woman *was* elevated above all other *women*: the Angel or Saint of the Household. Her feminine opposite was the Fallen Woman, embodied in the image of the Prostitute, who symbolized all the imperfections that had been avoided by the Angel or Saintly Woman. Prostitution was reconstructed as sin and, like all sin, was seen as a result of moral imperfection and personal weakness.

Female activists worked to spread their view that the problem of women was men. If true, this meant that prostitutes were more sinned against than sinning. Prostitution came to be understood less in moral terms and more in political ones. Women were viewed as having been forced into prostitution by ruthless men, so prostitution was reconstructed as "white slavery." Demands for criminalization and governmental control of it increased. Prostitutes were still punished, however, and little interest existed in exploring how class conflicts or sexual inequalities caused prostitution.

The final dichotomization came when the Ideal Woman was constructed as the Nurturing Mother, and the Prostitute was constructed as intrinsically pathological. Prostitute was defined as embodying the traits of hypersexuality, immorality, and impulsivity; she was defined as lacking any maternal instincts. The reconstruction went so far as to declare that the Prostitute was not a woman at all. Her incessant and inexorable sex drive meant that she was genetically closer to man than to woman (Ball, 2012).

In the United States, Nevada is the only state that permits legalized prostitution (and not in every county). The lynchpin of this world of impersonal sex is the *illusion* of intimacy, one more commodity to be peddled. Postmodern flesh peddlers have learned how to package physical intimacy and what seems to be authentic emotional engagement. They are able to make their clients feel that they are special. The women use a warm smile and engaging eye contact to seduce clients who really need little coaxing (Brents, Jackson, & Hausbeck, 2010, p. 120). Men who frequent prostitutes may be willing to pay for intimacy, but it is an *illusion* of intimacy, demarcated by its casualness and superficiality. (It is possible, Kipnis [2010, p. 2] observes, that what men are actually paying prostitutes for is not sex but the women's willingness to leave after the sex is over.)

A study of exotic dancers shows how nudity and seminudity, along with seductive sex talk, can be used to earn income, but the individual loses both power and self-respect in the process (Deshotels, Tinney, & Forsyth, 2012). Though exotic dancers do have some control over what they do and how much they work, thereby increasing personal wealth, they are still tightly boxed in by rigid expectations regarding how they should look and how they should express their sexuality (Hardy, Kingston, & Sanders, 2010). Their provocative dancing and overall sexiness does give them a measure of interpersonal power over their customers, but it is a hollow victory. The money tap only flows if they are willing to do whatever their patrons will financially reward. Exotic dancers must embrace a thoroughly other-directed view of their bodies and their sexual expression and be willing to do and be whatever the market demands (Pasko, 2009).

Female exotic dancers' sex work exists in a stratified and complicated world (Holland, 2010). Erotic value is contingent on the intersection of race, class, gender, appearance, and age. Darker-skinned Latinos and blacks do not fare as well as do whites in terms of pay or safety. Simply put, the "whiter" a dancer is—or is perceived to be—the more valuable she is defined to be and the greater her financial success (other things, such as age or appearance, being equal). Black women are stereotyped both as the most sexually insatiable and the easiest to attain (i.e., more sex for less money) (Brooks, 2010). Erotic capital, like other kinds of capital, is stratified along the dimensions of race and ethnicity.

Logan (2010) found that when it comes to gay male sex in the escort service, customers place a premium on masculinity, a penetrative sexual position ("topping"), aggressive sexual behavior, and muscular physiques. Generally, the closer a gay male sex worker is to embodying an image of hegemonic masculinity, the more coveted he is and the more handsomely he is paid. This spells substantial disadvantage for anything that hints of femininity, such as receptive sexual positions ("bottoming"); submissiveness; or a body build that is viewed as too fat, too thin, or too soft. Basically, when it comes to sex, masculine gay men are greatly valued, and effeminate gay men are not. Black men in the gay escort service do particularly well, because gay men are willing to pay the most for escorts whom they deem to fit the image of a large, muscular, aggressive, dominant, penetrating, insatiable sex brute. Though the sexually dominant black male may be frightening to heterosexuals (Lemelle, 2010), he is anything but to gays, at least when it comes to commercial sex (p. 698).

The term "effeminate" (or its derivatives, such as "sissy," "wimp," "faggot," "fag," "girly-man," "girly-boy") symbolizes all that is not masculine, representing therefore what is unattractive and unacceptable for men to do and be. Men, regardless of sexual orientation, are expected to eschew any traces of femininity in their own personal style of acting and being. This may be easier for straight men than for gays because of the influence of the effeminacy effect. The *effeminacy effect* is the belief, both stigmatizing and insulting, that gay men are in fact more feminine than straight men and that homosexuality is what men turn to who have failed at masculinity. This belief has played some role in how gays have forged their own sexual identities.

Some gay men will dress as women (known as "drag") but they are not "drag queens." They are a part of a subculture called *Faeries*. Though they enjoy dressing as women, they are neither overtly feminine in manner nor trying to be women or to be identified as them. Faeries' objective is to separate from the world, challenging conventional gender norms by doing something that heterosexual men do not do (i.e., dress like women). They are not dressing as women because it turns them on to pretend that they are women. The *Bears* display a different anti-effeminacy strategy. This subculture developed out of a larger organization in the 1980s known as Girth and Mirth. Their erotic ideal is a body type that is older, hairier, and heavier than the type that is valued in other parts of gay subculture. Bears are regular masculine men—and they present themselves that way—but regular masculine men who find masculinity and men sexually arousing (Hennen, 2008).

The Fairies and Bears are both different from the *Leathermen*. The gay leather community strongly condemns any suggestion that an association exists between homosexuality and femininity. They embrace a hypermasculine sexuality, and their dress and mannerisms embody a hegemonic masculinity (or at least how they define masculinity). A great deal of leather clothing, bravado, and sadomasochistic "kinky" sex are the mechanisms by which these men show the rest of the world who they really *are* at the same time that they show who they really are *not*. Rough sex, along with tough dress and mannerisms, reflects and adds to the Leathermen's principal objective, which is to show that they are real men—more so, in fact, than heterosexual men (Hennen, 2008).

A study by Gray (2009) of gay identity construction (i.e., queer identity) in parts of rural Kentucky shows how important situational elements are in the construction of sexual identity. Unlike their counterparts in urban metropolises, these rural gays and lesbians were more inclined to utilize a program of *circulation* rather than *separation* to show their opposition to conventional heterosexuality. Gray's research shows that the "we're here and we're queer" approach, based on gay congregation, visibility, and open confrontation with straights, is not the only way to establish a gay identity.

A mobile, fluid process was used by Gray's sample to express their queer identity while remaining sensitive to the feelings of others, taking account of community standards in regard to propriety, decency, and respect of others (p. 166).

A tradition of self-reliance and a suspicion and mistrust of outsiders characterized rural life along the back roads and byways traveled by Gray (2009). In this setting, one's sexual orientation—and the inclination to be open and honest about it with others—is less important than one's identity as a member of a particular family, a community member, or a native Kentuckian. Gays and lesbians in rural Kentucky received acceptance from others if they could authenticate their status as an insider or familiar. Individuals who might normally have been unsupportive of gays and their interests became more accepting upon learning that one of their own is a homosexual.

The Myth of the Universal Turn-On

Human Variability and Sexual Arousal

Though humans can separate everyday reality from erotic reality, experiencing them as two distinct realms, components of one realm can easily intrude on the other. We may alternate between the two without intending to do so, and the sexual can impact the everyday and vice versa (Davis, 1983, p. 10). It is also true that human sexual deviance overlaps with human sexuality so much that what is true about sexuality in general also tends to be true about deviant sexuality. There need be no intrinsic differences between sexual deviance and sexual conformity. All that is required for sexual deviance to exist is for some group to forbid certain kinds of sexuality and to condemn those individuals who participate in them.

For some people, the principal fascination with sexuality that is exotic, bizarre, or maybe even perverted is that it upsets or alarms representatives of conventional society. According to Davis (1983), it is the fact that this sexuality is impure that makes it worth doing in the first place. Woody Allen, in the film *Everything You Wanted to Know About Sex*, expresses just this sentiment when he states that the only time sex is dirty is when it's done right. Although most types of sexual deviance have no specific procreative function—though they may be a prologue to reproductive acts—this fact alone is insufficient to account for their deviancy. Sex for pleasure is an integral part of human sexual experiences, and even some nonhuman primates seem to participate in sexuality for purposes other than reproduction (de Waal, 2005).

Biology influences sexual expression in many ways. No amount of cultural conditioning or socialization is going to make it possible for a human to orgasm indefinitely. Physical limits exist regarding how many sexual episodes one can have in a day, a year, or a lifetime. We can predict that some things are more likely than other things to turn people on, and we will be right more often than not. This is true, but it's not the whole truth. Humans can gain access to an intricate world of sexual experiences, sexual objects, and sexual activities that is unique because it offers so much diversity and variation (Chodorow, 1994). Expanding sexual freedom and a culture of eroticism can lead to new sites of sexual pleasure and self-expression, along with new sexual identities and the formation of new sexual communities (Seidman, 1991, p. 194).

Biological sexual urges and drives are harnessed by social and cultural factors (Gagnon & Simon, 1970, p. 20). Goode and Troiden (1974) made an observation over 35 years ago, but it is still of value today.

> Sexual behavior is not dictated by the body, not by our animal chemistry, but by the mind, by our human relationships, by civilization, by what has historically come to be accepted as good or bad—in short, by convention. We do what we do in bed because we have learned to do so. And what we do *could* have been otherwise; by growing up surrounded by different customs, we would have been completely different sexual beings. At birth, the possibilities for what we could do in bed—or, for that matter, out of bed, or anywhere else—are almost boundless. (p. 14)

The array of human sexual experiences is considerable, and the degree of variability and flexibility in human sexual experiences surpasses what is found in *all* nonhuman animal species, even the more sexually playful ones. Human sexuality is *distinctly* human (p. 13).

Bullough's (1976) comprehensive exploration of sexual variance throughout history makes it quite clear that wherever human sexuality is found, so is human sexual deviance. In addition, what qualifies as sexual deviance varies considerably from place to place and time to time:

> Some [societies] emphasized chastity and tolerated intercourse only in a marriage relationship with procreation specifically in mind, others had a double standard in which almost everything was tolerated for the male but not for the female, and still others tolerated, if not encouraged, almost any sexual activity, there being all kinds of variation in between. (p. 19)

Even kissing, defined as a valued and necessary part of lovemaking in some cultures, is seen as aberrant and unnatural in others (Tiefer, 1978, pp. 29–37). What one group defines as the epitome of sensuality, sophistication, and normalcy, another group brands as obscene, dangerous, and in need of immediate eradication (Beisel, 1993, p. 148). Humans may not have yet imagined the boundaries of their sexual potential, let alone exhausted all the possibilities (Sanger, 2010). Standards of human sexual conduct "are especially warped, species-ist, and human-centric because human sexuality is so abnormal by the standards of the world's thirty million other animal species" (Diamond, 1997, p. 2).

Humans are continually finding new sexual turn-ons, using the same old body parts but in new ways, finding new sexual paraphernalia to increase their sensual pleasures, establishing new relationships that provide new pleasures in the old ways, or enjoying solitary sex. Alfred Kinsey, a biologist who eventually directed his attention to surveying and describing human sexuality, was more aware of the diversity of human sexuality than were many of his successors. He knew that practically any stimuli could be sexualized by someone (Kinsey, Pomeroy, & Martin, 1948; Kinsey, Pomeroy, Martin, & Gebhard, 1953). How else can we explain the fact that for some people riding horses is sexually arousing and for others smelling the exhaust fumes of automobiles is?

Some individuals may become part of what Gregersen (1983, p. 181) called the *chastity underground*. These are individuals who have an interest neither in sexual activities nor in forming sexual relationships. The scanty information available suggests that these people do not have any noticeable sexual dysfunction (e.g., impotence). They simply have a marked disinterest in sexual activities. The authors of *Sex in America* (Michael, Gagnon, Laumann, & Kolata, 1994) reported that approximately 1 out of 3 women and 1 out of 6 men report a lack of interest in sex (for at least 1 of the 12 months before data collection); in addition, 1 woman in 5 and 1 man in 10 report that sex gives them no pleasure (p. 126). Some of these individuals do worry about their lack of sexual interest, thinking it indicates that something is wrong with them. It may simply be that asexual individuals do not get sexually aroused as quickly as do other individuals (Kelly, 2011, p. 369).

The speed, anonymity, and reach of the Internet give sexual deviants of all stripes unprecedented opportunities for sexual thrills and vicarious titillation (S. T. Holmes & Holmes, 2009, p. 169). The Internet offers access to websites, chat rooms, discussion groups, newsletters, contacts, parties, names of potential participants/partners, and photos/videos, covering an incredible array of sexual interests and unusual turn-ons (Durkin, Forsyth, & Quinn, 2006). The Internet has an openness and accessibility that is lacking with most other parts of culture and society, with an almost unlimited capacity to expand its coverage of things sexual (Streeter, 2011). It is one of the most unregulated social domains ever created, and it offers quick access to the dark side of human sexuality to practically anyone who wants it (Sandywell, 2006). In fact, the more extreme or bizarre the sexual deviance is, the more valuable the Internet becomes (Adler & Adler, 2006, pp. 144–145).

Maratea (2011) collected data from an Internet message board oriented toward a discussion of *zoophilia* (sexual desire for, and emotional attachment to, nonhuman animals) and *bestiality* (sex with nonhuman animals devoid of any emotional attachments to them). The nonrandom sample (with unknown characteristics) consisted of 4,983 individual posts, made mostly between September and November 2008. Sex with nonhuman animals was justified in many ways, but most of these accounts claimed in one way or another that no harm was done to the animals. Some acts of *bestiosexuality* were declared to have been caused by the nonhuman animals themselves, making them out to be (at least in the human's mind) something consensual *and* positive for the nonhuman creature. These participants in bestiosexuality portrayed their sexual interests and activities as more normal and ordinary than they might appear to nonparticipants. They endeavored to convince others that they were misunderstood and doing nothing harmful to their nonhuman consorts. Participants on this message board condemned their critics for themselves doing cruel things to animals.

It is unknown how important these justifications are to chatters on the message board, but it is possible that attitudes like them provide motivating and rationalizing functions, along with ways to manage stigma. Most participants in bestiosexuality establish limits beyond which they will not go, which also helps in the normalization process. *Fence hopping*, which refers to having sex with another individual's nonhuman pet without the consent of the owner, and *hot swapping*, where several humans have sex with the same nonhuman animal in rapid succession over a short period of time, are both widely tabooed within the zoophile/bestiality community (Maratea, 2011). Anyone advocating either of these in chats on the message board was likely to receive condemnation and reprimand from other participants.

The Internet (and nodes on this information superhighway, such as YouTube and Facebook) plays another role in the construction of sexual deviance. It gives moral entrepreneurs abundant opportunities to find something new, disturbing, and seemingly out of control to worry about and condemn. The Internet—and what it makes possible—is fertile ground for the origination of new moral crusades and moral panics. The "threat" of cyberporn, for example, can be used by moral entrepreneurs as yet one more example of the many risks that youngsters face. This claim can then be used to substantiate the further claim that youngsters are growing up too fast, in a climate of self-indulgence and irresponsibility that can only be interrupted by strong parental monitoring of youngsters' leisure time and government oversight (Potter & Potter, 2009). Cyberporn is now added to the list of threats to the purity and innocence of childhood and adolescence.

Patterning Paraphilias

Some sexual turn-ons—such as *formicophilia* (sexual arousal from insects), *emetophilia* (sexual arousal from vomiting), *klismaphilia* (sexual arousal from enemas), *eproctophilia* (sexual arousal from flatulence), *urophilia* (sexual arousal from urine), *coprophilia* (sexual arousal from feces), or *necrophilia* (sexual arousal from corpses)—are found among a relatively small number of individuals (who may be suffering from psychological disorders of one type or another). Few, if any, group and cultural supports exist for these far-side sexual thrills. Once called perversions, things like this are now classified as paraphilias in much of the psychiatric literature.

The term *paraphilia,* which literally means "a love beside," is used to refer to sexual arousal in response to objects or situations that are considered to not be a part of the *usual* arousal-activity patterns. The term describes sexual arousal in response to "inappropriate" objects, "inappropriate" acts, or acts that occur in "inappropriate" settings (American Psychiatric Association, 2000, pp. 566–567). Paraphilias cover a wide range of far-side sexual turn-ons that involve nonconsenting partners, nonhuman animals, inanimate objects, or acts that can cause pain or humiliation for the individuals involved (Stoller, 1979, 1985). Although some individuals who have paraphilias may be found to be "sick" or "mentally ill" in the clinical sense of the term, this finding is of limited value for a relativist approach. What the existence of paraphilias and people who indulge in them *do* show is that there is incredible variety in what humans find sexually arousing and that new turn-ons are found (or made) all the time.

Paraphilias are predominantly a Western, culture-specific happening, and it is their social construction and medicalization that require analysis to parallel whatever interest exists in why people have them in the first place (Bhugra, 2008). Though some paraphilias are rigid and incomprehensible to most people most of the time, many are concordant with conventional sexuality and overlap with it quite a bit. At times, paraphilias are best viewed as inclinations that are followed, altered, modified, and amended, rather than as concrete, invariant, abnormal conditions.

Individuals dabble in paraphilic sex—Rosewarne (2011) calls them part-time perverts—who are neither physically sick nor psychologically maladjusted. They simply manage sexual fantasy by selecting far-side sex for its expression. For example, *fetish* (sexual arousal from inanimate objects, such as clothing) is common among men (and some women), and it is widely viewed as both normative and normal (Steele, 1996). Yet fetish is defined as a paraphilia (American Psychiatric Association, 2000, pp. 569–570). *Voyeurism* (sexual arousal from viewing forbidden things), another paraphilia, has a variant in which a number of voyeurs will get together to spy on people. Sometimes they use telescopes, and they may even be viewing people who know that they are being watched (Forsyth, 1996, pp. 286–291).

As can be seen from this brief discussion of paraphilias, the term is value-laden and judgmental. It transforms something that is inherently ambiguous and relative (not part of the *usual* arousal-activity patterns; *inappropriate* acts, objects, or settings) into something that is more likely to be viewed as sick or degenerate. Paraphilias are (or can be) done by people who make contributions to a society, are well-integrated in it, and have full consent of their sexual partners (i.e., no involvement with children or nonhuman animals). In addition, paraphilias can be done in ways that are neither dangerous nor hurtful for the participants. They can be done in ways that are neither coercive nor exploitative.

Beckmann's (2009) study of individuals involved in the subculture of BDSM (bondage/discipline/sadism/masochism) in London, England, concludes that these individuals are involved in sexual activities that are better understood as sexual variations than as inherent individual pathologies. Members of her sample used bondage, discipline, dominance, and submission, along with the physical and psychological pain that can accompany them, as ways to achieve altered mental states and emotional transcendence. It is true that BDSM sex is rarer than mainstream sex, but it is still found throughout the world and human history. Though at the margins, BDSM can be done in safe and responsible ways, Beckmann's study indicates.

The existence of sadomasochistic sex (SM) between willing partners shows that the same sexual act, no matter how bizarre or dysfunctional it might seem to some individuals, is evaluated in positive or even glowing terms by other individuals. When SM is consensual and done by fully informed adults—as it almost always is—then it is wrong to dismiss it out of hand as evidence of a mental illness or social pathology. For the bulk of SM practitioners, an interest in the sex practice developed well after childhood (i.e., in their twenties or later) and was not a response to some childhood trauma or abuse. The principal way that most SM practitioners get introduced to sadomasochism is by someone else rather than through private discovery and experimentation (Powls & Davies, 2012).

Newmahr (2011) did a participant observation study of sadomasochism being acted out at parties, clubs, and dungeons in various locales in a northeastern U.S. metropolis she calls Caeden. Her findings offer a counterpoint to an approach that paints SM as a sexual deviance that is inherently abnormal and essentially dysfunctional. She reports that sadomasochism is a way for participants to purposefully and voluntarily take extreme risks (physical, psychological, emotional) in the quest for novel experiences (p. 160). Newmahr reaches the arguable conclusion that sadomasochism, as the administration of extreme though controlled violence (e.g., whipping, spanking, beating, caning), expertly delivered, is a form of intimacy that allows females to develop a sense of empowerment by successfully surviving male sadistic acts (p. 183). The Eulenspiegel Society, founded in New York City in 1971, and the Pansexual Society of Janus, founded in San Francisco in 1974, are the oldest and most populated sadomasochistic organizations in the United States (p. 4).

In 2010, the American Psychiatric Association's (APA) Sexual and Gender Disorder work group was petitioned by the National Coalition for Sexual Freedom (NCSF, 2010) to remove all paraphilias from the *DSM-V*, due for release in 2013. The request by NCSF was based on its belief that the decision by the APA to include them in the manual is based on politics instead of science. The NCSF has concluded that BDSM practitioners, fetishists, and cross-dressers are the targets of discrimination, bias, and negative social sanctions because of APA diagnostic decisions.

The social and legal definition of specific forms of sexuality as "unnatural" or "crimes against nature" (technically known as *sodomy*) developed in colonial America to protect women and children—even livestock—from sexual assault, not to regulate the sexual acts of consenting adults, especially when they were done in private. However, the promise of greater political freedoms and economic prosperity attracted waves of immigrants to the United States. Sodomy laws were used increasingly against ethnic and racial minorities whenever necessary to maintain a generally conservative social order and the conventional morality on which it was based. Although sodomy laws were sometimes used to regulate the private sex acts of heterosexuals, their principal objective was to suppress the sexuality of homosexuals, particularly gay men (Eskridge, 2008). Gays experienced so much persecution at the hands of heterosexuals that they learned that they would have to hide their sexual orientation, establishing an identity-based community that was separate from heterosexual society (Adam, 1987).

A study of global trends in the criminal regulation of sexuality (rape, sodomy, adultery, and sexual abuse of children), in 194 nation-states from 1945 to 2005, clarifies what is a complex relationship (Frank, Camp, & Boutcher, 2010). A primary factor has been the worldwide movement away from the view that sex is only for reproduction and toward the view that sex is an expressive and enjoyable activity, tied to individual needs and personal

pleasures (p. 887). A principal decision rule in deciding whether to criminalize and punish some sexual act has been whether it was voluntary for its
participants. Consensual sex is treated more leniently, while sexuality that is
coercive and nonconsensual—or is viewed that way—is treated more
severely. (For example, adult-to-adult incest is more often defined as consensual and treated more leniently than is adult-to-child incest, which is more
often viewed as coercive and so sanctioned more severely.) The global trend
toward making the independent person the foundation of social order meant
that characteristics of families, communities, societies, and nations became
less important reasons for changing global sex laws.

Rigid rules of sexual conduct, coupled with punitive sanctions, have the
primary effect of causing individuals to talk less and less about their sexuality and to conduct their sexual activities with greater caution and secrecy
(Gay, 1986, pp. 201–202). It is less likely that a valued and enjoyable sexual
practice, done in private, will be given up no matter how harsh the penalties.
The restrictions on sexual expression in nineteenth-century U.S. culture were
rigid and uncompromising. Chastity before marriage and fidelity after it
were cultural imperatives. Sexual moderation was expected, and sexual
intercourse was allowed only if it was intended to lead to the birth of a child.
However, cultural rules against forbidden sex (e.g., masturbation, oral sex,
anal sex) were not as absolute as they appeared. Nineteenth-century
Americans enjoyed a wide range of sexual pleasures, and they privately
rejected the ideal culture that called for a monotonous and unemotional sex
life (Lystra, 1989, pp. 101–102).

Kinsey's studies of sexuality (Kinsey et al., 1948, 1953) indicated that the
sexual activities of Americans were far more flexible and diverse than ideal
culture permitted and more so than most people suspected. By the middle
of the twentieth century, ideal culture itself started to change. More was
learned about sexual pleasure and the multitude of ways that humans could
achieve it. Conception could be separated from sexual pleasure as more and
better methods of birth control became available. The double standard
began to erode as women experienced some movement away from their
traditional position as caretakers of home and children to seek their fortunes in jobs and attain advanced degrees in colleges and universities.
Homosexuals and prostitutes became better organized and more insistent
that they be left alone because their sexuality was their business and nobody
else's (Bullough, 1976, p. 635).

People felt freer than they ever had to embark on their own journey into
sexuality and to use their imaginations to discover new sources of sexual
pleasure with less concern for what prevailing sexual standards dictated.
People became confident (or brazen) enough to divulge publicly that they

violated traditional sexual standards at least some of the time. The acclamation of sexuality as a pleasurable and important human experience for both males and females went a long way toward legitimating the kinds of sexual experimentation—collective and individual—that would have been considered serious sexual deviance in earlier times (Peiss & Simmons, 1989, pp. 4–5).

Sexual Politics and the Transformation of Intimacy

As the twentieth century churned on, the whiff of revolution was in the air. Sexuality became more open and pleasure-oriented than it ever had been before. People discussed and reflected on sexual matters incessantly and publicly while they reassured one another that sexuality was a private and largely insignificant pastime (Foucault, 1978, p. 35). Women's pursuit of sexual pleasure, more effective contraceptive techniques, and changing feminine identities were correlated with increasing tensions between males and females, as well as between the young and the not-so-young (Giddens, 1992). Problems surrounding teenage pregnancy, both probable and improbable, were used as a way to justify the regulation of the sexuality of adolescent females because moral and medical controls were becoming less effective (Nathanson, 1991, pp. 163–164). People used sexuality as a way to achieve self-liberation and find rewarding personal experiences (Quadagno & Fobes, 1995, p. 183).

The civil rights movement and the Black Freedom movement provided the opportunity for both white and black females to liberate themselves from traditional sex roles and a stifling femininity by challenging male chauvinism, patriarchy, and the double standard through organizing demonstrations, giving speeches, and writing essays for public outlets (Giardina, 2010). Prominent African American women (e.g., Beyoncé Knowles, Janet Jackson, Jill Scott, Serena Williams, Tyra Banks) became erotic revolutionaries by embodying a "new feminist chic." They are smart, edgy, ambitious, socially conscious, and independent women who embody virtue while they inspire others to work toward greater empowerment, liberation, and sexual agency (Lee, 2010, p. xiv).

When members of the LGBT community engage in political work to further their interests (e.g., marches on Washington), they are most successful when what are multiple and often competing and incompatible concerns and objectives are framed in terms of broader issues of sexual diversity, civil rights, democracy, and public health (HIV/AIDS prevention) (Ghaziani & Baldassarri, 2011, p. 197; Gould, 2009). The outcome of political struggles over discrimination against gays in the workplace and in the military, hate crime laws, same-sex marriage/marriage equality, partnership benefits, adoption rights, and antisodomy laws reflects many things, some of which are unique to the particular issue in question. The elements that coalesce around the same-sex marriage issue, for example, are not identical to those that coalesce around survivor benefits or the passing of laws against gay-bashing. The outcome of any particular enterprise to further gay rights and opportunities is affected by how threatening the general public perceives the issue to be, how threatening politicians *think* the general public perceives it to be, and the political environment at a given place and time. What is most beneficial for gays and their interests is whether politicians will be encouraged to join the movement to further gay rights and opportunities and whether the judicial branch will play a proactive role in advancing them (Barclay, Bernstein, & Marshall, 2009; Mucciaroni, 2008).

Battles over the legality and morality of same-sex marriage will be a constant feature on the political and social landscape in the years ahead. This issue has been used by gays to further their interests more broadly in regard to equality and social acceptance (Taylor et al., 2009). Intolerance of same-sex marriage is highest in areas characterized by traditional gender roles, high rates of residential instability, high crime rates, and low levels of home ownership. These are sites of weak or nonexistent social capital. Residents are inclined to define same-sex marriages as yet one more threat to their interests and values at a time and place where they already feel weak and vulnerable. Though they may not know what to do about high crime rates or neighborhood instability, they do know what to do about same-sex marriage when given the opportunity to vote on the issue: reject it (McVeigh & Diaz, 2009).

The 2012 U.S. election was a historic one for gay equality, at least as far as marriage is concerned. The electorate in three states (Maryland, Maine, and Washington) voted to legalize same-sex marriage. The electorate in a fourth state (Minnesota), while not voting for marriage equality, did vote against a measure that would have amended the state constitution to read that marriage is only between a man and a woman. Though a minority of states already did recognize civil unions between same-sex couples, and an even smaller minority already had legalized same-sex marriage, this is the first time that same-sex marriage was approved in any U.S. state by a popular vote. Opponents of same-sex marriage predicted that legalizing it will lead to increasing homosexuality in schools, as well as endangering the entire fabric of the nation. Only further research and the passage of time will allow us to know how legalization of same-sex marriage in U.S. states will affect the entire nation.

With the arrival of what Janus and Janus (1993) called the *second sexual revolution* in the early 1980s, the casual sex of previous years was replaced by something close to a sexual anarchy. The cornerstones were increased sexual activities among the mature and older adult generations and the practice of more and more far-side sexual deviance. In a process of defining deviancy down, people were prepared to accept sexual activities among others—or even to try some themselves—that would have been extremely shocking to the moral sensibilities of earlier times (pp. 15–17). The specter of AIDS and other sexually transmitted diseases was one restraint (Burroway, 2010), but even the prospect of contracting a communicable—or even potentially fatal—disease was not enough for people to substantially alter their sexual activities. Sexual pleasure was just too important to individuals for them to allow too much to interfere with their pursuit of it.

The nuclear, heterosexual, patriarchal family, firmly ensconced in the middle-class U.S. home, at one time defined the American experience. It was considered to be one of the best ways to ensure social order and individual morality (Lewis, 2010). Whether it was a crusade against gambling, abortion, pornography, contraceptive devices, or even the dangers of skating rinks (where females might fall, assuming improper poses—feet in the air and clothing in disarray—which could lead to all kinds of mischief), the family was expected to play a pivotal role in social stability and whatever social reforms were necessary. The family has always played an important role in the way that class relationships are reproduced (Beisel, 1997).

The move toward greater sexual equality stalled a bit by the mid-1990s (Cotter, Hermsen, & Vanneman, 2011). The idea of co-nurturing was replaced by a view that the mother must once again become the pivotal player in the parenting trip. *The Battle Hymn of the Tiger Mother* (Chua, 2011) was originally supposed to be Chua's glorification of the skill of Chinese parents as compared to Western parents to raise their children. It became a book that glorified highly authoritarian and rigid, demanding and unyielding, *mother-centered* child-rearing techniques as the road to raising successful and perfect kids. (Chua's two daughters were only allowed to play the violin or piano and were never allowed to attend a sleepover or have a playdate.) The book could easily have been titled *A Message to My Daughters: My Way or the Highway.*

A counterpoint to tiger mothering is *attachment parenting.* Mothers still play the pivotal role, but a very different relationship exists between mother and child than is found between tiger moms and their cubs. Attachment parenting is fundamentally and totally child-centered (Sears & Sears, 2003). (Tiger mothering is based on the principle that the child must do the bidding of the mother no matter what she says because it is she who knows what is in the best interests of the child.) The trifecta of attachment parenting is a lengthy period of breastfeeding (sometimes for years, even into toddlerhood); co-sleeping (in the mother's bed or in a bed next to hers); and wearing (use of baby slings to keep infants in constant contact with their mothers and their mothers' body rhythms). Children are in charge, and every cry is considered to be a cry for help. These cries can only be ignored at the peril of both mother and child.

Attachment mothering, due to its intensity (derisively called "helicopter parenting" by its critics), puts mothers in a position where they are pressured to select either motherhood or careers. The response to this role conflict has *not* entailed a simple reversion back to the double standard of the 1950s where dads bring home the bacon and moms fry it up in a pan while raising children. The response has been a rise of a cultural frame of *egalitarian essentialism*. This allows mothers to stay at home to follow the principles of attachment parenting while still thinking that they embody the feminist ideals of choice and equality.

> We believe this cultural explanation [egalitarian essentialism] is . . . consistent with the broader changes that . . . shifted in the mid-1990s. Married mothers' labor force participation began to decline at about the same time. Women's entry into previously male occupations slowed in the 1990s. Even women's state-level political office holding seems to have peaked in that decade. The gender gap in earnings that had been narrowing since the late 1970s stopped changing in the 1990s. The convergence in husbands' and wives' housework time stopped well short of equality. (Cotter et al., 2011, pp. 261–262)

One outcome of these sociocultural changes has been a "mommy war," in which a central conflict has been between working mothers and stay-at-home mothers. Attachment mothers insisted that what seemed to be traditional gender roles and a sexual double standard really were not.

Attachment parenting was justified—if it needed to be justified at all—as a type of child rearing that was in the best interest of both the child and mother. Even though women gave up their career aspirations (at least for a while), making the family look traditional and the relationships between spouses seem unequal, this was an incorrect view. It was not a betrayal of the sisterhood. Because women's decision to stay at home to raise their children was voluntary and done in the best interest of their children, not specifically to further their husbands' career goals, it was both reasonable and constructive. The division of labor between husband and wife represented less an endorsement of tradition and the double standard than it did a new and better way to raise children.

Marriage does not have the same function or fascination that it once did—at least for some individuals—and family life is becoming increasingly diverse (Bergstrand & Sinski, 2010; Fox, 2009). In this setting, it becomes even more difficult to define alternate lifestyles (e.g., swinging or gay marriage) as inherently pathological and dysfunctional. Fewer people are getting married now than in the last century, more children are being born out of wedlock, and college graduates are now more likely to marry than are those individuals who never went to college (Luscombe, 2010). For women who are inclined to marry, their objective is not simply to find a mate. It is to have a *good* marriage, or the trade-off of giving up their independence is not worth it. Women want careers, good marriages, and children, but they realize it will be difficult to have all three successfully. More than ever before, modern U.S. women want to be able to have careers and to use the college degrees they have earned (Regnerus & Uecker, 2011).

Men were changing too (Aboim, 2010). Part of this change was in response to economic and political changes, and part of it was in response to criticisms of men and traditional masculinity.

> Buffeted by changes not of their making, increasingly anxious in an economic and political arena that erodes their ability to be breadwinners and confused by new demands about emotional responsiveness and involved fatherhood, men seem uncomfortable in that new spotlight, shifting uncomfortably, shielding their eyes, even railing against the glare. (Kimmel, 2010, p. 2)

As masculinity became ever more difficult for men to figure out, let alone embody, the declaration that full equality between the sexes offered the only real possibility for personal growth and social progress seemed truer than ever. A strong argument was made that gender equality is in the best interests of both sexes and that the transformation of masculinity would enrich both males and females. It was promised that it would lead to a greater capacity among men to develop richer emotional lives (Kimmel, p. 11). Modern intimacy, however, is filled with a multitude of anxieties and difficulties (Miller, 1995, pp. 12–13).

Deviantizing Sexual Matters

Moral enterprises have existed, do exist, and will continue to exist in regard to sexual matters. Whether it is gay marriage, erectile dysfunction, teenage pregnancy, pornography, extramarital sex, or cross-dressing, it is clear that patterns of sexuality generate a great deal of social distress and interpersonal anxiety for some people some of the time. Moral enterprises can reach the point of being moral panics, where worry evolves into something more widespread and disturbing (Lancaster, 2011). Some of the concern of moral entrepreneurs over sexuality, of course, may be both reasonable and justified, but history shows us that some of it is silly and irrelevant, nothing more than dust in the wind. At times, the reaction is so disproportionate to the actual threat, it is the *reaction* that is the real problem.

Genital Hysteria

Penis size seems to be a near-universal concern of men (and sometimes of their mates), which generally boils down to "the bigger the better" (at least up to a point). It is no surprise, then, that if males think that their penises are shriveling up and disappearing, it would cause enough concern, anxiety, and fear to qualify as a moral panic. Women, too, share a similar fear, but with different organs (i.e., vulvas, breasts, and nipples).

> In parts of Asia, entire regions are occasionally overwhelmed by terror-stricken men who believe that their penises are shriveling up or retracting into their bodies. Those affected often take extreme measures and place clamps or string onto the precious organ or have family members hold the penis in relays until an appropriate treatment is obtained, often from native healers. Occasionally women are affected, believing their breasts or vaginas [i.e., vulvas] are being sucked into their bodies. Episodes can endure for weeks or months and affect thousands. (Bartholomew, 2008, pp. 79–80)

The shrinking of the penis to the point of being absorbed back into the body—or the belief that this is what is happening—is known as koro (APA, 2000, p. 900). *Koro* is a word of Malayan-Indonesian origin that means "tortoise," which is used because of the similarity between the head and wrinkled neck of a tortoise and the tip and shaft of the human penis.

The belief that penis absorption is possible is widespread in Chinese culture, where medical texts as far back as the 1800s described the reality of penis shrinking and its deadliness if left untreated. (The origin of female anxiety over the absorption of their sex organs is unclear.) A number of "penis panics" occurred in regions of China, Singapore, Thailand, and India in the twentieth century (Bartholomew, 2008). The first well-documented one occurred in the fall of 1967 in Singapore, a small island in Southeastern Asia. Hospitals in the area were treating more and more anxious males who were convinced that they had koro, portending their immediate death. The sufferers had tried a number of remedies themselves—rubber bands and even clothespins—in a futile attempt to stop the shrinkage. The penis panic ended (amid a number of sore and injured penises) when the populace was assured by medical specialists that nothing out of the ordinary was happening. Another penis panic occurred in the Guangdong province of China, starting in 1984 and ending a year later (in August 1985). Approximately 5,000 inhabitants of the region believed they were experiencing genital-shrinking episodes. Between November and December of 1976, approximately 2,000 people in northeastern Thailand thought that they had koro, and in 1982, a koro epidemic occurred in northeastern India, where thousands of males and females were afflicted. A popular local remedy in the Indian epidemic was to have the sufferer hold the affected body part tightly while he or she drank lime juice and was thoroughly soaked with cold water.

Koro has tended to afflict individuals in rural regions of a country who were poorly educated and without much sophistication or an abundance of intellectual skills. However, in the examples given above, sociocultural factors were also at work. Rumors about the rapid spread of koro, coupled with the belief that humans could actually experience the absorption of a body part, set the stage for the panic. It helped that of all body parts, the penis, scrotum, breasts, and nipples, are the most physiologically capable of changing size in response to changes in climate, sexual arousal, stress, depression, anxiety, fear, illness, or the ingestion of certain drugs. Idiosyncratic events (e.g., anxiety) and a cultural system that authenticates koro as a real possibility made it possible for some humans to perceive and then believe that their sexual anatomy was undergoing an unwanted and dangerous transformation. When local remedies failed to work, medical intervention was required. In these cases, the individuals themselves, with the help of group and cultural supports, defined an ordinary and temporary change in sexual anatomy as more ominous than it actually was.

Attacking Autostimulation

Masturbation (also known as *autostimulation* or *automanipulation*) is a regular sexual practice. In one study, 40 percent of females and approximately 60 percent of males (ages 18 to 59) reported that they had masturbated at least once during the previous year; about 25 percent of the male and 10 percent of the female respondents reported that they masturbated at least once a week (Michael et al., 1994, p. 158). The Janus report on human sexuality indicated that 5 percent of the 1,338 males in their sample and 8 percent of the 1,398 females stated that their *preferred* way to achieve orgasm was through masturbation (Janus & Janus, 1993, p. 98). A survey of 223 college undergraduates about their masturbatory activities during the

3 months prior to data collection provides evidence that masturbation is a common way for individuals to achieve sexual pleasure or at least sexual release (Pinkerton, Bogart, Cecil, & Abramson, 2002). These researchers found that 2 percent of the males (*n* = 1) and 36 percent of females (*n* = 40) reported that they had never masturbated, meaning that 98 percent of males and 64 percent of females reported that they had masturbated. Men averaged 12 times per month, and women averaged 5 times per month (p. 111). People who are most likely to masturbate are individuals who have partners with whom they are sexually active (Michael et al., 1994, p. 165). This suggests that individuals with the *fullest* sex life are the ones who are most likely to masturbate.

Both Judaism and Christianity condemn masturbation. (The literal meaning of the word *masturbation* is "self-abuse.") The biblical inspiration for this denunciation is the sin of Onan. Rather than consummate a sexual relationship with his sister-in-law after the death of his brother, Onan spilled his semen on the ground, and the Lord struck him dead for his deed. It is not entirely clear if his sin was masturbation or his failure to honor the custom of *levirate* and impregnate his sister-in-law, but over the years the religious interpretation rigidified, and the cardinal sin of Onan came to be his masturbation. Good Christians quickly learned that all righteous sexuality had to be oriented toward reproduction, and even then it must be done with a minimum of excitement and pleasure. Spending the seed without a good reproductive reason led to tragic results.

The condemnation of masturbation gained a stronger foothold as it went from being branded as badness to sickness. The prevailing and authoritative medical view of human afflictions during the eighteenth century was that good health came from a perfect balance among bodily substances of blood, bile, and sexual fluids. Any practice that upset this balance, the story went, would cause harmful results. Masturbation especially was suspect. Not only did it lack any apparent reproductive purpose, but it also depleted the body of essential fluids and generated far too much excitement in the masturbator. Regardless of the real or imagined consequences of masturbation, its medicalization as a form of disease reflected in part the increasing power of medicine as a moral guide in regard to ethics of the flesh (Laquer, 2003, p. 16). Physicians in the eighteenth century blamed every physical, nervous, and mental illness that they could on masturbation. It is what explained pathological singularity (Foucault, 2003, p. 60).

One cornerstone of any moral crusade against sexuality—and the condemnation of masturbation certainly qualifies—is to disseminate the belief that certain sexual practices are immoral and have dire consequences for *all* of a society (Sherkat & Ellison, 1997, p. 974). Richard von Krafft-Ebing

(1947), a neurologist and psychiatrist born in Germany in the nineteenth century, concluded from his case studies that four categories of sexual deviation existed—masochism, sadism, fetishism, and homosexuality—all of which were abnormal and all of which were caused by masturbation. Male gynecologists were inclined to view women's sexual urges as quite unnecessary or even as dangerous distractions. The most troublesome of the lot was female masturbation. Once a female fell under its spell, all was lost, and her obsession with the "solitary vice" would know no bounds (Barker-Benfield, 1976, pp. 212–274). Even at the beginning of the twentieth century, female masturbation was still seen as a major cause of women's lack of sexual responsiveness in marriage (Jacquart & Thomasset, 1988).

The social reformers of the nineteenth century believed that the only way to halt the creeping social decay that they believed was plaguing U.S. society was for every individual to develop a strong personal moral code, especially with regard to food, drink, and sexuality. A moral man or woman was an individual who was safe from all temptations because of his or her ability to control the ever-present dangers posed by the unholy trinity of sexual desire, stimulating food, and unhealthy practices. No challenge or temptation was so great that it could not be bested by a well-managed body. Sylvester Graham (1794–1851) was confident that total individual control was the one virtue that could truly make people free (cited in Sokolow, 1983, p. 122). Graham's views were supported by others, such as John Harvey Kellogg (1852–1943). Kellogg identified 39 warning signs of masturbation in a book published in 1888 (cited in Money, 1985). Some of these were weakness, untrustworthiness, isolation, bashfulness, unnatural boldness, emaciation, paleness, colorless lips and gums, changes in disposition, underdeveloped breasts (females), gluttony, round shoulders, weak backs, pain in the limbs, stiffness of joints, use of tobacco by boys, acne, fingernail-biting, obscene talk, and bed-wetting (pp. 91–98). Kellogg believed that masturbation was the principal cause of most of the paleness, feebleness, nervousness, and general good-for-nothingness that he saw all around him.

Both Graham and Kellogg had great faith in the power of correct food and proper eating habits to keep humans morally upright. Both believed that masturbators were attracted to excessive amounts of spicy or upsetting foods, such as pepper, salt, cloves, mustard, horseradish, or vinegar. They also believed that chronic masturbators were inclined to consume non-nutritious substances, such as clay or plaster. If chronic masturbators avoided both nutritious and bland foods, as Graham and Kellogg believed, the path to salvation was clear. Masturbation was much less likely if individuals learned proper nutrition at an early age. Graham developed a mild foodstuff called the Graham cracker, and Kellogg developed the cornflake, to help keep individuals from touching themselves in sexual ways (Money, 1985).

If the dietary restrictions were unsuccessful, other things still might work. Parents were instructed to wrap up their children's genitals, cover the genitals with some protective device, or bind their children's hands to make self-touching impossible. Devices were invented and peddled that supposedly would prevent male masturbation. Most of these contraptions combated masturbation by making it difficult, if not impossible, for a male to have an erection. One of these, a large ring with sharp spikes on its inside, was positioned to encircle a male's penis while he slept. If the penis were to become erect (*tumescence*), the spikes would come in contact with the organ, and pain, along with a rapid *detumescence*, would result. Another device was more elaborate and far less painful. It sounded an alarm when an erection occurred, alerting the vigilant, who would take the necessary steps to stop whatever was happening (Gregersen, 1983, p. 30). One treatment that was guaranteed to cure female masturbation was for the masturbator's parents to apply pure carbolic acid to her clitoris (Michael et al., 1994, p. 161).

The rationale for maligning masturbation was based on how it was practiced and how it was understood. It was a sexual practice that was accessible to the young and to *both* boys and girls. The democratic nature of masturbation—its status as equal-opportunity sex, accessible to practically anyone at practically anytime—was compounded by the fact that it was defined as uniquely capable of excess (the "crack cocaine of sexuality," according to Laqueur [2003, p. 21]). The last straw in the demonization of masturbation was that it cut its practitioners off from the world of work and responsibility, moving them into the more dangerous world of fantasy and self-indulgence. Sex panics are less about protecting children, Lancaster (2011, p. 2) instructs, than they are about preserving adults' recollections about childhood—that it is supposed to be a time of innocence and purity.

Most people now define masturbation as relatively harmless, even though about half of the women and men who masturbate still report some guilt over it (Michael et al., 1994, p. 166). (Foucault [2003, p. 59] declares masturbation to be the "universal secret shared by everyone but disclosed to no one.") The comic David Steinberg once divulged on *The Tonight Show* that he felt guilty about his own masturbation. The reason was because he did it so badly (or so he said). Masturbation exists in a changing moral terrain. It is no longer viewed as the road to disease and moral decay. It is not even widely viewed as deviant unless it is excessive and comes to supplant other forms of sexuality that are defined as better and healthier. In general, masturbation is now viewed as a form of self-enhancement instead of self-pollution. However, could another Graham or Kellogg happen along and successfully attach new meanings to old practices?

Maligning Menstruation

A biological event such as *menstruation,* found only among women of a particular age and physical status, is one that can hardly be ignored, certainly not by a woman herself and likely not by her peers, either. The variable meanings attached to this natural event remind us once again that social groups and social relationships must be at the center of our under- standings of what is proper and improper. At some places and times, men- struation was taken as a sign of woman's high status, and menstruating women were treated with respect. Menstrual blood was believed to have the power to cure leprosy, warts, hemorrhoids, epilepsy, and headaches. It was used as a love charm, a sacrifice to the gods, and a protection against evil spirits. A virgin's first menstrual pad was saved and used as a curative for disease. At other places and times, this periodic bleeding was viewed as a sign of contamination and pollution. Pliny, the Roman naturalist, thought that menstrual blood could ruin crops, dull steel knives, make ivory tar- nish, cause iron to rust, and make new wine turn sour. Dogs were supposed to be driven mad from the taste of menstrual blood, and bees supposedly died from it. Women were disallowed from working in the Saigon opium industry in the 1800s because opium was supposed to acquire a bitter taste if menstruating women were near it (Delaney, Lupton, & Toth, 1988, p. 9). At still other places and times, menstruation was viewed as an ordinary part of everyday life, and people did not worry very much about it one way or the other.

Women's ability to produce blood that neither appreciably weakened nor killed them, and that was associated with life and living rather than with death and dying, produced a measure of envy among those men who were willing to think about it at all. Male initiation rites among native popula- tions in Melanesia, Africa, the Americas, and Australia contain rites of pas- sage in which men actually emulate female menstruation by slitting the underside of their penises to facilitate bleeding. Sometimes the incision is short, but at other times it extends the entire length of the shaft (Tannahill, 1992, p. 44). Why would men attempt to simulate female menstruation unless they viewed it as the source of a power that they wanted for them- selves (Knight, 1991, p. 37)?

The way menstruation came to be symbolized—its social construction— reflected, at least in part, the conflicts and struggles between men and women for power and control. Men tried to increase their influence over women by constructing an ideology that defined women as naturally inferior. A cultural establishment of what menstruation meant and how it should be handled by women and responded to by men was a central part of this ideology (Laws, 1990, pp. 28–29). Times and places can be found where women most certainly did suffer a loss of status. They were secluded and isolated in special dwellings where they had little to do other than to handle their menstrual cramps as best they could and follow the rules that regulated only them (Mead, 1949, p. 222).

Even when the seclusion was not entirely voluntary, women may have turned it to their own advantage (Buckley & Gottlieb, 1988, p. 14). It was usually a group event, and it provided opportunities for fellowship, relaxation, and growth. It was a time for women to get in touch with other women while they got in touch with themselves and the rhythms of their own bodies (Hathaway, 1998). The segregation of menstruating women was an important event in the life of the entire community, and men's activities were strongly influenced by the menstrual cycles of women. Some men even had illicit love affairs with menstruating women during their period of isolation (Buckley, 1988).

To those women and men who consider menstruation to be impure and debilitating, here is an alternative view of this very natural process. The biologist Margie Profet (1993) argues that it is most unlikely that women would lose as much blood and tissue as they do, and potentially be incapacitated for so long, simply to slough off unnecessary uterine lining. It is more likely that menstruation also evolved as a way for a female to purge herself of infectious microorganisms (p. 338). Bacteria can be carried from the woman's vagina into her uterus by getting on the heads or tails of swimming sperm, and seminal fluid can transport viruses from the male to the female reproductive organs (p. 341). Menstrual blood offers some protection to a female. It helps remove uterine tissue that might be infected, and it also contains chemicals that kill a wide range of pathogens in the uterus, cervix, vagina, and oviducts (pp. 345–346). This take on menstruation is part of an emerging image of female sexuality. It views females' sexual responses as having evolved to allow them to be sexually active with whomever they like, in rapid succession, without getting sick in the process from any intimate contact that they might have had with unclean or infected males.

> The composite picture is one of a female who seeks sexual pleasure and has developed biological defenses that protect her from the consequences of an active sex life, a creature designed by natural selection to improve her reproductive success by carefully directing her intimate life. (Small, 1995, p. 94)

In this view, the so-called "curse" comes to an end by being defined as more of a blessing.

Some individuals are convinced that the customary views of menstruation are bad for both women and the environment. These *menstrual activists* are convinced that menstruation has been socially constructed as a way to justify the subjugation and control of women. The bedrock of menstrual activism is the belief that menstruation is neither shameful nor unclean, a claim that leads to a critique of the political economy and the environmental impact of the feminine hygiene industry. Some menstrual activists believe that menstruation is an event that is integrative, binding women to one another. It is understood and defined as something to be celebrated instead of cursed or dreaded. Other menstrual activists condemn the feminine hygiene industry for relentless profiteering, manipulation of women, and environmental destruction, all perpetrated under the façade of care and concern for women. Menstrual activists are unified in their commitment to making women aware of the individual and collective injuries that come from defining menstruation as nothing more than an individual matter of discomfort and pain management. It makes women more susceptible to being conned and manipulated by the self-serving strategies of the feminine care industry (Bobel, 2010).

Conclusions

Various possibilities arise from the interplay of biology, personality, culture, and society in regard to attitudes, behaviors, and conditions. When pigeonholes are created, and people and what they do are forced into them, our ability to recognize the full range of human sexual diversity is restricted. When this sexual differentiation is coupled with differences in power between categories, one category of individuals is usually devalued more than the opposite category. Human sexuality—deviant and otherwise—and how it is defined are powerfully influenced by social and cultural factors. Because of this, sexual customs are relative, and the evaluations of sexual experiences and responses are variable.

The distinctive aspect of human sexuality is its relativity, as well as the importance it is given in practically every society. A wide range of things are sexually stimulating to humans, at least some of the time, from sexual intercourse to far-side paraphilias (e.g., necrophilia or coprophilia). Though many varied sexual acts are available to humans, the sex/gender roles that are available in U.S. culture are limited and limiting. Gender benders (like Dorothy/Billy Tipton) do not have easy access to a legitimate institutionalized status.

A crucial part of a relative understanding of sexual deviance is to know about moral enterprises and moral panics in regard to sexual matters. Groups of people develop views of the propriety or impropriety of sexual experiences, and they force these on other groups. Fluctuations in the social meanings of both masturbation and menstruation are particularly instructive. They show us that any human event or practice can be the source of differentiation and evaluation. Depending on place, time, and situation, people's sexual experiences and sex/gender attributes are the objects of reverence, scorn, or anything in between.

The experiences of people who are stigmatized and isolated for their sexual outlooks and sexual interests are not appreciably different from the experiences of people who are scorned for other reasons. Sometimes, humans even become mightily concerned over their own sexuality and do what they can to control what they view as unwanted sexual changes in themselves. This is clear with the genital hysteria and penis panics of the twentieth century. It is also clear in the way menstruation is defined and understood.

References

Aboim, S. (2010). *Plural masculinities: The remaking of the self in private life.* Burlington, VT: Ashgate.

Adam, B. (1987). *The rise of a gay and lesbian movement.* Boston, MA: Twayne.

Adler, P. A., & Adler, P. (2006). The deviance society. *Deviant Behavior, 27,* 129–148.

American Psychiatric Association. (2000). *Diagnostic and statistical manual of mental disorders* (4th ed., text revision). Washington, DC: Author.

Ball, R. A. (2012). Changing images of deviance: Nineteenth-century Canadian anti-prostitution movements. *Deviant Behavior, 33,* 26–39.

Barclay, S., Bernstein, M., & Marshall, A. M. (Eds.). (2009). *Queer mobilizations: LGBT activists confront the law.* New York: New York University Press.

Barker-Benfield, G. J. (1976). *The horrors of the half-known life: Male attitudes toward women and sexuality in nineteenth-century America.* New York, NY: Harper & Row.

Bartholomew, R. (2008). Penis panics. In R. Heiner (Ed.), *Deviance across cultures* (pp. 79–85). New York, NY: Oxford University Press.

Beckmann, A. (2009). *The social construction of sexuality and perversion: Deconstructing sadomasochism.* New York, NY: Palgrave Macmillan.

Beisel, N. (1993). Morals versus art: Censorship, the politics of interpretation, and the Victorian nude. *American Sociological Review, 58,* 145–162.

Beisel, N. (1997). *Imperiled innocents: Anthony Comstock and family reproduction in Victorian America.* Princeton, NJ: Princeton University Press.

Bergstrand, C. R., & Sinski, J. B. (2010). *Swinging in America: Love, sex, and marriage in the 21st century.* Santa Barbara, CA: Praeger.

Bhugra, D. (2008). Paraphilias across cultures. In R. Heiner (Ed.), *Deviance across cultures* (pp. 106–116). New York, NY: Oxford University Press.

Birken, L. (1988). *Consuming desire: Sexual science and the emergence of a culture of abundance, 1871–1914.* Ithaca, NY: Cornell University Press.

Bobel, C. (2010). *New blood: Third-wave feminism and the politics of menstruation.* New Brunswick, NJ: Rutgers University Press.

Brents, B. G., Jackson, C. A., & Hausbeck, K. (2010). *The state of sex: Tourism, sex, and sin in the new American heartland.* New York, NY: Routledge.

Brooks, S. (2010). *Unequal desires: Race and erotic capital in the stripping industry.* Albany: State University of New York Press.

Buckley, T. (1988). Menstruation and the power of Yurok women. In T. Buckley & A. Gottlieb (Eds.), *Blood magic: The anthropology of menstruation* (pp. 187–209). Berkeley: University of California Press.

Buckley, T., & Gottlieb, A. (1988). A critical appraisal of theories of menstrual symbolism. In T. Buckley & A. Gottlieb (Eds.), *Blood magic: The anthropology of menstruation* (pp. 3–50). Berkeley: University of California Press.

Bullough, V. (1976). *Sexual variance in society and history.* New York, NY: Wiley.

Burroway, R. (2010). Schools against AIDS: Secondary school enrollment and cross-national disparities in AIDS death rates. *Social Problems, 57,* 398–420.

Burstyn, L. (1997). Female circumcision comes to America. In L. Salinger (Ed.), *Deviant behavior 97/98* (2nd ed., pp. 19–23). Guilford, CT: Dushkin.

Buss, D. (1994). *The evolution of desire: Strategies of human mating.* New York, NY: Basic Books.

Byne, W. (1994, May). The biological evidence challenged. *Scientific American, 270,* 50–55.

Carrier, J. (2007). Homosexual behavior in cross-cultural perspective. In J. Macionis & N. Benokraitis (Eds.), *Seeing ourselves: Classic, contemporary, and cross-cultural readings in sociology* (7th ed, pp. 204–214). Upper Saddle River, NJ: Pearson/Prentice Hall.

Carter, S., & Sokol, J. (1989). *What really happens in bed: A demystification of sex.* New York, NY: M. Evans.

Chodorow, N. (1994). *Femininities, masculinities, sexualities: Freud and beyond.* Lexington: University Press of Kentucky.

Chua, A. (2011). *Battle hymn of the tiger mother.* New York, NY: Penguin.

Colapinto, J. (2000). *As nature made him: The boy who was raised as a girl.* New York, NY: HarperCollins.

Cornwell, B., & Laumann, E. O. (2011). Network position and sexual dysfunction: Implications of partner betweeness for men. *American Journal of Sociology, 117,* 172–208.

Cotter, D., Hermsen, J. M., & Vanneman, R. (2011). The end of the gender revolution? Gender role attitudes from 1977 to 2008. *American Journal of Sociology, 117,* 259–289.

Davis, M. (1983). *Smut: Erotic reality/obscene ideology.* Chicago, IL: University of Chicago Press.

Delaney, J., Lupton, M. J., & Toth, E. (1988). *The curse: A cultural history of menstruation* (Rev. ed.). Urbana: University of Illinois Press.

Deshotels, T. H., Tinney, M., & Forsyth, C. J. (2012). McSexy: Exotic dancing and institutional power. *Deviant Behavior, 33,* 140–148.

De Waal, F. (2005). *Our inner ape: A leading primatologist explains why we are who we are.* New York, NY: Riverhead Books/Penguin.

Diamond, J. (1997). *Why is sex fun? The evolution of human sexuality.* New York, NY: Basic Books/HarperCollins.

Dorkenoo, E., & Elworthy, S. (2007). Female genital mutilation. In J. Macionis & N. Benokraitis (Eds.), *Seeing ourselves: Classic, contemporary, and cross-cultural readings in sociology* (7th ed., pp. 425–432). Upper Saddle River, NJ: Pearson/Prentice Hall.

Durkin, K., Forsyth, C., & Quinn, J. (2006). Pathological Internet communities: A new direction for sexual deviance research in a post-modern era. *Sociological Spectrum, 26,* 595–606.

Epstein, C. F. (2012). Death by gender. In J. Naughton (Ed.), *Annual editions: Criminal justice 11/12* (35th ed., pp. 38–40). New York, NY: McGraw-Hill.

Eskridge, W. (2008). *Dishonorable passions: Sodomy laws in America, 1861–2003.* New York, NY: Viking.

Fields, J. (2008). *Risky lessons: Sex education and social inequality.* New Brunswick, NJ: Rutgers University Press.

Fine, C. (2010). *Delusions of gender: How our minds, society, and neurosexism create difference.* New York, NY: Norton.

Forsyth, C. (1996). The structuring of vicarious sex. *Deviant Behavior, 17,* 279–295.

Foucault, M. (1978). *The history of sexuality* (Vol. 1). New York, NY: Pantheon.

Foucault, M. (2003). *Abnormal: Lectures at the Collège de France* (V. Marchetti & A. Salomoni, Eds.; G. Burchell, Trans.). New York, NY: Picador.

Fox, B. (2009). *When couples become parents: The creation of gender in the transition to parenthood.* Toronto, Ontario, Canada: University of Toronto Press.

Frank, D. J., Camp, B. J., & Boutcher, S. A. (2010). Worldwide trends in the criminal regulation of sex, 1945–2005. *American Sociological Review, 75,* 867–893.

Gagnon, J., & Simon, W. (1970). Perspectives on the social scene. In J. Gagnon & W. Simon (Eds.), *The sexual scene* (pp. 1–21). New Brunswick, NJ: Transaction Publishers.

Gagnon, J., & Simon, W. (1973). *Sexual conduct.* Chicago, IL: Aldine.

Gates, G. J., & Newport, R. (2012, October 18). Special report: 3.4% of U.S. adults identify as LGBT. Retrieved October 29, 2012, from http://www.gallup.com/poll/158066/special-report-adults-identify-lgbt.aspx

Gay, P. (1986). *The tender passion: The bourgeois experience, Victoria to Freud* (Vol. 2). New York, NY: Oxford University Press.

Ghaziani, A., & Baldassarri, D. (2011). Cultural anchors and the organization of differences: A multi-method analysis of LGBT marches on Washington. *American Sociological Review, 76,* 179–206.

Giardina, C. (2010). *Freedom for women: Forging the women's liberation movement, 1953–1970.* Gainesville: University Press of Florida.

Giddens, A. (1992). *The transformation of intimacy: Sexuality, love and eroticism in modern societies.* Stanford, CA: Stanford University Press.

Goode, E., & Troiden, R. (Eds.). (1974). *Sexual deviance and sexual deviants.* New York, NY: William Morrow.

Gould, D. (2009). *Moving politics: Emotion and ACT UP's fight against AIDS.* Chicago, IL: University of Chicago Press.

Gray, M. L. (2009). *Out in the country: Youth, media, and queer visibility in rural America.* New York: New York University Press.

Gregersen, E. (1983). *Sexual practices: The story of human sexuality.* New York, NY: Franklin Watts.

Haney, L. (2010). *Offending women: Power, punishment, and the regulation of desire.* Berkeley: University of California Press.

Hardy, K., Kingston, S., & Sanders, T. (Eds.). (2010). *New sociologies of sex work.* Burlington, VT: Ashgate.

Hathaway, N. (1998). Blood rites: Myths, taboos, and the eternal rhythm of the female body. In L. Salinger (Ed.), *Deviant behavior 98/99* (3rd ed., pp. 22–25). Guilford, CT: Dushkin.

Hennen, P. (2008). *Fairies, bears, and leathermen: Men in community queering the masculine.* Chicago, IL: University of Chicago Press.

Holland, S. (2010). *Pole dancing, empowerment and embodiment.* New York, NY: Palgrave Macmillan.

Holmes, M. (Ed.). (2009). *Critical intersex.* Burlington, VT: Ashgate.

Holmes, S. T., & Holmes, R. M. (2009). *Sex crimes: Patterns and behaviors* (3rd ed.). Thousand Oaks, CA: Sage.

Irvine, J. (1990). *Disorders of desire: Sex and gender in modern American sexology.* Philadelphia, PA: Temple University Press.

Jacquart, D., & Thomasset, C. (1988). *Sexuality and medicine in the Middle Ages.* Cambridge, UK: Polity.

Janus, S., & Janus, C. (1993). *The Janus report on sexual behavior.* New York, NY: Wiley.

Jordan-Young, R. M. (2010). *Brain storm: The flaws in the science of sex differences.* Cambridge, MA: Harvard University Press.

Kelly, G. F. (2011). *Sexuality today* (10th ed.). New York, NY: McGraw-Hill.

Kemper, T. (1990). *Social structure and testosterone.* New Brunswick, NJ: Rutgers University Press.

Kessler, S. (1998). *Lessons from the intersexed.* New Brunswick, NJ: Rutgers University Press.

Kimmel, M. (1996). *Manhood in America: A cultural history.* New York, NY: Free Press.

Kimmel, M. (2000). *The gendered society.* New York, NY: Oxford University Press.

Kimmel, M. (2010). *Misframing men: The politics of contemporary masculinities.* New Brunswick, NJ: Rutgers University Press.

Kinsey, A. C., Pomeroy, W. B., & Martin, C. E. (1948). *Sexual behavior in the human male*. Philadelphia, PA: W. B. Saunders.

Kinsey, A. C., Pomeroy, W. B., Martin, C. E., & Gebhard, P. H. (1953). *Sexual behavior in the human female*. Philadelphia, PA: W. B. Saunders.

Kipnis, L. (2010). *How to become a scandal: Adventures in bad behavior*. New York, NY: Metropolitan Books.

Knight, C. (1991). *Blood relations: Menstruation and the origins of culture*. New Haven, CT: Yale University Press.

Krafft-Ebing, R. von. (1947). *Psychopathia sexualis* (12th ed.). New York, NY: Pioneer.

Lancaster, R. N. (2011). *Sex panic and the punitive state*. Berkeley: University of California Press.

Laqueur, T. W. (2003). *Solitary sex: A cultural history of masturbation*. Brooklyn, NY: Zone Books.

Laumann, E. O., Gagnon, J. H., Michael, R. T., & Michaels, S. (1994). *The social organization of sexuality: Sexual practices in the United States*. Chicago, IL: University of Chicago Press.

Laws, S. (1990). *Issues of blood: The politics of menstruation*. New York, NY: Macmillan.

Lee, S. (2010). *Erotic revolutionaries: Black women, sexuality, and popular culture*. Lanham, MD: Hamilton Books.

Lemelle, Jr., A. J. (2010). *Black masculinity and sexual politics*. New York, NY: Routledge.

LeVay, S. (1993). *The sexual brain*. Cambridge, MA: MIT Press.

Lewis, C. H. (2010). *Prescription for heterosexuality: Sexual citizenship in the Cold War era*. Chapel Hill: University of North Carolina Press.

Lewontin, R. (2000). *It ain't necessarily so: The dream of the human genome and other illusions*. New York, NY: New York Review of Books.

Lewontin, R., Rose, S., & Kamin, L. (1984). *Not in our genes: Biology, ideology, and human nature*. New York, NY: Pantheon.

Logan, T. D. (2010). Personal characteristics, sexual behaviors, and male sex work: A quantitative approach. *American Sociological Review, 75*, 679–704.

Luscombe, B. (2010). Marriage: What's it good for? *Time, 176*, 48–56.

Lystra, K. (1989). *Searching the heart: Women, men, and romantic love in nineteenth-century America*. New York, NY: Oxford University Press.

Maccoby, E. (1998). *The two sexes: Growing up apart, coming together*. Cambridge, MA: Belknap Press of Harvard University Press.

Mackie, G. (1996). Ending footbinding and infibulation: A convention account. *American Sociological Review, 61*, 999–1017.

Maratea, R. J. (2011). Screwing the pooch: Legitimizing accounts in a zoophilia on-line community. *Deviant Behavior, 32*, 918–943.

Martin, K. (1998). Becoming a gendered body: Practices of preschools. *American Sociological Review, 63*, 494–511.

McCarthy, B., & Grodsky, E. (2011). Sex and school: Adolescent sexual intercourse and education. *Social Problems, 58*, 213–234.

McVeigh, R., & Diaz, M. E. D. (2009). Voting to ban same-sex marriage: Interests, values, and communities. *American Sociological Review, 74,* 891–915.

Mead, M. (1949). *Male and female: A study of the sexes in a changing world.* New York, NY: William Morrow.

Michael, R. T., Gagnon, J. H., Laumann, E. O., & Kolata, G. (1994). *Sex in America: A definitive study.* Boston, MA: Little, Brown.

Middlebrook, D. (1998). *Suits me: The double life of Billy Tipton.* Boston, MA: Houghton Mifflin.

Miller, M. V. (1995). *Intimate terrorism: The crisis of love in an age of disillusion.* New York, NY: Norton.

Money, J. (1985). *The destroying angel.* Buffalo, NY: Prometheus.

Money, J. (1988, February). The development of sexual orientation. *Harvard Medical School Mental Health Letter, 4,* 1–4.

Money, J., & Tucker, P. (1975). *Sexual signatures: On being a man or a woman.* Boston, MA: Little, Brown.

Moon, D. (1995). Insult and inclusion: The term fag hag and gay male "community." *Social Forces, 74,* 487–510.

Moore, R. I. (1987). *The formation of a persecuting society: Power and deviance in Western Europe, 950–1250.* New York, NY: Basil Blackwell.

Mucciaroni, G. (2008). *Same sex, different politics: Success and failure in the struggles over gay rights.* Chicago, IL: University of Chicago Press.

Nathanson, C. (1991). *Dangerous passage: The social control of sexuality in women's adolescence.* Philadelphia, PA: Temple University Press.

National Coalition for Sexual Freedom (NCSF). (2010). *DSM-V Revision Project.* Retrieved August 30, 2012, from https://ncsfreedom.org/key-programs/dsm-v-revision-project/dsm-v-program-page.html

Newmahr, S. (2011). *Playing on the edge: Sadomasochism, risk, and intimacy.* Bloomington: Indiana University Press.

Park, A. (2008, June 17). What the gay brain looks like. *Time.* Retrieved December 20, 2009, from http://www.time.com/time/printout/0,8816,1815538,00.html

Pasko, L. (2009). Naked power: Stripping as a confidence game. In P. Adler & P. Adler (Eds.), *Constructions of deviance: Social power, context, and interaction* (6th ed., pp. 476–484). Belmont, CA: Thomson Wadsworth.

Peiss, K., & Simmons, C. (1989). Passion and power: An introduction. In K. Peiss & C. Simmons (Eds.), *Passion and power: Sexuality in history.* Philadelphia, PA: Temple University Press.

Pinkerton, S. D., Bogart, L. M., Cecil, H., & Abramson, P. R. (2002). Factors associated with masturbation in a collegiate sample. *Journal of Psychology and Human Sexuality, 14,* 103–121.

Plemons, E. (2010). Envisioning the body in relation: Finding sex, changing sex. In L. J. Moore & M. Kosut (Eds.), *The body reader: Essential social and cultural readings* (pp. 317–328). New York: New York University Press.

Potter, R. H., & Potter, L. A. (2009). The cyberporn and child sexual predator moral panic. In P. Adler & P. Adler (Eds.), *Constructions of deviance: Social power, context, and interaction* (6th ed., pp. 176–183). Belmont, CA: Thomson Wadsworth.

Powls, J., & Davies, J. (2012). A descriptive review of research relating to sadomasochism: Considerations for clinical practice. *Deviant Behavior, 33,* 223–234.

Profet, M. (1993, September). Menstruation as a defense against pathogens transported by sperm. *Quarterly Review of Biology, 68,* 335–386.

Quadagno, J., & Fobes, C. (1995). The welfare state and the cultural reproduction of gender: Making good girls and boys in the Job Corps. *Social Problems, 42,* 171–190.

Regnerus, M., & Uecker, J. (2011). *Premarital sex in America: How young Americans meet, mate, and think about marrying.* New York, NY: Oxford University Press.

Reiss, I. (1986). *Journey into sexuality.* Englewood Cliffs, NJ: Prentice Hall.

Ridley, M. (1993). *The Red Queen: Sex and the evolution of human nature.* New York, NY: Penguin.

Rosewarne, L. (2011). *Part-time perverts: Sex, pop culture, and kink management.* Santa Barbara, CA: Praeger.

Saadawi, N. (1982). *The hidden face of Eve: Women in the Arab world.* Boston, MA: Beacon.

Sandywell, B. (2006). Monsters in cyberspace: Cyberphobia and cultural panic in the information age. *Information, Communication & Society, 9,* 39–61.

Sanger, T. (2010). *Trans people's partnerships: Towards an ethics of intimacy.* New York, NY: Palgrave Macmillan.

Scheitle, C. P., & Hahn, B. B. (2011). From the pews to policy: Specifying Evangelical Protestantism's influence on states' sexual orientation policies. *Social Forces, 89,* 913–934.

Schur, E. (1988). *The Americanization of sex.* Philadelphia, PA: Temple University Press.

Sears, W., & Sears, M. (2003). *The baby book: Everything you need to know about your baby—from birth to age two* (2nd ed., Rev. ed.). Boston, MA: Little, Brown.

Seidman, S. (1991). *Romantic longings: Love in America, 1830–1980.* New York, NY: Routledge.

Sherkat, D., & Ellison, C. (1997). The cognitive structure of a moral crusade: Conservative Protestantism and opposition to pornography. *Social Forces, 75,* 957–982.

Shneer, D., & Aviv, C. (Eds.). (2006). *American queer, now and then.* Boulder, CO: Paradigm.

Simons, G. (1982). *The illustrated book of sexual records.* New York, NY: Delilah Books/Putnam.

Small, M. (1995). *What's love got to do with it? The evolution of human mating.* New York, NY: Anchor.

Sokolow, J. (1983). *Eros and modernization: Sylvester Graham, health reform, and the origins of Victorian sexuality in America.* Rutherford, NJ: Fairleigh Dickinson University Press.

Spain, D. (1992). *Gendered spaces.* Chapel Hill: University of North Carolina Press.

Steele, V. (1996). *Fetish: Fashion, sex & power.* New York, NY: Oxford University Press.

Stoller, R. (1979). *Sexual excitement: Dynamics of erotic life.* New York, NY: Pantheon.

Stoller, R. (1985). *Observing the erotic imagination.* New Haven, CT: Yale University Press.

Streeter, T. (2011). *The net effect: Romanticism, capitalism, and the Internet.* New York: New York University Press.

Tannahill, R. (1992). *Sex in history* (Rev. ed.). Chelsea, MI: Scarborough House.

Tavris, C. (1992). *The mismeasure of woman.* New York, NY: Simon & Schuster.

Taylor, V., Kimport, K., Van Dyke, N., & Andersen, E. A. (2009). Culture and mobilization: Tactical repertoires, same-sex weddings, and the impact on gay activism. *American Sociological Review, 74,* 865–890.

Tewksbury, R. (1994). Gender construction and the female impersonator: The process of transforming "he" to "she." *Deviant Behavior, 15,* 27–43.

Tewksbury, R. (1996). Cruising for sex in public places: The structure and language of men's hidden, erotic worlds. *Deviant Behavior, 17,* 1–19.

Tiefer, L. (1978, July). The kiss. *Human Nature, 1,* 29–37.

Van Buren, A. (1981). *The best of Dear Abby.* Kansas City, MO: Andrews McMeel.

Wade, L. (2011). The politics of acculturation: Female genital cutting and the challenge of building multicultural democracies. *Social Problems, 58,* 518–537.

Weinberg, M., & Williams, C. (1994). *Dual attraction: Understanding bisexuality.* New York, NY: Oxford University Press.

Weinberg, M., Williams, C., & Laurent, B. (2005). Medicalizing and demedicalizing hermaphroditism. In E. Rubington & M. Weinberg (Eds.), *Deviance: The interactionist perspective* (9th ed., pp. 472–486). Boston, MA: Allyn & Bacon.

West, C., & Zimmerman, D. (2000). Doing gender. In M. Kimmel (Ed.) (with A. Aronson), *The gendered society reader* (pp. 131–149). New York, NY: Oxford University Press.

Wijngaard, M. van den. (1997). *Reinventing the sexes: The biomedical construction of femininity and masculinity.* Bloomington: Indiana University Press.

Williams, W. (1986). *The spirit and the flesh: Sexual diversity in American Indian culture.* Boston, MA: Beacon.

Wolf, N. (2012). *Vagina: A new biography.* New York, NY: HarperCollins.

Ziv, L. (1997). The tragedy of female circumcision: One woman's story. In L. Salinger (Ed.), *Deviant behavior 97/98* (2nd ed., pp. 9–12). Guilford, CT: Dushkin.

9

Drugs and Drug Taking

The Social Reality of Drug Use

Get any textbook on drugs, and you will find that a *drug* is defined as a chemical substance that, when ingested, alters or changes the functioning of the mind or body. A textbook definition of drug gives the impression—incorrectly, as it turns out—that drugs have uniform and universal characteristics that make it possible for them to be classified as drugs. The truth is that no single uniform feature is found in all the substances called drugs that differentiates them from all the substances called nondrugs, except that all drugs have been classified as drugs by somebody.

> Some drugs, such as heroin, alcohol, valium, nicotine, and caffeine, may lead to withdrawal symptoms upon discontinuance of use; but drugs such as peyote, LSD, and marijuana do not. Some drugs, such as cocaine and amphetamines, stimulate the central nervous system while others, such as barbiturates and alcohol, depress it. Some drugs have medicinal value, others have none at all. In fact, efforts to argue that drugs are defined by their action on our bodies or mind[s] lead only into absurdity since everything we eat and drink is a chemical that affects our bodies and minds. (Matveychuk, 1986, p. 9)

The naming of some substance as a drug or a drug of abuse is a highly relative, value-laden, culture-specific, often personal judgment, and it cannot be separated either from the sociocultural context or from who is doing the defining. Practically any claim about drugs is contentious, and discussions about drugs are almost always highly charged.

The Greek word for drug, *pharmakon,* contained three images: The substance was a poison (bad), a remedy (good), or a magical amulet (wonderful). Drugs and drug use have been viewed in many different and often contradictory ways: as demonic, deadly, enslaving, monstrous, curative, spiritual, liberating, fun, or interesting (Montagne, 1988, pp. 418–419). It seems to be true that one group's medicine can be another group's poison and vice versa. A former Mississippi lawmaker and judge named Noah Sweat, Jr. (a.k.a. "Old Soggy") gave a short speech on the floor of the Mississippi state legislature in 1952. It was prompted by the issue of legalizing alcohol. The speech was masterful in the way it reconciled contradictory views of the drug by allowing Sweat to declare that he was *both* emphatically against whisky and emphatically for it. He shows how to straddle a fence with style and a satiric flair (Safire, 1997, p. 876), while showing that drugs can have multiple meanings. (His nickname "Old Soggy" came not from his love of liquor but from "sorghum top" because his appearance resembled a sugar cane plant.)

> If when you say "whisky" you mean the devil's brew, the poison scourge, the bloody monster that defiles innocence, dethrones reason, destroys the home, creates misery and poverty, yea, literally takes the bread from the mouths of little children; if you mean the evil drink that topples the Christian man and woman from the pinnacle of righteous, gracious living into the bottomless pit of degradation, and despair, and shame, and helplessness, and hopelessness—then certainly I am against it.
>
> But, if when you say "whisky" you mean the oil of conversation, the philosophic wine, the ale that is consumed when good fellows get together, that puts a song in their hearts and laughter on their lips, and the warm glow of contentment in their eyes; if you mean Christmas cheer; if you mean the stimulating drink that puts the spring into the old gentleman's step on a frosty, crispy morning; if you mean the drink that enables a man to magnify his joy, and his happiness, and to forget, if only for a little while, life's great tragedies, and heartaches, and sorrows; if you mean that drink the sale of which pours into our treasuries untold millions of dollars, which are used to provide tender care for our little crippled children, our blind, our deaf, our dumb, our pitiful aged and inform [*sic*]; to build highways and hospitals and schools—then certainly I am for it.
>
> This is my stand. I will not retreat from it. I will not compromise. (Sweat, addressing the Mississippi state legislature, 1952, quoted in Safire, p. 877)

It practically goes without saying that with a little effort and some fine-tuning, Old Soggy's speech could be extended to cover practically *any* chemical substance, not just whisky.

If the term *drug* is slippery, then the term *drug abuse* is even slipperier. Even if it is true that the use of a particular drug can be harmful to users—what chemical substance couldn't be abused if the user were to try hard enough?—the potential for harm is not the only or even the principal reason that one drug is branded as a substance of abuse and another is not. Scientific evidence about the harmfulness of a particular drug almost always comes *after* the declaration by authorities that it is a drug of abuse (Szasz, 1985). "People in positions of social responsibility have greater credibility and authority to prove, create and maintain their reality, while some have no credibility and must suffer the consequences of the reality created by others" (Matveychuk, 1986, p. 11).

Cultural meanings and personal experiences work together to help drug users perceive, interpret, discuss, respond to, and remember the pharmacological actions of drugs (Montagne, 1988, p. 420). This symbolic universe of discourse also makes it possible for drug users to share their private experiences with drugs with other people. Those societies that have an extensive drug-user culture are the ones most likely to provide users with positive images of their drug experience. Where this user culture is absent or poorly developed, an antidrug message is more common, and drug effects are more likely to be portrayed as dangerous and debilitating. Even users themselves may hold negative views of their own drug experiences (Becker, 1967).

Every drug experience reflects a user's expectations and experiences with regard to a chemical substance, called the *set,* as well as the *setting,* the history of where a chemical substance has been used, with whom, when, and why (Weil, 1972). The sociocultural environment and its repository of meanings and understandings, as well as a user's accumulated experiences with a particular drug, introduce a great deal of variability and relativity into *every* drug experience.

> To assume that the biochemical properties of a drug are the sole or major cause of drug behavior ignores the cultural and social variability of drug behavior and experience. In order to understand this variability, we must examine the individual's expectation of drug effects and the physical and social environment in which the drug is taken. (Matveychuk, 1986, p. 7)

Molecular structure of a drug is one factor that will help to determine its effects, but pharmacological effects of any drug are always mediated by social meanings, social contexts, and social relationships. The reality of drugs, drug use, and drug abuse is a socially constructed one. Images of the addict and addiction in the popular media usually stress the damage that drugs do to the body, both in regard to how the "addicted" body looks and how it functions. The addict is usually portrayed as a marginal "other," both geographically (i.e., a threat from abroad) and socially (Huggins, 2010, pp. 385–386).

Getting Stoned in the Animal Kingdom

Our human ancestors may have learned much of what they knew about intoxication from observing the kinds of effects that nonhuman animals derived from the plants they consumed. Getting "stoned" in the animal kingdom does seem to be influenced by something chemical and physiological because certain substances produce similar effects among dissimilar organisms.

> After sampling the numbing nectar of certain orchids, bees drop to the ground in a temporary stupor, then weave back for more. Birds gorge themselves on inebriating berries, then fly with reckless abandon. Cats eagerly sniff aromatic "pleasure" plants, then play with imaginary objects. Cows that browse special range weeds will twitch, shake, and stumble back to the plants for more. Elephants purposely get drunk on fermented fruits. Snacks on "magic mushrooms" cause monkeys to sit with their heads on their hands in a posture reminiscent of Rodin's *Thinker*. (Siegel, 1989, p. 11)

Siegel labeled intoxication the *fourth drive,* little different from the other basic drives of hunger, thirst, or sex (p. 10). He stated that the fourth drive does not simply motivate organisms to consume external substances to feel good. Rather, it motivates them to attain some altered state, and the direction of that change—up or down or good or bad—is of secondary importance. Sometimes nonhuman animals will stop their regular activities—eating, drinking, mating—and take psychoactive chemicals if they have the chance.

Studies of the drug use of nonhuman animals in the wild are interesting. They suggest that a part of the variation in drug-taking experiences is accounted for by the relationship between biological structures and chemical substances. However, naturalistic studies are flawed. They credit nonhuman animals with far too many human qualities, and they suffer from insurmountable problems of interpretation and measurement. It is impossible to know for sure exactly what is going on when a nonhuman animal gets intoxicated. Because little is known (or knowable) about the creature's needs, its unique biological characteristics, the quality of its group life, how much of a psychoactive drug is in its body, its stresses and strains, its specific body weight, its fat composition, its psychological characteristics, or its temperament, the demonstration that some nonhuman animal is intoxicated tells us little of value about drugs, drug use, or drug abuse.

Laboratory studies of drug-taking behaviors of nonhumans, though more artificial than studies in the wild, allow more precision in determining how drugs work. Test animals in laboratories do engage in drug-taking behaviors when given the opportunity. Monkeys allowed to press a bar to get an injection of morphine (a central nervous system depressant) will press it hundreds of times for one injection even if they only receive a small amount of the drug (Ray & Ksir, 1996, pp. 41–42). Rats, dogs, and several species of monkey will go through a series of complicated physical maneuvers and forgo practically all other pleasures if cocaine is the reward. A laboratory animal might have to press a bar 100 times for its first injection. On subsequent trials, the number of presses is then doubled to 200, 400, 800, and so on. At some point, an animal will either stop responding or be too exhausted to continue, and this is called the *breaking point*. Cocaine's breaking point is 2 to 16 times higher than that for other drugs, and some monkeys have been found to be willing to press a bar 12,800 times for one cocaine injection (Siegel, 1989, pp. 183–185). By contrast, laboratory animals do not seem to like alcohol or tobacco, and they will not use either of them to the point of addiction or dependency. However, humans in their natural settings like these two chemicals quite a lot (Goode, 2008a, p. 436).

Lab studies clearly show that certain drugs are powerfully reinforcing to laboratory animals with free access to them. They may indulge themselves to the point where other pursuits become irrelevant. What the lab studies mean, however, is not as clear. These studies do *not* prove that some inevitable, inexorable, physical addiction process exists to account for compulsive drug use among members of the animal kingdom (Peele, 1985, p. 77). The lab animals may self-administer drugs simply because they are attached to implanted catheters that make it easy for them to get drugs and are frightened, under stress, in pain, and living in overcrowded, uninteresting, and unfamiliar environments. Because these studies maximize the chance that a hapless creature will self-inject drugs, they really do not prove that drug-taking behavior is determined by the properties of drugs, reflecting some uniform breakdown of control. If animal research has any relevance for understanding *human* drug experiences, it is in its demonstration that one important source of a drug habit is a life filled with wretchedness. Humans may develop a drug habit when they do not have the kinds of rewarding experiences or quality relationships that make a drug-free life worth living.

Addiction: Imprecise Definitions and Arbitrary Meanings

How we define or label a human activity affects greatly the way we react to it (Orcutt, 1996). If drug use is classified as an addiction and the user as an addict, this designation alone makes it much less likely that the drug use will be viewed as anything other than a sickness or disease. If it were to be defined in some other way—as sin, psychological malfunction, an outgrowth of social disorganization, a problem in living, a central activity, a form of self-help, or ordinary behavior—it would generate entirely different understandings and evoke entirely different responses. Representing drug use as an addiction makes it appear inexorably and inherently compulsive, self-destructive, and in need of cure. The disease model of drug addiction, Schaler (2000) instructs, was created and actively promoted by individuals who had a lot to gain from widespread acceptance of it.

Before the twentieth century, the word *addiction* was used to refer to a habit that could be *either* good or bad but was most often good. Back then, addiction meant no more than a preference, interest, or inclination that people had (Alexander & Schweighofer, 1988). They might be addicted to religion, hard work, reading, sobriety, their families, or even the devil (Szasz, 1985, pp. 6–7). If addiction were to be viewed as something that could be positive or negative, drug-related or not, then it could be claimed that Beethoven was addicted to music, and da Vinci was addicted to painting; Mickey Mantle was addicted to baseball, and Buddy Holly was addicted to rock and roll; Proust was addicted to writing, and Goethe was addicted to reading. Schaler (2000) describes what he considers one of the most difficult and uncomfortable of all addictions, associated with upsetting physical reactions, which can be negative or positive depending on situational elements. The addiction is what we humans call "love" (p. 6). Goffman (1952) would agree with Schaler. He used the word "hooked" to refer both to persons who fall in love and those who take drugs (p. 453). The word *addiction* ultimately attained its current meaning as a relentless and self-defeating pursuit. The words *addict* and *addiction* were expanded to cover a large number of human activities and experiences that really had little in common with one another.

Changes in the meanings of addiction and addict always produce changes in the kinds of substances that are defined as addicting, the kinds of drug-taking patterns that are viewed as problematic, and the kinds of people who are classified as troublesome (Murphy, 2011). Some drugs that were once considered inconsequential and recreational are now considered dangerous and addicting, and some drugs that were once considered addicting and dangerous no longer are.

> Some people do use the terms "addiction" and "addict" indiscriminately to condemn whatever they think is bad, compulsive, and in need of correction, regardless of whether they are discussing sex, drugs, or some other activity that they do not like. When the brush sweeps this wide, it is probably time to rethink seriously our understanding and use of the terms "addiction" and "addict." Use of the addiction terminology does incorrectly make some things look intrinsically good and other things look intrinsically bad. (Szasz, 1985, p. xii)

Controversy and dispute seem to be the rule, and different groups will hold vastly different understandings about drug addictions and drug addicts. "The problem is that, although some drugs may be more likely than others to result in addiction, there is no clear distinction between substances that are addicting and those that are not" (Ray & Ksir, 1996, p. 43). One thing is clear: More is involved in the determination that an individual is addicted to a particular drug than close scrutiny of a drug's chemical properties (Staley, 1992, p. 99).

The meaning of addiction reached a point where it meant not only something generally bad but also something invariant, uniform, and universal. In order to make the process of addiction seem uniform and invariantly debilitating, physical changes supposedly associated with drug use and abuse were identified. These gave the impression that drug addiction could be objectively and factually determined. Drugs that were associated with (1) *withdrawal* (physical changes in heavy users if the drug were discontinued) and (2) *tolerance* (the physical capacity to withstand higher and higher doses of a drug; diminishing effects upon subsequent use at the same dose) were branded as addicting. Other drugs were defined as nonaddicting (i.e., only habituating) because users experienced neither tolerance nor withdrawal.

Drug use patterns continued to change throughout the twentieth century, and the meaning of addiction changed right along with them. Drug patterns were becoming more diverse, and more and more people were using more and more drugs. The traditional meanings of addict and addiction were considered too restrictive by authorities to include all the new drug users and patterns of drug use that they believed needed to be included. Addiction was transformed into more of a psychological process than it had been, but a psychological process that still had universal and uniform biological underpinnings.

An individual was defined as addicted if he or she craved a drug, used it uncontrollably, and remained indifferent to the actual or potential adverse consequences of its use. It became the prevailing scientific view that psychological dependence, based on reinforcement, was the driving force behind all drug addiction; physical changes could still occur, but these were no longer considered necessary to identify an addiction or an addict. By the 1980s, drugs like cocaine and marijuana were included in the category of addictive substances, whereas at one time they had been defined as only habituating.

The reinforcement that addicts receive, the story now goes, comes from a jolt of pleasure and exhilaration associated with the flow of brain chemicals (Volkow, Wang, Fischman, et al., 1997; Volkow, Wang, Fowler, et al., 1997). Experiences of the addict, such as craving, compulsion, and loss of control, may also be due to these same brain chemicals. The prevailing view is that practically anyone can become addicted to practically anything under the right circumstances because of something going on in his or her brain.

We can appreciate some of the difficulties with the terms *addiction* and *addict* by looking at their application to a type of behavior that at one time would never have been called an addiction: human sexuality. Are some people addicted to sex, or is the concept of sex addiction nothing more than a silly fad? Opinions vary, and different groups give different answers to these questions. Some people believe that no such thing as a sex addiction exists. Sexual behavior is not a substance, they claim, and it is not associated with tolerance and withdrawal symptoms at too-low doses. To call certain erotic feelings and behaviors "addictions" is to brand them as abnormal and as both uncontrolled and uncontrollable (Henkin, 1996). Does this contribute anything to our understanding of either addiction or sexuality, or does it merely stigmatize those people who are unhappy with their sex lives but feel powerless to change them?

Other people believe wholeheartedly in the existence of sex addictions. According to them, a sex addiction is a life-threatening condition where people's lives are dominated by a pattern of compulsive, destructive sex that they would like to change but cannot. Sex makes them "high" because it releases chemicals in the brain (Rice, 1998, p. 218). It is claimed that sex addictions lead to suicide, unwanted pregnancies, family disintegration, violence, major health care costs, and child abuse. People who refuse to believe that sexuality can be an addiction are themselves branded as suffering from an illness: the denial of an illness (Carnes, 1991, pp. 9–38).

A messy term like *sex addiction* gets even messier when it is applied to concrete cases. Who is a sex addict? This category seems to include a diverse group of people whose only qualification is that they have had their lives made difficult—tragically so, in some cases—by sex. Carnes (1991) offers the following as actual examples of sex addicts and their addictions: a woman who had burned herself using a vibrator and had to go to an emergency room for treatment; a priest who stole money from his parish to pay for visits to prostitutes; a dentist who drugged his unresponsive wife in order to have sex with her; a corporate technician who sexually harassed people; and a male youth leader who had sex with boys (pp. 9–10). What is true is that these individuals seem to be out of control in regard to features of their sexuality. It is not true, however, that our understanding of complex human activities and relationships is improved by calling them "addictions," applying the term indiscriminately to sexual activities that seem indecipherable in other ways.

Our most damaging addiction may be our addiction to the addiction terminology (Henkin, 1996, p. 64). The availability of the terms *addiction* and *addict* may offer some advantages to a person who is doing something that seems compulsive and destructive. However, faith in the addiction terminology can easily serve as a vocabulary of motive in which individuals become convinced that they have no capacity for self-control and no responsibility for the consequences of their actions (Schaler, 2000, pp. 8–9). How on earth can people control something that they truly believe is relentless and uncontrollable? Why would they even try? Regardless of how it is defined, addiction does not automatically denote danger: A substance that is nonaddictive can still be used destructively and harmfully, and an addictive substance can still be used safely and responsibly (Franklin, 1996). More kids die each year from ingesting the fragments of balloons than die from the use of marijuana (Trebach, 1987, p. 86).

Carr's (2011) study of an outpatient drug treatment program for homeless women in the Midwest (which she refers to as "Fresh Beginnings") shows how important it is to the lifeblood of a therapeutic agency that its members (therapists, clients, administrators, case managers) use the language of addiction and in similar ways. Agency personnel had an unshakable belief that addiction was real and that all of the clients' problems in living erupted from their enslavement to drugs. A major objective of the agency's personnel was for them to get their clients to fall into line and start using the addiction terminology to interpret their own personal experiences and habits. Central to this project was the expectation that clients would reach a point where they would be willing to disclose a personal history of suffering and misery that was caused by their addiction to drugs. Clients were expected to be able and willing to articulate the official view at Fresh Beginnings and come to speak like the addicts they were defined to be.

Unsurprisingly, clients learned on their own, as well as from more experienced and knowledgeable clients, how to use the vocabulary of addiction, helplessness, and recovery to please their caretakers. In Carr's (2011) words, they "flipped the script" (p. 191). *Flipping the script* involved a presentation of self in which clients were willing to use the narratives and vocabularies that agency personnel both wanted and expected to hear, without clients making any personal investment in the content or correctness of their statements (p. 3). It is recovery through impression management. These interpersonal strategies allowed clients to be better able to get things they wanted and were of value to them (e.g., housing, transportation vouchers, medical care, job training, legal protection, and therapeutic assistance). The therapy at Fresh Beginnings focused more on getting clients to use the words that agency personnel wanted to hear than it did on changing clients' actual relationship to drugs (p. 3).

The Social Dynamics of Human Drug-Taking Experiences

Organizing Drug Use

The addiction model fails to account for the diversity, uniqueness, and ineradicably social nature of human drug-taking experiences. Humans may use drugs because they expect them to bring pleasure, to eliminate psychic discomfort, or to interrupt the onset of physical pain and discomfort (Grilly, 1994, pp. 118–121; Lindesmith, 1968). Humans may even have a *psychogenic addiction,* believing that they are addicted and so must continue their drug use when no physical basis for their addiction exists; it is only in their minds (Inciardi, 1992, p. 92).

One thing that seems clear from careful studies of drug abusers and addicts is that they use drugs in order to get high and to stay in an altered state for as long as possible, not simply to maintain a habit or to avoid the onset of unpleasant withdrawal symptoms (Goode, 2008a, p. 437). Drug use, especially if the drugs are stimulants, is a form of *edgework*, risky behavior that overwhelms the body with a sense of exhilaration and excitement, combined with a measure of nervousness and fear (Pine, 2010, pp. 176–178). Far from being problematic, the risk is the reward that comes from the drug use, and the nervousness and exhilaration are viewed as ways to achieve new levels of freedom, knowledge, and self-determination. With certain drugs (e.g., methamphetamines), users may experience a sense of supreme, self-realized sovereignty (p. 177).

Of all living things, only humans use drugs because of peer pressure or because they want to be part of a drug subculture (Whaley, Smith, & Hayes-Smith, 2011). A drug-using group gives its members the opportunity to develop new identities, relationships, lifestyles, and ideologies, all centered on drug use (Anderson, 1995, p. 366). Users will be able to find others who are like them, and they may find this connectedness to be the most "intoxicating" part of their drug-taking experience. Only humans can self-consciously and willfully discontinue their drug use because it becomes unattractive to them or inconsistent with other self-images or values that they have developed.

With drugs that are illegal, difficult to get or use, or expensive, a *hassle factor* is present. As the burden of continuing some particular activity increases, it becomes less likely that it will continue for very long (Goode, 2008a, pp. 437–438). This is what increases in criminal penalties for drug abuse are supposed to do: make drug use so risky or inconvenient that it is no longer worth the hassle to use drugs. If drugs do become less of a hassle to get and use, it is likely that drug use will increase. This will be found, however, principally among the heaviest users (Goode, 2008b, p. 388).

On July 1, 2001, Portugal embarked upon a program of nationwide decriminalization of all drugs (e.g., no distinction was drawn between "hard" and "soft" drugs). Possession for personal consumption incurred no criminal penalties at all. It didn't matter if the drugs were used in private or in public or to maintain a habit or simply to get "high." Technically, use of controlled drugs continued to be prohibited under Portuguese law, but use was treated as an administrative matter, not a criminal offense. Decriminalization was adopted as public policy because it was clear that criminalization was making a serious social problem much worse. One major obstacle to effective government policies to deal with drug abuse and related problems was that criminalization drained resources that could have been used for prevention and treatment. Another obstacle was that users were scared to enter treatment because they feared arrest and the stigma that would come from being sanctioned by the criminal justice system.

A review and analysis of the success of the Portuguese program by Greenwald (2009) reports impressive results, leading to the conclusion that the decriminalization framework has been a resounding success. Drug use did not increase. In fact, it decreased in absolute terms in some categories of drugs and increased only slightly in other categories (e.g., for older groups). The capital city of Lisbon did not become a haven for drug tourists. Newly reported cases of AIDS and HIV among drug addicts declined substantially. Drug-related mortality rates went down. One *increase* is notable: More individuals sought treatment in the decriminalized setting than they ever did in the criminalized one, substantially *reducing* drug-related harms for the country.

By freeing its citizens from the fear of prosecution and imprisonment for drug usage, Portugal has dramatically improved its ability to encourage drug addicts to avail themselves of treatment. The resources that were previously devoted to prosecuting and imprisoning drug addicts are now available to provide treatment programs to addicts. Those developments, along with Portugal's shift to a harm-reduction approach, have dramatically improved drug-related social ills, including drug-caused mortalities and drug-related disease transmission. (p. 28)

Decriminalization made more resources available for treatment and education, and it increased users' willingness to take advantage of them. One lesson from the Portuguese experience is that stringent laws and harsh criminal penalties reduce neither the number of addictions nor the number of addicts very much (if at all). They also do not eradicate the harms that drugs do. In fact, the opposite may be the case.

The Limits of Criminal Penalties

The continuing and serious drug-related problems in the United States, existing in tandem with a highly criminalized approach to drug abuse, offer compelling evidence that criminalization is not going to *ever* work well enough to justify its use. The problem is not simply that it hasn't worked. The problem is that it *can't* work, and the Portuguese decriminalization program shows some of the reasons why. Criminalization of drugs can do more harm than good (Walker, 2011, pp. 315–316). It increases the profits from drug trafficking for those individuals who have no reluctance to break the law to benefit themselves; it increases drug-related violence; it corrupts law enforcement; and it keeps drug users away from seeking medical help, exposing them to intense pressures to break the law to support their habits. Arguably, in the end, criminalization does little to affect the demand for drugs and not much more to affect the supply. Disrespect for the law may go up, and the quality and safety of street drugs may drop even more.

The problems that can come from a policy of criminalization can be seen with what is happening with the federal approach to medical marijuana. Barack Obama, during his presidential campaign in 2008, pledged he would not use federal law enforcement to interfere with the selling of medical marijuana in the states where it had been legalized (which it has been in California and 17 other states, plus the District of Columbia, as of this writing). However, what he said as a presidential candidate is not what he did as a president. By 2012, a tough federal crackdown on the medical marijuana market was apparent and with predictable results. The market is going underground, leading to both a lack of information about what kind of marijuana the sick are receiving (in terms of quality and ingredients) and a diminished regulation of it. This has made it more likely that unscrupulous people will get involved in its manufacture and supply. The new crackdown has been justified by its supporters on the grounds that states were not doing enough to ensure that marijuana intended to help the sick was not getting into the hands of the pleasure-seeking well.

The U.S. prohibition of alcohol from 1920 to 1933 offers some lessons about *all* drug-taking experiences and the limits of criminal sanction (Goode, 2008b, p. 386). One lesson from Prohibition is that criminal penalties can work with some people, some of the time, to discourage their use of certain drugs. The demand for heroin is little affected by variations in criminal penalties associated with its use, but the demand for marijuana does drop when penalties for use increase (Goode, 2008b, p. 387). Another lesson from Prohibition is that criminalization of a drug *always* produces unanticipated consequences, some of which are counterproductive for achievement of the initial objective. A prohibition on drugs can, for example, produce a *crime tariff* in which criminalization of some commodity sets up barriers that actually protect criminal activities, financially rewarding anyone who is willing to break the law to supply drugs to users (Packer, 1968). When this happens, criminalization makes a bad situation even worse, and the efforts to stop drug use actually produce more problems, not fewer. Walker (2011, p. 311) concludes that convictions for drug offenses are the primary factor accounting for the "spectacular" increase in the U.S. prison population during the last 35 to 40 years.

A 2011 global commission on drugs and drug policy issued a report that concluded that the global war on drugs was a failure in reducing either consumption of illegal drugs or their supply (Global Commission on Drugs, 2012). Tougher policies did little to make the global environment safer, and they did little to promote healthier societies or healthier patterns of drug use. The commission's main recommendation was for nations to regulate drugs in such a way that organized crime's power would be decreased while the health and security of citizens would be increased.

The commission concluded that drug policies that are based on a war mentality and zero tolerance are counterproductive if sensible drug policies are our objective. Worldwide supply of opiates in illegal markets increased almost fivefold from 1980 to 2010, while the price of heroin in Europe and the United States dropped almost 80 percent from 1990 to 2009 (Global Commission on Drugs, 2012, p. 2). The power and profits of organized crime cartels have not been substantially reduced. The falling drug prices have been accompanied by an increase in drug potency in cannabis and cocaine. A war mentality in regard to drugs is incompatible with a treatment/public health model, and it can make the HIV/AIDS epidemic even worse (pp. 4–11). The commission concluded that legalization of cannabis would be a positive and beneficial change. Drum (2009) concurs. He argues that softening our laws on marijuana use would be a step in the right direction because too-harsh penalties for its use have destroyed too many lives and squandered too many scarce societal resources in a vain effort to stop people from smoking pot (p. 52).

The conclusions of this global commission should be viewed as serious information to be taken seriously. The honorary chair was George P. Shultz, secretary of state under Ronald Reagan, and the acting chair was the former president of Brazil, Fernando Henrique Cardoso. The membership included Paul Volcker, former chair of the United States Federal Reserve and of the Economic Recovery Board; as well as César Gaviria, former president of Colombia; Ernesto Zedillo, former president of Mexico; and Ricardo Lagos, former president of Chile. The report of this blue ribbon commission should serve as a warning to anyone who continues to think that a war on drugs is the best way to deal with drug abuse. Jablecki (2012) sees some light at the end of the tunnel. He thinks a harsh, retributive approach, making drug abusers into enemies of the state, is slowly being replaced by a more compassionate, forgiving approach to drug abuse.

In the 2012 U.S. election, referendums were passed by voters in the states of Washington and Colorado (but defeated in Oregon) that will legalize recreational marijuana for individuals 21 and over in those states. The National Organization for the Reform of Marijuana Laws (NORML) applauded this as a significant victory. How much will actually change for pot smokers remains to be seen because marijuana is still ranked as a drug that has high potential for abuse (Schedule I in the federal Controlled Substances Act) and no medical use (even though medical marijuana is legal in 18 states and D.C., as noted above). The efforts to normalize and legalize the recreational use of marijuana will undoubtedly continue in the years ahead, which will elicit reactions from police and drug enforcement agents to enforce federal laws to curtail its use.

Central Activities and Role Engulfment

In a book titled *Heavy Drinking,* Fingarette (1988) explores the human dimension of drug use as he critiques the claim that alcoholism is a disease. Though Fingarette concentrates on alcohol, his discussion has great value for understanding *any* human drug experience. Heavy drinking and alcoholism are not really physical disorders, he explains. They are labels that are attached to cover a wide array of social and individual problems that are the result of a complex and poorly understood interrelationship among biological, psychological, social, and cultural factors (p. 27). The cardinal feature of alcoholism is its seeming uncontrollability and dysfunctionality. Reaching for that next drink without considering the complications seems to make no sense. Why would anyone sacrifice health, wealth, and happiness for what seems to be a transitory pleasure? A common explanation is that drug use can become a disease. Just as an individual with a cold cannot stop sneezing, an individual with an addiction supposedly cannot stop drinking, smoking, snorting, or injecting (p. 32).

The core of the addiction model of human drug use is the concept of craving. Some people start using a drug and quickly reach a point where they throw all caution to the wind, doing things that are self-defeating. In these cases, it seems that a powerful momentum is at work and that no amount of persuasion, coercion, or self-control will be sufficient to create the level of self-restraint necessary to interrupt the bout of drug taking. The evidence strongly suggests, however, that even individuals who claim that they have uncontrollable cravings for drugs—and it doesn't seem to matter what kind of drug it is (e.g., heroin, cocaine, alcohol, or marijuana)—do moderate their use of them as the drugs become unavailable (Schaler, 2000, pp. 27–35).

Why would someone drink to excess again and again? Fingarette (1988) insists that heavy drinkers are neither sick nor addicted. They are simply those people for whom alcohol drinking has become a *central activity*, not all that different from other central activities around which people organize their lives, such as jobs, hobbies, families, or community service. When drinking alcohol evolves into a central activity, an individual's life is defined by drinking, and his or her major preoccupation becomes the pursuit of drink, drinking situations, and drinking companions. Central activities exert a great deal of power over us because they demand new relationships, new activities, new values, and new views of the self and of others. Research has shown that college students—some, at any rate—are inclined to view drinking alcohol as a central activity, and college drinking cultures exist that exert a powerful influence on college drinking patterns (Peralta, 2005).

A longitudinal study of 449 couples shows that romantic partners during adolescence can play a powerful role in creating and transforming an individual's drinking patterns into a central activity (Kreager & Haynie, 2011). They are conduits to the development of new friendships and new meanings, which set the foundation for learning new ways of acting, thinking, feeling, and being. Romantic partners can be an entrance into a new world of relationships, possibilities, and understandings about the self and others. These changes can lead to risky behaviors like illegal or excessive alcohol use. Even friends of an individual's romantic partner can exert an influence on one's drinking patterns (p. 756). This influence may continue even if the romantic relationship ends.

People cannot always (or easily) change what they are and what they do entirely by themselves. A great deal more than good intentions and personal resolve may be required to reconstruct one's life and to change one's central activities. However, it would be a mistake to discount the power and importance of willpower in the transformation of central activities. Determination and dedication are important parts of any change—personal or social—and they are important in moving from one central activity to another or in shifting the priorities of one's central activities. We must not allow the tenets of the addiction model to blind us to the important role played by will, determination, and true grit in human behavior.

It is unlikely that the future holds some remarkable scientific breakthrough that will prove indisputably that ongoing drug use either is or is not an addiction. People who believe human addictions exist have no trouble finding the elements of an addiction in drug-taking behavior, just as they do in sexual behavior, violence, gambling, nail-biting, and overeating. Likewise, people who believe that the term *addiction* fails to fit human drug-taking experiences have no trouble in finding inconsistencies and contradictions in the addiction model. One thing is true: The word *addiction,* if it is designed to describe drug use as a uniform, universal, biologically determined experience, is woefully inadequate to account for the relativity and variability that exists in human drug-taking experiences.

The best thing might be simply to admit that the words *addiction* and *addict* are so mired in controversy and confusion that they have no value and no purpose other than to criticize and discredit. They contribute little to a better understanding of human drug use. The words *addiction* and *addict* increase the likelihood that we will miss the huge impact of social, cultural, and personality factors on drug taking. They also make it more likely that we will see more uniformity and consistency in human drug-taking experiences than actually exist. It may be best to "just say no" to the terms *addiction* and *addict,* avoiding them whenever possible (Alexander & Wijngaart, 1992).

Moral Entrepreneurs and Drug Crusades

Demonizing Drugs

Drugs are nothing more than inert substances until they are ingested by people, who experience effects from them. What determines their moral status—good or bad—is how they are viewed and described by human groups.

> The use of antihistamines to avoid cold symptoms seems unlikely to be defined as deviant, that is, unless the user is a Christian Scientist or a member of any one of several other religions that advocate treating disease by spiritual means only. Drinking alcohol is permitted in our society, but its manufacture and sale were once illegal nationwide, and in some areas it is still illegal to sell alcoholic beverages. . . . Amphetamines are widely available through medical prescription, but taking them without a prescription makes one liable to imprisonment for using a dangerous drug. (McCaghy & Capron, 1997, pp. 283–284)

A drug of abuse at one time and place is not the same at another, and groups that are despised and harassed for their drug use in one situation may be ignored or even praised in some other situation. Because images of drugs and drug users change over time, and because so many groups have vested interests in what the images are, we must understand what we can about crusades against drugs and drug users.

A crusade against drugs and drug users will be unsuccessful without broad public support (Ryan, 1994, p. 218). To achieve this, drug crusaders must have sufficient time, influence, and resources to be able to define a chemical substance and its use as problematic; convince others that what the crusaders say is true; invent or find a way to cure or correct the problem that is affordable, effective, and acceptable to others; and overcome any resistance to the crusade that might be offered by other crusaders (Tuggle & Holmes, 1997, p. 80). Moral crusaders may subtly—and not so subtly—create new kinds of deviance and new profiles of deviants by hunting, catching, and sanctioning people who had never been punished before (Victor, 1994, pp. 308–309). They are helped mightily if they can garner the support of scientific, medical, religious, or legal authorities. Politicians and other representatives of government, along with media spokespersons, play a central role in creating and legitimating wars on drugs (Goode, 2008a; Wysong, Aniskiewicz, & Wright, 1994, p. 461). Without involvement of respected and powerful authorities, most moral crusades will sputter and die (Victor, p. 310).

Wars on drugs are usually legitimated on the grounds that they, like their military counterparts, can be won only if the cause is just and the soldiers are strong and noble (Kraska, 2003). The major outcome of drug wars, however, is not a victorious conquest. It is usually little more than increased social control over subordinate groups and greater surveillance of their patterns of drug use (Fagan, 1994). Drug crusades are almost always launched against groups of people who are already defined as a problem by some dominant group, and their patterns of drug use are used to justify an attack on them (Reinarman, 1996). These ceremonies of exclusion have less to do with the molecular structure or pharmacological effects of drugs than they do with what dominant groups want to encourage or discourage and with whom they want to interact. Drug users are almost always being persecuted for being members of a despised or threatening group, not because they use dangerous drugs. A war on drugs is a convenient smokescreen for waging a war on certain kinds of *people* (Helmer, 1975; Schaler, 2000, p. 120; Szasz, 1985, p. 65). A strange irony is that the war on drugs may do greater damage to the social fabric and ruin more lives than the drugs themselves ever could (Trebach & Inciardi, 1993, p. 42).

U.S. history is filled with examples of drug crusades that boiled over into public hysteria (Musto, 1987). Alcohol, cocaine, cigarettes, opium, morphine, methamphetamines, marijuana, and heroin have all been the targets of moral reformers in the past, and these chemical substances and those who use them continue to be the object of periodic concern and attack. Any usable chemical substance can be viewed as abusable by some group, somewhere, and its members can then set about to make things right (Acker, 1991; Brandt, 1991). People with long enough memories can usually recall when today's "most dangerous substance on earth" was at one time proclaimed to be a safe and effective corrective for some human affliction (Inciardi, 1992).

Prior to their criminalization as illegal and their designation as dangerous substances, the major psychoactive drugs—opium, heroin, morphine, cocaine, marijuana—were administered freely to get people to work harder and longer at dangerous and exhausting jobs. These drugs increased productivity because they were a reward for hard work, and they took some of the edge off the pain of backbreaking labor (Szasz, 1985, p. 75). In colonial times in the United States, alcohol was widely viewed as a cure-all for a range of psychological and physical ailments, and physicians and ministers encouraged its use (Levine, 1984). In the closing years of his life, Benjamin Franklin used laudanum (opium dissolved in an alcoholic drink) on a daily basis, principally to manage the pain he suffered from kidney stones. Narcotics were available through mail-order catalogs (e.g., Sears, Roebuck, & Co.), and the soda pop known as Coca-Cola started life (in 1886) as an alcohol-free beverage that contained cocaine as a key ingredient (cocaine was removed in 1900). Marijuana is a widely used, albeit generally illegal, chemical substance. In fact, no other illegal drug comes even close (Goode, 2008a, p. 240). In 2011, a total of 18.1 million individuals reported being current users of marijuana (during the past month) (Substance Abuse and Mental Health Services Administration [SAMHSA], 2012).

An excellent example of how a chemical substance can be demonized and its negative effects exaggerated, thereby producing a drug scare, is the portrayal of *phencyclidine (PCP)* in the U.S. media. At one time, phencyclidine was used as an anesthetic-analgesic in surgery (which dulled pain while the patient remained conscious), but it was eventually abandoned for use because of its side effects. It can produce hallucinations, disorientation, and a range of unpleasant or upsetting physical symptoms (vomiting, rashes, numbness, lack of coordination, and excitement). When mixed with other drugs, usually LSD, phencyclidine is known on the street as *angel dust*. PCP eventually earned a reputation as a "devil drug," and it came to be viewed as a substance capable of precipitating ghastly acts of violence and self-inflicted injury.

Descriptions of the drug in the print media and portrayals of it on television relied heavily on horror stories, especially ones that reported PCP users as being unusually prone to gouge out their own eyes. If a stronger image than this one exists, it is hard to know what it could possibly be. It shocks, scares, repels, and creates a sense of urgency, while conveying an image of a drug user who is insane, crazy, and totally out of control. Were the negative images of PCP and its users totally false? Probably not—drug crusades may contain a kernel of truth—but facts about drugs are not usually the driving force behind drug scares (Schaler, 2000, p. 39). A gruesome tale such as the gouged-eye story is told and retold so often that it comes to offer instant proof of the correctness of the fears of drug crusaders. Eye gouging is an image that is so meaningful *and* so horrendous that facts alone cannot constrain it (Morgan & Kagan, 1995, p. 210).

One thing worse than horrific instances of the self-inflicted injury that eye-gouging represents is when horrific injuries are inflicted on *others*. The bar was raised again over Memorial Day, 2012 (May 26), in Miami, Florida. Rudy Eugene, naked and growling, ate about 75 percent of a homeless man's face before he was killed by police when he refused to stop eating his victim. The homeless man was permanently disfigured from the mauling, but he survived it. The attack was blamed on "bath salts," a synthetic stimulant, described in the media as a cocaine substitute or synthetic LSD. The drug is poorly understood, but like all designer drugs, it can contain a variety of different chemical compounds that affect the human organism in multiple ways. (Usually, bath salts contain mephedrine, methylenedioxypyrovalerone, or other amphetamine-like substances.)

Another unusual feature of this admittedly bizarre happening is that the toxicology report on Rudy Eugene found no evidence of bath salts, synthetic marijuana, or LSD in the man's system. The only substance detected was marijuana, a substance that is currently believed to be incapable of provoking the kinds of things that occurred during the Memorial Day attack. This fact will probably mean little to those individuals who are prepared to conclude that bath salts are the newest "most dangerous substance on earth." The truth of this incident may be far less complicated and far less sensational. Rudy Eugene may simply have been a seriously disturbed individual who did not receive the kind of care he needed during his life, which led to his attack on the homeless man (Szalavitz, 2012).

A horror story about drugs can sensationalize or even demonize certain events and make new chemical substances and new patterns of drug use the object of heightened public concern. What it cannot do, however, is ensure that a demonized drug is actually the one thing responsible for all the bad effects blamed on it. Some of the problems associated with drugs exist because of how a drug is taken, how much is taken, where it is taken, who is taking it, and what impurities get into the body along with the psychoactive substance. Drugs purchased on the street, where a user can never be sure what psychoactive substance or how much of it is being taken, can be dangerous. Some people can do destructive things to themselves (or others) when they are under the influence. People use these substances at their own risk.

The demonization of drugs and the persecution of drug users, curiously enough, are not necessarily intended to create a drug-free world. The war *against* certain drugs is almost always a war *for* other drugs.

> The abuse of tobacco, alcohol, and prescription drugs leads to far more serious consequences in terms of public health, violent behavior, spiritual deterioration, family disruption, death and disease—consequences that are all but ignored in the quest for a so-called drug-free culture. The drug-free culture being pursued is in fact a culture which allows citizens to consume culturally integrated drugs but excludes the drugs of other cultures. (Johns & Borrero, 1991, p. 79)

Representatives of the pharmaceutical industry do more than push drugs legally. They push a faith in the power of drugs to cure the afflictions of human existence by constantly reinforcing the message that the solution to personal problems can be found in a tablet, capsule, syrup, or syringe.

The drug pushing of drug companies has serious consequences: death and injury to consumers from their use of inappropriate or dangerous legal drugs and a colossal waste of patients' money and national health resources (Chetley & Mintzes, 1992, p. 35). Drug companies do all they can to suppress reports of dangerous drugs or test results that are unfavorable to their economic interests. If this concealment fails, the results are whitewashed, and every effort is made to direct attention to the dangers of illegal drugs, rather than to the dangers of those drugs that are an important source of company profits (Clinard & Yeager, 1980; Coleman, 2006; Simon, 2008). Overdoses of prescription pain remedies and deaths from legal chemical substances (i.e., nicotine and ethyl alcohol) kill far more people than cocaine and heroin (Reiman & Leighton, 2010).

Drug Bans and Social Bedevilment

Helmer (1975) insists that deception is the core of U.S. drug policy. Past crusades against opium, marijuana, and cocaine were not only about the dangers—real or imagined—of psychoactive substances. Antidrug crusades were also perfect covers for relentless attacks on U.S. minorities, such as the Chinese, Mexicans, and African Americans, supposedly because these people were addicted to drugs and dangerous to themselves and to others. The primary objective of these drug crusades was actually the exclusion of U.S. minorities from social life and the eradication of any threats that they might have posed to moral crusaders' interests (Helmer, 1975, p. 8; Latimer & Goldberg, 1981; Musto, 1987; Szasz, 1985). A drug crusade generates new images of drug use and drug users, and these images become part of the weaponry that some groups use to battle other groups.

The 1970s and 1980s were a perplexing time in the United States. U.S. social diversity and cultural heterogeneity were frightening to those people who viewed them as disorganizing forces. A constellation of problems was particularly alarming: family breakdown, economic decline, disorder in schools, premarital sexuality, illegitimacy, pornography, adultery, community deterioration, crime, delinquency, violence, and America's loss of influence abroad. If the problems were many, so went the official view, the causes were few. Too many people had lost their moral rudders, turning on with drugs and thereby neglecting their social responsibilities and failing to honor the social contract.

Sensitization to the dangers of drugs, especially crack cocaine, provided a scapegoat for some of the social and personal problems that seemed to have increased dramatically as the years had passed. The transformation of the image of cocaine use from a harmless, recreational activity to a dangerous, if not deadly, addiction was accompanied by shifts in the symbolization of both cocaine and its users (Scheibe, 1994, p. 209). Stricter drug laws and harsher punishments of drug offenders became a central part of the overall plan to rebuild the United States.

In September 1986, the U.S. House of Representatives passed a sweeping anti–drug abuse act. It allocated more monies for enforcement than treatment, increased sentences for drug-related crimes, and increased penalties for foreign nations that refused to cooperate with the U.S. effort to eradicate foreign sources of illicit drugs coming into the United States. This act authorized the *100-to-1 rule*, which provided a glaring (and illogical) discrepancy between the penalties for crack cocaine and powdered cocaine use by penalizing users of crack cocaine more severely (100 times, to be exact) than it did users of powdered cocaine. The criminal penalty was the same for someone possessing 5 grams of crack as it was for someone possessing 500 grams of powdered cocaine. Although the way a drug is taken (e.g., swallowed, inhaled, or injected) does influence the speed and duration of its effects, this is insufficient justification for penalizing users of crack cocaine so much more harshly than users of powdered cocaine. The Fair Sentencing Act of 2010, passed by the 111th Congress and signed into law by President Obama that same year, reduced the disparity between mandatory minimums for users of crack cocaine and powdered cocaine from 100 to 1 to 18 to 1. Under this new law, the threshold to be charged with a felony for possession of crack is 28 grams, but it remains at 500 grams for powdered cocaine. (In June 2012, the U.S. Supreme Court ruled that the new law applied retroactively, covering people who had been convicted before the act was passed.)

George H. W. Bush, forty-first president of the United States, delivered his first major prime-time speech to the nation from the Oval Office of the White House (on September 5, 1989). The core of his address was his pledge that he and his administration would achieve a victory over drugs. To show the nation just how accessible drugs were, he held up a clear plastic bag of crack cocaine marked "EVIDENCE." He reported to the nation that the bag had been seized by drug enforcement agents in Lafayette Park, directly across from the White House. The implication was clear: No place was safe from drugs. Bush insisted that "crack" was destroying our cities, turning them into battle zones and killing our children. A picture of the president, cocaine bag held defiantly aloft, appeared on the front pages of newspapers all across the country (Reinarman & Levine, 1997).

The president, however, was not telling the truth. His handlers and speech writers thought he needed a prop to show his viewing audience to enhance his message. The president had agreed. He even wanted the drug to be seized from someone (anyone) in Lafayette Park so that he could claim that "crack" was everywhere, even right in front of the White House. Reinarman and Levine (1997) tell us what happened next.

White House Communications Director David Demarst asked Cabinet Affairs Secretary David Bates to instruct the Justice Department "to find some crack that fit the description in the speech." Bates called Richard

Weatherbee, special assistant to Attorney General Dick Thornburgh, who then called James Millford [*sic*], executive assistant to the DEA chief. Finally, Milford phoned William McMullen, special agent in charge of the DEA's Washington office, and told him to arrange an undercover crack buy near the White House. (pp. 22–23)

The president's plan may have been good politics, but it was based on bad sociology and even worse economics. Drug agents could find nobody selling crack or any other drug anywhere near the White House, because nobody would be there to buy it. The sale of crack cocaine was concentrated in the poorer neighborhoods of Washington, D.C.

All was not lost, however. Drug enforcement agents were able to find someone who was willing to journey to the White House to make the sale. They enticed Keith Jackson, an 18-year-old African American high school student, to make the trip. He had to be coached, however, because the man did not even know where the White House was, let alone how to get there. The agents did not actually seize the cocaine, either. They bought it from Jackson for $2,400 and then sent him on his way. When reality did not conform to the script, the speech, or the wishes of the president and his advisors, things were done to create a reality that would fit the scripted image.

One claim that received strong support in scientific writings and the popular press was that cocaine poses exceptional threats to a user's health and well-being. Leading authorities asserted with confidence and usually much fanfare that cocaine was too dangerous to be tried even once and posed extraordinary threats to any user. These claims, especially because they seemed beyond dispute, were used as one more bit of ammunition in the war on drugs in general and the war on cocaine in particular. Fewer and fewer people were willing to speak on behalf of cocaine (Erickson, Adlaf, Murray, & Smart, 1987; Trebach, 1987). The indisputable fact that certain drugs at high enough doses are deadly was transformed into a more general and bogus indictment of *all* illicit drugs at any dose as unusually dangerous.

Cocaine is a heart stimulant, so any imprudent or recreational use is cause for concern. However, *moderate* use of cocaine seems to be no more cardiotoxic than other stimulating activities, and the claim that no safe dose of cocaine exists is false. A link does seem to exist between *prolonged* and *heavy* use of cocaine and cardiotoxicity, but even here we must be cautious if truth is our objective. If a heavy user were to die from a heart attack while using cocaine—a rare event—it still would not prove that cocaine was the cause. The death might have been an atypical reaction to the drug, comparable to the deaths some people experience from using aspirin. It might also have been due to an already existing health problem, such as high blood pressure or arteriosclerosis. If this person had tried to jog, had sex, or had gotten too excited over a sporting event, the outcome likely would have been the same. Another possibility is that it was not the cocaine itself but some adulterant in the street variety of the drug, or some other drug used along with it, that caused the death (Alexander & Wong, 1990, p. 260).

A prominent scare story associated with cocaine use is the claim that large numbers of children are born addicted because of their mothers' use of the drug. The initial studies of babies who were born to mothers who used cocaine during pregnancy were not at all encouraging. They reported that these infants were more likely to be born prematurely; have a significantly lower birth weight; have smaller heads; suffer seizures; have genital and urinary tract abnormalities; suffer poor motor ability; have brain lesions; and exhibit behavioral aberrations, such as impulsivity, moodiness, and lower sensitivity to environmental stimuli (Goode & Ben-Yehuda, 1994, p. 216). Findings such as these were picked up quickly by the media and just as quickly transmitted to the general public. However, according to Goode and Ben-Yehuda, enough evidence had accumulated by the 1990s to suggest strongly that the *crack-baby syndrome* is a medical fiction (p. 217). Mothers who smoke crack are more likely to engage in a variety of practices that strongly correlate with poor infant health, such as smoking tobacco, drinking alcohol, using other psychoactive drugs, refusing to exercise, following poor eating habits, failing to visit physicians regularly, and maintaining a generally reckless lifestyle.

> With crack babies, what we saw was [sic] pathological conditions *associated with* the use of cocaine that was [sic] automatically *assumed to have been caused* by the drug which later, careful research indicated, were in fact caused by very conventional conditions *about which there was very little subjective concern.* (p. 216)

Many things work together to determine the health of a newborn, and a mother's use of crack cocaine is just one of them.

Not only were helpless infants defined as an at-risk population, but so were the hale and hearty. In the 1980s, increasing attention was directed toward the illicit drug use of professional athletes (Leiber, Jamieson, & Krohn, 1993). Once again, the reason has less to do with drugs than it does with social relationships and group interests. Drug use among professional athletes, real or imagined, was used by owners as a trump card in the difficult and contentious contract negotiations that were under way. Players were mainly concerned with their freedom to determine with which team(s) they would play and other features of their professional careers, as well as their pension plans, but management artfully focused most of the attention on illicit drug use among players.

The players' wish to be free from the intrusion of drug testing was branded by the owners as an example of their selfishness and irresponsibility. Their thinking was, why not go along with the plan unless something was being hidden? Media representatives tended to side with owners and portrayed players as the deviant ones for being generally ignorant of, or indifferent to, how damaging their drug use was to themselves and to the game. This alignment of the media with owners increased the owners' power and effectively undercut players' demands for higher salaries, more control over the game, and even more control over their own personal careers.

Professional and nonprofessional athletes alike are increasingly being singled out for their illegal use of steroids. Any objective analysis of athletes' use of steroids must conclude that legitimate health risks exist, but that the risks have been exaggerated (Perry, 2008, p. 167). Physicians have used steroids to treat patients since the 1930s with a reasonable measure of safety. The current claims of horrible side effects from steroid use correctly describe the experiences of only long-term, heavy users who use steroids without medical advice and supervision. Making steroids more difficult to get by making their use a crime did have a predictable effect: It produced a black market for steroids in which prices went up and quality went down.

The lack of medical supervision and oversight of what athletes were putting into their bodies, due principally to the criminalization of steroid use, made a dangerous situation even worse. Once steroid users concluded that most of the claims they were hearing about the dangers of steroids were lies, it was hard for them to believe other claims, even true ones, about the dangers. Drug testing in professional athletics, ostensibly to get rid of illegal steroid use, was done principally for public relations purposes by a business that is highly interested in protecting its image and its profits.

The sense of panic and urgency that the war on drugs generates may be one of its biggest liabilities. The use of *club drugs* or *designer drugs,* specifically by adolescents and young adults at nightclubs, raves, or concerts, has generated a disproportionate amount of public attention and concern. The use of designer drugs, such as Ecstasy (MDMA), GHB, Rohypnol ("the date rape drug"), and ketamine, has involved a relatively small number of individuals, even among the drug-using population, and the frequency of use has declined with the passage of time (Goode, 2008a, p. 268). Although the club drugs are a heterogeneous collection of psychoactive chemicals, each one having distinctive effects, they are still (mistakenly) lumped together into the same category. This mistake, however, pales in comparison to a more serious one, namely, treating these drugs as uniformly the same in terms of the potential to hurt or kill users.

A study in the state of Florida reported that from 1994 to 2000, exactly 254 individuals had died from their use of rave or club drugs (discussed in Goode, 2008a, p. 267). However, it turns out that the study was flawed, and the panel that prepared the report had based their conclusions on dogma and political interest. Too many types of drugs were included in the category of club drugs, some of which did not even fit the panel's *own* working definition of what qualified as one (e.g., nitrous oxide or laughing gas was included, and though it is sometimes abused, it does not qualify as a club drug). In addition, some of the 254 deaths the panel blamed on club drugs stretched things a bit too far. One woman died after being hit by an automobile, and she was included in the deaths. Another man committed suicide after losing his job. His blood tested positive for amphetamine, so he was included in the tally, too (p. 267). Although some of the club drugs can be dangerous, condemnation of a chemical substance for the purpose of public relations or political advancement may do more harm than good if it breeds distrust. Even a well-meaning lie is still a lie.

Portrayals or conceptualizations of drug use that pathologize or demonize adolescent drug use give pictures of it that are too distorted to do us much good if we wish to understand users' motivations and methods. The typical participant in the rave scene is neither an enslaved victim of a drug epidemic desperately in need of therapy nor a self-centered risk taker desperately in need of being locked up for the protection of others. Adolescents' drug-use patterns are flexible and almost always voluntary—meaning they simply want to take them rather than having a physical need for them—and adolescent nightlife behaviors change all the time (Hunt, Moloney, & Evans, 2010).

Any evidence of an increase in drug use, no matter how slight and no matter what drug it is, or any evidence of a shift in drug-use patterns, is dramatized by the U.S. press (Lotz, 1991). The U.S. print media created a cocaine drug scare in the summer of 1986 by using "shocking numbers and graphic accounts" to make cocaine use, especially crack cocaine, appear widespread and dangerous. These media representatives took raw data from surveys of drug use among high school seniors and young adults and fiddled with the numbers until they could be used to prove the existence of a drug epidemic.

We found ample evidence of media workers snatching at shocking numbers from ISR [Institute for Social Research at the University of Michigan] press releases, smothering reports of stable or decreasing use under more ominous headlines, and distorting the cocaine problem to epidemic proportions as high as 40 percent of high school seniors. (Orcutt & Turner, 1993, p. 203)

When cocaine use could no longer be portrayed as an epidemic—drug stories about it had disappeared from all the major news magazines by the end of 1986—media magicians simply produced a new plague from the ashes of the old. *Newsweek* reported in its February 3, 1992, issue that LSD use was "rising alarmingly" among U.S. teens (quoted in Orcutt & Turner, p. 201). Like previous media claims, this one was based on omissions, exaggerations, and distortions. According to Orcutt and Turner, the "alarming rise" in LSD use from 1989 to 1990 was countered by a much larger *drop* in cocaine use, but little was made of this decrease (p. 201). It seems that decreases in drug use are not nearly as newsworthy as increases.

Practically any claim or declaration about patterns of drug use or the social or personal consequences of it must be tentative. Users of most drugs are inclined to be deceptive or evasive about their drug use, so estimates of drug use patterns are very likely to be unreliable and invalid to an unknown degree (Andreas & Greenhill, 2010; Page & Singer, 2010). A substantial number of people understate on surveys the extent of their drug use, and some people are more likely to lie on surveys than others.

Drug Fears

A growing concern in the twenty-first century combines societal distress over drugs with societal distress over international terrorism. The term *narcoterrorism* covers a multitude of activities in which terrorist groups manufacture and distribute illegal drugs in order to accrue capital to further their terrorist activities. With the end of the Cold War and the relative decline in the influence of communism on world events, state-sponsored terrorism started to fade in importance. U.S. retaliation against Islamic radicals for the terrorist attacks of September 11, 2001, has crippled their ability to raise funds from mosques and charities. Today, surviving as a terrorist requires the ability to raise funds in independent ways, and trafficking in drugs is one of the most profitable activities around. Al-Qaeda's leadership has avoided involvement in drug smuggling, but practically nobody else has. Despite bad weather and blight, which hurt Afghanistan's poppy harvest in 2012, renewed planting efforts and increasing profits from heroin trafficking are still likely (Kaplan, 2009; Rubin & Rosenberg, 2012). The United States now officially views drug trafficking and terrorism as sharing the same ground of geography, money, and violence (Winslow & Zhang, 2008, p. 510). The war on terror now goes hand in hand with the war on drugs.

(The two countries that are currently principal sites of narcoterrorism are Afghanistan and Pakistan.)

Drugs, even without their tie to terrorism, are still associated with global crime and violence. Mexican drug lords and the cartels they command are engaged in an ongoing, bloody turf war, fueled both by guns and money. The weapons can be assault rifles or even grenade launchers, and the targets are rival gang members, police officers, soldiers, or even civilians. Anybody in the way of their relentless profiteering is fair game (Gibler, 2011). The death and destruction from these power struggles seem never-ending, a threat to the entire fabric of a society. The tremendous profits to be made from drug trafficking have led to widespread corruption in Mexico of the police, judiciary, and military. The local police can be working for one cartel, the state police for another, and the federal police for still another (Vulliamy, 2010, p. 20).

Ordinary citizens—even journalists—may be reluctant to travel in Mexico for fear that they will be stopped at a checkpoint, robbed of what they have, and then murdered and left to rot on the side of the road. Even when the criminal justice system is free from corruption, convictions are difficult to get because evidence is lacking and witnesses are either afraid to testify or are simply murdered prior to trial. This unchecked violence and cartel competition has spawned an arms race than can only lead to further violence and bloodshed. It may be tempting to conclude that Mexico's drug problems are its own, better dealt with at a local level. This kind of thinking, however, would be a mistake. The huge U.S. demand for drugs is what fuels much of the profit engine in Mexico—giving cartels economic incentives to put money first—and arms imported from the United States are what help to make the violence as deadly as it is (Vulliamy, 2010, pp. 9–10; Young, 2011, p. 251).

Two Mexicos exist. One is a place where Mexican authorities fight drug cartels by waging a war on drugs, where U.S. financial aid plays a role, and where the Mexican Army is a central part of the fight. This Mexico has both laws and a criminal justice system that is enlisted in the war on drugs. The U.S. government views this society as its ally in the international effort to stop drug abuse. This is the Mexico reported on by U.S. media. The other Mexico, however, is the real deal. It is a place where the war is fought to *get* drugs, and the police and military actively go after as much money as they can get from drugs and the U.S. demand for them. In this latter Mexico, the coin of the realm is fear, intimidation, bribery, and corruption. Murder of the innocent is a common occurrence, and survival is either a matter of luck or of brute force. It is a lawless place, pervaded by violence and greed (Bowden, 2009). The drug cartels have expanded their influence into the United States, bringing not only drugs but also murder, kidnapping, and corruption of U.S. law enforcement.

The ties between Mexico and the United States are real, and the border between the two countries is porous. In 2008, over 50 victims of drug violence in Ciudad Juárez were treated at Thomason Hospital in El Paso, Texas, and U.S. and Mexican firefighters help out one another (Vulliamy, 2010). Narcotics running across the border and along the borderland between the United States and Mexico—it is 2,100 miles long and 50 miles wide, stretching from the Pacific Ocean to the Gulf of Mexico—has made this vast area even more forbidding and dangerous than it once was. It is a world unto itself (which Vulliamy calls *Amexica*). The drug war in Mexico, according to Vulliamy (pp. 10–12), is unique because it is about nothing that matters. It lacks both a propelling cause and any convincing ideology. "Mexicans are mutilating, decapitating, torturing, and killing each other ostensibly over money and the drug-smuggling routes that provide it" (p. 11). It is a war only to show who is the coolest by making it possible for drug pushers and drug traffickers to own and display symbols of conspicuous consumption.

Conclusions

Though animals, regardless of species, are sensitive to certain chemical substances, for humans it is their cognitive and symbolic abilities and their complex and intricate social lives that are most responsible for their drug-taking experiences. Ongoing disputes over fundamental questions are real and important: What is a drug? What is addiction? What is abuse? Who is an addict? These questions are at the foundation of the interpretation of drug experiences.

Some groups advocate using an addiction terminology to interpret the use of drugs; other groups advocate staying clear of the words *addiction* and *addict* because of the fact that they believe these terms are used more to criticize than to explain. Human drug experiences are unique and show a great deal of relativity. Understandings about drugs and drug use are forged in the context of struggles between different groups, some of which take charge of interpreting social reality for everybody else.

What is most valuable is to develop an understanding of the cause, course, and consequence of the many crusades that have been initiated against drugs and drug users. Opiates, alcohol, marijuana, cocaine, PCP, steroids, designer drugs, and stimulants have all been the target of moral entrepreneurs at some point in U.S. history. These crusaders have done what they could to have their drug of concern identified as the most dangerous substance on earth. A "new" menace is narcoterrorism, which merges two of our fears together: the fear of terrorist attack and the fear of drug addicts. Mexico-based drug cartels are having an influence on the relationship between the United States and Mexico. The war on drugs, whatever it is designed to do, is not going to usher in a drug-free world. The war is simply filled with too many contradictions and ironies for it ever to be able to accomplish its intended objectives.

References

Acker, C. (1991). Social meanings of disease: Changing concepts of addiction in the twentieth century. *Magazine of History, 6,* 28–29.

Alexander, B. K., & Schweighofer, A. (1988). Defining "addiction." *Canadian Psychology, 29,* 151–162.

Alexander, B. K., & Wijngaart, G. F. van de. (1992). The disease of addiction: It's sick and tired. In A. Trebach & K. Zeese (Eds.), *Strategies for change* (pp. 275–279). Washington, DC: Drug Policy Foundation.

Alexander, B. K., & Wong, L. S. (1990). Adverse effects of cocaine on the heart: A critical review. In A. Trebach & K. Zeese (Eds.), *The great issues of drug policy* (pp. 257–267). Washington, DC: Drug Policy Foundation.

Anderson, T. (1995). Toward a preliminary macro theory of drug addiction. *Deviant Behavior, 16,* 353–372.

Andreas, P., & Greenhill, K. M. (Eds.). (2010). *Sex, drugs, and body counts: The politics of numbers in global crime and conflict.* Ithaca, NY: Cornell University Press.

Becker, H. (1967). History, culture and subjective experience: An exploration of the social bases of drug-induced experiences. *Journal of Health and Social Behavior, 7,* 163–176.

Bowden, C. (2009). We bring fear. *Mother Jones, 34,* 28–43.

Brandt, A. (1991). Up in smoke: How cigarettes came to be a controlled substance. *Magazine of History, 6,* 22–24.

Carnes, P. (1991). *Don't call it love: Recovery from sexual addiction.* New York, NY: Bantam.

Carr, E. S. (2011). *Scripting addiction: The politics of therapeutic talk and American society.* Princeton, NJ: Princeton University Press.

Chetley, A., & Mintzes, B. (Eds.). (1992). *Promoting health or pushing drugs? A critical examination of marketing of pharmaceuticals.* Amsterdam, Netherlands: Health Action International.

Clinard, M., & Yeager, P. (1980). *Corporate crime.* New York, NY: Free Press.

Coleman, J. W. (2006). *The criminal elite: Understanding white-collar crime* (6th ed.). New York, NY: Worth.

Drum, K. (2009). The patriot's guide to legalization: Have you ever looked at our marijuana policy? I mean really looked at it? *Mother Jones, 34,* 49–52.

Erickson, P., Adlaf, E., Murray, G., & Smart, R. (1987). *The steel drug.* Lexington, MA: Lexington.

Fagan, J. (1994). Do criminal sanctions deter drug crimes? In D. L. MacKenzie & C. Uchida (Eds.), *Drugs and crime: Evaluating public policy initiatives* (pp. 188–214). Thousand Oaks, CA: Sage.

Fingarette, H. (1988). *Heavy drinking: The myth of alcoholism as a disease.* Berkeley: University of California Press.

Franklin, D. (1996). Hooked/not hooked: Why isn't everyone an addict? In H. Wilson (Ed.), *Drugs, society, and behavior 96/97* (11th ed., pp. 54–65). Guilford, CT: Dushkin.

Gibler, J. (2011). *To die in Mexico: Dispatches from inside the drug war.* San Francisco, CA: City Lights Books.

Global Commission on Drugs. (2012, June). *The war on drugs and HIV/AIDS: How the criminalization of drug use fuels the global pandemic.* Report of the Global Commission on Drug Policy. Retrieved September 4, 2012, from http://global commissionondrugs.org/wp-content/themes/gcdp_v1/pdf/GCDP_HIV-AIDS_2012_REFERENCE.pdf

Goffman, E. (1952). On cooling the mark out. *Psychiatry, 15,* 451–463.

Goode, E. (2008a). *Drugs in American society* (7th ed.). Boston, MA: McGraw-Hill.

Goode, E. (2008b). Legalize it? A bulletin from the war on drugs. In J. Goodwin & J. Jasper (Eds.), *The contexts reader* (pp. 384–391). New York, NY: Norton.

Goode, E., & Ben-Yehuda, N. (1994). *Moral panics: The social construction of deviance.* Cambridge, MA: Blackwell.

Greenwald, G. (2009). *Drug decriminalization in Portugal: Lessons for creating fair and successful drug policies.* Washington, DC: Cato Institute.

Grilly, D. (1994). *Drugs and human behavior* (2nd ed.). Boston, MA: Allyn & Bacon.

Helmer, J. (1975). *Drugs and minority oppression.* New York, NY: Seabury.

Henkin, W. (1996). The myth of sexual addiction. In R. Francoeur (Ed.), *Taking sides: Clashing views on controversial issues in human sexuality* (5th ed., pp. 58–65). Guilford, CT: Dushkin.

Huggins, R. (2010). Images of addiction: The representation of illicit drug use in popular media. In L. J. Moore & M. Kosut (Eds.), *The body reader: Essential social and cultural readings* (pp. 384–398). New York: New York University Press.

Hunt, G., Moloney, M., & Evans, K. (2010). *Youth, drugs, and nightlife.* New York, NY: Routledge.

Inciardi, J. (1992). *The war on drugs II.* Mountain View, CA: Mayfield.

Jablecki, L. T. (2012). The death of the war on drugs. In J. Naughton (Ed.), *Annual editions: Criminal justice 11/12* (35th ed., pp. 16–18). New York, NY: McGraw-Hill.

Johns, C. J., & Borrero J. M. (1991). The war on drugs: Nothing succeeds like failure. In G. Barak (Ed.), *Crimes by the capitalist state* (pp. 67–100). Albany: State University New York Press.

Kaplan, D. (2009). Paying for terror. In T. Badey (Ed.), *Violence and terrorism 08/09* (11th ed., pp. 28–33). Boston, MA: McGraw-Hill.

Kraska, P. (2003). The military as drug police: Exercising the ideology of war. In L. K. Gaines & P. B. Kraska (Eds), *Drugs, crime, and justice: Contemporary perspectives* (2nd ed., pp. 288–308). Prospect Heights, IL: Waveland Press.

Kreager, D. A., & Haynie, D. L. (2011). Dangerous liaisons: Dating and drinking diffusion in adolescent peer networks. *American Sociological Review, 76,* 737–763.

Latimer, D., & Goldberg, J. (1981). *Flowers in the blood: The story of opium.* New York, NY: Franklin Watts.

Leiber, M., Jamieson, K., & Krohn, M. (1993). Newspaper reporting and the production of deviance: Drug use among professional athletes. *Deviant Behavior, 14,* 317–339.

Levine, H. (1984). The alcohol problem in America: From temperance to alcoholism. *British Journal of Addiction, 79,* 109–119.

Lindesmith, A. (1968). *Addiction and opiates.* Chicago, IL: Aldine.

Lotz, R. E. (1991). *Crime and the American press.* New York, NY: Praeger.

Matveychuk, W. (1986). The social construction of drug definitions and drug experience. In P. Park & W. Matveychuk (Eds.), *Culture and politics of drugs* (pp. 7–12). Dubuque, IA: Kendall/Hunt.

McCaghy, C., & Capron, T. (1997). *Deviant behavior* (4th ed.). Boston, MA: Allyn & Bacon.

Montagne, M. (1988). The metaphorical nature of drugs and drug taking. *Social Science and Medicine, 26,* 417–424.

Morgan, J., & Kagan, D. (1995). The dusting of America: The image of phencyclidine (PCP) in the popular media. In J. Inciardi & K. McElrath (Eds.), *The American drug scene: An anthology* (pp. 204–213). Los Angeles, CA: Roxbury.

Murphy, J. (2011). Drug court as both a legal and medical authority. *Deviant Behavior, 32,* 257–291.

Musto, D. (1987). *The American disease: Origins of narcotic control* (Expanded ed.). New York, NY: Oxford University Press.

Orcutt, J. (1996). Deviance as a situated phenomenon: Variations in the social interpretation of marijuana and alcohol use. In H. Pontell (Ed.), *Social deviance* (2nd ed., pp. 215–222). Englewood Cliffs, NJ: Prentice Hall.

Orcutt, J., & Turner, J. B. (1993). Shocking numbers and graphic accounts: Quantified images of drug problems in the print media. *Social Problems, 40,* 190–206.

Packer, H. (1968). *The limits of the criminal sanction.* Stanford, CA: Stanford University Press.

Page, J. B., & Singer, M. (2010). *Comprehending drug use: Ethnographic research at the social margins.* New Brunswick, NJ: Rutgers University Press.

Peele, S. (1985). *The meaning of addiction: Compulsive experience and its interpretation.* Lexington, MA: D. C. Heath.

Peralta, R. (2005). Race and the culture of college drinking: An analysis of white privilege on campus. In W. Palacios (Ed.), *Cocktails and dreams: Perspectives on drug and alcohol use* (pp. 127–141). Upper Saddle River, NJ: Pearson/Prentice Hall.

Perry, D. (2008). Pumped-up panic. In R. Heiner (Ed.), *Deviance across cultures* (pp. 166–176). New York, NY: Oxford University Press.

Pine, J. (2010). Embodied capitalism and the meth economy. In L. J. Moore & M. Kosut (Eds.), *The body reader: Essential social and cultural readings* (pp. 164–183). New York: New York University Press.

Ray, O., & Ksir, C. (1996). *Drugs, society, and human behavior* (7th ed.). St. Louis, MO: C. V. Mosby.

Reiman, J., & Leighton, P. (2010). *The rich get richer and the poor get prison: Ideology, class, and crime.* Upper Saddle River, NJ: Pearson.

Reinarman, C. (1996). The social construction of drug scares. In E. Goode (Ed.), *Social deviance* (pp. 224–234). Boston, MA: Allyn & Bacon.

Reinarman, C., & Levine, H. (1997). The crack attack: Politics and media in America's latest drug scare. In C. Reinarman & H. Levine (Eds.), *Crack in America: Demon drugs and social justice* (pp. 18–51). Berkeley, CA: University of California Press.

Rice, R. (1998). The startling truth about sexual addiction. In L. Salinger (Ed.), *Deviant behavior 98/99* (3rd ed., pp. 217–219). Guilford, CT: Dushkin.

Rubin, A. J., & Rosenberg, M. (2012, May 26). U.S. efforts fail to curtail trade in Afghan opium. *New York Times.* Retrieved March 29, 2013, from http://www .nytimes.com/2012/05/27/world/asia/drug-traffic-remains-as-us-nears-afghanistan-exit.html?pagewanted=all

Ryan, K. (1994). Technicians and interpreters in moral crusades: The case of the drug courier profile. *Deviant Behavior, 15,* 217–240.

Safire, W. (1997). *Lend me your ears: Great speeches in history* (Rev. & expanded ed.). New York, NY: Norton.

Schaler, J. (2000). *Addiction is a choice.* Chicago, IL: Open Court.

Scheibe, K. (1994). Cocaine careers: Historical and individual constructions. In T. Sarbin & J. Kitsuse (Eds.), *Constructing the social* (pp. 195–212). Thousand Oaks, CA: Sage.

Siegel, R. (1989). *Intoxication: Life in pursuit of artificial paradise.* New York, NY: Dutton.

Simon, D. (2008). *Elite deviance* (9th ed.). Boston, MA: Allyn & Bacon.

Staley, S. (1992). *Drug policy and the decline of American cities.* New Brunswick, NJ: Transaction Publishers.

Substance Abuse and Mental Health Services Administration (SAMHSA). (2012). *Results from the 2010 National Survey on Drug Use and Health: Summary of National Findings,* NSDUH Series H-41, HHS Publication No. (SMA) 11–4658. Rockville, MD: Author. Retrieved February 1, 2013, from http://www.samhsa .gov/data/NSDUH/2k11Results/NSDUHresults2011.pdf

Szalavitz, M. (2012, June 27). The cannabis cannibal? Miami face-eater didn't take "bath salts." *Time Health & Family.* Retrieved September 3, 2012, from http:// healthland.time.com/2012/06/27/the-cannabis-cannibal-miami-face-eater-didnt-take-bath-salts

Szasz, T. (1985). *Ceremonial chemistry: The ritual persecution of drugs, addicts, and pushers* (Rev. ed.). Holmes Beach, FL: Learning Publications.

Trebach, A. (1987). *The great drug war.* New York, NY: Macmillan.

Trebach, A., & Inciardi, J. (1993). *Legalize it? Debating American drug policy.* Washington, DC: American University Press.

Tuggle, J., & Holmes, M. (1997). Blowing smoke: Status politics and the Shasta County smoking ban. *Deviant Behavior, 18,* 77–93.

Victor, J. (1994). Fundamentalist religion and the moral crusade against Satanism: The social construction of deviant behavior. *Deviant Behavior, 15,* 305–334.

Volkow, N. D., Wang, G.-J., Fischman, M. W., Foltin, R. W., Fowler, J. S., Abumrad, N. N., . . . Shea, C. E. (1997). Relationship between subjective effects of cocaine and dopamine transporter occupancy. *Nature, 386,* 827–830.

Volkow, N. D., Wang, G.-J., Fowler, J. S., Logan, J., Gatley, S. J., Hitzemann, R., . . . Pappas, N. (1997). Decreased striatal dopaminergic responsiveness in detoxified cocaine-dependent subjects. *Nature, 386,* 830–833.

Vulliamy, E. (2010). *Amexica: War along the borderline.* New York, NY: Farrar, Straus & Giroux.

Walker, S. (2011). *Sense and nonsense about crime, drugs, and communities* (7th ed.). Belmont, CA: Wadsworth/Cengage.

Weil, A. (1972). *The natural mind.* Boston, MA: Houghton Mifflin.

Whaley, R. B., Smith, J. M., & Hayes-Smith, R. (2011). Teenage drug and alcohol use: Comparing individual and contextual effects. *Deviant Behavior, 32,* 818–845.

Winslow, R., & Zhang, S. (2008). *Criminology: A global perspective.* Upper Saddle River, NJ: Pearson/Prentice Hall.

Wysong, E., Aniskiewicz, R., & Wright, D. (1994). Truth *and* dare: Tracking drug education to graduation as a symbolic politics. *Social Problems, 41,* 448–472.

Young, J. (2011). Moral panics and the transgressive other. *Crime, Media, Culture, 7,* 245–258.

Index

About the Author

John Curra is a professor at Eastern Kentucky University, where he has taught since 1975. He received both his bachelor's and master's degree from San Diego State College (now San Diego State University) in sociology, and his doctorate from Purdue University, also in sociology. He has taught courses in introductory sociology, social deviance, criminology, sociological analysis, social problems, social psychology, juvenile delinquency, and criminological theory. In 1981, he received the prestigious Excellence in Teaching Award from the College of Social and Behavioral Sciences. In 2005–2007, he was chosen as a Foundation Professor, one of the highest honors a professor can receive at Eastern Kentucky University. In 2012, Curra moved to the Department of Criminal Justice in the School of Justice Studies. That same year, he was awarded the Excellence in Teaching Award by the Department of Criminal Justice in the College of Justice and Safety. Curra has authored or coauthored several books, an instructor's manual, and a reader.

⑤SAGE researchmethods

The essential online tool for researchers from the world's leading methods publisher

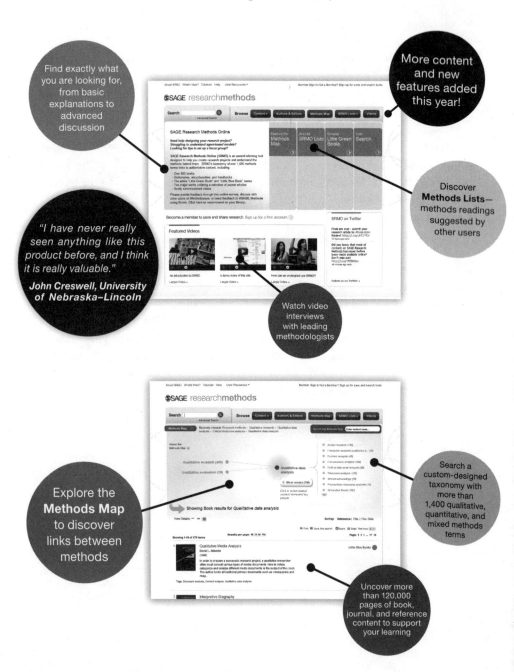

Find exactly what you are looking for, from basic explanations to advanced discussion

More content and new features added this year!

"I have never really seen anything like this product before, and I think it is really valuable."

John Creswell, University of Nebraska–Lincoln

Discover **Methods Lists**— methods readings suggested by other users

Watch video interviews with leading methodologists

Explore the **Methods Map** to discover links between methods

Search a custom-designed taxonomy with more than 1,400 qualitative, quantitative, and mixed methods terms

Uncover more than 120,000 pages of book, journal, and reference content to support your learning

Find out more at
www.sageresearchmethods.com